Understanding Russianness

In today's world where other cultures are being tapped to a greater extent than ever before, the processes of mixing and matching are especially relevant in making sense of Russia. Not only do borrowing and assimilation, interaction between the Own and the Alien, constitute a venerable tradition in Russian culture, but during the last two post-Soviet decades a notable Western influence has become apparent.

This book provides means for understanding Russianness in this new situation. By bringing together Russian and Western, eminent and younger scholars it provides insights from both inside and outside the country. By extending its perspectives to three fields – linguistics, cultural studies, and social sciences – it covers different dimensions of creative misunderstandings, hybrids, tensions, and other modes of adaptation in the Russian culture. By offering concrete case studies it avoids easy stereotypes, deconstructs clichés, problematizes accepted truths, and identifies points of interaction between Russia and the West.

Risto Alapuro is Professor Emeritus of Sociology at the University of Helsinki, Finland, and the head of the Helsinki Research Group for Political Sociology. His recent publications include the co-edited volumes *Beyond Post-Soviet Transition: Micro Perspectives on Challenge and Survival in Russia and Estonia* (2004), *Nordic Associations in a European Perspective* (2010), and *Political Theory and Community Building in Post-Soviet Russia* (2011).

Arto Mustajoki is Professor of Russian Language and Literature at the University of Helsinki, Finland. His research interests include functional syntax, features of contemporary Russian, corpus based research, intercultural communication, and identities. He has published seven books and over eighty related research articles.

Pekka Pesonen is Professor Emeritus of Russian Literature at the University of Helsinki, Finland, and the head of several international research projects including Modernism and Postmodernism in Russian Literature and Culture, and St Petersburg/Leningrad: History–Narration–Present. Among his research interests are Russian literature and culture (especially modernism and postmodernism), and cultural semiotics. He has published three monographs, eighteen edited books, and about one hundred research articles.

Routledge advances in sociology

Understanding Russianness

Edited by
Risto Alapuro, Arto Mustajoki,
and Pekka Pesonen

 Routledge
Taylor & Francis Group

LONDON AND NEW YORK

First published 2012
by Routledge
2 Park Square, Milton Park, Abingdon, Oxon, OX14 4RN

Simultaneously published in the USA and Canada
by Routledge
711 Third Avenue, New York, NY 10017

Routledge is an imprint of the Taylor & Francis Group, an informa business

British Library Cataloguing in Publication Data
A catalogue record for this book is available from the British Library

Library of Congress Cataloging in Publication Data
Understanding Russianness/edited by Risto Alapuro, Arto Mustajoki, and
Pekka Pesonen.
p. cm.
Includes bibliographical references and index.
ISBN 978-0-415-60415-4 (hardback)
1. Social psychology--Russia (Federation) 2. Group identity--Russia (Federation)
3. Ethnicity--Russia (Federation) 4. Russia (Federation)--Social life and customs.
I. Alapuro, Risto, 1944- II. Mustajoki, Arto S. (Arto Samuel), 1948- III.
Pesonen, Pekka.
HM1027.R9U53 2011
306.0947--dc22
2011004697

ISBN: 978-0-415-60415-4 hbk
ISBN: 978-0-203-83414-5 ebook

Typeset in Baskerville
by Taylor & Francis Books

Printed and bound in Great Britain by
CPI Antony Rowe, Chippenham, Wiltshire

Contents

Tables and Figures

Table

Figures

Contributors

Risto Alapuro was Professor of Sociology at the University of Helsinki, Finland, from 1991 to 2010, and Academy Professor at the Academy of Finland 2005–9. His publications include *State and Revolution in Finland* (1988), other monographs, and edited or co-edited anthologies, including *Nordic Associations in a European Perspective* (2010) and *Political Theory and Community Building in Post-Soviet Russia* (2011).

David R. Andrews is Professor of Slavic Languages at Georgetown University in Washington, DC, USA. He specializes in contemporary Russian socio- and psycholinguistics, with a particular focus on émigré Russian, standard versus nonstandard speech forms, and language attitudes.

Evgenii Bershtein is Associate Professor of Russian and Chair of the Russian Department at Reed College in Portland, Oregon, USA, where he teaches twentieth-century Russian literature and culture. He has published on Western sexual ideologies in Russian Symbolism (the topic of his forthcoming book), as well as eighteenth-century Russian poetry, and contemporary Russian literature and film.

Anna Colin Lebedev is a postdoctoral researcher at the École des Hautes Études en Sciences Sociales, Paris, France. She received her PhD from the Paris Institute for Political Science. She works on collective action in the post-Soviet context.

Boris Gasparov is Professor of Russian and East European Studies at Columbia University, USA. He is the author and editor of a number of books on Slavic and general linguistics and on Russian literature and culture. His latest work is *Speech, Memory, and Meaning: Intertextuality in Everyday Language* (2010).

Jukka Gronow is Professor of Sociology at the University of Helsinki, Finland, specializing in modern consumption. His publications include *The Sociology of Taste* (1997), *Ordinary Consumption* (2000, co-edited with Alan Warde), and *Caviar with Champagne* (2003).

Tomi Huttunen, PhD, is a postdoctoral researcher and a *docent* of Russian literature and culture at the Department of Modern Languages, University of Helsinki, Finland. He specializes in the Russian avant-garde, semiotics of culture, and rock poetry.

Markku Lonkila works as an Academy of Finland research fellow at the Department of Social Research, University of Helsinki, Finland. His interests include social networks in post-Soviet Russia, Russian voluntary associations and social movements, and the role of information and communication technology in the development of Russian society and economy. Lonkila's publications include articles in international journals and the monograph *Networks in the Russian Market Economy* (2011).

Arto Mustajoki is Professor of Russian Language and Literature and Head of the Department of Modern Languages, University of Helsinki, Finland. He has done research on contemporary Russian language, the theory of functional syntax, communication failures, and cross-cultural communication.

Gennady Obatnin, PhD, is Senior Lecturer in Russian Literature at the University of Helsinki, Finland and the author of the monograph *Vyacheslav Ivanov as a Mystic* (2000). His main field is Russian modernism, including the entire range of its manifestations and intellectual roots.

Vesa Oittinen is Professor of Russian Philosophy and History of Ideas at the Aleksanteri Institute, University of Helsinki, Finalnd. His latest publications include studies on German, Scandinavian, and Russian philosophy.

Ekaterina Protassova, PhD, *docent*, is a University Lecturer at the Department of Modern Languages, University of Helsinki, Finalnd. Her main scholarly interests are the acquisition, development, and maintenance of Russian as a first and a second language, bilingualism, intercultural communication, and education, and varieties of spoken Russian.

Lara Ryazanova-Clarke is Head of Russian and Academic Director of the Princess Dashkova Russian Centre at the University of Edinburgh, UK. She has published widely in the fields of Russian socio-cultural linguistics and discourse analysis.

Alexei Shmelev is Professor of Russian Linguistics at the Moscow Pedagogical State University, Russia and Head of the Department of Linguistic Standards of Russian at the Institute of Russian Language, Russian Academy of Sciences. His research interests cover a number of disciplines, including cultural studies and linguistics.

Sergey Shtyrkov is a senior researcher at the Peter the Great Museum of Anthropology and Ethnography, Russian Academy of Sciences, and Assistant Professor at the European University at St Petersburg, Russia. His fields of expertise are religious nationalism and popular religion. He has co-edited *Sny Bogoroditsy: Issledovaniya po antropologii religii* (2006).

Ilya Utekhin, PhD in anthropology, is Associate Professor in the Department of Anthropology at the European University at St Petersburg, Russia. He works on the ethnography of communication and on cognitive science, and conducts research on the use of technology in everyday life.

Vadim Volkov, PhD in sociology (Cambridge, UK), is Vice-Rector for International Affairs and Professor of Sociology at the European University at St Petersburg, Russia. He is the author of *Violent Entrepreneurs: The Use of Force in the Making of Russian Capitalism* (2002) and articles in scholarly journals on sociology.

Introduction

Risto Alapuro, Arto Mustajoki, and Pekka Pesonen

Russia is a great challenge for Western people. The Iron Curtain is away, but Russia still stands behind a mental barrier. There is something mysterious in the behaviour of Russia as a state; the Russians tend to surprise us at the very moment when we start to think that they have changed and become like us. The political events in Moscow may seem distant to us, but more visible new contacts arise from the presence of Russians in our countries. They seem to be everywhere in the world, both as tourists and as immigrants. We hear them, we see them, and we ask ourselves what they are like and whether they are different from us. And if they are different, we ask why.

There is something special about Russianness, but in today's world, where foreign cultures are being tapped to a greater extent than ever before, the processes of mixing and matching are especially relevant in making sense of Russia. Not only do borrowing and assimilation, interaction between the Own and the Alien, constitute a venerable tradition in Russian culture; the Russians also have a peculiar way of building from this the Third, something in-between. The last two post-Soviet decades have inevitably accelerated the process of Western influence. However, we see some typically Russian paradoxical tendencies: Western ideas seem to penetrate Russian society very quickly, yet at the same time ancient Russian traditions and patriotic thinking are experiencing a renaissance. Perhaps there is nothing stunning about this; such attitudes and desires fuel one another.

This book provides means for understanding Russianness in this new situation. By bringing together Russian and Western, eminent and younger scholars, it provides insights from both inside and outside the country. By extending its perspectives across three fields – linguistics, cultural studies, and social sciences – it covers different dimensions of creative hybrids, tensions, misunderstandings, and other modes of adaptation in Russian culture. By offering specific case studies, it avoids easy stereotypes, deconstructs clichés, problematizes accepted truths, and identifies points of interaction between Russia and the West. The aim of the book is not to give ready-made answers, but to challenge the reader to recognize the many dimensions of the issue.

Through chapters based on concrete examples of the complexity of Russianness, the authors of the book believe that we can look deeper into the souls of the Russians. The Russians themselves like to emphasize the specific qualities of their society and culture. This spirit is well expressed in the Russian attitude towards the West, an attitude whose underlying idea is *Polyubite nas chernen'kimi, belen'kimi nas vsiaky polyubit* (literally, 'Love us black – anybody will love us white'). In other words, the Russians want to be accepted as they are, but not through the glasses of a Western person.

In each part of the book, Russianness has been approached by the methods and traditions of a given research field: linguistics, cultural studies, and social sciences. As will be seen on the basis of the chapters, the approaches are in fact very close to each other, illuminating the same object from slightly different perspectives.

This volume grew out of the workshop *Understanding Russianness*, held on 17–18 October 2008 at the University of Helsinki and made possible by the financial support of the Rector of the University. A related seminar for young scholars, funded from the same source, was organized on 3–4 December 2009. We would like to thank all those who contributed to the arrangement of the two events, notably Hanna Ruutu and Irja Vesikko. Thanks are also due to Olga Timofeeva and Sergey Zavyalov for their valuable help in editing the final manuscript of the book.

For the transliteration of the Russian Cyrillic alphabet the simplified BGN/PCGN 1947 System was followed, except for cases where it contradicts generally accepted forms, for example, *Dostoevsky* is preferred to *Dostoyevskiy*.

Part I

Language

The chapters in this section give an idea of the major changes that have taken place in the use of the Russian language and in the rethinking of Western concepts after the collapse of the Soviet Union.

In the long and sudden leap into 'the new era of public language', many features are shared with Western countries, but in a more pronounced form. As in the West, these result from phenomena like the expansion of entertainment in the mass media, the personalization of politics, and the expansion of colloquial speech in areas where the previous tradition was to stick to more formal language.

A feature typical of Russia is the concern about international influences on contemporary Russian. To be sure, Russian has always been very open to foreign influences, from Tsar Peter I to the Bolsheviks, but despite this background, the issue is seen today in the concern of the intelligentsia over the purity of the Russian language. The phenomenon as such is known in almost all non-English-speaking countries, but in Russia these discussions have a more emotional tone and are coloured by a controversy involving a strong desire to use loanwords on one side, and a strong inclination to comment upon and criticize their use on the other.

Another typical Russian feature is the rethinking of Western concepts. Ideas and words are borrowed, but they gain a slightly different meaning on Russian territory. For example, *piar* (as the Russians spell PR, public relations) is nowadays a very popular word in Russian with a great variety of derivatives, but it is used mainly in a negative sense. The expression *political will* came into the Russian rhetoric some years ago, but the direct translation does not work because *volya* – the Russian equivalent of *will* – has a special meaning, with connotations of despotism.

All these linguistic aspects of the encounter between the Own and the Alien – the impact of the 'new era of public language', international influences, and, more specifically, the use of Western concepts – are illuminated in the four chapters of Part I.

The first chapter goes straight to the point. Lara Ryazanova-Clarke discusses the way the Russians interpret the notion of 'the West'. In her analysis she uses both public narratives and texts by the chief Kremlin ideologist Vladislav Surkov. The West has always had a double function in Russian discourse. It serves as a contrast to the uniqueness of Russian culture and identity, but at the same time it feeds Russian society with new ideas and trends.

David R. Andrews focuses on each country's perception of its own and the other's language, the correlation of these perceptions with larger socio-cultural and socio-political factors, and their evolution from the late Soviet era through to the present day. Using evidence from literature and from his own life, he shows that neither of the two parties can avoid strong subjectivism in their attitude towards the language of the great enemy.

The chapter by Arto Mustajoki and Ekaterina Protassova starts with an overview of the Russians' way of interpreting various new phenomena in language use. The dualistic attitude of the Russian intelligentsia towards new linguistic features and their reverence for the common old traditions leads to a perennial debate on the matter. More specific analyses of the way the Russians use their own words for *political will* and *crisis* show that even these ostensibly simple concepts have special Russian readings.

Alexei Shmelev continues in the same vein by attesting semantic shifts in the use of some loanwords. Using a rich authentic material from works by several writers, he considers the complex Russification process of three words and concepts: 'honour' (in Russian, *gonor*), 'courage' (*kurazh*), and the French word 'aventure' (*avantyura*). Shmelev also shows that words like 'successful', 'effective', 'ambitious', and 'career' have special nuances in Russian.

1 The 'West' in the linguistic construction of Russianness in contemporary public discourse

Lara Ryazanova-Clarke

For centuries, the notion of the 'West' has occupied a special place in public narratives about the Russian national self. It is the 'West' that called on Peter the Great to embark on his 'grand embassy', after which he implemented his interpretation of the 'West' by building St Petersburg, shaving his subject's faces, introducing European dress, and building a Dutch-style fleet. It was the 'West' that was the cornerstone of the nineteenth-century debate between the Westernizers and Slavophiles, sparked by Petr Chaadaev's *Philosophical Letters*. The answers to the debate's major question, whether Russia should progress along the European path of development, drove the Russian intelligentsia into two different camps. According to one, Russia was backward, ever catching up with the 'West', while the other believed in Russia's special path and spiritual light and contrasted it to the morally decadent 'West'. The twentieth-century grand narratives of Russia and the 'West' included Vladimir Solov'yev's and Nikolay Berdyayev's concept of 'the Russian idea', ideas of the Eurasianism movement, which originated among Russian émigrés, and even the Soviet doctrine of the Cold War, a specific form of rejection of the 'Western' civilizational route.

The collapse of the Soviet Union and the emergence of post-Soviet Russia did not seem to have dispensed with the centuries-long concepts of Russianness incorporating the notion of the 'West'. Opening up the country to the outside world, Mikhail Gorbachev initiated the narrative of the 'common European home/ house', of which he saw Russia to be an equal member, while in 1996, the first president of independent Russia, Boris Yel'tsin, articulated the need to manufacture a new 'Russian idea' and formed a Kremlin think-tank tasked with drafting yet another variant of a Russian 'special path', a notion further developed under Vladimir Putin's rule. Thus, the public discourse of contemporary Russia continues to debate and negotiate the imaginative 'West': as Vera Tolz notes, the comparison with the 'West' has been 'the most important ingredient of modern Russian identity' (Tolz 2001: 69).

The writings of Stuart Hall may offer some explanation for the Russian preoccupation across the centuries with the 'West'. Elaborating on Jacque Lacan's idea of the mirror stage in human psychological development, Hall argues that identity arises from some lack of wholeness in the individual or society, which causes the need for its articulation from outside the self (Hall 1992: 287). He concludes that 'identities are constructed through, not outside, difference, through the relation to the Other' (Hall 1996: 4).

Much of contemporary scholarly work investigating Russian identity explores its 'Western' component from cultural, historical, political, and anthropological perspectives. Berlin (1963) McDaniel (1996), Neumann (1996), Paramonov (1996), Shalin (1996), and Smith (2002) among others discuss the 'West' over different historical periods as a compound of an unfading myth, which Russia has constructed and reconstructed for specific purposes of the time. Linguistic approaches have produced numerous works which debate how Russianness is reflected in various strata of the Russian language.[1] However a discursive perspective with regard to the analysis of the 'West' in the Russian identity narrative has been applied to a lesser degree, with Paul Chilton and Mikhail Ilyin's (1993, 1998) analysis of the *perestroika* metaphor of the 'common European house' and Zhdanova's (2006) exploration of the notions of *chuzhbina* 'alien land' and *rodina* 'fatherland' in the language of Russian speakers in Germany being a few notable exceptions. Yet, it is discourse analysis that specifically reveals the ways in which language use is constitutive of institutional practices and the social ordering of institutional domains, such as national identity (Slembrouck 2001: 36). This chapter expands on the existing research on various aspects of Russian discourse and identity (Ryazanova-Clarke 2006, 2008a, 2008b, 2008c, 2009) and deals with identification of specific discursive strategies employed for the contemporary portrayal of the 'West' that contributes as its significant Other to the construction of Russianness.

It has been pointed out that during the last decade, public discourse attempted to formulate varied versions of Russian identity. The dominant discourse associated with the voice of the authorities produces its own picture of Russianness, which diverges from that depicted by the counter-discursive stream located, during Putin regime, at the margin of the public space (Ryazanova-Clarke 2008a, 2009). In order to identify the specific strategies of these self–Other depictions, the following presents two case studies of contemporary Russian public discourse, exploring the linguistic construction of the 'West' in the narratives of the national self. The dominant discourse is represented by the programmatic speech given in February 2006 by the chief Kremlin ideologist Vladislav Surkov who was at the time the Deputy Head of the Presidential Administration and Aide to the President (Surkov 2006).[2] The speech was addressed to students of the 'United Russia' Party Centre for Staff Development and, according to some analysts' interpretations, constitutes the central and most comprehensive articulation of contemporary ideology conceived by the Russian authorities (Radzikhovsky 2006). The counter-discourse is exemplified by the text 'Velikaya reka ekonomiki' by Yuliya Latynina, an investigative journalist, a daring political commentator, and the Putin regime's leading critic. Latynina writes for the liberal *Novaya Gazeta* and *Kommersant* (2006–7), participates in several internet publications including *Gazeta.ru* and the demonstratively oppositional *Ezhednevny Zhurnal*, and presents the political phone-in programme *Kod dostupa* on the last remaining free-thinking national radio channel *Ekho Moskvy*. Known for her conspicuous criticism of the authorities, and branded for that a 'fifth column traitor' on the Kremlin controlled Russian television

(Aron 2008: 6) Latynina was among those who founded the '2008 Free Choice Committee' which campaigned for free and democratic presidential elections for 2008. The article 'Velikaya reka ekonomiki' ('The great river of economics') was published in *Ezhednevny Zhurnal* on 22 May 2007 (Latynina 2007).

Ascribing meanings from the Kremlin: Russia and the 'West' in Vladislav Surkov's speech

Speaking in front of a future generation of 'United Russia' party leaders, Vladislav Surkov centres his rhetoric upon the contrast between in- and out-groups, or 'us' and 'them'. Throughout the speech his vision of Russia is pitted against the 'West', which is continuously evoked in order to both facilitate and complement his articulation of Russianness. In particular, Surkov takes the 'West', also phrased as 'Europeanism', as a point of departure, thus marking its intrinsic importance for his defining of Russian qualities.

In general, this portrayal of Russianness through the mirror of a significant 'Other' incorporates two major strategies with regard to the notion of the 'West': one of assimilation and the other of relativization, including the negative presentation.[3] The speech starts with the topos of similarity which allows the speaker to begin constructing his version of Russian identity through the strategy of legitimization: here, the notion of European civilization is called upon in order to ascribe a positive value to Russia, for example:[4]

(1) Никакого секрета не открою, если скажу, еще раз повторившись, что Россия - это европейская страна.

('I will reveal no secrets if I say once again that Russia is a European country.')

This notwithstanding, the metalinguistic asides and hedges (such as *Nikakogo sekreta ne otkroyu* ('I will reveal no secrets') and *yeshche raz povtorivshis'* ('I say once again'), that accompany Surkov's articulation of commonality, give away a good deal of his unease and uncertainty towards the above categorization.

(2) Начиная издалека хочу сказать, что развитие европейской цивилизации, частью которой является цивилизация российская, показывает, что люди на протяжении всех наблюдаемых эпох стремились прежде всего к материальному благополучию.

('Starting from some distance, I want to say that the development of European civilization, of which Russian civilization is a part, demonstrates that in all the epochs observed people strove first of all for material wealth.')

Further into the text, Vladislav Surkov on the one hand maintains the topos of similarity by continuing to connect Russia and the 'West', while on the other, he turns to a 'distancing' strategy. Thus in (2), in a genuinely post-communist spirit, he picks the aspiration towards personal material wealth as a key characteristic connecting the Russian national character with European civilization. A far cry from the Soviet rhetoric that vilified Western bourgeois acquisitiveness and contrary to the centuries-long narratives embedded in Russian culture, claiming the non-material spirituality of the Russian character, it is the prioritization of material prosperity above all that Surkov, with the help of the notion of Europe, now attributes to Russianness. Describing this quality as natural and common sense, the speaker uses the normative framing of the 'West': Russia is measured in terms of Western norms and, as a result, the existing status quo of wealth distribution in contemporary Russia looks natural, justified and even equitable.

Despite this strategy of assimilation, in a distancing move, the West is also depicted as a corrupter of the earlier asserted quality of Russian materialism (3). As regards those oligarchs who move their assets offshore, Surkov ascribes to his audience an assumption that they are to be placed into the category of the 'enemy', and then argues against that view, normalizing them as the 'business community'. Initially the super rich are referred to by an ironically hued 'Western' set of categorizations – aristocratic titles qualified by attributive references to foreign lands: *offshornaya aristokratiya* ('offshore aristocracy'), *grafy Bermudskiye i knyaz'ya ostrova Men* ('Counts of Bermuda and Princes of the Isle of Man'). However, by constructing them as 'our citizens', Surkov uses a contrast between the Westernized nature of 'them' and their 'real' quality of being 'us' as he suggests that those oligarchs have a duty to become properly integrated into Russian society – and moreover, to become its stalwart supporters, guarantors of its prosperous future. However in order to achieve that status, they need to undergo a patriotic transformation. The speaker linguistically constructs this transformation by shedding the oligarchs' 'Western' attributes, and by modifying references to them with 'nationally coloured' expressions such as *natsional'naya burzhuaziya* ('national bourgeoisie').

(3) Если наше деловое сообщество не трансформируется в *национальную буржуазию*,[5] то, конечно, будущего у нас нет. Причем даже называя многих этих людей '*оффшорной аристократией*', отнюдь не нужно считать их *врагами*: все эти *графы Бермудские и князья острова Мэн наши граждане*, у которых есть масса причин так себя вести … Трансформировав *оффшорную аристократию в национальную буржуазию и постсоветскую бюрократию в современную, успешную, гибкую бюрократию*, общество может быть спокойным за будущее нашей страны.

('If our business community does not transform into a national bourgeoisie then of course we do not have a future. Also to mention that even if we call these people "the offshore aristocracy" we should not consider them enemies. All these Counts of Bermuda and Princes of the Isle of Man are our citizens who have masses of reasons to behave like that … Only having transformed the offshore aristocracy into a national bourgeoisie and the post-Soviet bureaucracy into a contemporary, successful, flexible bureaucracy, can society be confident about the future of our country.')

Surkov's framing of the 'West' receives a further blow as the speaker applies strategies of relativization when it comes to mentioning the more traditional Western characteristics – democratic rights, freedoms, and institutions. Relativization occurs through the mechanisms of downplaying and minimization which are manifested in such linguistic devices as the 'yes – but' figure, further hedging, and the topos of a small number, among others.

(4) Напомню, что всеобщее избирательное право, всеобщее право участвовать в политической жизни - это *изобретение недавнее.*

('To remind you, the right of universal suffrage, the universal right to take part in political life is a recent invention.')

For example, in (4), the common assumption that the universal rights of suffrage and political activism are unquestionable 'Western' values is relativized by stressing that they have a short history. These democratic rights are referred to as *izobreteniye* ('an invention'), a noun that is often used to relate a whimsical quality, modified by the temporal adjective *nedavneye* ('recent'). The speech act of reminding articulated by the first person verbal form *napomnyu* ('to remind you') re-focuses the listeners' attention on the relativized quality. Thus, Surkov's verbalization of the short length of the Western democratic tradition can be seen as a version of the 'small number' device, a tool of downplaying. Furthermore, this accent on the 'novelty' quality of democracy has an implication that this Western habit may be untested and unreliable.

(5) Но мы все *вроде бы* согласны, что изобретение это прогрессивное, и в таких обществах жить и *выгоднее, и интереснее.* Естественно, человек, у которого есть знания, человек, который может участвовать *в той или иной степени (кто-то больше, кто-то меньше)* в принятии решений по демократическим процедурам, у такого человека и больше свободы выбора, и больше чувство собственного достоинства.

('But we sort of agree that it is a progressive invention: it is more profitable and more interesting to live in such societies. Naturally, a person who has knowledge, a person who can take part to one degree or another (some more and some less) in taking decisions on democratic procedures, that person has more freedom of choice and more sense of self respect.')

As he positively constructs the 'Western' principles of democracy in further statements (5), Vladislav Surkov pre-empts that with linguistic hedging: the modal particles *vrode by* ('sort of') mark uncertainty, the multiple relative markers *v toy ili inoy stepeni (kto-to bol'she, kto-to men'she)* ('to one degree or another (some more and some less)') contribute to the concept's relativization and ultimately cast doubt on the notion of unequivocal and full democratic participation. In addition, the speaker uses a strategy of evasion when he does not mention the basic notions of equality and fairness usually attached to the concept of 'Western' democracy. Instead, the benefits of living in a democratic society are formulated here through the arguments of profitability and a rather vague 'interest': *vygodneye* ('more profitable') and *interesneye* ('more interesting'). At the same time, the category of participation is linguistically limited to the bureaucratically phrased 'taking decisions on democratic procedures' – *prinyatiye resheniy po demokraticheskim protseduram* – in contrast to the use of procedures to exercise the people's will, which is not mentioned here at all.

In implementing strategies of avoidance and euphemization towards 'Western' democratic qualities, the noun *demokratiya* ('democracy') is replaced by the less specific term *vseobshcheye pravo uchastvovat' v politicheskoy zhizni* ('the universal right to take part in political life'), and rephrased with pseudo-synonyms, such as *tekhnologii* ('PR technologies'), modified by attributes underscoring the manipulative qualities of the described system: *slozhnyye, myagkiye, izoshchrennyye* ('complex, soft, sophisticated'). These linguistic substitutes create an impression that Western democracy is nothing but a craftily managed political manipulation:

> (6) В связи с этим и *социальная технология, и технология власти, и технология самоорганизации общества* становятся все более сложными, все более, если угодно, *мягкими и изощренными*.
>
> ('In connection with that, social technology, the technology of power and the technology of self-organization of society are becoming more complex, softer and more nuanced if you wish.')

Following a strategy of disassociating Russia from the 'West', Surkov mixes or rather swaps around the distinctive attributes that historically defined the 'Russian' side of the dichotomy Russia–the 'West'. Raising the spectre of Soviet sophistry and stripping the term *ideologiya* ('ideology') down to its etymology as well as, in addition, furnishing his point with the emphatic quantifying prefix *sverkh-* and the particle *kuda boleye*, he attributes more ideology to 'Western' democracy than to totalitarianism:

> (7) Как ни парадоксально, демократическое общество, по моему мнению, сверхидеологизировано, куда более идеологизировано, чем тоталитарное, где страх заменяет идею.
>
> ('Paradoxical as it may sound but in my opinion, a democratic society is superideologized, much more ideologized than a totalitarian society where fear replaces the idea.')

As he continues attributing unreliability and negative value to the 'West', Vladislav Surkov explains 'Western' peoples' convictions regarding democracy and human rights in terms of the success of 'Western' propaganda technologies. Metaphoric constructions – the passive participle unit *gvozdyami vbity* ('nailed in') and the idiom *ikh noch'yu razbudi* ('you wake them up at night') – serve as tools to portray those inhabiting the 'West' as passive, brain-washed unthinking experiencers rather than conscientious citizens:

> (8) И насколько '*гвоздями вбиты*' основные ценности демократии гражданам США, Англии, Франции. *Их ночью разбуди* - они вам начнут рассказывать про права человека и так далее.

('And you see how the main values of democracy are nailed into the heads of citizens of the USA, England and France. You wake them up in the middle of the night and they will begin to tell you about human rights and so on.')

While he linguistically downgrades the 'Western' notion of democracy, surrounding its discourse referent with markers of hesitation, or even recasts it as false, Surkov uses the term *demokratiya* ('democracy') unreservedly when he moves on to talk about Putin's Russia. It is attributed the quality of being genuine without any possible doubt or evidence, and it is described almost ecclesiastically as a word whose real sense the president personally rediscovers and hands down to institutions:

(9) Просто *демократия в России - это всерьез и надолго*; Президент *возвращает реальный* смысл слова 'демократия' *всем демократическим институтам*.

('Simply democracy in Russia is serious and for a long time; the President returns the real sense of the word "democracy" to all democratic institutions.')

As Surkov moves on to describe the details of the Russian brand of democracy, it appears that the speaker's understanding of the term relates not to the whole of the post-communist Russian period but only to the period of Vladimir Putin's presidency. The period of the 1990s marked by Boris Yel'tsin's presidency, at the time associated with democratic rule, is described here through strategies of delegitimization and demontage. In particular, similar to the narration of the 'West', it is qualified as not a democracy: *demokratiya* is framed as a failed expectation by the complex conjunction *vmesto togo, chtoby* ('instead of'), and is deconstructed and redefined with the help of a chain of its local antonyms: *zoologichesky period* ('the zoological period'), *oligarkhiya* ('the oligarchy'), *pridvornyye intrigi* ('court intrigues'), *manipulyatsiya* ('manipulation'). The animal metaphor of the first reference is demeaning and by contrast highlights the 'civilized', 'human character' of the period that followed (10).

(10) И одно из самых важных достижений 90-х, мне кажется, то, что в такой достаточно *зоологический период нашего развития* к ведущим позициям пробились по-настоящему активные, стойкие, целеустремленные и сильные люди, материал для формирования нового ведущего слоя нации; *То есть вместо того, чтобы* двигаться к демократии, мы получили то, что справедливо названо *олигархией* ... В результате все основные идеи демократии были искажены. Вместо общественной дискуссии мы получили сплошные *придворные интриги*. Мы получили *манипуляцию* вместо представительства.

('So my impression is that one of the most important achievements of the 1990s is that in such sufficiently zoological period, people who are really active, firm and determined managed to push themselves into the leading positions and became material for the formation of the new layer of the nation's leaders: That is instead of moving towards democracy we received what may fairly be called an oligarchy ... As a result, all the main ideas of democracy were distorted. Instead of public debate we got complex court intrigues. We got manipulation instead of representation.')

Surkov thus chooses vagueness in his various definitions of democracy, which also forms a distancing strategy regarding Russia and the 'West'. The notion of democracy becomes even more blurred when he attempts to attribute democratic values to the Soviet regime, thus revoking and reconstructing the legitimacy of the latter. Using the topos of 'history as a teacher', he finds roots of the present variant of Russian democracy not in the 'West' but back in the Soviet period and in particular, in the Soviet constitution. The present desire of Russians to live in a democratic society is interpreted by the use of the verb *vernut'sya* as a movement back in history to the Soviet past, 'a return' to the letter of Soviet legislation. That the Soviet regime is a ready made successful model to follow is additionally emphasized by the use of the first person parenthesis *zamechu* ('I will note') and the adverbial *podrobno* ('in detail'):

(11) И он (народ) попытался *вернуться к демократическим ценностям*, которые, *замечу, были подробно прописаны в советской конституции.*

('And they (the people) attempted to return to the democratic values that, I must note, were outlined in detail in the Soviet Constitution.')

The dominant discourse of the Putin era habitually equates the notion of the 'West' with globalization and contrasts the commonality of the 'Western' globalized world with the supposed uniqueness of Russia. Similarly, Surkov realizes a strategy of demontage towards the 'West' through the contrasting qualities of 'globalized'–'non-globalized.' Thus, *globalizatsiya* ('globalization') is presented here as the main threat to a dominant qualifier of modern day Russian identity, the non-globalized quality called *suverenitet* ('sovereignty'). In Surkov's speech, 'sovereignty' is constructed to be fragile, in need of protection and guarding, while the temporal frame for this state renders it constant and unevolving (*vse vremya* 'all the time'):

(12) Что касается *суверенитета*: почему мы, собственно, должны *все время о нем помнить и его беречь*? Есть такое явление - *глобализация.*

('As concerns sovereignty: why in fact do we need to remember about it all the time and treasure it? There is such a thing called globalization.')

In (13), the 'West' is portrayed as a source of the dangers and problems befalling Russia. In particular, the demontage of the 'West' continues as Russia is described as a potential victim of the 'West'. The qualifier *mezhdunarodny* ('international') used for 'terrorism' blurs the real, experienced danger of domestic terrorist activity connected to the conflict in the North Caucasus with the Western narrative of Muslim terrorism, which emerged after the September 2001 attacks on the Twin Towers in New York. This recasts the outside world, including the 'West', as a place from which danger emerges, rather than from the local territories. The description of Russia's hypothetical involvement in a direct military clash leaves the enemy unspecified, however the phrasing including the noun *ugroza*, which usually implies an existence of an aggressor, evokes the subject positions established in the Soviet discourse of the Cold War. So, underspecification here works towards the depiction of the 'West' cast in the role of an aggressive enemy. Anthropomorphic metaphors also contribute to conveying the idea that the 'West' is a dangerous Other, against whom it would be prudent to sharpen one's alertness. In this vein, the digestive metaphor *myagkoye pogloshcheniye* ('easy consumption') conceptualizes the 'West' as some predatory entity able to consume other countries as if they were food. Russia, on the other hand, is constructed through the metaphor of a feeble body with a low immunity, which might be, like Ukraine, unable to resist the 'Orange' disease which in its turn is nothing but political spin arriving from the scheming 'West'. There is also a rhyming connection between *suverenitet* ('sovereignty') at the beginning of the paragraph and *immunitet* ('immunity') at the end. This rhyming game perhaps bears a specific additional sense coming from Surkov, who in addition to his Kremlin duties apparently engages in literary pursuits.[6]

(13)   Что угрожает суверенитету как составной части нашей существующей и будущей политической модели? Основные *угрозы суверенности* нашей нации - это *международный терроризм*; это (к счастью, пока очень гипотетическая) *угроза прямого военного столкновения*; ... *мягкое поглощение* по современным 'оранжевым технологиям' *при снижении национального иммунитета* к внешним воздействиям.

('What threatens the sovereignty as an integral part of our present and future political model? The main threats to our nation's sovereignty are international terrorism, the threat of a direct military clash (fortunately still very hypothetical), ... the possibility of being easily consumed following the contemporary "orange technologies" in case the national immunity to outside influences falls.')

Finally, Surkov's discussion of Russian participation in global information systems reveals further still the duality and incoherence of his vision of the place that the 'West' occupies in relation to Russian identity. As (14) demonstrates, despite building up the sense of the 'Western' threat he also uses an ameliorative personification in his reference to it as *prilichnoye obshchestvo* ('a decent society'), which Russia is apparently keen to join. Here we see an element of construction of the 'West' within the normative frame; however, it is also clear that Russia is to achieve a favourable position in the outside world not by joining but by circumventing the norm. To relate this, Surkov's choice of imagery for depicting the options for Russian behaviour towards the global 'West' comes from an arsenal of animalistic metaphors. Constructing a Darwinian model of the world and expanding on the earlier metaphor of consumption he imagines the interacting nations either in the role of a predatory spider or an object of its digestion, a fly. This leads to the understanding that for Russia, the route to 'the decent society' and possibilities of engagement with the 'West' are limited and can only be achieved through one swallowing the other, through rivalry, mistrust, and trickery.

> (14) Что касается средств связи, то только прямое участие российских компаний в создании глобальных информационных сетей сможет обеспечить *место России в приличном обществе*. От этого *зависит наш суверенитет, и кто мы в мировой паутине - пауки или мухи.*
>
> ('As far as the communication technologies are concerned, only direct participation of Russian companies in the creation of the global information networks can ensure the Russian place in decent society. Our sovereignty depends on this and who we are in the world web, spiders or flies.')

Given Vladislav Surkov's official role and influence, he is certainly instrumental in developing patterns of identity constructed and perpetuated in the dominant discourse. The pattern that emerges from this case study regards the 'West' as a constant comparator against which Russian national qualities are interpreted. While some instances of narration of commonalities are present in the text, the preference of the discursive tools seems to focus on the othering, that is, on stressing the distinction of Russia from the 'West', with a predominantly negative attribution to the latter. Such a construction of the 'West' occurs with the implementation of discursive strategies of distancing and demontage and with the production of ambiguity. Specific meanings which attribute to the 'West' a normative quality and positive categorizations are overshadowed by the more prominently positioned meanings that negate and relativize the former, while Russia is described as a rival and a vigilant, mistrusting counterpart of the 'West'.

The West versus Russia: metaphors of counter-discourse

The counter-discourse is 'always interlocked with the domination' it contests (Terdiman 1989: 16). In other words, by its very nature of voicing opposition the counter-discourse is in dialogical and interpretative relation to the dominant discourse. Signs with images embedded in them and meanings attributed to them present a field of struggle for signification, or what in Spivak's words is 'an elemental *machine for domination*' (1998). In principle, Russian counter-discourse tends to display strategies of demontage towards the dominant meanings and, conversely, constructive strategies for the articulation of the oppositional senses (Ryazanova-Clarke 2009). However, as Spivak reminds us, the negotiated signs incorporate displacement that breaks the binary opposition of the dominant and the dissident, which allows the sign to both follow the 'trace' of the dominant and to oppose it. She writes, interpreting Derrida's difference from the 'completely other', located in a sign: 'Such is the strange "being" of the sign: half of it always "not there" and the other half always "not that"' (Spivak 1998: xvii). This section looks into the use of the metaphor as a major counter-discursive meaning negotiator and the strategies this mechanism services. The metaphor is a particularly powerful tool for linguistic interpretation of novel phenomena as it always links it to the familiar and resorts to past experiences (Lakoff and Johnson 1980; Nerlich et al. 2000; Zinken 2003). In the interpretative capacity, the metaphor plays a key role in discourses to frame ideologies and viewpoints. Recent research has identified a specific type of discourse metaphor which are to a high degree socially and culturally situated and embedded in the networks of power (Zinken et al. 2008). As discourse metaphors organize narratives of politics, so in both dominant and the oppositional discourses they are placed to present the focal point of contestation of the relevant dominant sense (Koteyko and Ryazanova-Clarke 2009).

Latynina, who is also a fiction writer and who uses figurative language as her favoured mode of writing,[7] often resorts to metaphors for the realization of strategies of identity construction in relation to both Russianness and the 'West'. In the article 'Velikaya reka ekonomiki', she consistently builds a system of verbal images known as extended metaphors, or megametaphors, which together work as a strategy of both reconstructing and dismantling the dominant voice of othering the 'West'. According to Paul Werth, the megametaphor is a system of interconnected metaphors in the undercurrent stratum of the text that all together provide a condensed way for relaying meaning and guide the reader's interpretation of the central meanings of the text (Werth 1994: 79, 1999: 323). So, in Latynina's text, the sides in the Russia-versus-the-'West' identity concept are constructed through a system of discourse megametaphors which are mapped to domains with both contrasting and common elements.

The article's narrative, which is an ironic stylization of a Chinese parable, maps Russia and the 'West' respectively to two kinds of water realm. Latynina follows the dominant meanings in reconstructing the notion of a separate unit called the 'Western' world and, as in Surkov's speech, it is rephrased as the world of global economy. But the globally engaged 'West' in Latynina's model is associated not with the web of spiders and flies but with a powerful river, highlighting the semantic elements of freedom and the natural, inevitable character of its behaviour:

(15) Есть единый, экономически целый мир – Большая Река Экономики, которая течет куда-то в будущее.

('There exists a single, whole economic world – the Big River of Economics which flows somewhere into the future.')

As the law of nature dictates, the Western river flows freely and confidently into the future, as it takes along with it small islands and bits of turf that stand in the way and temporarily obstruct the flow. This image is contrasted with a group of countries defined by their isolation from the global economy. The author uses the strategy of participant categorization through association, grouping them in a particular way (van Leeuwen 1996: 50). Russia joins this category, together with authoritarian Belarus and North Korea, all of which are metaphorically conceptualized as still and stagnant water forms: ponds, weirs, and dams (16). Stillness though does not necessarily mean calmness or peacefulness: the metaphorical ponds are also attributed the semantic characteristics of aggression and are portrayed fighting with each other, and brandishing their dubious greatness.

(16) И в изоляции от этой Большой Реки есть несколько *Прудов.* Эти *Пруды* разные. Одни слегка сообщаются с Большой Рекой. Другие от нее отрезаны полностью … Часть *Реки* не может победить Реку. Часть Реки может только вырыть себе *запруду,* воздвигнуть *плотину* и *кричать с нее:* '*Наша запруда - самая прогрессивная, самая великая, самая нанотехнологическая в мире!*' С Рекой *воевать* бессмысленно вообще. Между собой воюют только *Пруды … Обитателям Прудов* нечего предложить друг другу. Президент Белоруссии может летать в гости к президенту Венесуэлы; Ахмадинежад, Путин и Ким Чен Ир втроем могут обличать американский 'четвертый рейх.' Но предложить им друг другу нечего.

('And isolated from this Big River are several Ponds. These Ponds are varied. Some of them are slightly connected with the Big River. Others are completely cut off from it … A section of the River cannot win over the River, the section of the river can only dig a dam for itself, to erect a dyke and to yell from it: "Our dyke is the greatest, the most progressive, the most nano-technological in the world!" It is totally senseless to fight with the River. Only Ponds fight with each other … The inhabitants of the Ponds have nothing to offer to each other. President of Belorussia may fly to visit the President of Venezuela. Three of them: Ahmadinejad, Putin and Kim Jong Il may castigate the American "Fourth Reich". But there is nothing that they can offer to each other.')

As the discourse progresses, this complex metaphorical structure is elaborated and further fields are added to both the meanings of the 'West' and of Russianness. For Latynina, the local synonym of the 'Western' notion, *reka* ('river') is *okean* ('ocean'), as she links the two concepts by the semantic elements of 'openness', 'strength of current', and 'movement'. Conversely, the negative referencing progresses on the 'Russian' side, and a chain of metaphorical synonyms characterized by a descending trajectory in quality is constructed. *Prud* ('pond') turns into *bolota* ('swamps'), later categorized with the features of smell and colour as *chernaya vonyuchaya voda* ('black and stinking water') and finally, downgraded as *kanalizatsiya* ('sewage'), whose interaction with the clean and lively river can only be interpreted as poisoning.

Elaborating the megametaphor further, Latynina also contrasts the two types of liquid habitat through a description of the two kinds of species inhabiting them. The ocean of the 'Western' metaphorical domain is full of graceful creatures – the author populates it with *morskiye kon'ki* ('sea horses'), *zolotyye rybki* ('gold fish'), and *netoroplivyye transnatsional'nyye kity* ('the majestically slow transnational whales'). The metaphor of the ocean is constructed as the normative frame while against this Western norm, the notion of 'the Other' is attributed to Russia, clearly depicted as a distortion and aberration. Mutants of a primitive and clumsy crustaceous form dominate the 'Russian' waters, living among slime and green algae. The metaphor of aberrant mutation is cleverly lexicalized by the mutant name compounds *rakokraby*, blending 'crabs' and 'crayfish', and *raboraki*, combining in one word 'crayfish' and a component which could be understood as truncated 'crab', or possibly, 'slave'. In addition, the mutant compounds are characterized by a cluster of consonants /k/, /r/, and /b/, sounding screechy and ominous:

(17) На самом деле китов волнует только одно. Если эти *ракокрабы* и *рабораки* решили жить в *канализации* - пусть эта *канализация не отравляет Реку*.

('In fact, whales worry only about one thing: if these crab-cancers or crabcrustaceans decided to live in sewage, let this sewage not poison the River.')

The device of referential assimilation in (18) allows Latynina to extend the chain of screechy compounds with the real names of leaders of dictatorial regimes – Kim Jong Il of North Korea, Mahmud Ahmadinejad of Iran – and influential members of the Russian administration, Gennady Onishchenko and Igor' Sechin.[8] Linguistically downgrading these characters as *tvari* ('lowly creatures') of the bogs, Latynina plays with their names to form mutant compounds: capitals are omitted, transferring proper nouns into common nouns, and several names are merged into one. Thus, the meaning of 'abnormality, undesirability' created through the mutant names and metaphorical contrast of the water creatures is transferred to the above persons associated with the imagery represented as the dominant version of Russianness.

(18) В одних [прудах] еще *есть черная вонючая вода*. Другие полностью превратились в *болота*, где водятся невиданные в Большой Реке *твари – кимчениры, ахмадинежады, онищенкосечины*.

('In some [ponds] there is still some water, albeit black and stinky. Others completely transformed into bogs where creatures exist that are unseen in the Big River: kimjongils, ahmadinejads and onishchenkosechins.')

According to Latynina's conceptualization, the freedom of the self-cleansing flow in the 'Western' river (or the ocean) is prohibitive for authoritarian regimes, that is, the Russian pond and those akin to it. The key characteristics of primitiveness and clumsiness associated through imagery with Russianness are expanded by further metaphorical elaborations in which animals representing Russia are described through specific parts pointing to predatory, aggressive, and parasitic functions: for example, jaws, blood sucking polyps, poisonous tails, and exoskeletons (19):

(19) В Реке такая фауна не выживет. Несмотря на имеющиеся у нее в изобилии *челюсти, кровососущие присоски, ядовитые хвосты, хитиновый покров* и пр., она умирает от простой проточной воды.

('This kind of fauna will not survive in the River. Despite the abundance of jaws, blood sucking polyps, poisonous tails, and exoskeletons, etc., it dies from simple running water.')

So, in Yuliya Latynina's counter-discourse, the megametaphor implements with regard to the dominant discourse both the strategy of continuation in the representation of the 'West' as the global 'Other' of Russia, as well as the dismantling strategy. In articulating the latter the megametaphor links together the unflattering semantic characteristics derived from a series of source domains conceptualized as an interpretation of the dominant vision of Russianness. In particular, the series of water metaphors acts to contradict the neo-Slavophile, isolationist view that Russia needs a special path to achieve a successful future away from the international integration processes on terms defined by the globalized 'West' and in that way contradicts the knowledge frames found in Surkov's speech. As Latynina's metaphorical meanings deconstruct the dominant portrayal of Russianness they also attribute normative and superior qualities to the 'West'. As opposed to Russianness, Yuliya Latynina describes the 'West' within the normative frame through the benign, happy and commonsensical qualities manifested in the images of clean water and friendly animals.

To conclude, after centuries of history, the 'Other' orientation towards the 'West' continues to be a crucial factor in identity construction in Russian public discourses. The lack of wholeness that Hall was referring to is demonstrated by both discourses. Yuliya Latynina's liberal counter-discourse falls within the parameters of the Westernized tradition as it continues to define Russianness as deficiency, while holding up the West as the normative model for Russia to follow and requiring it to adjust its practices and ways accordingly. The dominant discourse represented by Vladislav Surkov's speech displays even more duality and incompleteness in the construction of Russianness through the image of the 'West'. Surkov's discourse demonstrates a combination of attraction and repulsion, but ultimately the 'West' emerges as an unreliable, scheming, and deceiving 'Other', a place that needs to be constantly debunked for its spurious qualities, which in general are far inferior in comparison with those of Russia; but also as a place of decency and standards to be aspired to and as a model for reluctant followers to pursue.

Notes

1 For examples of contemporary literature on Russianness reflected through the Russian language, see Wierzbicka (1997); Savel'yeva (2000); Kolesov (2002); Shmelev (2002); Zaliznyak et al. (2005).
2 http://www.kreml.org/media/111622794?mode=print
3 For details of discursive strategies of national identity construction see Wodak et al. (2009).
4 Here and below, quoted passages are indicated and referred to by numbers.
5 Here and in examples below the emphasis is added.
6 It is claimed that Vladislav Surkov has written poetry under pseudonyms. In particular he was the author of the lyrics for the rock group Agata Kristi's album *Peninsulas*: 'Vremya ugryumoye, konchilis' prazdniki' (*Komsomol'skaya Pradva*, 29 December 2003). His image of a man of letters is confirmed by the current assumption in cultural circles that he is also the author of the novel *Okolonolya* ('Aboutzero') published in 2009 under the pseudonym Natan Dubovitsky.

7 Yuliya Latynina has written fantasy fiction and has created a new literary genre, 'the oligarchic novel'. Her best selling novels *Okhota na Izyubrya* ('Stag Hunting'), which appeared in 1999 and *Promzona* ('The Industrial Park'), published in 2003, have been made into popular television series.

8 Gennady Onishchenko is the Head of the Russian public health service and has been known for using public health reasons for politically motivated bans on exports. In 2007, Igor' Sechin was a presidential aide.

Bibliography

Aron, L. (2008) 'The Georgia Watershed', *Russian Outlook*, Fall: 1–10.

Berlin, I. (1963) 'The Silence of Russian Culture', in P.E. Mosley (ed.) *The Soviet Union, 1922–1962: A Foreign Affairs Reader*, 337–60, New York: Praeger for the Council of Foreign Relations.

Chilton, P. and Ilyin, M. (1993) 'Metaphor in political discourse: the case of the "common European house"', *Discourse and Society*, 4/1: 7–31.

Chilton, P.A., Ilyin, M.V., and Mey, J.L. (eds) (1998) *Political Discourse in Transition in Europe 1989–1991*, Amsterdam/Philadelphia: John Benjamins.

Dubovitsky, N. (2009) *Okolonolya*, Moscow: OOO Media-gruppa Zhivi.

Hall, S. (1992) 'The Question of Cultural Identity', in S. Hall, D. Held and T. McGrow (eds) *Modernity and its Futures*, 274–327, Cambridge: Polity Press.

——(1996) 'Who needs identity?', in S. Hall and P. du Gay (eds) *Questions of Cultural Identity*, 1–17, London: Sage.

Kolesov, V.V. (2002) *Filosofiya russkogo slova*, Sankt-Peterburg: Yuna.

Koteyko, N. and Ryazanova-Clarke, L. (2009) 'The path and building metaphors in the speeches of Vladimir Putin: back to the future?' *Slavonica*, 15/2: 112–27.

Lakoff, G. and Johnson, M. (1980) *Metaphors We Live By*, Chicago: University of Chicago Press.

Latynina, Yu. (2006 [1999]) *Okhota na Izyubrya*, Moscow: Eksmo.

——(2003) *Promzona*, Moscow: Olma-Press Ekslibris.

——(2007) 'Velikaya reka ekonomiki', *Ezhednevny Zhurnal*, 22 May.

McDaniel, T. (1996) *The Agony of the Russian Idea*, Princeton, NJ: Princeton University Press.

Nerlich, B., Clarke, D.D., and Dingwall, R. (2000) 'Clones and crops: the use of stock characters and word play in two debates about bioengineering', *Metaphor and Symbol*, 15: 223–40.

Neumann, I.B. (1996) *Russia and the Idea of Europe: A study in Identity and International Relations*, London: Routledge.

Paramonov, B.M. (1996) 'Historical culture', in D. Shalin (ed.) *Russian Culture at the Crossroads: Paradoxes of Postcommunist Consciousness*, 11–40, Boulder, CO: Westview Press.

Radzikhovsky, L. (2006) 'Yevropeytsy sverkhu', *Nezavisimaya Gazeta*, 7 May.

Ryazanova-Clarke, L. (2006) '"The state turning to language": power and identity in Russian language policy today', *Russian Language Journal*, 56: 37–55.

——(2008a) 'On the satirical counter-discourse of *Processed Cheese*', *Russian Language Journal*, 58: 93–112.

——(2008b) 'Putin's nation: discursive construction of national identity in "Direct line with president"', in A. Mustajoki, M.V. Kopotev, L.A. Biryulin, and E.Yu. Protassova (eds) *Instrumentariy rusistiki: korpusnyye podkhody*, 311–31, Helsinki: Helsinki University Press.

——(2008c) 'Re-creation of the nation: orthodox and heterodox discourses in post-soviet Russia', *Scando-Slavica*, 54, 223–39.

——(2009) 'How upright is the vertical? Ideological norm negotiation in Russian media discourse', in I. Lunde and M. Paulsen (eds) *From Poets to Padonki: Linguistic Authority and Norm Negotiation in Modern Russian Culture*, 288–315, Bergen: Bergen University Press.

Savel'yeva, L.V. (2000) *Russkoye slovo: konets XX veka*, Sankt-Peterburg: Logos.

Shalin, D. (1996) 'Intellectual culture', in D. Shalin (ed.) *Russian Culture at the Crossroads: Paradoxes of Postcommunist Consciousness*, 41–98, Boulder, CO: Westview Press.

Shmelev, A.D. (2002) *Russkaya yazykovaya model' mira*, Moskva: Yazyki slavyanskoy kul'tury.

Slembrouck, S. (2001) 'Explanation, interpretation and critique in the analysis of discourse', *Critique of Anthropology*, 21/1: 33–57.

Smith, K.E. (2002) *Mythmaking in the New Russia: Politics and Memory during Yeltsin Era*, Ithaca, NY: Cornell University Press.

Spivak, G.Ch. (1998) 'Translator's preface', in J. Derrida *Of Grammatology*, trans. by G.Ch. Spivak, ix–lxxxix, Baltimore, MD: Johns Hopkins University Press.

Surkov, V. (2006) 'Stenogramma vystupleniya zamestitelya rukovoditelya administratsii Prezidenta – pomoshchnika Prezidenta RF Vladislava Surkova pered slushatelyami Tsentra partiynoy ucheby i podgotovki kadrov VPP "Yedinaya Rossiya" 7 fevralya 2006 goda.' Online. Available: www.edinros.ru/news.html?id=111148 (accessed 20 September 2008).

Terdiman, R. (1989) *Discourse/Counter-Discourse: The Theory and Practice of Symbolic Resistance in Nineteenth-Century France*, Ithaca, NY: Cornell University Press.

Tolz, V. (2001) *Russia*, London: Arnold.

van Leeuwen, T. (1996) 'The representation of social actors', in C.R. Caldas-Coulthard and M. Coulthard (eds) *Texts and Practices*, 32–70, London: Routledge.

Werth, P. (1994) 'Extended metaphor: a text world account', *Language and Literature*, 3/2: 79–103.

——(1999) *Text Worlds: Representing Conceptual Space in Discourse*, London: Longman.

Wierzbicka, A. (1997) *Understanding Cultures through Their Key Words: English, Russian, Polish, German, and Japanese*, New York/Oxford: Oxford University Press.

Wodak, R., de Cillia, R., Reisigl, M., and Liebhart, K. (2009) *The Discursive Construction of National Identity*, 2nd edn, trans. by A. Hursch and R. Mitten, Edinburgh: Edinburgh University Press.

Zaliznyak, A.A., Levontina, I.B., and Shmelev, A.D. (2005) *Klyuchevyye idei russkoy kartiny mira*, Moskva: Yazyki slavyanskoy kul'tury.

Zinken, J. (2003) 'Ideological imagination: intertextual and correlational metaphors in political discourse', *Discourse and Society*, 14/4: 507–23.

Zinken, J., Hellsten, I., and Nerlich, B. (2008) 'Discourse metaphors', in R. Frank, R. Dirven, T. Ziemke, and E. Bernárdes (eds) *Body, Language and Mind*, vol. 2: Sociocultural Situatedness, 363–86, Amsterdam: John Benjamin.

Zhdanova, V. (2006) 'Russkaya kul'turno-yazykovaya model' prostranstva i osobennosti individual'noy orientatsii v ney', in V.V. Krasnykh (ed.) *Russkiye i Russkost'*, 5–178, Moskva: Gnozis.

2 Attitudes toward the Russian and English languages in Russia and the United States: perceptions of self and the other

David R. Andrews

'Why are they always so angry at one another?' my godfather asked me shortly after I had returned from my first study-abroad trip to Moscow in 1979. 'Who?' I asked. 'The Russians', he answered. 'Whenever I hear people speaking Russian, it seems as if they're arguing or threatening one another. It's such a harsh language!' My godfather, of course, understood no Russian and was reacting only to his opinion of its sound. In any case, I was perplexed and rather offended. By that time I had not only lost my heart to the Russian language but had also decided to devote my future professional life to it. In the spirit of a budding sociolinguist, I tried to tease out of my godfather how and why his feelings had originated. He finally admitted that his attitudes toward Russian had most likely been formed by American media portrayals of the Soviet Union. In particular, he mentioned Nikita Khrushchev's banging his shoe in anger at a 1960 meeting of the UN General Assembly and his threat to 'bury' the capitalist world, actually an earlier utterance which had become conflated with the UN incident in the American consciousness (see Frankland 1966: 154–70; Hyland and Shryock 1968: 3–17). In other words, my godfather's feelings were almost entirely politically motivated, although he still maintained that there was something about the sound of the Russian language that he simply disliked.

The counterpart to the above episode occurred during a subsequent year I spent in Moscow. I was the dinner guest of a local family with whom I had grown quite close. That evening, for the first time, I had brought along another American student to meet them. I cannot recall the subject of the conversation, but at one point my compatriot and I were attempting to explain some bit of American realia to our hosts. While discussing the best way to do so, we briefly slipped into English, until the mother of the family stopped us rather abruptly. Her objection was not so much that we had begun speaking in a language she did not understand, but rather that I sounded so very different from the person she had come to know. In fact, with English on my tongue I seemed downright unpleasant to her. When challenged by another family member, the woman admitted that her encounters with the English language had been limited mostly to snippets from television or film in which the speakers were depicted in an unfavourable light. Still, however, she was adamant that there was something about the sound of the English language that she simply disliked.

These and similar incidents throughout my almost thirty-five years as an American student, teacher, and scholar of Russian have inspired me to reflect upon certain broad-based language attitudes in Russia and the United States. In this chapter I explore them more systematically, focusing on each country's perceptions of its own and the other's language, the correlation of these perceptions with larger sociocultural and sociopolitical factors, and their evolution from the late Soviet era through to the present day. The Cold War engendered by no means universal, but nevertheless widespread, mutual misunderstanding and suspicion, and the vicissitudes of Russian–American relations since then have done little to ameliorate this situation, at least for certain segments of each populace. Reciprocal attitudes toward the Russian and English languages, then, are partly an outgrowth of differing worldviews and of each society's popular image of itself and the other. Nevertheless, there are important differences between conditions now and thirty years ago, which we will explore below.

These language attitudes are also connected to some highly charged questions with exceedingly complex answers. Exactly to whom does each language belong? What is the role of each language in this era of rapid globalization? If English truly is the new global language, what does that mean for native speakers of both English and Russian (not to mention of other European languages)? How do Russians and Americans view the nature and function of language? What do they think about standardization and proper versus improper usage? How does the intelligentsia in each country contribute to discussions of language and culture, and how does each society regard its intellectual elite? At the same time, language attitudes may be reinforced by purely linguistic factors, such as differences in intonation, vowel length, use of active versus passive constructions, and the semantics of individual words. Often overlooked because they are primarily subconscious, these variables are no less important in a thorough examination of the problem. They help explain, for instance, the residual negativity toward Russian and English respectively of the man and woman featured in the first two paragraphs.

At this point the reader may object that we are dealing here with generalizations and stereotypes. Even during the darkest days of the Cold War, there were certainly many Russians and Americans who admired and respected the achievements of the other culture and bore no ill will toward its language. First, however, it is precisely of stereotypes that linguistic prejudices, whether internal to any one country or cross-cultural, are made. One need think only of the deeply ingrained biases against nonstandard pronunciations and/or dialects in most societies, although modern linguistics has thoroughly demonstrated that standard languages are a social convention and that any variety of human speech is an equally valid means of communication. A cross-cultural example is the common Anglo-American reaction to French as 'pretentious' or 'snobby', no doubt conditioned by centuries of cultural insecurity in certain specific domains. Second, the attitudes discussed here were not shaped by the relatively small percentage of Russians or Americans who are well acquainted with the other language and culture, but by the broader masses. The number of Americans who know Russian even cursorily, apart from the émigré community, is infinitesimal. How else could

'Russky' have become a derogatory term for 'Russian' in American English during the Cold War?[1] By comparison, many more Russians have traditionally studied English, and today it has increasingly become the foreign language of choice. Knowledge of the language, however, is still quite shallow, at least by European standards.

There was fear-mongering, of course, even by the elites. *Kak my portim russky yazyk* ('How We Are Ruining the Russian Language'), a widely read polemic by K.F. Yakovlev (1974), was a full-throttled denunciation of (by that time, mostly English) borrowings in Russian. While part of a more than two-hundred-year tradition of combating foreign influences on the Russian language, it certainly imparted the impression that there was something sinister about English. An earlier piece by Solzhenitsyn, '*Ne obychay degtem shchi belit'*, *na to smetana*' ('It is not the custom to lighten cabbage soup with tar, for that we have sour cream') (Solzhenitsyn 1965), although not singling out English specifically and also concerned with Russian stylistics more broadly, helped set an us-versus-them tone by its very title. Given Solzhenitsyn's anti-Soviet writings and subsequent exile, it is possible that his propositions here were even more influential in some quarters, for they clearly showed that negative views of foreign linguistic influences could stand apart from purely political concerns.

On the American side the furore was less language-specific, as there was no comparable Russian influence on the English language. However, the anti-Soviet zealotry of the late 1940s and early 1950s, associated most prominently with the work of the Committee on Un-American Activities in the US House of Representatives and of Joseph McCarthy in the US Senate, certainly had a negative effect on public perception of the Russian language. The former is best remembered for its 1947 hearings on possible communist propaganda in the entertainment industry, including even wartime-era films with positive depictions of the Soviet Union (Carr 1952). Clearly, affection for things Russian could be construed as 'un-American'. Three years later, in asserting that there were large numbers of Soviet sympathizers and even outright spies in various arms of the federal government, McCarthy and his allies cast suspicion on speakers of Russian. It was certainly no coincidence that *Voice of America*, which beamed broadcasts in Russian to the Soviet Union, was a specific target of these accusations (Griffith 1970; Matusow 1970).

After the launch of sputnik in 1957, when Americans famously became worried that they were lagging behind the Soviets in technology, attitudes toward the Russian language began to change. As noted in a 1959 article on the scarcity of Russian-language programmes in American schools, 'McCarthy-era opposition to Russian on political grounds' had largely subsided (Parry 1959: 506), and Americans had grown more amenable to the study of the language. This acceptance, however, was firmly set in terms of national security and the need to understand and compete with the Soviet adversary. Indeed, the National Defense Education Act, passed in 1958 to advance the teaching of science, mathematics, engineering, and critical foreign languages (especially Russian), originally contained a loyalty oath. Financial beneficiaries had to pledge that they would not try to overthrow the US government and would defend the country 'against all its enemies, foreign and domestic' (National Defense Education Act, *United States Statutes at Large*, 72: 1602).

This programme evolved considerably over the next two decades and became a major source of graduate-level funding in several different foreign languages and cultures. Loyalty oaths were quickly discarded, and reformulated guidelines emphasized the importance of cross-cultural competence and a global perspective in all spheres of human activity, not only the political. Previous attitudes, however, lingered in the popular imagination. In the small American town where I was raised, some friends and neighbours were palpably uneasy over my decision to become a college Russian major in the mid-1970s. This uneasiness usually grew when I affirmed that I was motivated more by a genuine interest in the language and culture itself than by strictly utilitarian goals.

The tenacity of Cold War impressions is vividly illustrated by two phenomena in the contemporary American zeitgeist. The first is the charge by the political opposition that Barack Obama is a covert socialist and that the policies he is trying to implement amount to 'creeping socialism'. Nowhere is this charge more invoked than in the fight over universal health care, derided as 'socialized medicine', a term that elicits a negative reaction from a substantial percentage of the American populace ('Poll: U.S. Split on Socialized Medicine', Online). In the many organized protests over the past year, participants have often carried signs referring to the Soviet Union, as if it were still a living entity. Once again, affinity for things Russian remains suspect. The other example is the recent spate of books and articles commemorating the fall of the Berlin Wall, and by extension, the collapse of European socialism. Some of these are self-congratulatory commentaries in which it is implied that Americans, especially the political right, 'won' the Cold War. Among these is *Tear Down This Wall: A City, a President, and the Speech That Ended the Cold War*, by Romesh Ratnesar (2009). The allusion, of course, is to Ronald Reagan and his 1986 address in Berlin, when he urged Mikhail Gorbachev to 'tear down this wall'.[2] This sort of rhetoric is not conducive to mutual respect and understanding between Russians and Americans. It feeds the Russian suspicion that the United States is gloating over the demise of the Soviet Union as a great power, and it also encourages a dismissive attitude toward Russia among Americans.

The Cold War may have officially ended with the dissolution of the Soviet Union in 1991, but its legacy is very much extant. As the dominant paradigm during the formative years of the generations presently in power in both countries, it helped shape their political, economic, and cultural outlooks. Old ways of thinking cannot be put aside immediately, and even a rejection of the past is a reaction to it. Moreover, in some respects the Russian and American governments still seem to be fighting the Cold War. Mutual accusations over issues ranging from the expansion of NATO to the origin of the current global economic crisis resonate in much the same way as thirty years ago. For many on both sides, there may remain a direct link between dislike for such criticisms and the language in which they are spoken.

One important change since the end of the Cold War is the greatly accelerated pace at which English is becoming the language of global commerce, diplomacy, scholarship, and cross-cultural communication in general. While English had been emerging as the international language of choice for most of the twentieth century (with the possible exception of the socialist countries between 1945 and 1990), its dominance in this regard has solidified over the past twenty or so years. The conditions leading to the almost universal embrace of English, from the centuries-long spread of the language worldwide by the British Empire to American economic hegemony after World War II, have been well documented and need not be repeated here. With the rise of computer technology and the prominence of English in that domain, the trend may well be irreversible. In any case, it seems that much of the world is obsessed with learning English, including the Russians. Advertisements for instruction in the language, often promising a particular variant or pronunciation and/or specialized vocabulary in a given field, abound in the Russian press and Internet, on city billboards, and in public transportation.

The desire to master English, however, is sometimes coupled with resentment at having to do so in the first place, for the elevation of one language may imply the denigration of another. Such backlash against English is quite astonishing to Americans, a nation of immigrants in which acquisition of the language has always been viewed as natural and normal. I can offer a particularly telling example from my own teaching experience. Every spring I offer History of the Russian Language to advanced undergraduates of Russian and beginning graduate students of Russian Area Studies, virtually all of whom have a functional command of Russian, have lived and studied in Russia or elsewhere in the former Soviet Union, and are generally well-disposed to the language and culture. During the semester we read two articles (Pool 1980; Nyirady 1980) dealing broadly with the role of the Russian language in the multi-ethnic Soviet state and the many hats that Russian wore simultaneously: ethnic language of the Russian people, potential second native language of the non-Russian peoples, the language of interethnic communication within the Soviet Union, the language of the Warsaw Pact, and even the symbolic language of socialism, at least in its European variant. Both articles treat the fact that the majority languages of all fifteen republics were officially equal, that even small minority languages were promised support and protection, and that the use of Russian by non-Russians was supposedly voluntary, as well as the large disconnect between ideology and reality in these matters. When I ask my students to comment, they gravely agree that other Soviet languages were equal to Russian only in theory, and they enumerate the ways in which mastery of Russian was a prerequisite for educational, political, and/or socioeconomic advancement. I then turn the question around and ask them about the status of English as a global language today. The whole world may be learning English, but is this truly voluntary? Are other languages equal to English not only in theory, but also in practice? The initial reaction to this question is amazement and the ensuing discussion lively and dramatic. Even such linguistically savvy, highly educated young Americans have rarely stopped to consider the element of coercion in having to learn English for upward mobility and professional survival.

This ambivalence toward English is not unique to Russians, of course. Witness the ubiquitous Euro-English joke that has been making the rounds on the Internet ('Proposed EU Spelling Changes', Online). It begins with the statement that the European Commission has chosen English over German as its official language, but only on the condition of major spelling revisions in English. The joke continues with the various year-by-year spelling reforms, with each piece of text written in the new style. After each change, English more and more resembles German. Some versions of the joke, such as the one I cite here, end with the prediction that finally 'we will all be speaking German like they wanted in the first place'. Although couched in jest, this is a clear example that the predominance of English is not always welcome.

If this is the case even in Western Europe, the unease over global English is likely to be more acute in Russia, in light of Russian–American tensions that date back to the Cold War. The extensive investigation of Anglicisms in contemporary Russian by A.Yu. Romanov (2000) supports this contention. In a statistically verified survey, Romanov (2000: 63, 123–24) found that 76 per cent of respondents had a somewhat or very negative reaction to widespread borrowing from English. Equally important, there was no statistically significant correlation between this attitude and the respondents' age, level of education, or knowledge of English. Two additional comments, in a test of respondents' knowledge of new Anglicisms, were especially illuminating. One person wrote in the margins of the answer sheet that *bebisiter* meant the same thing as *sidelka* or *nyanya*, only that the former's services would cost more. Another wrote that the identical vodka sold in a bottle with an English label would be more expensive than in one with a Russian label (Romanov 2000: 67). These findings clearly indicate a dislike of English influences on Russian, even among people who know and use this type of language.

Another factor was the larger identity of English and Russian during the Cold War. If indeed there was a sense of competition between English as the language of world capitalism and Russian as the concomitant language of socialism, as Nyirady (1980) and Pool (1980) claim, then the current economic order may facilitate a perception of English as the conquering language and Russian as the vanquished. Such an outlook contributes to the broader frictions between Russians and Americans described earlier. The expansion of the European Union, in which English has become the major administrative language, also plays a significant role. In the former Warsaw Pact countries and Baltic republics that have joined the EU, English has decisively replaced Russian as the most widely studied foreign language, and English influences abound in the local languages (see, for instance, Srpová 2008; Mańczak-Wohlfeld 2008). This fascination with English extends even to Ukraine, not a current EU member but perhaps an aspiring one. According to Krouglov (2008: 19–20), the growing popularity of English there derives precisely from the desire among much of the population for integration with Europe. Official concerns over the expansion of Western economic, political, and military institutions, especially the worry that Ukraine may be pulled into these orbits, feeds a potential dislike in Russia for global English.

In the United States the rise of global English complicates an already ambivalent attitude toward the study of foreign languages. On the one hand, many Americans have come to understand that our prevailing monolingualism is a detriment in an increasingly interconnected world. There have been concerted efforts to expand the teaching of foreign languages to more learners and at earlier ages at least since the 1983 publication of *A Nation at Risk*, an influential report on the deficiencies of the American educational system by the National Commission on Excellence in Education. Encouraging the study of foreign languages because it 'introduces students to non-English-speaking cultures, heightens awareness and comprehension of one's native tongue, and serves the Nation's needs in commerce, diplomacy, defense, and education', the Commission specifically recommended that instruction should begin in primary schools (*A Nation at Risk*, Online: Recommendations, A6). On the other hand, these efforts have met with only limited success, and foreign-language programmes are among the first to face budget cuts in difficult economic times. Many Americans continue to view foreign languages as an educational add-on or frill rather than as a core academic discipline, often precisely because 'everyone in the world speaks English'.

The tendency to question the utility of foreign languages in general bears directly on American attitudes toward Russian. Interest in the language is fickle and largely dependent on world events. The high point came near the end of the glasnost' era, after the fall of the Berlin Wall. In 1990 there were 44,626 students of Russian at American institutions of higher learning, with increases from 23,987 in 1980 and 33,961 in 1986. By 1998, however, peak numbers had declined by almost one half, to a mere 23,791 (Furman, Goldberg and Lusin 2007:10; Schillinger 2009: 16). This, of course, was also the year of the rouble collapse, when many in the United States seemed to be giving up on Russia altogether. Even in the best of times, however, there have been far fewer students of Russian in the United States than of the Romance languages or German. Part of the reason is that Russian has retained its reputation among Americans as exotic and difficult to learn, but this cannot be the entire explanation. In 2006, the last year for which nationwide figures are available, enrolments in Chinese and Japanese were more than twice those in Russian, and in Arabic they were almost identical (Furman, Goldberg and Lusin 2007: 10–11). Unresolved feelings toward Russia and uncertainty over the future of Russian–American relations are also root causes of Americans' relative indifference toward the Russian language. Even today, when Russia has reasserted itself on the international stage far more vigorously than many Americans would have predicted ten or eleven years ago, one of the most frequent questions that my students hear about their study of Russian is: 'But what are you going to *do* with it?'.

Until this point we have treated self-perceptions mostly in the context of each nation's reactions to the other language. Let us now examine more closely the attitudes of Russians and Americans toward their own language as well as toward the cultural significance of language per se. Only by doing so can we paint a fuller picture of both societies, for internal and external impressions interact and mutually reinforce one another in shaping language attitudes as a whole. They are, so to speak, opposite sides of the same coin.

As is well known, many commentators in Russia are greatly alarmed by the erosion of language standards there over the past two decades. These complaints include the large influx of English borrowings discussed earlier (Velichko 1995; Bazylev and Sorokin 1998; Fedorova 2001) but extend far beyond that, from previously impermissible usages in verbal government (Chulaki 1999) and word stress (Velichko 1995) to the proliferation of vulgarities (*mat*) and other non-standard lexicon (Romanov 2004; Komarova 2006). It is unsurprising that these developments are so disturbing to the intelligentsia, for whom the Russian language has traditionally held enormous symbolic power. Indeed, for many it has been a virtual object of veneration, along with Russian literature. If literature is regarded as the crowning achievement of Russian culture, then these perceived assaults on the standard language are a threat to the very culture itself. The connection with literature is even encoded in the language directly; what English-speaking specialists refer to as 'Contemporary *Standard* Russian' is, of course, the '[*kodifitsirovanny*] *literaturny yazyk*' in Russian. However, although they are unwelcome by many, these drastic changes were only to be expected. With the transition from Soviet power came the relaxation of rigid controls in many different aspects of Russian life, language among them. In any case, after a brief comparison to American English, I will argue that we are now witnessing not the total dissolution of standard Russian, but rather the gradual emergence of a new type of norm.

In the United States issues of language do not reverberate in quite the same way as in Russia. First, it cannot be said that English belongs to or uniquely characterizes the American people, for Americans are not its originators and are only one of many nations for whom it is the majority language. This was true even before the rise of global English but is perhaps more so now, when one could argue that English belongs to the entire world. Furthermore, literature has nowhere near the cultural significance in the United States that it has in Russia. The most sacred American texts are not literary, but founding documents like the *Declaration of Independence* and the *Constitution* or great historical pronouncements like Lincoln's *Gettysburg Address* during the Civil War or F.D. Roosevelt's *A Day That Will Live in Infamy* speech after the Japanese bombing of Pearl Harbor. The symbolic power of English in the United States, therefore, is sociopolitical. Quite simply, English is the language of American civic life, and knowing the language is a prerequisite for full participation in that life.

This combination of factors has resulted in the relative absence of linguistic purism among Americans, even the intellectual elite. Discussions of usage, such as the former 'On Language' columns in the *New York Times Magazine* by the late William Safire (Safire 1980), are more descriptive than prescriptive. Other writers openly deride so-called 'nitpickers' and the 'language police'. This does not mean, however, that educated Americans are free of linguistic prejudices. To the contrary, they react very negatively to violations of General American, which functions in the United States as a sort of standard language. Unlike a traditional standard, however, it is what Millward (1988: 325–26) has called a 'negative dialect', or one that it is defined not so much by the specific features that it has but by the recognizably unacceptable ones that it lacks. A negative dialect permits a great deal of variation within certain boundaries, but anything beyond is an unambiguous deviation from the norm. In fact, in a cross-cultural sociolinguistic experiment that I conducted in the early 1990s (Andrews 1994), I demonstrated that speakers of General American were even less forgiving of such norm violations than were speakers of standard Russian.[3]

In other work (Andrews 2006) I have argued that recent developments in the Russian language are indicative of a transition from a well-defined standard to a negative dialect among educated speakers. In effect, it is the imposition of a new norm, less restrictive in some ways and more in others. Nevertheless, it is a jarring change for many Russians. It helps explain, therefore, why some Russians today are particularly sensitive about language in general and remain suspicious of English, since English influences are an important and much debated component of current usage. A final comparison with English, however, suggests that language will always have a special place, if also a different and evolving one, in Russia. Consider the *padonki*, or 'low-lifes', who with their self-proclaimed *padonsky* or *padonkafsky dialekt* (the non-standard spellings here are reflective of their usage) deliberately distort and play with the Russian language on the Internet. They have become quite the phenomenon, inspiring a wide variety of discussion groups, chat rooms, and their own dictionaries. Although there are many abbreviations, slang terms, and other innovations in English as used on the Internet, there is nothing that quite matches the range and influence of the *padonki*. Their 'dialect' may be one of the very things that the Russian intelligentsia is despairing over now, but there is also comfort in the fact that only gifted and accomplished users of the language could manipulate it in this way.

Let us now bring the discussion full circle and return to the American man and Russian woman at the beginning of the chapter. Both of them continued to claim that there was something they simply disliked about the other's language, even after admitting that sociocultural presuppositions might have been the primary motivation of their negative perceptions. This suggests that there are intrinsic features of each language that, while not responsible for shaping these language attitudes alone, can intensify and reinforce them. It is my opinion that the 'something' in this particular case was intonation and, where it is tied to intonation, vowel length. Even in one's native language, reactions to intonation occur primarily at the subconscious level. This is all the more so in a cross-cultural listening situation in which neither person understands the language itself.[4]

Unmarked declarative utterances in Russian are characterized by a simple falling tone, or Intonation Construction-1 (IC-1) in the Bryzgunova (1980) nomenclature. It differs from the corresponding contour in American English, where a slight rise or step-up precedes the fall. American English does have a simple fall that is acoustically quite similar to IC-1, but it marks non-neutral declaratives, with connotations of brusqueness, disapproval, or boredom. Another difference occurs in typical yes-no questions. Standard Russian uses IC-3, a steep rise on the tonic syllable followed by an equally abrupt fall on any post-tonic material, whereas the most prevalent contour in American English is a post-tonic gradual rise to the end of the utterance. There is no intonation contour in American English with the acoustical range and sharp reversal of IC-3. To the untrained American ear, it sounds highly emotional. The closest contour is used in exclamations of frustration or anger, including exclamatory questions. My god-father, therefore, was misinterpreting neutral Russian statements and questions based on what such intonation would convey in English. There is little wonder that he thought Russians were always rude to or angry at one another.

The Russian woman experienced similar perceptual problems. The use of the rise-fall in American declaratives is accompanied by increased vowel length and is especially prominent in diphthongs, or what English speakers call the 'long vowels'. The step-up contains the first part of the diphthong and the fall the second, with the demarcation between the two acoustically distinct. A similar phenomenon occurs in yes-no questions, where the first part of the diphthong is spoken on the tonic syllable and the second part is slowly drawn out into the gradual rise. To the untrained Russian ear, both American contours can create the impression of an artificially elongated vowel, which is highly marked in Russian. It characterizes the plaintive speech of children and sounds particularly petulant and disagreeable when used by an adult. American intonation, therefore, most likely contributed to this woman's assessment of English as unpleasant.

Even Russians and Americans who do know the other language may sometimes misunderstand one another because of inherent linguistic differences. In a recent article on the psychology of language learning, Dewees and Nelson (2009), citing Wierzbicka (1988), note that Russians use 70 per cent more passive constructions than do English speakers. They also point out that the use of the passive voice is growing in Russian, especially in written style, while it is decreasing in English. This could lead to problems in official correspondence, they conclude, because overuse of passive constructions in English makes a document seem 'evasive' or 'unclear', whereas overuse of the active voice in Russian might convey an 'abrupt or even rude tone' (Dewees and Nelson 2009: 15–16).

More important than this, I believe, is another type of potential interference that Wierzbicka (1992, 1997) has explored at length. In her analysis of so-called 'key words' in several different languages, Wierzbicka argues that human concepts often thought to be universal are actually understood in a culturally specific way. A full discussion is beyond the scope of this article, but a particularly good illustration is her juxtaposition of English *friend* and its usual Russian gloss of *drug* (1997: 32–84). By carefully dissecting the full meaning of each term, she proves unequivocally that they denote fundamentally different relationships in each culture. The picture becomes even more complicated if one adds semantically related words, such as English *acquaintance* and Russian *znakomy*, *priyatel'*, and *tovarishch*. Direct translations from one language into the other can therefore lead to serious cross-cultural misunderstanding. Wierzbicka discusses other important concepts as well, demonstrating that English *freedom*, *liberty*, *soul*, *heart*, and *fate* are not at all identical to their standard glosses of *svoboda, volya, dusha, serdtse,* and *sud'ba.* These differences can be pitfalls even for people who know the other language quite well, and the problem is compounded the less a speaker is aware of them.

Because they are deeply ingrained and mostly subconscious, language attitudes are rarely given explicit attention. Within a given culture they are connected to delicate matters of social class, economic status, and educational achievement, and cross-culturally they evoke easily challenged perceptions of national character. For these reasons most people choose to ignore them. However, mutual understanding could be significantly enhanced if more of us gave thought to how language attitudes are formed and perpetuated, including the purely linguistics factors that may exacerbate them. I hope that this discussion has shed some light on why Russians and Americans have been misunderstanding one another for many decades now, and how this misunderstanding is reflected in language. Perhaps it will provide food for thought as Russians and Americans continue to face one another across the linguistic divide.

Notes

1 I still encounter well-educated, but linguistically naive, Americans who assume that 'Russky' must also have a negative connotation in Russian, if indeed they know it is a real Russian word.

2 The full contents of the book present a more detailed analysis than suggested by the title, but the author's arguments always lead back to Reagan.

3 It is important to note that Millward's description of General American is based on pronunciation alone, as was my own experiment. However, the concept of a negative dialect can extend to grammatical features as well. Someone who says 'between you and I' might still be considered a speaker of General American, despite the obvious case error, because that expression has become so ubiquitous. A double negative, however (e.g. 'He didn't do nothing'), is a clear norm violation.

4 Descriptions of Russian intonation here are based on Bryzgunova (1980). There is no single system for the treatment of English intonation. See Trager and Smith (1951), Trager (1964/1972), Ladd (1978), Cruttenden (1986), and Bolinger (1989). For comparisons of Russian and English intonation, see Leed (1965), Holden and Hogan (1993) and Andrews (1999: 120–38).

Bibliography

Andrews, D.R. (1994) 'Subjective reactions to non-standard pronunciations in Great Russian and American English', *Language Quarterly,* 32/3–4: 149–64.

——(1999) *Sociocultural Perspectives on Language Change in Diaspora: Soviet immigrants in the United States,* Amsterdam/Philadelphia: John Benjamins.

——(2006) 'The role of émigré Russian in redefining the "Standard"', *Journal of Slavic Linguistics,* 14/2: 169–89.

Bazylev, V. and Sorokin, Yu. (1998) 'O nashem novoyaze: ot chuzhih slov my stanovimsya agressivneye', *Nezavisimaya gazeta* 25 September.

Bolinger, D. (1989) *Intonation and Its Uses: Melody in Grammar and Discourse,* Stanford, CT: Stanford University Press.

Bryzgunova, E.A. (1980) 'Intonatsiya', *Russkaya grammatika,* vol. 1, 96–122, Moskva: Nauka.

Carr, R.K. (1952) *The House Committee on Un-American Activities: 1945–1950*, Ithaca, NY: Cornell University Press.

Chulaki, M. (1999) 'Vozmushchayus' o tom, chto skazano', *Literaturnaya gazeta*, 17 March.

Cruttenden, A. (1986) *Intonation*, Cambridge: Cambridge University Press.

Dewees, M. and Nelson, S. (2009) 'Culture, language and worldview. Educational aspects', *AATSEEL Newsletter*, 52/3: 15–16.

Fedorova, Ye. (2001) 'Global'ny yazyk kak global'ny vyzov', *Nezavisimaya gazeta*, 25 May.

Frankland, M. (1966) *Khrushchev*, Harmondsworth: Penguin Books.

Furman, N., Goldberg, D., and Lusin, N. (2007) 'Enrollments in languages other than English in United States institutions of higher education, fall 2006', *Modern Language Association of America*. Web publication, 13 November. Online. Available: www.mla.org/2006_flenrollmentsurvey (accessed 29 March 2011).

Griffith, R. (1970) *The Politics of Fear: Joseph R. McCarthy and the Senate*, Lexington: The University Press of Kentucky.

Holden, K.T. and Hogan, J.T. (1993) 'The emotive impact of foreign intonation: an experiment in switching Russian and English intonation', *Language and Speech*, 36: 67–88.

Hyland, W. and Shryock, R.W. (1968) *The Fall of Khrushchev*, New York: Funk and Wagnalls.

Komarova, O. (2006) 'Zametki po povodu diskussiy o russkom yazyke', *Polyarny vestnik*, 9: 7–20.

Krouglov, A. (2008) 'Globalization and Ukrainian language in the 21st century', in E. Andrews (ed.) *Linguistic Changes in Post-Communist Eastern Europe and Eurasia*, 14–35, Boulder, CO: East European Monographs.

Ladd, D.R., Jr. (1978) 'Stylized intonation', *Language*, 54/3: 517–40.

Leed, R.L. (1965) 'A contrastive analysis of Russian and English intonation contours', *Slavic and East European Journal*, 9/1: 62–75.

Mańczak-Wohlfeld, E. (2008) 'Influences of English in contemporary Polish', in E. Andrews (ed.) *Linguistic Changes in Post-Communist Eastern Europe and Eurasia*, 88–102, Boulder,CO: East European Monographs.

Matusow, A.J. (ed.) (1970) *Joseph R. McCarthy*, Englewood Cliffs, NJ: Prentice Hall.

Millward, C.M. (1988) *A Biography of the English Language*, Fort Worth, TX: Harcourt Brace Jovanovich.

A Nation at Risk: The Imperative for Educational Reform (1983) Online. Available: www.ed.gov/pubs/NatAtRisk/index.html (accessed 29 March 2011).

National Defense Education Act (NDEA) (1958) Public Law 85–864 – Sept. 2, 1958, *United States Statutes at Large*, 72: 1580–1605. Online. Available: wwwedu.oulu.fi/tohtorikoulutus/jarjestettava_opetus/Troehler/NDEA_1958.pdf (accessed 7 April 2011).

Nyirady, K.E. (1980) 'Language purity and Russian ethnic identity', in E. Allworth (ed.) *Ethnic Russia in the USSR: the dilemma of dominance*, 266–77, New York: Pergamon Press.

Parry, A. (1959) 'Russian language courses in American grade schools', *International Review of Education*, 5/4: 505–7.

'Poll: U.S. split on socialized medicine' (n.d.) Online. Available: www.webmd.com/news/20080214/poll-us-split-on-socialized-medicine (accessed 29 March 2011).

Pool, J. (1980) 'Whose Russian language? Problems in the definition of linguistic identity', in E. Allworth (ed.) *Ethnic Russia in the USSR: the Dilemma of Dominance*, 237–48, New York: Pergamon Press.

'Proposed EU Spelling Changes' (n.d.) Online. Available: www.musicalenglishlessons.com/jokes/correction/spellingchanges.htm (accessed 29 March 2011).

Ratnesar, R. (2009) *Tear Down This Wall: A City, a President, and the Speech that Ended the Cold War*, New York: Simon and Schuster.

Romanov, A.Yu. (2000) *Anglitsizmy i amerikanizmy v russkom yazyke i otnosheniye k nim*, Sankt-Peterburg: Izdatel'stvo Sankt-Peterburgskogo universiteta.

——(2004) *Sovremenny russky molodezhny sleng*, München: Verlag Otto Sagner.

Safire, W. (1980) *On Language* [a compilation of columns from the *New York Times Magazine*], New York: Times Books.

Schillinger, J. (2009) 'Russian enrollments: a roller coaster ride', *AATSEEL Newsletter*, 52/3: 16.

Solzhenitsyn, A.I. (1965) 'Ne obychay degtem shchi belit', na to smetana', *Literaturnaya gazeta*, 4 November.

Srpová, H. (2008) 'The Czech language in the post-velvet revolution period', in E. Andrews (ed.) *Linguistic Changes in Post-Communist Eastern Europe and Eurasia*, 58–87, Boulder, CO: East European Monographs.

Trager, G.L. (1964/1972) 'The intonation system of American English', in D. Abercrombie, D.B. Fry, P.A.D. MacCarthy, N.C. Scott and J.L.M. Trim (eds) *In Honour of Daniel Jones: Papers Contributed on the Occasion of his Eightieth Birthday*, 266–70, London: Longmans; reprinted in D. Bolinger (ed.) (1972) *Intonation: Selected Readings*, 83–86, Harmondsworth: Penguin Books.

Trager, G.L. and Smith, H.L. Jr. (1951) *An Outline of English Structure*, Norman, OK: Battenburg Press.

Velichko, A.V. (1995) 'O "russkosti" russkogo yazyka nashih dney', *Russkaya rech'*, 6: 54–57.

Wierzbicka, A. (1988) *The Semantics of Grammar*, Amsterdam/Philadelphia: John Benjamins.

——(1992) *Semantics, Culture and Cognition: Universal Human Concepts in Culture-specific Configurations*, New York/Oxford: Oxford University Press.

——(1997) *Understanding Cultures through Their Key Words: English, Russian, Polish, German and Japanese*, New York/Oxford: Oxford University Press.

Yakovlev, A.F. (1974) *Kak my portim russky yazyk*, Yaroslavl': Verkhne-Volzhskoye izdatel'stvo.

3 Russification of Western concepts: political will and crisis in a Russian way

Arto Mustajoki and Ekaterina Protassova

The purpose of the present chapter is to shed light on how the Russians interpret foreign concepts. The peculiar behaviour of the Russians in adopting influences from foreign cultures has aroused attention among both Western and Russian scholars. The conclusion usually drawn by researchers is that the Russians try to combine Russian and foreign cultural elements to produce something called the *third* (see, e.g., Huttunen and Pesonen 2003). We do not object to this interpretation: in our view it corresponds very well to reality. Nevertheless, we believe that it is important to go beyond this explanation, because creating something 'in-between' is quite a common feature in other cultures as well. Let us take a very simple example. It is true that the Russians have established the concept (and trade mark) of *Rostik's*, which is a 'Russified' version of *McDonald's*, but a very similar localization has taken place in Finland, where the *Hesburger* chain of fast-food restaurants has actually overtaken its original competitor in popularity. Thus, creating 'the third' is not *the* feature which makes the Russians different; there must be some other pattern of behaviour peculiar to the Russians.

In this chapter we try to give a more detailed picture of the contemporary way in which the Russians adopt foreign concepts. After some general remarks on the Russian attitude towards Western ideas, we present case studies of two Russified concepts, namely 'political will' and 'crisis'. When a point of comparison is needed, we take Finland as a representative of a Western-type society. We make two methodological assumptions. First, we take into account the fact that language use, as the most powerful tool in the distribution of ideas and opinions, also reflects people's thinking and attitudes. Being a very flexible means of communication, language adjusts itself to the needs of its users. Second, we are convinced that media texts mirror the real thinking of people, and sometimes even of whole populations. In answering questions posed by authorities or researchers, the Russians tend to think that they are obliged to help the survey providers to obtain the results that they are searching for. We therefore use Russian newspaper texts as our main source of evidence for the concept of Russianness that we are trying to tackle. Contrary to common opinion outside Russia, and in contrast to Russian TV, the Russian printed media is rather free and bold (cf. Rosenholm et al. 2010); it also reacts quickly to various phenomena in society.

The mixed, ambiguous, and emotionally loaded

Sociologists talk increasingly about the stratification of Russian society not only as one of its inherent characteristics, but also as a strategy employed by those in power to safeguard their own position. Russian society is divided into layers and segments which stand in opposition to one another to the extent that even a mythical (ideological) or real threat of invasion cannot reconcile them (as happened before and after the 1917 revolution and during the two world wars). Russian society as a whole does not seek unity, but some segments of it declare that they have found or are looking for a common idea as the goal of their activity. Ideological disunity may be seen as a reason for the absence of solidarity among the citizens (cf. Dubin 2007).

From the point of view of communicative strategies, Russian media texts, by comparison with Finnish ones, contain more clues reflecting the author's underlying ideological position. Moreover, the author's aim is to ensure that this position, which belongs to a particular segment of society, cannot be misinterpreted by the recipient of the message. Therefore, the concept of one representative 'public opinion' is less applicable to Russia than to Finland. There is an underlying assumption that the reaction of all Finns to the news will be more or less similar. It may be emotionally coloured, but not in the same way as the reactions of the Russians. In Russia, news is hardly ever reported in a neutral way: the headlines, the newsreader's intonation, even 'dry' genres such as weather forecasts always reflect the point of view of the 'powers' behind the media. Yet one single piece of news can provoke very different reactions in society: some share the point of view of the source of information, others categorically disagree, yet others remain indifferent. A good example of this is the *Right and Truth* manifesto written by the famous film director Nikita Mikhalkov in October 2010. His idea of *enlightened conservatism* has raised a huge debate. He maintains the tradition of the great authors of the nineteenth century, continued by Solzhenitsyn, of writing moralizing all-nation pamphlets.

The positions adopted by the citizens are based on cultural preferences coloured by the opposition between 'the own' and 'the other': East/West, authoritarianism/democracy, sympathy/opposition to the powers, collectivism/individualism, and so on. In every case, self-positioning on the value continuum is dependent on the emotions displayed. The emotional colouring of Russian discourse is part of a scale on which various authorial assessments of the events are placed. There are, in fact, many cultures where emotions are expressed even more vividly in media discourse than in Russia. Still, it cannot be assumed that the expression of one's perceptions is of an individual nature: the points of view adopted are chosen from a given set of options, presenting the opinions of a certain *gruppirovka* (a group of people with the same ideology and behaviour).

In every country the government and the opposition tend to focus on the same issues in their political discourse, although their priorities may differ. Any given text will normally include a number of clues signalling the author's ideological position (Wagnsson 2000; Yelenevskaya 2006). Here the contemporary Russian media, influenced to some extent by the West, is seeking to find its own paths (Hutchings 2002). In the Bakhtinian tradition, based on the notions of polyphony and the text being addressed to a listener, the perception of a verbal message inevitably calls forth associations based on all previous textual occurrences of the quotation (which may consist of no more than a single word) (Bakhtin 1984). This makes the Russian discourse tradition famous for its saturation with sub-textual meanings. There is, in fact, no freedom of discourse production: any utterance is part of a long tradition of texts (Sadovskaya 2008).

Democracy and fashion in language

If we look at the development of media texts in Western countries during the last few decades, we notice similar trends everywhere, but the scale and speed of change varies in different cultures. The process can be characterized by two interlinked denominators. First, public texts have become less official and have acquired features of colloquial speech. Second, all text and discourse types have adopted more and more elements of entertainment. Russia has undergone the same change, but at an accelerated tempo. After the Soviet-type media climate with rigid rules of language use, Russia jumped into a total freedom in a couple of years at the beginning of the 1990s. Thus, the democratization of language and a general shift towards lower style levels is a reality in Russia now. Lapteva (2003, 2004) shows how colloquial variants come to be accepted as part of the norm, producing internal transformations in the language, which thus reorganizes itself at a new stage of development.

The dyadic pair of contemporary leaders, Medvedev and Putin, has left its mark on the democratization of the Russian language use. Even before starting his first term of office as Prime Minister and before his presidency, the current Prime Minister Vladimir Putin astonished the public media by using an expression from army slang, *mochit' v sortire terroristov*, which can be translated to standard English as 'kill terrorists in the outhouse' (Kostomarov 2005: 237–38). President Dmitry Medvedev has his own style of speaking. Sometimes he adds computer jargon to official speeches. His favourite word is *moshchny*. It is a perfectly normal Russian word with the meaning 'powerful', 'strong'. Medvedev, however, puts the word into unusual contexts. During a single speech in Helsinki 2009 he used this word three times, and all of these occurrences were rather odd from the point of view of the standard language: *moshchny zal* ('hall'), *moshchnaya ekspertiza* ('expertise'), *moshchnoye razvitiye* ('development') (Mustajoki 2009).

If the democratization of the media language is due to the shift to a Western-type society, there are other trends in language use which derive from common undercurrents in human interaction. One of these is the speakers' desire to be regarded as smart; this need equally concerns journalists and people in everyday speech. An elegant and effective way to show one's smartness is to demonstrate the knowledge of the latest 'fashionable' words (*modnyye slova*). In talking about these expressions, we are indeed dealing with some kind of fashion, that is, expressions which have recently become frequent and attract by their novelty.

Reflections on contemporary linguistic phenomena (Gekkina 2006; Krongauz 2008) and a search for the typical key phrases of the present moment (Vepreva 2002; Kharlamova 2008) enjoy a great popularity among researchers and speakers of Russian.

Although there have always been purist tendencies in Russian, the language as a whole has been rather open to foreign influence over the past centuries. In fact, Russian turns out to be more receptive to English loanwords than other Slavonic languages (Pfandl' 2003). The contemporary Russian sport terminology is a good example of a readiness to accept loanwords: borrowings from English include not only the names of various sports (*boks, futbol, basketbol, biatlon, bobsley, slalom, vaterpolo*), but also many other basic words (*sportsmen, start, finish, final*), not to mention more specific terminology: *golkiper, taymaut, raketka* ('racket'), *pas*. During the last twenty years the Russian language has faced a new invasion of English loanwords, such as *glamur, autsorsing, klaster, kreativ, spitchrayter, ivent*. Indeed, the absence of a potential loanword can sometimes appear striking. One such lacuna is *challenging*, which has no direct equivalent in Russian. Following the idea expressed by Shmelev in this volume, the absence of a word speaks of the irrelevance of the notion behind the word.

The battle against foreign elements in the language

The dualistic way of thinking is realized in the attitude to foreign elements in Russian. As we have already mentioned, these words are very frequent, which means that at a certain level the Russians like them. On the other hand, there is a great resistance to them. At the personal level this appears in auto-reflective commenting on one's own speech. This kind of meta-discourse is very typical of the Russians, especially those representing the *intelligentsiya* (Vepreva 2002, 2003). When Russians use foreign words that have been foisted on them from above, they feel a strange need to make excuses and to fend off various accusations that might result from the use of such words. The reader or listener might, for example, suspect that the writer or speaker is too much of an insider in the current discourse – or, conversely, that he or she has an inadequate knowledge of the present situation. One might also end up being accused of excessive devotion to the authorities, or disrespect for one's own people and kowtowing to the West – or again, for being simply uncivilized. To shield themselves from possible reproaches, authors use a variety of linguistic devices.

Therefore, the use of foreign 'fashionable' words is often followed by comments such as: *as it is in fashion to say nowadays; as people tend to say; I apologize for this word; here I am using a word I hate; I wouldn't like to use this word but cannot find a Russian one* (Mustajoki and Vepreva 2006). Quotation marks also serve to highlight the special meaning of a (loan)word, or to mark the speaker's attitude to it (cf. Zaliznyak 2007). People's attitudes to foreign elements in languages sometimes sound comical. They may protest against the use of the loanword *sendvich*, arguing that the good old 'Russian' word *buterbrod* should be used, not recognizing its German origin. If in the case of *sandwich* a new word can be justified by the new shape of the object in comparison to the Soviet type of *buterbrod*, the description of the famous old hotel *Oktyabr'skaya* by the 'Russian' word *otel'* instead of *gostinitsa* 'hotel, guest-house' seems rather contrived.

Overall, words of Russian origin that have previously appeared in a multitude of texts are saturated with their textual history and are not perceived as 'empty' to the extent that foreign words are. The degree of assimilation and topicality of a word is demonstrated through meta-reflection. For example, the Russian verb *obshchat'sya* 'to communicate' and its foreign counterpart *kommunitsirovat'* have different connotations: the native Russian word may be defined as 'to talk to someone for a certain length of time in order to maintain friendly contact with this person' (Zaliznyak, Levontina and Shmelev 2002: 249), whereas the loan-word, increasingly used in day-to-day discourse, has the sense 'to exchange information'.

The same thing happens when a word from a local language is borrowed into the Russian spoken by emigrants or representatives of Russian-speaking minorities in diaspora (Protassova 2004): speakers and writers often feel a need to explain why they are using a loanword, in what sense, and why a Russian word with a similar meaning will not do ('as they say here', 'they have this word for it', etc.). This happens because the use of a word that draws attention to itself needs to be clarified.

At the state level, the discussion about the purity of Russian had led to heavy debate on the new language law. The process lasted for several years but the discussion did not come to an end when the law was adopted. The futile battle for correctness in language is reflected in specialized studies, which themselves become a form of meta-reflection (Ryazanova-Clarke and Wade 1999; Gusejnov 2005; Lunde and Roesen 2006; Pyykkö 2010). The law includes some striking paragraphs. It prohibits not only the use of foreign words in cases where a Russian equivalent exists, but also the use of vulgar expressions outside artistic contexts. In addition, the law gives the government the right to determine the norms of the Russian language. In September 2009, the government made use of this opportunity by compiling a list of authorized dictionaries and guidebooks and by giving new normative regulations that accept some variants which used to be regarded as incorrect. Among other regulations, the colloquial neuter gender is now accepted also as a literary norm for the word *kofe* 'coffee'; and with this rule a well-known pitfall for Russian learners, both native and foreign, has disappeared. The clause forbidding the use of foreign loanwords (if Russian ana-logues are available) has generated sneering comments in the media because the clause itself includes the international loanword *analog*.

Writers as norm makers

In the tradition of Russian linguistics, language norms are set by authoritative writers. This principle has been implemented in dictionaries until recent years by using examples from the works of Pushkin, Tolstoy, and Dostoevsky, instead of contemporary texts. At the same time the *intelligentsiya* used to have a salient role in determining language norms (cf. Mustajoki 2010: 36). They may use non-standard phrasing, but they do this consciously in the form of borrowings from other registers. The notion of a native speaker has a special interpretation in Russian tradition: from the point of view of the norm, standard language speakers (*nositeli literaturnogo yazyka*) are given the decisive role. The norm-oriented approach is essential for Russian society as a whole: norm always stands over usage (as A. Shmelev puts it in the present volume).

Bearing in mind the circumstances mentioned above, the position of literature is contradictory in contemporary Russian society with regard to its role as the norm maker and a reliable source for 'good' language. The attitude to foreign linguistic elements is a good test. On 24 February 2009, Viktor Yerofeyev said in the *Apokrif* programme on the *Kul'tura* channel that 'we speak tenderly of *superman* [using the English loanword], but *sverkhchelovek* [the Russian equivalent] puts us on our guard.' Both words are also used in special contexts (e.g. in the well-known films and in Nietzsche; cf. the references to Minayev and Pelevin below). This seems to us to be yet another case of how Western loanwords are much more attractive on the surface and ready for use in an intellectual game, while words of Russian origin require a more thoughtful attitude. Western values always seem glossy, superficial, and artificial, unable to grow in native soil.

As an example of the third in-between culture, we may consider the reasoning of the author Viktor Pelevin in a novel that has been published with the title *Empire V.* in the Roman alphabet on the cover, even though the publication has been officially registered as *Ампир В.* (the same title in Cyrillic letters), with the subtitle *Povest' o nastoyashchem sverkhcheloveke* 'A novel about a real superman', which every Russian connects with the old book *A Story of the Real Man* by Boris Polevoy and the film based on it. Incidentally, the author does not use different quotation marks for Russian and non-Russian text, as would be customary.

> I have, by the way, noted a most vulgar sign of our times: the habit of giving foreign names to shops, restaurants, and even novels written in Russian, as if to say: we're not like some others, we're more advanced, offshore, renovated to European standards. This has long since become something that I find completely nauseating. But I have now seen names like 'LovemarX' and 'Archetypique boutique' so many times that the irritation has passed and, willy-nilly, I have started to analyse them.
>
> From a theoretical course I knew that the word 'lovemarks' is applied in the world of glamour to trademark goods that one becomes whole-heartedly attached to, seeing them no longer as objects exterior to one's own being, but as the skeleton of one's personality. Apparently, the final 'X' was a tribute to juvenile orthography – or to Komsomol roots (a bust of Marx occupied a prominent place in the trade hall).
>
> (Pelevin 2006: 75)

Pelevin's play on alphabets is far from being the only one of its kind. There is a whole series of novel titles combining Roman and Cyrillic letters. This is found in titles like *Casual. Повседневное* (Robski, 2005) and *Welcome to жизнь, о Которой Вы Всегда Мечтали* (Sergeyeva 2008 'Welcome to the Life You Have Always Been Dreaming of'). Even more striking are combinations at the morpheme level: *Духless* (Minayev, 2006; *dukh* = 'spirit'), *Gламурный дом* (Robski, 2006a, 'glamour house'), *Про ЛЮБОff/on* (Robski, 2006b, 'On love and lack of love'). Established Russified forms, their English originals, and their native Russian counterparts are a constant source of wordplay, for example: *VIP – ВИП – ЗОЛД* (abbreviation for *Zal Ofitsial'nykh Lits i Delegatsiy*, literally 'hall for officials and delegations', meaning VIP lounge).

We will not look at the texts of contemporary writers in detail, but even these few illustrations show their new role as the source for the right linguistic norm. They are no longer maintaining the old norm, but rather grasping new linguistic phenomena from media texts and colloquial speech. At the same time they are faithful to the Russian way of using many allusions to the common cultural background of Russian people. Minayev's work *Духless* has a subtitle *Povest' o nenastoyashchem cheloveke* 'A Story of the Unreal Man' (again an allusion to Boris Polevoy).

The Russian 'political will'

The expression *political will* has become popular throughout the world. It is used when there is a common desire to improve living conditions or to reach other positive goals. For political discourse, the expression is very handy because it sounds solid and impressive, but as a matter of fact is unclear and vague. We do not know where political will comes from and who is behind it, it just floats in people's minds and speech. For decision makers political will plays a dual role: they can both shape it and respond to it. According to the former US vice-president Al Gore, political will is a renewable resource.

Expressions like *political will* sooner or later find their way to the Russian language through translations of official documents (UN, UNESCO etc.) and media texts referring to speeches by foreign politicians. However, the concepts behind the expression are never adopted as such; they undergo changes when touching the Russian soil. Changes may be caused by features of the Russian language or by the Russian way of thinking. In this case the linguistic shift of the notion is substantial. Neither of the two words of the Russian equivalent *politicheskaya volya* corresponds to the meanings of the original English expression. In Russian there is only one word, *politika*, for both *politics* and *policy* in English. People's opinion on politics, however, is even more important. In Russian, as a result of the experience that has been accumulated over time, *politika* is usually associated with something negative and far removed from the people, yet unavoidable. Of course, we meet similar attitudes in other cultures as well, but in Russia they are directed, more than elsewhere, to the whole political system, and not only to some parties or politicians.

However, there are more substantial differences in the interpretation of the words *will* and *volya* (Bulygina and Shmelev 1997: 481–90; Vezhbitskaya 1999: 434–99). Dictionaries give the Russian word the meanings 'freedom, space, independence', while the English noun has multiple meanings, including a person's 'last will and testament', and the notion of 'free will', which enables us to make conscious choices, perform actions, and so on. It is clear that in the majority of cases, in both English and Russian, the basic idea is that of channelling one's efforts towards the attainment of a goal, but apart from this the two notions may differ. For a Russian, if no explanation is given to the contrary, political will (*politicheskaya volya*) belongs to someone in a position of power, and in a centralized state this always means a highly placed individual to whom others pay deference. The relationships are of a vertical nature. 'Political will' in the Russian understanding cannot be diffused in society; it is wholly inconceivable that it could become the expression of the desires of several different, though interconnected groups of people.

Although a loan translation of this nature could easily be seen as a free combination of two perfectly familiar Russian words, it is our hypothesis that it stands out in the process of assimilation as something alien, becomes a marked element in discourse, develops connotations of its own, becomes dispersed in the flow of the text, and is processed according to models characteristic of contemporary Russian media language. This hypothesis will be tested by the methods of quantitative and qualitative analysis.

For the Russians, participation in global processes has always been and still remains a source of ambivalent feelings. On the one hand, it makes them feel part of a global community; on the other, it highlights their separateness from the citizens of other countries. The Russians are not inclined to believe that someone from the outside might wish them well, or that global documents are addressed to them as much as they are to people of all other nations. They have little faith in either Russian or foreign leaders: they have been inculcated since childhood with the notion that individual superiors will not look after them (only 'the state' will do so, and will do it badly). Attempts to build a civil society have so far been unsuccessful for various reasons, although there are particular cases where citizens' initiatives have been successfully implemented, as witnessed by many of the chapters in this volume.

Using the Integrum database (Mustajoki 2006), we made a search for occurrences of this collocation (*politicheskaya+volya*) in central Russian newspapers and magazines.

Figure 3.1 shows that the use of the construction *politicheskaya volya* started to expand rapidly in the mid-1990s; over the last five years or so, the number of occurrences has been in decline. The quantitative data show very well how the adaptation of Western concepts to Russian political life happens. Both the quick expansion of new ideas and the stabilization period after a while are typical of these processes.

It is even more interesting to have a closer look at the particular uses of the new expression. We will start with one reference where the term is used in a way that fully corresponds to international usage (we will use English translation unless the Russian expression contains specific linguistic features; all the examples are from Moscow-based Russian printed media):

> the problem is elsewhere, in legislation and *political will* not only among political leaders but also in society itself
>
> (Alyeshkina et al. 2005)

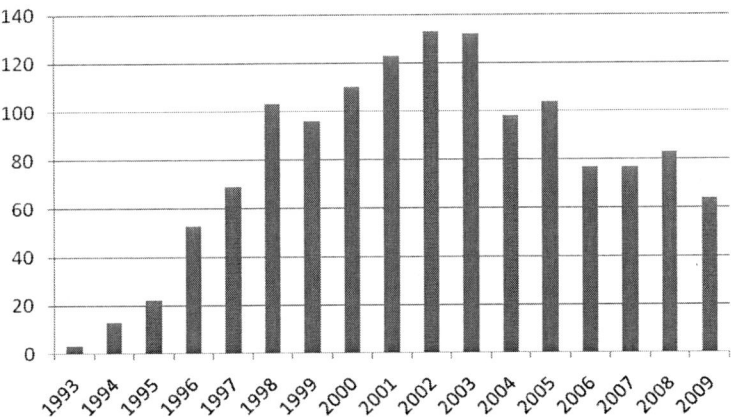

Figure 3.1 Number of occurrences of the construction *politisheskaya volya* in Russian media.

Turning to more Russian-like use of the expression, let us first take some examples which confirm the need that people feel to comment on a popular (or excessively popular) way of speaking. In the following examples, this word combination is no longer an international term, but an expression picked up in Russian discourse and independently reinterpreted:

> everything could have been done, there were people available, as well as computers, what was lacking was, *as they say, political will*
>
> (Lysenko 2004)

> As a whole, *as the officials of this service say*, the most important thing here is *political will*
>
> (Sivkova 2005)

> Where there's a will, or, *as it is now fashionable to say, 'political will'*
>
> (Kryshtanovskaya and Zyat'kov 1999)

> Usually at this moment our dear executors of different rank like to refer to *so-called political will*
>
> (Titov 2006)

The same dismissive and sceptical tone can be illustrated by the following instance:

> In Russia the thing with such progressive endeavours is, of course, more complicated, however there exists even some sort of *political will*.
>
> (Gazaryan 2006)

In the Russian original *kakaya-nikakaya* ('some sort of') expresses a high degree of vagueness and creates an ironic effect when combined with an international political term. Reservations and mistrust are often openly expressed. The attitude resembles Chernomyrdin's famous saying *Khoteli kak luchshe, a poluchilos' kak vsegda* ('We were hoping for the best, but it worked out as it always does'). Sometimes they say that political will is not the point; what is needed is common sense. A political scientist observes that:

> the expression 'political will' has returned to political parlance, although it is no longer connected to the aim of achieving something through choices, preferences, or aspirations, but is used now as a purely psychological characterization of a readiness to ignore others, use force, and go right through to the end.
>
> (Il'in 1995: 75)

The headline *Zemlya i politicheskaya volya* ('Land and political will'; Kravchenko 2006) is an example of the transformation of a pre-existing text: it is based on the name of a nineteenth-century political organization, *Zemlya i volya* (usually translated as 'Land and Liberty'). Examples whose general meaning is 'a need for political will' are very numerous: *nuzhna/neobkhodima politicheskaya volya* 'political will is needed/necessary'; *potrebuyetsya politicheskaya volya* 'political will is required'; *byla by politicheskaya volya* 'if the political will was there'; *glavnoye – politicheskaya volya* 'the main thing is political will'. The expression combines with the adjectives *sil'naya* 'strong', *zhestkaya*, *tverdaya* 'firm', and *bespretsedentnaya* 'unprecedented'. Political will is shown by those in power: *nachal'stvo* 'the leaders', *vlasti* 'the powers that be', *avtoritety* 'the authorities'. Ironic uses are found in many contexts, for example:

> No iz-za otsutstviya chetkoy *politicheskoy voli* proyekt so vremenem 'svernuli' ('But in the absence of a distinct political will, the project was in due course "wrapped up"')
>
> (Oludina 2008)

> Smertnaya kazn' i *politicheskaya volya* ('Capital punishment and political will')
>
> (Margelov 2007)

> *Politicheskaya volya* ili byurokraticheskaya otgovorka? ('Political will or bureaucratic evasion?')
>
> (Krasnov 2008)

The expression has gradually become synonymous with the will of the political leaders; in the regions it is commonly understood as referring to some higher authority that runs the country, while President Medvedev himself has stated that he has political will. It is emphasized in many documents that Europe is losing its political will, and that Russia does not have enough of it. In the last three years, the contraction *politvolya* is occasionally used in place of *politicheskaya volya*. The official media do not always provide objective information about the situation in Russia, and ordinary citizens have no way of knowing about what is happening; so, they mistrust and create their own theories.

A Russian-style crisis

Recession and economic crisis struck the global economy in an unexpected way. Let us consider the Russian version of this mega-phenomenon. The first observation by looking at the Russian context can be made by comparing the frequency of the word *retsessiya* (recession) with that of *krizis* in Russian media. The word *retsessiya* is surprisingly rare; in fact, the word *krizis* occurs fifty times as often. The unpopularity of the word *retsessiya* can be interpreted in different ways, but an obvious explanation here is the Russian connotations. For the Russians, *retsessiya* is too mild a word to be used in serious circumstances. The business review *Arbat Kapital* comments that 'recession' does not sound as frightening in Russian as 'crisis', even though 'crisis suggests something short-lived and easily overcome by effective measures, whereas recession is there for at least a year or a year and a half' (Golubovich et al. 2008: 2).

In Western countries the crisis very quickly became the number one topic of discussion between people in the streets, in pubs, and at home, but considering the depth of the crisis and its enormous consequences, the debate on its origin and causes calmed down remarkably quickly. It seems that people wanted to forget it as soon as possible and to believe in the vitality of the market economy, which had been only briefly called into question. In this respect, the Russian version of the global crisis is very different from what was found in many Western countries, but the speed with which it became the most popular media topic was the same. Let us start again with statistics (Figure 3.2).

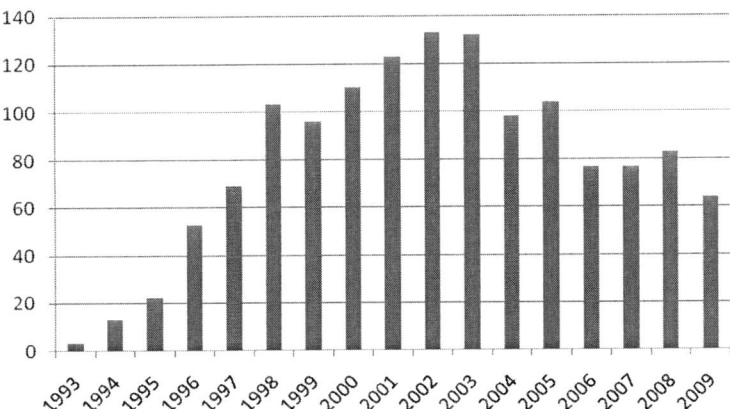

Figure 3.2 Number of occurrences of the word *krizis* in Russian media.

If we compare the global crisis with Russia's own monetary crisis in August 1998, we see a substantial difference between them. The globally initiated crisis (mainly of American origin) has been a more suitable thing to talk about. There are good reasons for this. It had a great deal of symbolic power. Strangely enough, it showed that Russia sits in the same boat with the rest of the world and is an essential part of the global market, given that its economy was hit by the same phenomenon. At a summing-up meeting of the government on 29 December 2008, Vladimir Putin stated this clearly:

> From the beginning of the 90s we kept repeating like an incantation that we must integrate into the global economy. Now we've integrated. As the popular Russian saying goes, *za chto borolis', na to i naporolis'* ['we cut ourselves on the very thing we fought for', i.e. more or less 'we had it coming to us']. Now our economy cannot exist outside global tendencies, whether positive or negative.
>
> (Putin 2008)

An inevitable feature of any Russian economic crisis is its apparent connection with the price of oil. Previous studies have shown that peaks in the occurrence of this word in Russia are connected to an intensified search for a national idea, and that there is an inverse correlation with oil prices (Fruchtmann 2006). Bearing this in mind, the 2008 crisis was, however, different because it had other explanations as well. It was also different in the sense that the number of people with relatively high income levels had substantially increased (the generation that grew up after *perestroika* had reached middle age and acquired middle-class habits), with those generations that remember the war against fascism gradually dying out. At the same time the experience of 1998 had been assimilated: more successful times always follow a crisis, leading to the stimulation of industrial development and potentially bringing about a redistribution of wealth.

The significance of the crisis for the Russian people led to the use of this word in advertising to make people spend money as they tried to clutch at straws amid the surrounding panic. Kachkayeva (2008: 1) cites the following advertising slogans:

> *Father's anti-crisis programme* (from the advertisement of a restaurant called *Otets* 'Father').
> The crisis hasn't hit us – a free loaf for everyone;
> A new flat, thanks to the crisis;
> Keep out the crisis – buy new windows!
> Facing the crisis in a new suit.

According to specialists, the word *anti-crisis* is used in marketing goods for people of the older generation, in the hope that they will be frightened into purchasing such goods in large quantities. Studies show that 96 per cent of all Russians pronounce the word *crisis* twice a day. Advertisers who initially intended not to waste money on advertising turned the crisis to their profit, because:

> the word is so close to us all. Listen to what the people are talking about today in the metro, in offices … It's all about the crisis! And so the ball started rolling … It's clear enough that a fashionable word is another

cunning stratagem. There have always been discounts on various goods. But now a new name has been invented for them, in the spirit of the times.

(ibid.)

Further uses of the word *crisis*: A restaurant has launched a campaign with the slogan *Skovorodkoy po krizisu* ('beating the crisis with a frying pan'). Other popular slogans include: *Zarabotay na krizise – kupi zemlyu* ('make money on the crisis – buy land'); *Poka krizis ne s"el vashi sberezheniya, vkladyvayte ikh v tekhniku* ('before the crisis eats up your savings, invest them in electrical appliances'). There are T-shirts bearing messages like *Krizis? Who is this?* (partly in English), *Ya sam krizis* ('I am myself a crisis'), *Perezhivem krizis. Bystro i nedorogo* ('We'll get through the crisis. Quick and cheap'). According to specialists, the phenomenon of anti-crisis advertising will last for a few months and will then fade away. In advertising agencies, 'crisis' is talked about as a new topical word that has been specially invented (Kuznetsova 2009).

There are advertisements for anti-crisis bricks, crockery, hire-purchase agreements, special offers, investments, bargain sales, trips, seminars, and medicines. *Krizisnyye* (the adjective from *crisis*) is used as an attribute of *tseny* 'prices', replacing words like *vygodnyye* 'favourable', *razumnyye* 'reasonable', *smeshnyye* 'ridiculous', *dostupnyye* 'affordable', and *nizkiye* 'low': there are advertisements for sweatshirts, concrete, machinery, package tours, parties, and so on 'at crisis prices'. Compounds like *krizis-lanch* 'crisis lunch' are also being created in accordance with a new tendency in word-formation. The adjective *antikrizisny* 'anti-crisis' is even more popular; apart from appearing in the phrase 'anti-crisis prices', it often occurs in various defiant slogans with the general meaning of 'We can beat the crisis.'

The Orthodox Church has taken up a powerful position in Russian politics. Thus, it is not a surprise that on 7 January 2009 Metropolitan Kirill, then *locum tenens* of the patriarchal throne (subsequently Patriarch of Moscow and all Russia), made the crisis the subject of his Christmas sermon, calling on believers to be firm in spirit. He observed that the Greek word *krisis* has the meaning of 'judgement'.

> Every crisis in life is God's judgement, and God's judgement separates truth from falsehood, God's judgement reveals human untruthfulness. And if there is an economic crisis in the world today, this judgement reveals a human untruthfulness of a global nature.

(Kirill 2009)

The crisis did not begin in Russia; it is 'a judgement on the desire to get rich by whatever means, while forgetting that everything genuinely valuable, including money, is a result of human labour, not of financial schemes and operations'. People should pray God 'to help all countries of the world to emerge from the crisis purified and enlightened, with a sound understanding of how we must live without sinning against God, in the economic sphere as well as all others' (ibid.). Another philosophical hint is found in a recommendation made by the journalist A. Arkhangel'sky: 'What to do in a time of crisis? Read the classics!' It is a profitable investment and a way of improving the general level of education (Arkhangel'sky 2009).

E. Sibirko presents a modern version of Russian patriotism and emotional stance on an insurance site:

> It is no secret that 'crisis' has recently become the most widely used word in our country, yet at the same time the initial shock of its appearance has now faded away. The redundancies and anxieties about the future have been effaced in our minds by the tons of work that must be coped with, not just in order to hold on to your job, but quite simply because your boss has assigned you a task and a deadline – and that's that, there's nowhere to retreat, Moscow is behind us!
>
> (Sibirko 2009)

Allusion is made here to well-known catchphrases used during the war; the crisis is thus placed in a historical context as another episode in the Russian people's struggle for independence in the face of foreign (Western) invaders. After citing some local examples, the author makes a suggestion:

> Turn on the telly or the radio – they're talking about the crisis even in the commercials. And why shouldn't they? It's a fashionable word, and people are milking it for all it's worth. Though for my own part, from an economic point of view, I can only see positive consequences of the crisis – such as an optimization of production costs. No more idleness and feet-dragging in the lives of ordinary citizens. Things are not as they were during the war, of course, but in any case the people now have a sense of the seriousness of what's happening, many have come down to earth and have started to look at the world more rationally. One would rather not think of the price that has been paid for these changes in people's consciousness – but it's all happened now, and there's no need to think about it any more. We must live in the new circumstances, work hard and with maximum dedication – that's the only way the country can leave the crisis behind – by making a lot of money.
>
> (ibid.)

In other words, the war now being waged by the Russian people is not in defence of an idea: the objective is money and the right of the young generation to live as they please. The article ends with a plea for unity between the generations in defending their country: 'I would very much like to wish everyone optimism, belief in ourselves, and belief in our country. Russia survived the Great Patriotic War. The Crisis is a mere trifle by comparison. We'll deal with it!' A nationalistic approach to the resolution of the crisis-related problems is something that the political leaders of the nation also tend to advocate in their speeches.

The crisis has also turned out to be convenient as a pretext for inaction and as an explanation for the ineffectiveness of one's efforts. In the words of the governor of Krasnodar region, A. Khloponin: 'The crisis provides a very convenient screen for inefficient bureaucrats, political charlatans and speculators to hide behind. As social tension mounts, all kinds of extremists and terrorists become active' (Khloponin 2009). A critical attitude to the crisis is found on various forums: 'it's all due to the crisis … – that's all you ever hear when they start making excuses … Perhaps we should talk about how to avoid stepping on the rake again? There's always plenty of fraud, speculation, and traps around' (*Forum* 2009). One gets the impression that people are ready to face the crisis because they were expecting one all along, but they will not believe those who claim to be innocent of bringing it about, or who claim that people abroad are to blame. On the other hand, people become tired of talking about the crisis because life as a whole is a hard struggle, and times of crisis are neither worse nor better than other times.

For a long time it was commonly said in Russia that the country would not be touched by a general crisis because there is a stabilization fund and a gold and foreign exchange reserve, but in the autumn of 2008 it was announced that the country had entered a crisis, although for the time being this was only felt by those whose salaries were not being paid. People tried to borrow money from the banks, which in their turn tried to raise interest rates on investments in an effort to attract clients.

International forums in the Russian language give a Russian view of the crisis as seen from abroad. It is asked whether the crisis is making itself felt in different countries, and the conclusion is that something has changed (things have become cheaper or more expensive, or have disappeared), but the reasons are unclear. There are suggestions that China or stupid political leaders are to blame (*Profit* 2009). In another internet discussion, the consequences of the crisis for the car industry are examined; readers are also urged to remember Karl Marx, who predicted forthcoming crises, and to seek ways of surfing the wave and emerging from the struggle stronger than before. The username Elena writes that she is in correspondence with people from abroad, who have told her that there is no such hysteria in their countries as in Russia. Her conclusion is: 'Someone very much needs a crisis in Russia: after all, it's easy to do dirty things in turbid water.' An absence of genuine competition is regarded as a special characteristic of the Russian crisis. Restaurants and casinos have remained as popular as before, but their glamour has been toned down (*Avtomatizatsiya zdaniy* 2008). In its issue 5 for 2010, the Russian version of the *Forbes* journal, one of the most widely read publications in Russia, enumerated banks and bankers who received enormous donations from the state during this period and let their capital multiply; indeed, the time of the crisis was the most successful in the world for the Russian banks.

A light-hearted look at the crisis is found in some sources: there are tales of how the populace does not believe what the officials say and prefers to do the exact opposite of what is advised on television. The film director Nikita Mikhalkov had this to say about the crisis: 'the most optimistic thing for us is that this *heavy wave* that has struck the cinema will *wash away what is unworthy*' (*samoye optimistichnoye dlya nas, chto eta tyazhelaya volna, kotoraya segodnya nakryvayet kino, smoyet to, chto nedostoyno*) (Mikhalkov 2008). A special site, *worldcrisis.ru*, has also been created: apart from financial and economic problems, it discusses intrigues in the Kremlin and their real background.

It turns out, then, that the Russians are in some ways scared of the crisis, but they also like to laugh at it and try to derive profits from it. Either corrupt political leaders or foreigners are regarded as having caused it. The explanations of those in power are widely disbelieved, and experts are suspected of being corrupt, insincere, and dishonest, regardless of whether they are talking about the crisis or not. The 'domestication' and 'taming' of an alien crisis that has been thrust upon the people takes place at the linguistic level through the incorporation of the word *krizis* into ready-made idiomatic formulas with a folklore flavour. A distinguishing feature of the current crisis is its global nature: for the first time Russia has been included among the 'big ones' and the Russians can feel the same as people in other countries, including both old and new democracies. Some are happy about this, as it shows that equality with other states has been achieved; others, remembering the crisis-free Soviet times, are nostalgic about the socialist economy and curse the West. If someone says that the crisis cannot be felt, this causes offence: the person making such a claim will be seen as unpatriotic, as someone wishing to stand out from the crowd, or to be suspected of independent thinking or of obtaining income by dishonest means. The fear of those who know the real nature of the crisis and are able to foresee subsequent development makes people tremble in the face of power – though it is unclear whose power. In a situation of scaremongering, where the crisis is used for frightening people and is presented as the root of all evil, the Russians want, on the one hand, to outwit the government and see through its secret designs – yet on the other hand they know that things are as they always have been, and the people will in any case end up being cheated.

Conclusion

We considered some common features in the adoption of Western ideas by Russians. We then made a more detailed study of the use of two frequent expressions of our days, *political will* and *(economic) crisis*. Summing up the main observations and claims, the following striking characteristics of the Russian version of making *the third* are worth mentioning.

1. **Scepticism towards the political elite.** In Western countries people tend to have faith in democracy, but not so much in the leaders elected through a democratic procedure. In Russian society this trend has its special nuances. During the Soviet period the citizens created covert means to criticize the political elite. The circumstances produced ingenious ways of writing and reading between the lines. Jokes told among best friends were another safety valve which helped in a society where overt reactions towards politicians were impossible. Jokes are still told, but their role is less important. Censorship, usually exercised by journalists themselves, still exists, but cannot be compared with that of the Soviet times. People's way of thinking and writing about political issues (e.g. notions like 'political will' or 'economic crisis') is characterized by a deeper antipathy towards decision makers than in Western countries.

A comparison of the processes whereby two Western terms have been introduced into contemporary Russian political discourse shows that, apart from interpretations characteristic of the Russian-language community as a whole, each of the two traditional currents of political thought (conventionally known as 'Slavophile' and 'Westernizing') assimilates the available concepts in its own way and uses them to defend its own views and to discredit those of the opposing side. An inalienable feature of the world of Russian politics is the presence of an unfathomable supreme power, which apparently cannot be identified with any of the actors on the political scene, but which stands behind all of them and brings new words into common use. Yet it is possible to oppose this power, and this can be done in a traditional way: by interpreting the neologisms from one's own point of view, by laughing at them and thereby also laughing at one's own agonizing fears, thus standing aside from the unknown and deciphering it in one's own mind.

2. **Scepticism towards the West.** The Russian way of thinking involves positioning oneself constantly in relation to a hypothetical West, regardless of the position adopted by the author (pro, contra, or neutral). This strange West – pernicious, hostile, and stupid – is of course a virtual construct. It is a great disappointment for many to discover that the West is not what they had imagined it to be – that it is diverse, capable of self-criticism, and so on. The West is and is not; it was there in the Soviet period and remains to this day. Whatever comes from the West is beautiful but dangerous; outwardly attractive but shallow (which is natural in the case of loanwords, because they have not developed a set of associations and connotations); entertaining but unserious, or too serious; not amorphous, but terminologically precise; in a word, 'not ours'. Unfamiliarity with foreign languages and an inability to use foreign sources in many fields of science and scholarship (including pedagogy) is still widespread, and a failure to keep abreast of global discussion has lamentable consequences in how the 'Own' is contrasted with the 'Alien' ('this is how we do it', 'we understand it in our own way'). At the same time Russia does not exist outside the global community, where certain laws apply, no matter how much the Russians would like to renounce them.

3. **Fuzziness, polyphony, yes-and-no attitude.** The Russian style of thinking demands a large array of concepts, which become inexact and fuzzy as they are interpreted in different ways in accordance with each author's intentions. The exact concept is at first enclosed in quotation marks and inserted into a variety of contexts; it is then applied to a range of different phenomena, acquires connotations, ceases to be identical to itself, is understood ambivalently, and, in the end, becomes Russian.

The Russian style of thinking is polyphonic. Objectivity may be replaced by an abundance of material, a plethora of quotations and conclusions. Reference must be made to earlier thinkers (whose thoughts are a priori better than any new ones), and it must be shown that different opinions exist and that the author is aware of the arguments in today's debate. An unconditional belief in something good is necessary (this is analogous to a national idea – something to fill a vacuum), and emotional proof is the strongest proof. An honest person is better off in opposition because those in power are constantly making mistakes, yet it is necessary to believe in something. A neutral position implies that it is possible to take responsibility for one's own actions and not for anyone else's; yet devotion to one's friends means that their actions must be defended as well. Russian meta-reflection is not neutral, even if the author adopts a neutral position.

4. **Strong ties with history.** A return to the sources, which is constantly called for, often means a desire to return to an earlier stage of scientific and scholarly thought, to renounce everything that happened in the twentieth century, to think as our great-grandmothers thought, and to do as our great-grandfathers did (for some reason with this particular gender distribution) – in other words, to return to superstition and to proving one's honour (compare, for example, the positive evaluation of the duel as a means of searching for the truth in the *Apokrif* programme on the *Kul'tura* channel on 10 December 2009). The fear of finding oneself under the fire of criticism, and the inability to overcome such shame (if they discuss you, it means you must be wrong) also plays a significant role in making people fearful of expressing their opinions.

5. **Word-centrism.** Russian thinking is word-oriented. Words, rather than thoughts, enchant; they also attract bitter criticism. The material world is not so important; what is important is the way that it is talked about. People do not see and do not know the greater part of what is discussed. In writing down some words, an author performs an action. What happens afterwards, how the words are understood and incarnated, is no longer important. But one should not lend too much credence to words, for they may turn out to be deceitful. To safeguard oneself, it is necessary to turn what has been said inside out, to subject it to various form of irony – from gentle banter to outright mockery. The way the Russians comment on their own speech by making auto-reflective explanations derives partly from the significance of particular words and sayings. When a person pronounces a word, (s)he can be regarded as a supporter of it. Therefore, by commenting on its use, the speakers keep it at a respectable distance.

As a final comment we would like pay attention to the absence or unpopularity of some Western concepts in Russia. Indeed, some imported concepts never become fully assimilated in Russian society: for example, 'peace education' was once translated into Russian as *vospitaniye v dukhe mira* (literal back-translation: 'education in the spirit of peace'), but this formulation, which allows for a variety of interpretations, simply does not work in Russian.

Another typical example of the false adaptation of an alien term is *ekologicheskoye vospitaniye* ('ecological education'). This term is understood, in accordance with the Russian attitude to the world, as 'love of nature', that is, children are taught to respond emotionally to animals, plants, and natural phenomena, for example through poetry. Educators at kindergarten and at school attribute human feelings to animals, trees, and even inanimate objects (pedagogical animism): 'the birch is in pain', 'the guinea-pig is suffering', 'the school desk is in agony'. An ecologically educated person knows the names of animals and plants, does not pick flowers, experiences a personal relationship with the natural world in the process of discovering it and communicating with it through the emotions (delight, joy, astonishment, tenderness, anger, indignation, compassion, etc.) and strives to preserve wildlife, thus manifesting a love for the world of nature, and knows items of folk wisdom such as the maxim that the season for sleigh rides begins on St Catherine's day (7 December), without in the least doubting the usefulness of such information in our day, regardless of climate change and the differences between climate zones within the country. This is practically the full extent of ecological education. Some Westerners are also taken aback at the Russian expressions 'good ecology' and 'bad ecology', understood as 'a small/large quantity of toxic emissions hindering the growth of plants, diminishing the animal population, and damaging people's health'.

Bibliography

Alyeshkina, A., Selivanova, M., and Savkin, A. (2005) 'Lekarstvo ot korruptsii', *Biznes*, 27 January.

Arkhangel'sky, A. (2009) 'Menedzher – za knigu!', *Vzglyad*, 29 January. Online. Available: www.vz.ru/columns/2009/1/29/251055.html (accessed 29 March 2011).

Avtomatizatsiya zdaniy (2008) Internet-forum 'Krizis i kak s nim borot'sya', 1 December 2008–13 May 2009. Online. Available: www.autobuilding.ru/phorum/viewtopic.html&f=9&t=52&archive=1 (accessed 29 March 2011).

Bakhtin, M.M. (1984) *Problems of Dostoevsky's Poetics*, Minneapolis: University of Minnesota Press.

Bulygina, T.V. and Shmelev, A.D. (1997) *Yazykovaya kontseptualizatsiya mira (na materiale russkoy grammatiki)*, Moskva: Yazyki russkoy kul'tury.

Dubin, B. (2007) 'Ot traditsii k igre: kul'tura v sotsiologicheskom proyekte Yuriya Levady', *Novoye literaturnoye obozreniye*, 5/87: 237–46.

Forum (2009) Internet-forum 'Eto modnoye slovo "krizis".' Online. Available: www.voditeli.ru/forum/index.php?topic=8117.0 (accessed 29 March 2011).

Fruchtmann, J. (2006) 'Correlating linguistic and extralinguistic developments', in G. Nikiporets-Takigava (ed.) *Integrum: tochnyye metody i gumanitarnyye nauki*, 165–92, Moskva: Letny sad.

Gazaryan, K. (2006) 'Iz zony v delo', *Biznes*, 1 March.

Gekkina, Ye.N. (2006) 'Izmeneniye yazykovykh norm v nablyudeniyakh i otsenkakh govoryashchikh', in L.P. Krysin (ed.) *Russky yazyk segodnya*, 4, 120–28, Moskva: Institut russkogo yazyka RAN imeni V.V. Vinogradova.

Golubovich, A., Orlov, A., Fundobny, S., Pavlov, A., Gromadin, V. and Bakhtigozin, A. (2008) 'Eto modnoe slovo – retsessiya', *Arbat-Kapital*, 19/12: 2–14.

Gusejnov, G. (2005) (ed.) *Language and Social Change: New Tendencies in the Russian Language*, Bremen: Forschungsstelle Osteuropa.

Hutchings, St. (2002) 'Ghosts in the machine: Literature as translation mechanism in post-Soviet television representations of western-ness', *International Journal of Cultural Studies*, 5/3: 291–315.

Huttunen, T. and Pesonen, P. (2003) 'Understanding the *Third*', in E. Tarasti, P. Forsell, and R. Littlefield (eds) *Understanding/Misunderstanding: Contributions to the Study of the Hermeneutics of Sign*, 491–500, Acta Semiotica Fennica 16, Helsinki: International Semiotics Institute at Imatra.

Il'in, M.V. (1995) 'Slova i smysly: volya', *Polis (Politicheskiye issledovaniya)*, 3/9: 68–77.

Kachkayeva, E. (2008) 'Kak nazhivayutsya na slove "krizis"', *Komsomol'skaya Pravda*, 20 December.

Kharlamova, T.V. (2008) 'Klyuchevyye slova tekushchego momenta *sil'noye gosudarstvo, sil'naya vlast'* na rubezhe vekov', in M.A. Kormilitsyna and O.B. Sirotinina (eds) *Problemy rechevoy kommunikatsii*, 8, 138–44, Saratov: Saratovsky gosudarstvenny universitet.

Khloponin, A. (2009) 'Tema krizisa – udobnaya shirma dlya sharlatanov i aferistov', *Komsomol'skaya Pravda*, 6.2.

Kirill (2009) 'Mitropolit Kirill posvyatil rozhdestvenskuyu propoved' krizisu', *Khristianskoye agentstvo novostey*, 7 January. Online. Available: http://jesuschrist.ru/news/2009/1/7/15557 (accessed 29 March 2011).

Kostomarov, V.G. (2005) *Nash yazyk v deystvii: Ocherki sovremennoy stilistiki*, Moskva: Gardariki.

Krasnov, M. (2008) 'Politicheskaya volya ili byurokraticheskaya otgovorka?', *Osobaya bukva*, 6 September.

Kravchenko, S. (2006) 'Zemlya i politicheskaya volya', *Izvestiya Udmurtskoy Respubliki*, 26 December.

Krongauz, M. (2008) *Russky yazyk na grani nervnogo sryva*, Moskva: Znak/Yazyki slavyanskikh kul'tur.

Kryshtanovskaya, O. and Zyat'kov, N. (1999) 'Regiony zabirayut vlast', *Argumenty i fakty*, 9 February.

Kuznetsova, K. (2009) 'Spasibo "krizisu"', *Vash tayny sovetnik*, 2 February.

Lapteva, O.A. (2003) 'Samoorganizatsiya dvizheniya yazyka: vnutrenniye istochniki preobrazovaniy (stat'ya pervaya)', *Voprosy yazykoznaniya*, 6: 15–29.

——(2004) 'Samoorganizatsiya dvizheniya yazyka: vnutrenniye istochniki preobrazovaniy (stat'ya vtoraya)', *Voprosy yazykoznaniya*, 5: 17–31.

Lunde, I. and Roesen, T. (2006) (eds) *Landslide of the Norm: Language Culture in the Post-Soviet Russia*, Bergen: University of Bergen.

Lysenko, A. (2004) 'Chto ostayetsya lyudyam?', *Shakhmatnoye obozreniye*, 15 November.

Margelov, M. (2007) 'Smertnaya kazn' i politicheskaya volya', *Rossiyskaya gazeta*, 10 October.

Mikhalkov, N. (2008) 'V krizis vyzhivut samyye dostoynyye kinematografisty', *RIA Novosti*, 21 November. Online. Available: www.rian.ru/culture/20081121/155591216.html (accessed 29 March 2011).

Minayev, S. (2006) *Dukhless*, Moscow: AST.

Mustajoki, A. (2006) 'The Integrum database as a powerful tool in research on contemporary Russian', in G. Nikiporets-Takigava (ed.) *Integrum: tochnyye metody i gumanitarnyye nauki*, 50–75, Moskva: Letny sad.

——(2009) 'Venäjän kielen monet kasvot', *Idäntutkimus*, 2: 70–74.

——(2010) 'Types of non-standard communication encounters with special reference to Russian', in M. Lähteenmäki and M. Vanhala-Aniszewski (eds) *Language Ideologies in Transition Multilingualism in Russia and Finland*, 35–55, Frankfurt am Main: Peter Lang.

Mustajoki, A. and Vepreva, I.T. (2006) 'Kakoye ono, modnoye slovo: k voprosu o parametrakh yazykovoy mody', *Russky yazyk za rubezhom*, 2: 45–63.

Oludina, Ye. (2008) 'Politicheskaya volya protiv korruptsii', *Parlamentskaya gazeta*, 14 October.

Pelevin, V. (2006) *AmpirV. Povest' o nastoyashchem sverkhcheloveke*, Moscow: Eksmo.

Pfandl', Kh. (2003) 'O sile i bessilii purizma: anglitsizmy i internatsionalizmy i ikh vozmozhnyye al'ternativy (na materiale russkogo, slovenskogo i khorvatskogo yazykov)', *Voprosy yazykoznaniya*, 6: 108–22.

Profit (2009) Internet-forum 'Komu vygoden krizis', 15 June 2009–18 May 2010. Online. Available: http://profit-maker.ru/archive/index.php/t-756.html (accessed 29 March 2011).

Protassova, E.Yu. (2004) *Fennorossy: zhizn' i upotrebleniye yazyka*, Sankt-Peterburg: Zlatoust.

Putin, V.V. (2008) 'Putin: krizis – eto sledstviye integratsii v mirovuyu ekonomiku. Za chto i borolis', *Novosti ekonomiki*, 29 December. Online. Available: www.newsru.com/finance/ 29dec2008/putincrisis.html (accessed 29 March 2011).

Pyykkö, R. (2010) 'Language policy as a means of integration in Russia', in M. Lähteenmäki and M. Vanhala-Aniszewski (eds) *Language Ideologies in Transition Multilingualism in Russia and Finland*, 81–99, Frankfurt am Main: Peter Lang.

Robski, O. (2005) *Casual. Povsednevnoye*, Moskva: Rosmen.

——(2006a) *Glamurny dom*, Moskva: OlmaMediaGrupp.

——(2006b) *Pro Lyuboff/on*, Moskva: Rosmen.

Rosenholm, A., Nordenstreng, K., and Trubina, E. (2010) (eds) *Russian Mass Media and Changing Values*, London: Routledge.

Ryazanova-Clarke, L. and Wade, T. (1999) *The Russian Language Today*, London: Routledge.

Sadovskaya, Ye.V. (2008) 'Interdiskurs. Intertekstual'nost'. Metadiskurs. K probleme formirovaniya vyskazyvaniy "drugogo" v metadiskurse', *Vestnik Samarskogo gosudarstvennogo universiteta*, 1/60: 167–75.

Sergeyeva, P. (2008) *Welcome to Zhizn', o Kotoroy Vy Vsegda Mechtali*, Moskva: AST.

Sibirko, E. (2009) 'K slovu "krizis" uzhe privykli!', *Gruppa INEC*. Online. Available: http:// insuranceblog.ru/k-slovu-krizis-uzhe-privykli (accessed 13 October 2009).

Sivkova, V. (2005) 'Bukhta ne nashey radosti', *Argumenty i fakty*, 29 June.

Titov, S. (2006) 'Ya ne ponimayu', *Argumenty i fakty*, 31 May.

Vepreva, I.T. (2002) *Yazykovaya refleksiya v postsovetskuyu epokhu*, Yekaterinburg: Ural'sky universitet.

——(2003) 'Verbalizatsiya metayazykovogo soznaniya kak realizatsiya printsipa tolerantnosti', in N.A. Kupina and M.B. Khomyakov (eds) *Filosofskiye i lingvokul'turologicheskiye problemy tolerantnosti*, 155–67, Yekaterinburg: Ural'sky universitet.

Vezhbitskaya, A. (1999) *Slovarny sostav kak klyuch k etnofilosofii, istorii i politike: 'Svoboda' v latinskom, angliyskom, russkom i pol'skom yazyakh: Semanticheskiye universalii i opisaniye yazykov*, Moskva: Yazyki russkoy kul'tury.

Wagnsson, Ch. (2000) *Russian Political Language and Public Opinion on the West, NATO and Chechnya: Secularisation Theory Reconsidered*, Stockholm: University of Stockholm.

Yelenevskaya, M.N. (2006) 'Language as a reflection of ideology in Russia', *International Sociology*, 21/3: 359–70.

Zaliznyak, Anna A. (2007) 'Semantika kavychek', in *Trudy mezhdunarodnogo seminara 'Dialog'2007' po komp'yuternoy lingvistike i yeye prilozheniyam*, Moskva: RGGU.

Zaliznyak, Anna A., Levontina, I.B., Shmelev, A.D. (2002) 'Klyuchevye idei russkoy yazykovoy kartiny mira', *Otechestvennye zapiski*, 3, 248–65.

4 A Russian view of Western concepts

Alexei Shmelev

Introduction

In what follows, I will deal with linguistic data indicative of how Russian culture perceives 'Western' concepts. The expression 'Western culture' is based on the stereotypical opposition of Russia and the 'West', which has become common-place in a plethora of publications dedicated to comparative cultural studies. As any stereotype, this opposition is a generalization (even though rough and inexact) based on an actual state of affairs deserving thorough investigation. This stereo-type was supported by an evident contrast between Russia under the communists and the free Western world over many years. However, this contrast, along with any other stereotype, cannot be used as a tool for scholarly analysis. It takes no account of deep differences between different 'Western' cultures (say, Finnish culture and Italian culture), which are in many cases no less significant than the differences between Russian culture and any of those 'Western' cultures. As for the general mechanisms governing the reception of 'Western' concepts by the Russian language, we may deal with them without posing the question as to which of the 'Western' cultures is the source of the particular concept under consideration.

The analysis that follows (of necessity concise and sketchy) is based on the assumption that if a concept is salient in a given society, the language spoken in that society normally has a linguistic unit that encodes this concept. Accordingly, if a concept is absent from Russian culture (even though similar concepts may be found there), the Russian language does not have a linguistic unit that would correspond to this concept. This means that in situations where Russian needs to be spoken, there arises the problem of how to use the resources of the Russian language to encode the required meaning. There are two options: (a) borrowing a word or expression from the language that serves the cultural sphere to which the concept belongs, and (b) using a Russian analogue of the foreign word. For example, a goalkeeper in a football game may be referred to in Russian by (a) the loanword *golkiper*, or (b) the analogous Russian word *vratar'* (of Church Slavonic origin). The Russian analogue may be formed on the basis of the foreign word by morphological or semantic calquing; a special case of semantic calquing is 'secondary borrowing', which takes place when a pre-existing loanword is given a new meaning in order to convey a notion arising from the reception of a 'Western' concept (for example, the words *interes* and *interesny* were initially borrowed in the sense of 'advantage' or 'profit', but subsequently acquired the meaning of 'attention' or 'curiosity', also based on a Western model. What happens in all cases, though, is the appearance in Russian of a new linguistic unit: even if the expression has previously existed in the language, a new lexical item is created at the level of content. Moreover, it is significant that the content of the new Russian expression generally differs to a greater or lesser extent from the meaning of the corresponding expression in the source language. The new meaning is created as the result of a reinterpretation of the 'Western' concept, and it contains features based on the adaptation of this concept to the Russian linguistic picture of the world. The various ways in which this adaptation takes place are examined below.

Two main methods of adaptation must be distinguished: 'assimilation', or 'integration' of the borrowed concept into the Russian linguistic picture of the world (whereby the concept undergoes a greater or lesser transformation); and 'adoption' of the borrowed concept (in which case it is the relevant fragment of the linguistic picture of the world that is transformed to some degree). Overall, it can be said that the 'assimilation' of the borrowed concept usually happens when loanwords are used, while 'adoption' takes place when a Russian analogue (possibly itself an earlier loanword) is used; however, this is not a straightforward correspondence. We will now examine different subtypes of each of these methods of adaptation.

Assimilation of the concept

It often turns out that 'assimilation' does not take place at once. Initially, both the phonetic shape (with the necessary modifications) and the semantics of the foreign expression are borrowed; it is only then that the meaning of the expression undergoes a process of assimilation. Thus, the loanword *delikatny* was initially used in Russian (in the eighteenth and early nineteenth centuries) in accordance with the full spectrum of meanings conveyed by the French original *délicat*. It was especially common in describing culinary delicacies (cf. the noun *delikates*, which has retained this meaning in Russian). Compare this to:

> Я нигде не видал деликатнее ['вкуснее'] стола, как в нашем трактире.
> ('Nowhere did I see a more delicate ['tasty'] cuisine than in our tavern')
>
> (Denis Fonvizin)

> Вы будете в большом, большом счастии, в золотом платье и ходить и деликатные разные супы кушать
> ('you will be very, very happy, you will be wearing golden dresses and eating various delicate soups')
>
> (Nikolay Gogol')

However, such close attention to gastronomic refinement is uncharacteristic of Russian culture, and it is not surprising that by the latter half of the nineteenth century the meaning of this adjective became considerably narrower: it came to be used mainly with reference to tactful behaviour in the sphere of human relations. This corresponds to a characteristic tendency of the Russian linguistic picture of the world whereby particular attention is paid to the nuances of interpersonal relationships (this is reflected in a number of language-specific Russian expressions (cf. Zaliznyak et al. 2005: 11)). Someone described as *delikatny* takes particular care not to place anyone in an awkward situation and not to become a source of mental anxiety to others. The essence of the notion of *delikatnost'* is explained in this excerpt from Konstantin Paustovsky's memoirs, *The Distant Years*:

> Попутно Селиханович учил нас и неожиданным вещам – вежливости и даже деликатности. Иногда он задавал нам загадки. 'Несколько человек сидят в комнате', – говорил он, – 'Все кресла заняты, Входит женщина. Глаза у нее заплаканы. Что должен сделать вежливый человек?' Мы отвечали, что вежливый человек должен, конечно, тотчас уступить женщине кресло. 'А что должен сделать не только человек вежливый, но и деликатный?' – спрашивал Селиханович. Мы не могли догадаться. 'Уступить ей место спиной к свету', – отвечал Селиханович, – 'чтобы заплаканные ее глаза не были заметны.'

> ('In the meantime Selikhanovich also taught us unexpected things – politeness and even *delikatnost'*. Sometimes he gave us riddles. "Several men are sitting in a room", he would say, "all the chairs are occupied. A woman enters. Her eyes are red with weeping. What should a polite man do?" We answered that a polite man should, of course, offer her his chair at once. "And what should one do if one is not just polite, but also *delikatny*?" Selikhanovich asked. We could not guess. "Offer her a seat with its back to the light", Selikhanovich answered, "so that nobody could see her red eyes".')

The adjective *delikatny* is also used with reference to situations requiring a tactful approach (e.g. *delikatnoye delo, delikatny vopros, delikatnoye porucheniye*), but this meaning is less common. Other meanings of the adjective have gone almost completely out of use (and are not, for example, mentioned in the dictionary of Ozhegov and Shvedova 1992). The 'Western' concept has thus been reinterpreted and 'integrated' into the Russian linguistic picture of the world as a designation for one of its central cultural values.

An interesting shift in meaning has taken place with the French word *courage*, which has, in its Russian form *kurazh*, significantly changed its meaning and has been drawn into the semantic field that includes language-specific words like *udal'*, *razmakh, zagul*, associated with the major cultural motif of 'broadness'. As a result, *kurazh* has become a Russian word that is difficult to translate. Its Russian meaning is not primarily that of bravery, but rather 'lack of restraint/inhibitions'; it is the quality required of actors and sportsmen, for example. There is a notion in Russian culture that this mental state can be attained by means of consuming alcoholic beverages (cf. the expression *vypit' dlya kurazha* or *dlya kurazhu*).[1]

Сотрудник, оставшись один, налил себе еще для большего куража и независимости, выпил, закусил

('When alone, the clerk poured himself some more to add to his *kurazh* and independence, drank, got a bite')

(Fedor Dostoevsky)

Да она и не была пьяна, просто чуть выпила для куражу.

('No, she wasn't drunk, she'd just had a small drink to gain *kurazh*')

(Yury Trifonov)

There are similar examples in the *Russian National Corpus*:

Было видно, что он к тому же еще и выпил для куража.

('moreover one could see that he had had a drink to gain *kurazh*')

(Sergey Osipov, *Strasti po Fome*, I (1998))

This has led to *kurazh* being persistently associated with drinking sprees – compare this to the expression *p'yany kurazh* (reminiscent of the English expression 'Dutch courage'), which is understood in Russian as a state of being into which one can fall (*vpast'*) or which it is possible to arrange (*ustroit'*):

Да что об этом толковать в пьяный кураж впавшему человеку.

('Why talk about this to a man who is in his drunken *kurazh*')

(Viktor Astaf'yev)

А ведь тоже был пьяный. Крепко поругались в семье. Все на него: жена, дочка и сын. И тот же хмельной кураж: 'Не уважаете'

('But he was tipsy too. There was a bad row in the family. Everyone against him: wife, daughter and son. And the same drunken *kurazh*: "You don't respect me"')

(Boris Yekimov)

Compare this to examples from the *Russian National Corpus*:

Однажды я в пьяном кураже наставил на нее пистолет и прохрипел: 'Щас пристрелю тебя, паскуду интеллигентскую!'

('Once in a drunken *kurazh* I aimed the gun at her and wheezed, "I'll shoot you down at once, you filthy intellectual!"')

(Eduard Volodarsky, *Dnevnik samoubiytsy* (1997))

повод для пьяного куража и большой драки

('an excuse for a drunken *kurazh* and a big fight')

(Yury Buyda, *U koshki devyat' smertey* (2005))

Moreover, the word *kurazh* in the first half of the nineteenth century referred not only to unrestrained behaviour under the influence of liquor, but also to the beverages themselves and the state of intoxication brought about by them (however, this usage failed to establish itself in the language):

он любил что-либо заказывать Петровичу тогда, когда последний был уже несколько под куражем, или, как выражалась жена его, 'осадился сивухой, одноглазый чёрт.'

('he liked to order something of Petrovich when the latter was already somewhat under the *kurazh*, or, as his wife would phrase it, "had had his raw vodka, the one-eyed devil".')

(Nikolay Gogol')

Interestingly, the state of *kurazh* is often perceived as something specifically 'Russian', alongside *toska* (approximately 'melancholy') and *nadryv* ('a violent display of emotion'), as in the following examples from the *Russian National Corpus*:

В далеком полутемном углу кто-то с тоской и куражом рвал гармошку и надсадно пел что-то

('In the half-dark far corner someone was torturing the accordion with *toska* and *kurazh* and singing something in a hacking voice')

(Mit'ki, *Zimnyaya mukha* (1992))

Ее низкий грудной голос нельзя назвать концертным, но в нем есть все, что так близко русской душе: и кураж, и свобода, и тоска о чем-то безвозвратно ушедшем.

('Her low chest voice cannot be called a concert voice, but it has everything that is so dear to the Russian soul: *kurazh* and freedom and *toska* about something irrevocably lost.')

(Varvara Sinitsyna, *Muza i general* (2002))

Here, as in the case of *delikatnost'*, 'Western' content has been reinterpreted in the process of borrowing and has entered the sphere of 'one's own' culture.

It often happens, however, that a reinterpretation of a 'Western' concept reflects an alienated and, as a rule, distorted perception of the relevant 'Western' phenomenon. Thus, the Polish language has the word *honor* (not equivalent to 'honour' in English) designating one of the central values of Polish culture (and, correspondingly, of the Polish linguistic picture of the world). *Honor* implies the notion of sacrifice and personal dignity, which prevents one from demeaning oneself or compromising one's principles in the hope of material gain or to escape from danger. A good illustration of the underlying meaning of this concept in Polish culture can be seen in Aleksandr Solzhenitsyn's screenplay for the film *The Tanks Know the Truth*. When the prisoners' rebellion is quashed by the tanks, it is only the Pole Gavronski who does not lose his dignity:

= Бьют, как попало, над головами! над самыми головами!! И кричат остервенело сами же:

–На землю! … Ложи-ись! … Все ложись! …

= Как ветер кладет хлеба - так положило волной заключенных. В пыль! на дорогу! (может, и убило кого?) Все лежат!

Нет! Стоит один!

Пальба беспорядочная.

= Лежат ничком. Плашмя. И скорчась. С-213, жирнощекий; смотрит зло из праха наверх - как продолжает стоять

Р-863, Гавронский. Вскинутая голова! Грудь, подставленная под расстрел! Гонор - это честь и долг!

С презрительной улыбкой он оглядывает стреляющий конво

(' = They shell just anyhow, over the heads! over the very heads!! And shout in a frenzy themselves:

–To the ground! … Down! … All down! …

= As the wind flattens the corn, so the inmates were knocked down by the wave. Into the dust! on to the road! (Perhaps, someone got killed?) So all of them are down!

No! One is standing!

Disorderly firing.

= Lying face down. Prone. And squirming. S-213, fat-cheeked, staring evilly up from the dust as he remains standing.

R-863, Gavronsky. His head jerked up! His chest held up to execution! *Gonor* is honour and duty!

With a scornful smile he is looking at the escort firing')

However, the use of the loanword *gonor* in this episode does not correspond to the standard meaning of this word in Russian: Solzhenitsyn consciously employs it in a sense that corresponds almost exactly to its Polish meaning. In the Russian perception, conduct based on such premises is very often seen as conceited and arrogant, reflecting a lack of genuine humility. The word *gonor* in Russian has therefore come to be associated with negative concepts like *spes', kichlivost', samouverennost', samonadeyannost'*, and *samomneniye* (all of which refer to haughtiness and excessive self-esteem); manifestations of *gonor* are therefore not in the least encouraged.

> каждый еще норовит свой гонор показать, и каждый из себе прынца строит.
>
> ('and everyone wants to show his *gonor* and to make a prince of himself.')
>
> (Vladimir Voynovich)

Gonor is very often mentioned alongside other negative traits, passions, or even sins (examples from the *Russian National Corpus*):

> преходящие страсти: честолюбие, гонор, жажда власти, денег, успеха или фантастическая вера в идею
>
> ('transient passions: vanity, *gonor*, thirst for power, money, or success; or a fanatical faith in an idea')
>
> (Oleg Kurayev, *Territoriya* (1970–75))

Сколько прегрешений, совершенных и несовершенных было за мою жизнь, тут и гордыня, и гонор, и кощунства, и грех уныния, глупость, и запутанность в мелочевке

('How many transgressions, committed and uncommitted, were there in my life, here comes pride and *gonor*, and blasphemies, and despair, stupidity, and preoccupation with petty things')

(Andrey Voznesensky, *Na virtual'nom vetru* (1998))

Even the construction of the Tower of Babel may be associated with *gonor*:

Я почему-то подумал о том, как дорого обходятся человечеству гонор и заносчивость предков. Следовало бы высечь тех олухов, которые когда-то затеяли строить Вавилонскую башню, а в результате все мы говорим на разных языках.

('For some reason I thought, how dearly mankind has to pay for the *gonor* and insolence of the ancestors. Those blockheads who once decided to build the Tower of Babel should have been whipped, because we now have to speak different languages.')

(Viktor Konetsky, *Nachalo kontsa komedii* (1978))

At the same time the notion of *gonor* as a specifically Polish trait is retained, and this keeps alive the stereotype of the haughty Pole and Polish arrogance (*kichlivy lyakh, shlyakhetsky gonor*):

поляк, уже совершенно чисто говоривший по-русски, одетый джентльменом, хотя все-таки смахивавший на лакея, с огромными усами и с гонором.

('the Pole, who by then had learnt perfect Russian, dressed as a gentleman, although still looking a bit like a footman, with a huge moustache and with *gonor*.')

(Fedor Dostoevsky)

в нём было много этакого шляхетского гонора.

('he had a lot of that Polish *gonor*.')

(Anatoly Rybakov)

A similar disapproval of having a high opinion of oneself has led to the words *ambitsiya* and *ambitsiozny* acquiring a negative meaning: instead of corresponding to *ambition* and *ambitious*, they have come to refer to an unfounded self-confidence and vanity, and indeed a pursuit of personal gain (which is traditionally disapproved of in Russian culture). For example:

был спесив, горд и амбициозен до крайности.

('[he] was haughty, proud and ambitious in the extreme.')

(Fedor Dostoevsky)

The definition given in the shorter Academy dictionary well reflects this negative evaluation: *ambitsiozny* (marked as dated) is defined as 'excessively, keenly ambitious'. The disapproving expression *udarit'sya v ambitsiyu* may also be noted. The negative implications can be clearly seen in the following examples from the *Russian National Corpus*:[2]

> амбициозный и бездарный интриган
>
> ('an ambitious and talentless intriguer')
>
> (Lev Trotsky, *Moya zhizn'* (1929–33))

> оставляя меня один на один со сворой рвущихся к власти и деньгам амбициозных проходимцев
>
> ('leaving me face to face with a pack of ambitious rascals lusting for power and money')
>
> (Boris Levin, *Inorodnoye telo* (1965–94))

> из-за нескончаемой грызни людей, получивших вместе с разумом амбиции и подлость
>
> ('because of the endless squabble of people who have received their intellect together with ambitions and meanness')
>
> (Vyacheslav Rybakov, *Vecher pyatnitsy* (1990))

The adaptation of a borrowed concept to the Russian linguistic conceptualization of the world is less common in those cases where the means of expression is a Russian analogue of the foreign word. This does, however, occur from time to time. For example, the notion of *sobornost'* (approximately 'collectivism'), which is often regarded as one of the most original concepts created by Russian culture, is expressed by a word that was formed to convey an important notion common to all Christians: the corresponding adjective, *soborny*, is simply a translation of the Greek *katholikos*. Language-specific in form (the importance of the underlying notion of 'gathering together' in the Russian conceptualization of the world is discussed, for example, in Shmelev (2002)), the words *soborny* and *sobornost'* express a concept which is frequently perceived as specifically Russian, and *sobornost'* is indeed often qualified by the adjective 'Russian' (*russkaya* or *rossiyskaya*):

> Русский 'коллективизм' и русская 'соборность' почитались великим преимуществом русского народа, возносящим его над народами Европы.
>
> ('The Russian "collectivism" and Russian "sobornost" were considered a great advantage of the Russian people, which raised it above the nations of Europe.')
>
> (Nikolay Berdyayev)

> идея личности, вроде бы западная, показана у Бахтина на творчестве русского писателя Достоевского, а идея соборности, вроде бы русская – на творчестве западного писателя Рабле.

('the seemingly Western idea of personality is illustrated by Bakhtin with reference the Russian writer Dostoevsky, while the seemingly Russian idea of *sobornost'* is discussed in relation to the Western writer Rabelais.')

(Sergey Averintsev)

Compare this also to examples from the *Russian National Corpus*:

именно соборность определяет русский народный дух (менталитет)
    ('it is *sobornost'* that defines the Russian national spirit (mentality)')
        (Valery Andreyev, *Natsional'nyye modeli ekonomiki* (2004))

наша неизбывная российская соборность, генетически заложенное в нас стремление жить и выживать сообща, миром
    ('our inescapable Russian *sobornost'*, our genetically defined strive to live and survive together, communally')
        (I.A. Arkhipova, *Muzyka zhizni* (1996))

Another similar example is the third member of Uvarov's famous triad of *pravoslaviye, samoderzhaviye, narodnost'* ('orthodoxy, autocracy, and nationality'): apparently the word *narodnost'* was constructed by Count Uvarov to convey the meaning of the French *nationalité*, but the Russian word came very soon to be perceived as referring to a specifically Russian value.

Adoption of the borrowed concept

What happens in other cases (and on a particularly massive scale since the 1990s) is that the 'Western' concept is adopted with practically no assimilation. In this case the Russian linguistic picture of the world comes under the influence of the semantic system of the source language. This happens particularly often in connection with semantic calquing, when a word that has previously existed in the language (in some cases an assimilated loanword) acquires a secondary meaning under the influence of a secondary meaning expressed by the equivalent word in another language. Numerous examples of this kind were examined in our article Zaliznyak et al. (2006); here I will confine my attention to a few brief illustrations.

A number of borrowings and semantic calques are connected with the dissemination in contemporary Russian society of an ideology of success, consumption, and enjoyment. Traditionally in Russian culture, pleasure and success have not been regarded as fundamental life values. At the same time, the high axiological status of success, wealth, and the possibility of enjoyment is frequently attributed to 'Western' culture. In his acceptance speech at the ceremony where he was presented with the Aleksandr Solzhenitsyn Literary Prize in 2007, Academician Zaliznyak characterized the saying 'If you are bright, why are you poor?' as a 'Western formula' and (referring to an advertisement with the text 'Everything can be bought!') described it as a 'salvo aimed at the traditional moral values of Russia'.

In complete accord with this interpretation, the poet Naum Korzhavin, in poems written shortly after his emigration, transcribes with Russian letters the English words corresponding to the notions of pleasure and success, thus foregrounding the alien character of these American cultural values, which he is unable to accept. In the poem *Reministsentsiya* (1978), he writes: 'vot zhivu za krayem sveta, / V tot mir bespechny zanesen, / Gde redko trebuyet poeta / K svyashchennoy zhertve Apollon. / Gde zhizn' – "indzhoy"' and adds the footnote explaining the meaning of *indzhoy*, which is the English word *enjoy* written in Russian characters (incomprehensible to a Russian with no knowledge of English). In the long poem *Spleteniya*, he uses a thoroughly exotic transcription *saksesyfulmen*, which he explains in a footnote as *uspeshlivy chelovek*, that is, a 'successful man'. It is noteworthy that he uses the rare Russian word *uspeshlivy*, which has a slightly negative connotation; at the time it seemed impossible to use the more frequently used, or familiar, word *uspeshny* in combination with a noun referring to a person. The word *uspeshlivy* is also used (with the same negative connotation) by Aleksandr Solzhenitsyn in his characterization of Yury Nagibin as a highly successful Soviet prose writer.

A suspicious attitude to success is even more clearly illustrated by the verb *preuspevat'* and its derivatives, the noun *preuspevaniye* and the adjective (of participial origin) *preuspevayushchy*. The following examples, in which the adjective is used, show that the negative connotations have remained to this day:

Нашей социальной средой теперь стали диссиденты и люди, вообще настроенные критически или не интегрировавшиеся в слой преуспевающих карьеристов.

('Dissidents, and people of a generally critical disposition, or unintegrated into the stratum of successful careerists, have become our social environment.')

(Aleksandr Zinov'yev)

Он был трусливый, преуспевающий, хлипкий московский барчонок, орущий на секретарей и швыряющий об пол дорогие ручки.

('He was a cowardly, successful, fragile Moscow lordling, shouting at his secretaries and flinging expensive fountain-pens on the floor.')

(Tat'yana Ustinova, *Podruga osobogo naznacheniya* (2003))

It must be emphasized that the negative attitude does not relate to success as such: when one wishes someone success (*zhelayu uspekha*), there is no negative implication. What is viewed in a negative light is the pursuit of *preuspevaniye*, where a person's goal in life is to attain success at any price.

Today the situation has changed: the hero of our time is the person who has attained success in life – that is, in contemporary terminology, the *uspeshny chelovek*, the very *saksesyfulmen* of Naum Korzhavin's poem. Numerous advertisements are specifically addressed to 'successful people' (*uspeshnyye lyudi*), although it was formerly considered impossible in Russian to combine the adjective *uspeshny* with *chelovek* 'person' or *lyudi* 'people'. A similar shift in meaning can be seen in the case of the adjective *effektivny*, which was also considered impossible with reference to people; in contemporary parlance it is used in combinations like *effektivny menedz-her*[3] (to a large extent under the influence of the English word *efficient*; *menedzher* is also a loan word from the English *manager*). A number of words have lost their negative connotations under the influence of their foreign analogues: for example, *kommersant, biznesmen, ambitsiozny, kar'yera*. What is common to all these changes is the acceptance of an orientation towards success, which is supplanting attentive-ness to the nuances of interpersonal relationships. It is understandable that these linguistic innovations irritate people whose attitudes are based on traditional Russian values, and that these people tend to perceive such changes as instances of linguistic decay. Linguists adopting a strong ideological position are even talk-ing about alien values being foisted on the Russian people as a means of 'manipulating the individual and social consciousness' (Vasil'yev 2003: 132).

The history of the word *problema*, described in Zaliznyak (2006), is a prime example of how a pre-existing Russian word (which is itself an earlier loanword) can be used to express a new concept that arrives from the 'West'. Schematically, the history of this word may be presented as follows. The word *problema* entered Russian from West European languages in the eighteenth century as a 'learned' word, and meant something like 'a difficult question to be resolved'. Subse-quently, the word gradually became part of everyday vocabulary, and at some point it developed a new meaning – 'a practical aim that is difficult to attain'. Significantly later (in the second half of the twentieth century), the word acquired yet another meaning as a result of semantic calquing from West European lan-guages: *problema* now came to be used in the sense of 'a circumstance that disrupts the smooth, normal, untroubled course of events'; in other words, something that must be eliminated in order to reinstate the 'normal' course of events which enables people to gain pleasure from life. The new meaning of the word *problema* has become deeply rooted in Russian, and a number of idiomatic clichés are now based on this meaning (many of them also calques):[4] *net problem, ne problema, bez problem, eto ne moya problema, eto tvoi problemy*, and *sozdavat' sebe problemy*. All these expressions are based on a picture of the world where the norm is an unhindered and untroubled movement along the path of life.

In all the cases noted so far, the Russian word (which may be a loanword, but has in that case been adapted to the system of values characteristic of the Russian linguistic picture of the world) has changed its meaning under the influence of a foreign analogue (i.e. a kind of semantic calquing has taken place), and this has led to some modifications in the corresponding fragment of the Russian linguistic picture of the world. Less often, the borrowing of a 'Western' concept takes place by the adoption of the external shape of a word that has had no previous exis-tence in Russian. An example of such borrowing is the word *empatiya*, recently discussed by Anna Gladkova in an article where she contrasts the Russian word *soperezhivaniye* with the English word 'empathy' (Gladkova 2007). Gladkova draws the conclusion that collocations including the word *empatiya* in Russian are a mirror-like reflection of English collocations with 'empathy', which leads her to ask whether the Russian emotional scripts might not be altered if the word *empatiya* becomes widely current in Russian. In other words, the borrowing of a word leads to a change in the corresponding fragment of the linguistic picture of the world if the concept behind the word is not subjected to assimilation.

It should be noted that changes of this nature are prime examples of genuine language change because they must inevitably be reflected in the lexicographical description of the language. Traditional dictionary entries for words like *uspeshny* 'successful', *effektivny* 'effective', *ambitsiozny* 'ambitious', or *kar'yera* 'career' do not correspond to the way that these words are used in contemporary discourse. For example, Ozhegov's dictionary (1972) gives two meanings for the word *kar'yerny* (as an adjective from *kar'yer*[1] 'career, full gallop' and from *kar'yer*[2] 'quarry'), but this word is not listed as an adjective from *kar'yera* '(professional) career'. However, if we examine contemporary texts, the overwhelming majority of examples with the adjective *kar'yerny* are seen to be based on the noun *kar'yera*; in other words, the lexicographical description of the word *kar'yerny* and of the other words that we have mentioned needs to be updated so as to reflect contemporary usage. Indeed, the use of *kar'yerny* as an adjective derived from *kar'era* has been noted in the more recent dictionary (Ozhegov and Shvedova 1992).

Concluding remarks

The reception of a Western concept in the Russian cultural sphere may lead to an assimilation of the concept whereby it is adapted to the peculiarities of the Russian linguistic picture of the world; but there is another option, borrowing the concept in an unmodified form, which leads to a restructuring of the corresponding fragment of the linguistic picture of the world. Such restructuring is perceived by the guardians of a strict linguistic norm as an adulteration of the language. For the linguist, however, both varieties of the reception of foreign concepts are of substantial value. In tracing the conflict between the value systems that find their incarnation in various languages, and the ways in which this conflict is resolved as words are borrowed, the linguist can discover the peculiarities of each of the linguistic pictures of the world that come into interaction. In particular, by observing the ways in which 'Western' concepts are received by the Russian linguistic consciousness, we are able to penetrate into those specific characteristics of the Russian linguistic picture of the world that might remain unnoticed if such material were not available.

Notes

1 This is also the case in English where one says 'Dutch courage' when one takes a drink before going into some intimidating situation such as a job interview or when one is expecting to be told off, or criticized, for doing something wrong (Godfrey Weldhen, personal communication).

2 It should be noted that the words *ambitsiya* and *ambitsiozny* are at present losing their negative colouring and are starting to be used with reference to qualities that are regarded in a favourable light. This is due to a shift in the linguistic picture of the world, which will be discussed in the next section.

3 Consider Dmitry Bykov's forceful protest against the value judgement implied by this word combination (*Russkaya zhizn'*, 30 April 2007).

4 It is noteworthy that Lidiya Chukovskaya, while generally appreciative of Solzhenitsyn's work, regarded his use of the word *problema* in this sense in a late nineteenth–early twentieth century context in *The Red Wheel* as a kind of anachronism ('he does not know the language of that time').

Bibliography

Gladkova, A. (2007) 'New and traditional emotion terms in Russian: semantics and culture', in A. Padgette (ed.) *Transcultural Studies: A Series in Interdisciplinary Research*, vol. 2–3, Special double issue on Discourses of Aesthetics, Ethics and Power in Old and Emerging Societies, 123–37, Idyllwild, CA: Charles Schlacks, Publisher.

Ozhegov, S.I. (1972) *Slovar' russkogo yazyka*, Moskva: Sovetskaya entsiklopediya.

Ozhegov, S.I. and Shvedova, N.Yu. (1992) *Tolkovy slovar' russkogo yazyka*, Moskva: Az Ltd.

The Russian National Corpus (2003–10). Online. Available: www.ruscorpora.ru (accessed 29 March 2011).

Shmelev, A.D. (2002) *Russkaya yazykovaya model' mira: materialy k slovaryu*, Moskva: Yazyki slavyanskoy kul'tury.

Vasil'yev, A.D. (2003) *Slovo v rossiyskom teleefire: ocherki noveyshego slovoupotrebleniya*, Moskva: Flinta/Nauka.

Zaliznyak, Anna A. (2006) 'Russkiye kul'turnyye kontsepty v yevropeyskoy lingvisticheskoy perspektive: slovo *problema*', in N.I. Laufer, A.S. Narin'yani, and V.P. Selegey (eds) *Komp'yuternaya lingvistika i intellektual'nyye tekhnologii: trudy mezhdunarodnoy konferentsii 'Dialog 2006' (Bekasovo, 31 maya-4 iyunya 2006 goda)*, 152–56, Moskva: Izd-vo RGGU.

Zaliznyak, Anna A., Levontina, I.B. and Shmelev, A.D. (2005) *Klyuchevye idei russkoy yazykovoy kartiny mira*, Moskva: Yazyki slavyanskoy kul'tury.

——(2006) 'Evolyutsiya klyuchevykh kontseptov russkogo yazyka v XX veke: aspekty izucheniya', *Vestnik RGNF*, 50/1: 120–27.

Part II

Society

The social dimension of our subject is examined through reflections on the Russian version of modernity, and above all political modernity. This is done through case studies that mainly concern the prospects of democracy in Russia.

One side of the issue is that the Russian 'sovereign democracy' is deficient if measured by Western yardsticks. The crucial problem is the apparent lack of autonomy of what is called civil society. Usually the notion refers to the social conditions that must be fulfilled for people to be able to act independently of state authority, or in opposition to it, in a sustained way; this capacity is necessary for democracy to prevail. The point is that a sphere of life is needed which is distinct from the state and the market and in which people can organize around interests that they communicate by making claims to other actors or to the state. Moreover, in linking themselves to one another, they produce social identities in this process. But these two interrelated aspects of civil society, interests and identities, and their mutual recognition, are not easy to develop. In the West the consolidation was preceded by a long period of institution-building.

The other side of the question is the emphasis in this approach on the *lack* of something, notably on the lack of autonomy of civil society and the related deficiency of the public sphere as the forum for free and well-developed interest articulation and identity formation. It is certainly appropriate that the perspective directs attention to tendencies in Russian political life that undermine civil society, such as the vertical structuration of interests and elements of clientelism. Yet the problem is that the Western view may obscure the perception of those aspects of joint action which are peculiar to Russia. It may not be sensitive enough to capture adequately the specific features of interest- and identity-formation in Russia and the ensuing responses to the specifically Russian problems of democracy.

The four democracy-related chapters aim to overcome this problem. They adopt different perspectives, all of which relate the respective subjects to Western experience but at the same time take into account their specifically Russian character. One chapter (Oittinen) is an overview sensitizing the reader to the historical dimension of the issue, while the other three (Colin Lebedev, Volkov, and Alapuro and Lonkila) adopt a micro-perspective in examining (respectively) a social movement, a conflictual incident, and two instances of associational activity. The micro-perspective seems especially relevant here, because it is above all at the level of everyday practices that people adopt their specific ways of pursuing common ends. The fifth chapter (Gronow) completes the picture by reflecting, through an example, on the broader question of the character of Soviet modernity and its implications for our time.

In his examination of the construction of Russia as the 'Other' in relation to the West from the nineteenth century to the Slavophile doctrines and recent theories, Vesa Oittinen reminds us that Slavophile thinking does not primarily stress national or ethnic disparities in relation to Western Europe, but refers to deep-seated differences in the whole conception of rationality. From this perspective a prospect presents itself for Russia to continue its own path and create a society on a basis different from Western modernity.

Anna Colin Lebedev's subject, the *Committee of Soldiers' Mothers of Russia*, is likely to be the most widely studied instance of popular action in present-day Russia. Contrary to previous analyses that present it as a social movement in the Western sense, this chapter shows its specific character by looking at ways of justification and by stressing the peculiar role of personal concerns in joint action. In elaborating a compromise between 'proximity attachments' and 'civic action', the organization provides access to the public sphere for people who are not able to act collectively. This is different from the Western viewpoint, which holds that dependence and proximity attachments must be overcome as a precondition for access to the public sphere. The author maintains, moreover, that the *Soldiers' Mothers'* activity leads us to consider more generally the importance of proximity in building the collective in contemporary societies.

In his case study of the spectacular but (as it turned out) temporary closure of the European University at St Petersburg in the winter of 2008, Vadim Volkov adopts as the central conceptual tool the notion of 'opposition substitute'. Derived from the conventional term of 'opposition', it is modified to capture an essential feature of Russian political culture today. Volkov interestingly shows how a civic campaign can succeed precisely because it is able to escape the label of (political) opposition.

Risto Alapuro and Markku Lonkila take as their starting point the way(s) in which people, when acting jointly, make the transition from their personal concerns to public demands. A thematic link connects their contribution to Anna Colin Lebedev's analysis. Different modes in the 'rise in generality' of demands are largely neglected in the comparative research dealing with social movements and action. The adequacy of this view is shown by comparing a diabetes association and a car drivers' association in St Petersburg with their counterparts in Helsinki, Finland. The approach puts in a new perspective those conventional findings which portray Russian associations as inner-directed and dominated by personal ties.

Finally, by exploring the nature of Soviet fashion, Jukka Gronow reflects in a concrete way on the question of the modernity of Soviet society: was it modern, and if so, was it modern in the same sense as the West, and what implications does its character have for present-day Russia? Gronow finds that in a kind of zigzag movement the modern (so to speak) homogenizing influence of the Soviet period in Russian culture has made room for opposite tendencies. Under the present conditions of increasing social inequality, such forms of fashion proliferate that quite directly reveal the status of their adepts, thus making the adoption of fashion more reminiscent of practices in traditional societies or early modernity than of those now prevalent in the West.

5 Russian 'otherness': from Chaadaev to the present day

Vesa Oittinen

To describe Russia and Russian culture as the Other in comparison to Western Europe is a commonplace. In academia, the impact of this mode of thinking can be seen in the fact that in the 'West' there are specialized research institutions that focus on Russia (such as, for example, my 'own' institute, the Aleksanteri Institute at the University of Helsinki), and special scientific journals on Russian issues – so, for example, the journal *Studies in East European Thought* publishes material on philosophy like any other philosophy journal, but concentrates exclusively on Russia and Eastern Europe. One might conclude from these examples that the Russian language and Russian culture is considered so alien to the West, that it cannot be researched on the same terms as the corresponding Western phenomena but has to be located in a special sphere of its own.

However, a second look at the problem of Russian otherness reveals intricate anomalies. To begin with, Russia has not always been considered as the Other. In order to prove this, one does not need to resort to the period of Kievan Rus', which was treated by the (albeit, still semi-barbaric) European states as *al pari* with them. In fact, the thesis put forward by the American historian of ideas, Larry Wolff, that the whole concept of an *Eastern Europe/Russia* as a contrast to the West was invented as late as the eighteenth century (Wolff 1994), is, although somewhat provocative, not at all ill-founded. Wolff remarks that earlier, in Antiquity and the Middle Ages, the main cultural divide of Europe was to be seen in the difference between the barbaric North and the civilized, Mediterranean South. The North was populated by such frightening or pitiful people as the Goths, Vandals, or Finns, while the crafts, arts, and philosophy thrived among the Greeks and Romans. Only as late as the eighteenth century was this traditional divide broken down to be replaced with another, this time vertical, divide between West and East. Wolff interprets this process as the 'construction of Eastern Europe' during the Enlightenment.

Although Wolff's basic observation – the radical shift of a European cultural divide – is convincing, he does not ask what the deeper socio-historical reasons underlying this process might be. I would, for my part, suggest one obvious candidate for such an explanation: this new geographical grouping is a result of the development of the *modern world* since the 1500s, a process during which the economic, political, and demographic point of gravity of the Old Continent shifted from the Mediterranean area to the north-west, to the areas surrounding the North Sea, where new, modern nations began to emerge, through the suggestive stages of the Renaissance, Reformation, and Enlightenment (as indicated by Jürgen Habermas in his seminal studies on the subject).

However, although this explanation at first glance might seem obvious, indeed almost trivial, its consequences are not, or at least have not been, thematized inthe field of Russian studies to the extent they deserve. Of course, the geopolitical aspects of modernity have been discussed in many centre–periphery models of the world economy, such as the theory of Immanuel Wallerstein. But despite the fact that Wallerstein himself has stressed that these global centre–periphery structures are very persistent (according to him, the present world order began to form over 500 years ago), the impact of these structures on local civilizations and cultures surprisingly often gets neglected in macro-sociological and historical analyses of modernity, which put its economic conditions in brackets, so to speak. The geographical factor which expresses itself in the international division of labour has been considered as something more or less external and contingent in relation to the more essential constituents of a social order and culture.

Thus the manner in which modernity has emerged seems to have produced an insoluble contradiction: on the one side, it has been brought forth in the geographically limited area of Western Europe (and North America), bearing even today the hallmarks of this restricted cultural area; but on the other side, the values of modernity are conceived as universal, to be shared by the whole of humanity.

Antinomity of Russian modernization 1: the *rencontre* of Diderot and Empress Catherine

Already in the heyday of the Enlightenment this antinomy could be discerned as Denis Diderot made his famous visit to Russia in the 1770s. Almost immediately on arriving in St Petersburg, Diderot reminded Empress Catherine II of the fact that she was but a representative of the *people*, and demanded that she give up autocratic rule, liberate the serfs, and call for parliamentary elections. On discovering that Catherine was not immediately enthusiastic about his suggestions, Diderot became disappointed and said that instead of the enlightened ruler he had expected, he had found a tyrant. Catherine, in turn, reproached Diderot: 'In order to please M. Diderot, my *nakaz* [the sketch for a Russian Constitution] should have turned the whole of Russia upside-down.' Shortly after their first meeting (a couple of months), Diderot ceased to talk about politics with the Empress and their meetings became less frequent. However, both Diderot and Catherine kept up appearances, and the Empress gave the philosopher 3,000 roubles to cover his travelling expenses back to Paris, plus an elegant fur, a golden ring, and a bust of herself. Back in France, Diderot summed up his experiences of Russia by saying that the Russians:

seem always to live as if they were expecting an earthquake to happen or as if it just had happened, and they always look as if they were trying to unravel whether they really had solid ground beneath their feet.

(Dlugach 1984: 38 ff)

Diderot refers here to the social tensions which were soon to lead to the mutiny of Pugachev, but his comment can be generalized: the superficial modernization of Russian society, driven violently from above, produced a constant threat to the social equilibrium.

Diderot and Catherine's meetings thus showed both horns of the dilemma of attempting to apply the ideas of a modern social order to a geographical periphery. One horn, represented by Diderot, was the assertion of the universality of the ideas of the Enlightenment and modernity, that is, the conviction that its ideas are generally applicable to all men, no matter what their ethnic, geographic, or cultural background might be. The other horn was defended by the Russian Empress, who maintained – with equal credibility – that Diderot's ideas would have hurled her country into chaos. Catherine had few illusions about the true nature of the Russian peasantry, later so idealized by the naïve Slavophiles, and she regarded the rebel Pugachev as an ogre who had to be suppressed at all costs.

But where Diderot, and following him, the Western Enlightenment tradition, saw in Russia only a despotic country stubbornly resisting liberal reforms and individual liberty (before the 1870s even Marx shared this general Enlightenment view, denouncing Russian society as 'a bloody morass of Mongol servitude' in one of his pamphlets),[1] Russian thinkers became more and more conscious of the specific character of their country, as the Enlightenment discourse produced an Eastern Europe as the Other to the modern West. This Other, Eastern Europe, seemed to have some constant traits in its social structures and culture, which in turn led to the necessary conclusion that the precepts of reason, naïvely held by the eighteenth-century Enlightenment as universal, could not immediately be applied to the realities of these societies. The suppression of the Decembrist insurrection in 1825 only seemed to reinforce the assessment that Russia and those substantial parts of Eastern Europe attached to it would remain long into the future a world where all was otherwise than in the enlightened West.

Antinomy of Russian modernization 2: paradoxes of Chaadaev

The first Russian thinker of merit, who clearly recognized the antinomy of Russian culture and life, was Petr Chaadaev. His *Philosophical Letters*, on which he had begun to work – in French – already in the 1820s, immediately after the defeat of the Decembrists, amounted to the entrée of Russian thematics to world philosophical literature and were in this sense quite unprecedented. The first and only *Letter*, which Chaadaev managed to publish in 1836 in the journal *Teleskop*, created a scandal, as his opinion concerning the state of Russia was in no way a flattering one. There is something highly ironic in the fact that the first work of truly original Russian philosophy is one which strongly underscores the non-originality of the Russians:

> [W]e have never advanced along with other people; we are not related to any of the great human families; we belong neither to the West nor to the East, and we possess the traditions of neither. Placed, as it were, outside of the times, we have not been affected by the universal education of mankind. This ... history of the human spirit which led men to the position which they occupy in the rest of the world today had no effect upon us.

Chaadaev characterizes Western development as the *'mouvement universel de l'humanité'*,[2] as the model of a 'normal' history, and gives a sketch of the 'average', enlightened *'homme de l'Europe'*. Among the European nations:

> there is a common bond which unites them in one whole, evident to anyone who has profoundly studied their history ... So you want to know what these ideas are? They are ideas of duty, justice, law and order. They originate in the very events which have built up society; they are the integral elements in the social world of these countries. This is the atmosphere of the West; it is more than history, more than psychology; it is the physiology of the European. What have you to substitute for that in our country?
>
> (Chaadaev 1991a: I, 93–94; Chaadaev 1991b: 22–23)

In contrast to this picture of the 'occidental', rational Man, the Russians seem to possess a devious form of civilization:

> As a result, you will find that we all lack certain self-confidence [*applomb*], method of thought, and logic. We are unfamiliar with the western syllogism. There is something close to frivolity in our best minds. The best ideas are paralyzed like sterile visions in our heads for lack of any relationship and consistency ... There are some of those lost souls in every land, but in ours it is a common characteristic ... ; it is really the carelessness of a life without experience and conjecture [*l'étourderie d'une vie sans expérience et sans prévision*], one which is unrelated to anything more than the ephemeral existence of the individual detached from the species.
>
> (Chaadaev 1991a: I, 94–95; Chaadaev 1991b: 23)

These became the classical formulations, which fixed the opposition of Russian and Western/Modern civilization, staking out the path of development of Russian historiosophic thought from the Slavophiles to the Russian Idealists, *Narodniks*, Marxists, and Eurasianists. The first reaction of the Russian public to Chaadaev's *Philosophical Letters* consisted, however, of consternation and indignation. Only a few would agree with the views of this thinker who had soiled his own nest. The first *Letter* was the last to be published, since Tsar Nicholas I was furious with both Chaadaev and the entire journal *Teleskop*, which was immediately suppressed by imperial decree; Chaadaev himself was officially declared insane.

This humiliating treatment (which, by the way, became a tradition in Russian history – it suffices to recall the political use of psychiatry against dissidents in the Soviet Union) did not, however, break Chaadaev, who, although he was a complex and extravagant personality,[3] nevertheless insisted on his right to think independently. He continued to write down his thoughts, which circulated in handwritten copies in the circles of St Petersburg's and Moscow's intelligentsia. His interpretation of history challenged the picture of Russia as depicted by the official historiography, for example in the extensive work *Istoriya gosudarstva Rossiyskogo* (1816–24, 1829) by Nikolay Karamzin, the court historian of Alexander I and favourite of Nicholas I, or by the well-known triple formula *autocracy–orthodoxy–nationalism*[4] of the Minister of People's Education, Count Uvarov. The view sketched by Chaadaev in his *Letters* was innovative not only in the sense that it raised the Russian theme to the level of philosophical discussion for the first time, but because it put the question in the context of universal history. It was Chaadaev who gave original Russian philosophy that historiosophic touch that it has retained ever since. It is no exaggeration to say that for Chaadaev the philosophy of history was – in contrast to the Western view of philosophy – the proper *philosophia prima*, the clue to the explanation of the world.

Russia's place in history presents itself to Chaadaev as a series of paradoxes, which might be interpreted as further deductions from the 'original paradox' that had been evident at least since the *rencontre* of Diderot and Catherine. They are formulated already in the only published *Letter* of 1836, where Chaadaev repeatedly compares Russia with its counterpart the West, the happy continent favoured by history. He never tries to give any geographically accurate definition of what he means by 'West' or 'Europe', showing thus that they are for him historico-philosophical, not geographic categories:

1) The *first paradox* lies already there, that Russia seems not to follow even the fundamental law of the development of Mankind. History is led by 'a divine, eternal power', and to become aware of it constitutes the deepest essence of Christian faith. By this, Providence gives every nation its specific and historic task which it has to realize. But Russia does not have any such historical task; *la loi général de l'humanité* does not apply to Russia, and Providence has seemingly not given Russia any task.

2) Providence in the form of certain spiritual leaders is leading the nations of the West, which represent 'l'intelligence collective de la nation' and make it progress. But in Russia there are no such persons. *[J]e vous le demande, où sont nos sages, où sont nos penseurs?* ['I am asking you, where are our sages, where are our thinkers?']

3) The nations of the West are developing by accumulating a tradition which is transmitted from one generation to another, and so every individual feels that he is in contact with the whole of humanity. But the Russians? *Nous ... venus au monde comme des enfants illégitimes, sans héritage, sans lien avec les hommes qui nous ont précédés sur la terre* ['We ... came to the

world as illegitimate children, without inheritance, without any bonds to the people who had preceded us on earth'].

4) It is characteristic of nations that develop normally (and Western Europe is for Chaadaev the measure of normality), that after an intense, effervescent and romantic juvenile phase, from which later they may even draw material for their poetry, there comes a phase of mature, regular and serene life. In Russia it is, again, otherwise: Russia is lacking both the heroic early period and the subsequent period of peaceful and even development. The 'moral world' (i.e. the world of civic life) is in Russia still in a state of 'chaotic fermentation', a state *semblable aux révolutions du globe qui ont précédé l'état actuel de la planète* [similar to the revolutions of the globe that preceded the current state of the planet] (one sees, by the way, here the echo of Diderot's observation of the Russians, made fifty years earlier, 'as if they were expecting an earthquake to happen or as if it just had happened').

5) Whereas the nations of the West gathered around the one, universal and Catholic Church, Russia adopted the Christian faith from the 'miserable Byzantium', a country profoundly despised by the builders of modern European civilization, and clung to its own schismatic orthodoxy under the pretext of petty theological disputes. So even a deviant form of religion separated Russia from Europe. *Nous n'avons rien à démêler avec la grande affaire du monde* ['We have nothing to do with the grand course of the world'].

(Chaadaev 1991a: I, 86–106)

After the catastrophe of the *Philosophical Letters*, Chaadaev continued to analyse the Russian problem in letters and drafts of articles for two decades, until his death in 1856. Sometimes he seemed to become more optimistic about the prospects for Russia, as in his next article *Apologie d'un fou* (1837), where he toyed with the idea that Russia's failure to share Western culture might even become an advantage: Russia had remained a blank sheet,[5] on which History can write something quite new and unprecedented (see Chaadaev 1991a: I, 301 and Chaadaev 1991b: 109–10).

But this optimism does not last long: already in the mid-1840s Chaadaev begins to return to his original austere views. In a fragment composed a couple of years before his death (1856) there is no mention of Russia's limitless perspectives: now he sees Russia as '*un fait tout nu*', and this fact, stripped of all wishful thinking, is that Russia '*tend à se dérouler sur la carte du globe en proportions de jour en jour plus gigantesques*' ['tends to unfold itself on the world map in the proportions that become daily more and more gigantic']. Chaadaev's conclusion is clear: the expansion of Russia must be stopped and its attack against the old civilized world reversed ['*il faut, par conséquent, empêcher s'il se peut de grandir outre mesure, d'empiéter sur le vieux monde civilisé*'] (Chaadaev 1991a: I, 312). The deepening reaction of the later years of Nicholas I's reign and the international role of Russia as the self-assumed 'gendarme of Europe' in the spirit of the Holy Alliance, in for example suppressing the revolutionary movement of 1848 in Poland and Austria, made Chaadaev think that Russia had no hope without a profound renewal of its social structure and culture.

Despite his critique of Russia's backwardness and the politics of the autocracy, Chaadaev cannot be called a radical, or even a revolutionary. His great veneration towards religion is a trait that distinguishes him both from the Enlightenment's atheism or deism and from the early socialists of the nineteenth century. In Chaadaev's view, religion – albeit in its Western, Catholic form – was a central constituting factor of civilization. This manner of stressing the importance of religion for the emergence of modernity makes him foreshadow Sergey Bulgakov, who later, in the beginning of the twentieth century, would seek to renew Russia's national way of life and economy by means of a 'reformed Orthodoxy'. It seems beyond doubt that Chaadaev had been influenced by such French catholic and conservative thinkers of the restoration period as Bonald, Lamennais, and de Maistre. But was Chaadaev a conservative? For a Conservative, he was too scandalous a person in his home country. As Andrzej Walicki remarks:

> [although] the author of the *Philosophical Letters* would undoubtedly have been a conservative seen against the background of the European milieu, he could not be such in his native country: on the contrary, he stresses that there are not to be found the fundamental requisites of a real conservativism in Russia: a feeling of traditions and stability, deep historical ties.

(Here again, by the way, Diderot's observation about Russians expecting an earthquake every day reappears!) Thus Chaadaev's ideas, instead of reinforcing the Russian status quo, on the contrary threatened to destroy it (Walicki 1973: 101).[6]

A special trait in Chaadaev was, as the editors of the latest Russian edition of his works point out in their excellent introduction, his situation as a kind of 'free-floating' intellectual between the Tsarist autocracy, on the one side, and the revolutionary democrats, on the other, so that 'leaving the shore of his home he did not find a new haven' (*Paradoksy* in Chaadaev 1991a: I, 10). But precisely because of this ambivalence, both the conservatives and the radicals could appeal to him and his writings with equal right. That Chaadaev remains to this day an enigmatic thinker, whose message has not been successfully 'deciphered' but remains instead constantly stuck in the clichés of ideological interpretations, is very eloquently shown by the fact that in the 1990s, during the demolition of the Soviet system, the old disputes of the nineteenth century on 'what Chaadaev really said' again emerged as if no consensus had ever been reached on this question.[7]

To my mind, it is obvious that Chaadaev has not been studied to the extent he deserves. He is a quite extraordinary figure in the history of Russian thought. But much in the same manner as the Russians have never thoroughly analysed the Pugachev phenomenon, so too Chaadaev has more remained an icon in Russian intellectual history than become the object of a really critical study. It became possible to publish Chaadaev's papers only after the revolution of 1905, and to date, Mikhail Gershenzon's *P.Ya. Chaadaev – Zhizn' i myshleniye*, published in 1908, remains the main comprehensive biography. Although a valuable collection of facts, Gershenzon's biography suffered from many flaws in its interpretation of

Chaadaev's position, which were later remarked on by some Russian scholars, such as, for example, Dmitry Shakhovskoy, an early Soviet Marxist student of literature, at the turn of the 1920s and 1930s.[8]

The Slavophiles

In Chaadaev's *Apologie d'un fou* there are some allusions to 'our fanatical Slavs', who are digging up 'all kinds of curiosities' from Russian history – in vain, for the 'emptiness of the Russian soul' will not be overcome by such stuff. Here Chaadaev was speaking about the movement which later came to be called Slavophilism and which represented the next generation of original Russian thinkers. Already by the 1840s, the complex of Chaadaev's ideas was divided along conservative and progressive lines, whose first form was the well-known dichotomy of the Slavophiles and the *Zapadniks*, 'Westerners'. There is so much literature available on this theme that I will not go into details here. The main point to be remembered is that the Slavophile and *Zapadnik* interpretations of Russia's place in universal history are complementary and that both rely on Chaadaev, while stressing different sides of his intellectual heritage. But while the *Zapadniks* saw Russia's otherness as something epiphenomenal and accidental, which would be overcome in the future course of history, the Slavophiles took the Russianness of Russia to their heart. Russia to them was *essentially* different from Western modernity. Moreover, the Slavophiles now conceived the otherness of Russia in comparison to the West in a quite positive sense, not as an occasion to lament the backwardness of Russia, as Chaadaev had done. In his now classical study, Andrzei Walicki has characterized the thought of the Slavophiles as a 'conservative utopia' (1973).

Slavophilism should not be confounded with other conservative and nationalist movements in Russia, such as Panslavism, or the *pochvennichestvo* ('earthiness') of Dostoevsky, not to mention the Great Russian chauvinism of the end of the nineteenth and early twentieth centuries. Slavophilism proper existed in fact for only a rather short period, from the last years of the 1830s to 1861, when the reforms initiated by the regime of Alexander II started a new cycle of modernization which finally revealed the utopianism of Slavophile constructions.

The ideological roots of Russian Slavophilism are often, especially in Western reference literature, seen in Romanticism. It is of course true that German idealism, above all the middle and late periods of Schelling, were an important point of reference for the Slavophiles. Ivan Kireyevsky was in his younger days a member of the so-called *lyubomudry* circle in Moscow, to which the well-known Schellingians V.F. Odoyevsky and D.V. Venevitinov belonged, too.[9] But despite all the respect shown towards Schelling and German idealism, Kireyevsky and other Slavophiles thought that the Russians should distance themselves from Western rationalism and instead develop their own original ways of thinking, drawing from the experience of Russian life. In fact, there are quite definite differences between Slavophilism and Western Romanticism. It suffices here to say that despite all their admiration for the Middle Ages, the German Romantics reverted to the then most-modern philosophy, namely, Kantian–Fichtean transcendentalism (especially Novalis) and German idealism. The relation of the Slavophiles to modernity is clearly much more retrograde than that of the Western Romantics. The Slavophiles would in all earnest have had a return to the pre-Petrine life forms of old Russia, and despite the (rather superficial) influences from Schelling they believed that it was possible to find in the Orthodox tradition solutions even for the intricate problems of modern Western philosophy, which according to them had gone astray since Descartes, who put the individual subject at the centre of his contemplations.

Walicki's characterization of Slavophilism as a form of 'conservative utopism' is more to the point. His analyses remain to this day indispensable for anyone wishing to study Russian Slavophilism, which in many respects was so extravagant a phenomenon. However, it should be borne in mind that such concepts as 'radicalism' and 'conservativism', like 'right' and 'left' in politics, having been formed in the West during and after the French Revolution, do reflect the conditions of the modern political and social order – conditions which did not exist in Russia at the time Slavophilism proper was thriving. If we accept the thesis of Russia's otherness in comparison to the West, it is obvious that Western political categories and classifications cannot be directly applied to Russian circumstances. So even Slavophile conservativism is a conservativism *sui generis*, as a short overview of the chief aspects of their ideas will quickly show.

Russia and her historical role was the focus of Slavophile thought. According to them, Russia differed from the West in several decisive ways. First, there was no private property in land, as in the West; instead the peasants lived in so-called *obshchinas*, autonomous agricultural communities which owned the soil collectively. (Actually, however, this system, so admired by the Slavophile ideologists, encouraged the tendency towards serfdom: because the authorities did not have to cope with the resistance of independent land-owning peasants, as the Russian peasant was already tied to his community, it was easy to turn him into a serf by making the landlords the heads of the communities.) A second point of difference was, according to the Slavophiles, that in Russia there had not been such severe internal conflicts and wars of conquest as were characteristic of the history of Europe. In most European countries the elite was formed by conquerors from abroad (the Franks in France, the Normans in Italy and England), while Russia was ethnically homogeneous. Even this assertion was clearly a product of wishful thinking, as it is well known that Russia was and is an extremely mixed country ethnically, and that foreign conquests have played a central role in Russian history – one needs only to mention the *Varyags*, Mongols, and Tatars. A third point of divergence was religion; Chaadaev had already mentioned this, but had seen in it a negative factor, isolating Russia from the West. For the Slavophiles, on the contrary, Orthodox Christianity was the Alpha and Omega of all Russianness. Thanks to Orthodoxy, Russian culture and even the modes of thinking and morality were – in a positive sense – different from the Western forms. The Russians had preserved the original, genuine forms of sociality, whereas the West had alienated itself from the true values of life.

These points might give reason to classify Slavophilism simply as a form of conservatism – and moreover, not a very bright one, when one considers their self-deceptive views which totally ignored the realities of Russian peasant life. But there are other components in their ideology which make the picture more complicated. Although keenly Orthodox, the Slavophiles had a problematic and tense relationship with the official church. The cause of their dissent was not only that the Slavophiles criticized the collaboration of the church with the state authorities, but also because the church thought that the Slavophiles were trying to dominate the doctrines of Orthodox faith. Attempts to reform the received Orthodox faith in accordance with the utopistic social concepts of the Slavophiles as the main ideological expression of Russianness (even at the cost of the universal Christian concerns of the church) was then during whole of the nineteenth century a distinctive trait of Russian idealistic philosophy. Seen from a Weberian perspective, which stressed the connection between Protestant rationality and the birth of capitalism, one could say that in this respect the Russian idealist thinkers *nolens volens* assumed a similar function towards orthodoxy as the sixteenth-century Protestant reformers in the West had towards traditional Catholicism. A remarkable example of this line of thought was the book by Sergey Bulgakov, *Filosofiya khozyaystva* ('Philosophy of Economy', 1912), mentioned above, a grandiose attempt to sketch a kind of Orthodox counterpart to Max Weber's theory of Protestantism as the world outlook of modern capitalism. Bulgakov wanted a Russian industrial capitalism which would differ from its Western counterpart in that it would reject the Benthamian idea of *homo oeconomicus* and build instead on the religious idea of service, which it should take from the Orthodox monarchs and apply to social and industrial life. Thus Russian industrial society would have a moral foundation which would make it quite different from Western capitalism and the supremacy of the (merely) formal rationalism described by Weber. With this work Bulgakov brought the Slavophile idea of Russia as a parallel world and alternative to Western modernity to its logical completion.[10] The big difference to the Protestant reformers was, however, that the attempts to renew orthodoxy with philosophical ideas did not lead to any significant changes in the religious consciousness of the ordinary Russian people, but remained an ideological toying of a small circle of intellectuals.

Slavophiles and the modern world

Following the exposition by a recent Russian researcher, A.M. Peskov (1993: 62–72),[11] one could draw a table of cultural oppositions depicting the differences between East and West in the Slavophile imagination (Table 5.1).

A study of the table leads to rather interesting conclusions. Of course, the Slavophile self-image of Russian pureness as contrasted to Western decadence is, in an unintended manner, comical, but the main point is elsewhere. It is striking that the problematic character of the relations between Russia and the West *does not*, according to the Slavophiles, *have any strictly ethnic or national causes*, contrary to the common opinion, which still today seems to prevail in the West when Russian

Table 5.1 Differences between East and West in the Slavophile imagination

	Europe	*Russia*
Origin of the State	By conquest and violence	Peacefully
Development of the State	Through antagonisms, via revolutions	Through peaceful growth
Relations between people and the estates	Founded on juridical agreements, that is, on mistrust	Founded on love, that is, natural, free, and peaceful
Law, jurisprudence	Formal legalism, the form is all-important	Jurisprudence according to tradition, according to conscience
Way of life and property relations	Private property, a privatized way of life, people longing to acquire private wealth; family ties disconnected	Collective and family property; the meaning of life is the well-being of the family
Interrelation of material and spiritual factors	The material side of life is more important; longing for luxury and riches	The spiritual side of life is more important; simplicity, modesty
Present state of religion	Disappearing faith; pluralism of opinions, freethinking and secularization	A true Christian faith (among the people)
Historical causes of the present state of religious life	The pagan heritage from Antiquity; rationalism	Absence of a pagan heritage; loyalty to the traditions of the Orthodox church
Concept of personality	A cult of personal freedom; personal discretion, inclination to make rebellion, pride	Self-sacrifice as the highest Christian form of freedom; humility
Mode of thinking	Rationalism, formal knowledge, supremacy of analysis	A holistic world view
Prospects	Spiritual resources are exhausted	The principles of Orthodoxy and Community will spread to the whole of Europe

nationalism is discussed. One can say that the traits attributed to the West are but general characteristics of modernity and modern forms of rationality (in contrast to the traditional, or organic rationality, in the terminology of Weber). 'Russianness' thus refers not only to a national difference in the sense the European nations differ from each other, but goes much deeper: it represents another form of rationality, which has preserved substantial parts of a pre-modern tradition. Russia would, accordingly, have the possibility of continuing on its own path of development and creating a society which differed from Western modernity. Some Slavophiles even imagined that the moral and intellectual attraction of the Russian model would become so big that the West, too, would understand that it had gone astray and that it would be best to follow Russia's path.

This is an important result. There are, of course, all kinds of cultural differences between Russia and the West, ranging from religious practices to the use of the Latin vs the Cyrillic alphabet, in costumes, clothing, eating habits, and so on. However, it is not Western culture per se which is the real *bête noire* of the Slavophile imagination, but certain traits of a modern society, such as individualism, the prevalence of formal rationality, and secularization, which present a threat to traditional forms of life. Because *modernity* is a concept of a different level to that of *culture* or *civilization*, it would in this respect be a grave mistake to interpret the Slavophile critique of the West only as a form of xenophobia or vulgar nationalism. Of course, even the latter phenomena occur in Russia, but they do not form the sources of Slavophile anti-modernism.

Andrzej Walicki had already come to the same conclusion in his study of Slavophilism. According to him, it is quite possible to characterize Slavophilism, following the Weberian scheme of pre-modern (traditional) vs modern, as 'an ideology which idealizes the structure of a *traditional*, communitarian society'. He adds that Slavophile ideology does not give expression so much to feudal as to patrimonialistic sentiments. While feudalism is a system of a warrior organization, patrimonialism is a wider concept, referring to forms of a personal and authoritarian use of power. Weber, in fact, thought that patrimonialism is the most suitable candidate for an ideal type of a traditional society – an assessment with which Walicki agrees (Walicki 1973: 168–69). His references to Weber remain, however, sporadic and he does not place his observations in the context of a more comprehensive theory of modernization; so his seminal analysis of Slavophilism remains much in the *niveau* of the ordinary history of ideas, seeking to reconstruct the influences that various Russian thinkers have obtained from abroad.

I think it is important to realize that not only 'conservative utopias' (if we maintain Andrzej Walicki's term) count upon the otherness of Russia; even the radical projects of the *Zapadniks* had to cope with the same dilemma of Russia's history since the reforms of Peter I. One could say that the Bolshevik project of 'socialism in one country' builds on this otherness of Russia, too, and on the perspectives it seemed to open for the construction of an alternative modernity much in the way of Sergey Bulgakov's utopia. But this is another story, too long to be told here.

Notes

1 See Karl Marx, *Revelations of the Diplomatic History of the Eighteenth Century*. This pamphlet, originally published in *The Free Press* 1856–57, and reprinted in 1899, was not included in the official editions of Marx and Engels in the USSR, nor in the East German *Marx – Engels Werke*. It will appear in the new MEGA (*Marx-Engels Gesamtausgabe*) but even now one may consult the Internet publication: www.archive.org/details/secretdiplomatic00marxuoft. In about 1870, there came a change in Marx's views on Russia, as his contacts with various Russian revolutionaries deepened.

2 *Lettres philosophiques, Lettre première*, in: P.Ya. Chaadaev, *Polnoye sobraniye sochineniy i izbrannye pis'ma*, I, Moskva: Nauka, 1991, p. 91. I cite here the English translation by R. McNally and R. Tempest (eds), *Philosophical Works of Peter Chaadaev*, Dordrecht/ London: Kluwer 1991, p. 20.

3 Chaadaev indeed reminds one somewhat of Kierkegaard, who was roughly his contemporary: both represented the type of an 'odd' thinker, outside a university career and on the 'fringe' of conventional social life. It was precisely this social status of a 'free-floating' intellectual, which enabled them to employ the gaze of an outsider when considering the social and philosophical questions of their time, giving important insights, but the psychological toll to be paid for such a position seems to have been considerable. For a recent psychological portrait of Chaadaev, see Cherepanova (2009: 222–36).

4 The nuances of the Russian original *samoderzhaviye–pravoslaviye–narodnost'* are not easily translated. *Narodnost'* does not, in effect, mean 'nationalism' in the Western sense, but something like 'allegiance to the spirit of the people'.

5 Andrzej Walicki even sees here a direct analogy with Locke's concept of *tabula rasa* (Walicki 1973: 104). In fact, the same idea was later, and quite independently, brought forth by Mao Zedong, who described the people of China as a blank sheet, waiting for somebody to write characters on it. Indeed it seems that this idea of a 'blank sheet' is a typical rhetorical device in the vocabulary of many modernizers.

6 The Polish original *W kręgu konserwatywnej utopii* was published in 1964.

7 Cf. the contrary interpretations of Boris Tarasov, defending a 'Slavophile' lecture of Chaadaev, and the 'Zapadnik' critique on Tarasov's interpretations by Zakhar Kamensky, documented in Chaadaev (1998: 601 ff, 620 ff, and especially 669–87).

8 Shakhovskoy showed that Chaadaev was not such a religious mystic as Gershenzon had depicted him, and not a pessimist with regard to the future of Russia. Shakhovskoy made, too, the important assertion, that '*la société moderne* was for Chaadaev a quite definite concept, signifying European society, which developed – constantly – in the light of Christianity'. Shakhovskoy fell victim to the Stalinist purges (he was executed in 1939) and his highly interesting assessments of the role of Chaadaev in Russian intellectual history did not exert much influence on the received picture of him.

9 This circle was formed in the early 1820s. *Lyubomudry*, 'lovers of wisdom', is a Russian translation of the Greek term *philosophia*, and the name thus points to the programmatic intention of the circle to promote indigenous philosophical thought and culture.

10 Bulgakov develops these ideas yet more pointedly in a programmatic article *Narodnoye khozyaystvo i religioznaya lichnost'*, published for the first time in 1909, where he relies heavily on Weber and 'other researchers on the early history of capitalism' and laments at the same time that in Russia such research has hitherto been carried out only by the *Narodniks* and Marxists, who are not interested in the 'spiritual factors of economic development' (Bulgakov 1993: 360–61). For a more detailed analysis of Bulgakov's relationship to Weber's theories see van Kessel (2010).

11 I have taken this somewhat modified quotation of Peskov's exposition from my introduction in Oittinen (2007: 33).

Bibliography

Bulgakov, S.N. (1993) 'Narodnoye khozyaystvo i religioznaya lichnost'', *Sochineniya*, vol. 2, 343–67, Moskva: Nauka.

Chaadaev, P.Ya. (1991a) *Polnoye sobraniye sochineniy i izbrannye pis'ma*, vol. I, Moskva: Nauka.

Chaadaev, P. (1991b) *Philosophical Works of Peter Chaadaev*, R. McNally and R. Tempest (eds), Sovietica, vol. 56, Dordrecht/London: Kluwer.

Chaadaev, P.Ya. (1998) *Pro et contra: antologiya*, Sankt-Peterburg: Izdatel'stvo RKhGI.

Cherepanova, R. (2009) 'Bezumets v maske mudretsa, mudrets pod maskoyu bezumtsa – Sluchay Petra Chaadaeva', *Neprikosnovenny Zapas*, 63/1: 222–36.

Dlugach, T. (1984) *Deni Didro*, Moskva: Progress.

Kessel, J. van (2010) 'Protestant rationalism and Orthodox Sophia as ideal types of sociological rationalization' in V. Oittinen (ed.) *Max Weber and Russia*, Helsinki: Aleksanteri Papers.

Marx, K. (1899) *Revelations of the Diplomatic History of the Eighteenth Century*, E.M. Aveling (ed.), London: Sonnenschein & Co. Online. Available: www.archive.org/details/secretdiplomatic00 marxuoft (accessed 20 November 2010).

Oittinen, V. (ed.) (2007) *Venäjä ja Eurooppa*, Tampere: Vastapaino.

Peskov, A.M. (1993) 'Germansky kompleks slavyanofilov', in *Rossiya i Germaniya: opyt filosofskogo dialoga*, 53–94, Moskva: Medium.

Walicki, A. (1973) *Una utopia conservatrice: Storia degli slavofili*, Torino: Einaudi.

Wolff, L. (1994) *Inventing Eastern Europe: The Map of Civilization on the Mind of the Enlightenment*, Stanford, CT: Stanford University Press.

6 From a mother's worry to *Soldiers' Mothers'* action: building collective action on personal concerns

Anna Colin Lebedev

Introduction

One of the ideas frequently used in the analysis of Soviet and post-Soviet Russian society is the importance of interpersonal connections and networks in social regulation. Personal relationships are seen as an alternative to State or market-based official institutions. In the economic sphere, the importance of the economy of favours is emphasized (Ledeneva 1998, 2006). In the political sphere, personal relations and informal group belonging are seen as key resources in attaining positions of power (Kryshtanovskaya 2005; Ledeneva 2006). As for collective action, analysts underline its weakness and point out that escape and alternative solutions are preferred to mobilization and collective protest. The lack of social frames for protest, the vagueness of discontent, the lack of a clear differentiation of interests, and the local and limited character of protest are seen as specificities of collective action in Russia (Levada 2000).

The emphasis on the informal and interpersonal in contemporary Russian society is based on an implicit opposition between a 'Western', 'ordinary', 'classical' way and a 'specific', 'Russian' way of living in common in a society. The case of Russia challenges social science as elaborated in Western societies, and questions the universality of its concepts. This chapter will try to avoid both declaring the specificity of the Russian case, and adapting major mobilization and protest concepts to a form of action that does not perfectly fit the Russian context.

The case studied here is the *Committee of Soldiers' Mothers of Russia*,[1] more precisely the way people address this organization to ask for help, and consequently the transformation of their worries into formal complaints and collective demands. The *CSM* is a well-known organization, one of the oldest social movements in any of the post-Soviet countries, which was created at the end of the 1990s and continues to exist today, in 2010. In some ways, the *CSM* is seen as an exception among forms of social activism in Russia because of its grassroots nature, its institutionalization, and its reference to human rights in the Russian context where grassroots movements are rare and short-lived, and where reference to human rights is not very widespread. This chapter will try to overcome the debate on the sameness or the particularity of this Russian social movement by presenting a generally valid model of collective action illustrated by the *CSM*'s case. The argument is based on extensive qualitative research conducted within the Moscow office of the movement, between 2003 and 2006 (Colin Lebedev 2009). It combines an analysis of written requests sent to the *CSM*[2] and a long-term observation of the activities of the organization.

The Soldiers' Mothers: *a short presentation*

The *Committee of Soldiers' Mothers of Russia* was created in 1989 in Moscow by a group of mothers whose sons were conscripts in the Russian army. Conscription is compulsory in post-Soviet Russia, as it was in the Soviet Union for all men between eighteen and twenty-seven. In most cases conscription lasted two years. At the end of the 1980s, in the context of a growing openness in society, the violence perpetrated on conscripts and the bad conditions of military service were revealed by the media, and alerted mothers who decided to create an organization dedicated to the soldiers' defence.

Mothers based their claims both on a reference to human rights and on the affirmation of the right and duty of a mother to protect her child. At the beginning of the 1990s, these demands were heard by the political authorities.

Nevertheless, the reforms asked by the *Soldiers' Mothers* were introduced at a slow pace. Other problems appeared and were revealed by mothers who came to the *CSM*'s meetings: the conscription of young boys who were manifestly ill and unfit for service; the use of unprepared soldiers in armed conflicts within or outside Russia; and desertions due to physical and psychological violence perpetrated on conscripts. The organization continued to develop and branched out in two directions: assistance to individual soldiers encountering problems, and lobbying for reforms of the Russian army.

The *CSM* became famous in Russia and abroad during the first war in Chechnya, in 1994–96, especially when mothers whose sons were soldiers in this conflict decided to go, on their own, straight into the war zone in order to retrieve their sons from the Russian army or to release them from captivity. Since the middle of the 1990s, numerous local *CSM*s have been created by mothers all around Russia. As the organization has gained visibility abroad, it has benefited from grants and awards from international institutions for its activity in the defence of human rights.

Nevertheless, as the situation of the conscripts in the Army remained problematic, the *CSM* continued to develop its activities. Since 1993 the Moscow *CSM* benefited from a small permanent office, where visitors could present their requests in person or send a letter. In responding to the families' requests, the *CSM*'s volunteers have chosen to use the specific means offered by legislation of the Russian Federation. For example, a conscript who wants to avoid military service will be advised to look for some aspect of his situation that allows a deferral or an exemption, such as his state of health or his family situation. In order to facilitate communication with military institutions concerning these cases, the *CSM* cooperates with some military officials, such as the Military Prosecutors (*Prokurory*). This cooperation, conducted both with upper-level (Ministry of Defence officials) and with ordinary officers, does not prevent the *CSM* from publicly criticizing the situation in the Russian army. Opposition to the Army is often expressed in public interviews and also presented to visitors to the *CSM* as a principle of action.

The visible professionalization of the movement and the persistent reference to human rights in its public discourse contrast, for an external observer, with the motherly dimension of the organization. The reference to motherhood in the *CSM*'s name is manifest in its everyday functioning because visitors as well as volunteers are mostly mothers of soldiers or former soldiers. The *CSM*'s volunteers address visitors as mothers, emphasizing their motherly feelings, capacities, and duties. While references to motherhood are frequent in questions asked by journalists, however, they are scarce in the volunteers' answers and in the *CSM*'s public discourse.

Between human rights and maternal care: the Soldiers' Mothers' case as a challenge for collective action theories

The combination of motherhood and human rights in the *CSM*'s activities have made this movement an attractive object of investigation.[3] This interest can be explained by the great visibility of the *Soldiers' Mothers* since the war in Chechnya and by the lack of active social movements on the Russian public scene during the same period. The *CSM* is mostly analysed from three conceptual standpoints: the research on civil society in Russia, the viewpoint of gender studies and the frame theory approach.

From the first point of view, the *CSM* is seen as an example of an emerging civil society in post-Soviet Russia. Civil society, defined as a sphere of organized social activity independent from the State, is one of the key concepts used to describe the social evolution of Russia after the fall of the Soviet Union (Colas 2002: 31). At the beginning of the 1990s when the Soviet regime collapsed, autonomous social movements were seen as the main actors of social and political change and great attention was then paid by the social sciences to the new-born associations, seen as the basis of an emerging civil society in Russia. But by the middle of the 1990s, social organizations remained weak in influence and few in number. The academic debate then moved from an affirmation of the development of civil society to seeking the reasons why it had not proceeded more quickly. In this debate, the *CSM* was used most often by researchers as a counterexample against the argument that no change was occurring.

The second point of view on *Soldiers' Mothers* is the gender studies approach. The *CSM* appears as a paradoxical organization, feminine but not feminist, because the woman is not the object, but the subject of the *CSM*'s action (Sperling 2003). At the same time, the researchers notice that the *CSM*'s activists use an essentialist conception of motherhood and womanhood in their public discourse (Zdravomyslova 1999a). While most analysts note the double reference of the *CSM*'s action, human rights and motherhood, understanding the combination of the two is a challenge for researchers (Danilova 2004).

Researchers have tried to overcome this contradiction in their analyses. Caiazza argues that in post-Soviet Russia, as was the case in the USSR, citizenship is still gendered (Caiazza: 2002). The civic obligations and possibilities of action are different for men and women. While the main civic duty of women is to give birth and bring up new citizens, the civic contribution of men is military service. In this context, an essentialist vision of motherhood becomes a political resource for a particular group of people, and is expressed by the *CSM*.

The frame theory (Snow, Rochford et al. 1986; Benford and Snow 2000) is the third theoretical approach used here to explain the combination of motherhood and human rights in the *Soldiers' Mothers'* action. Zdravomyslova proposes an incisive analysis of *Soldiers' Mothers'* action in terms of frames, distinguishing two major self-identity frames in the organization of the *Soldiers' Mothers of St Petersburg*: the liberal human rights frame and the responsible motherhood frame (Zdravo-myslova 2007). The purpose of the human rights frame is to introduce the ideology of human rights 'to the ex-Soviet citizenry, which is not knowledgeable about their legal rights and the ways to defend them' (Zdravomyslova 2007: 217). In this analysis, the leaders and the key volunteers of the movement are the sole reposi-taries of the human rights frame, when the visitors are perceived by the leaders as being without resources. The very small group of volunteers then tries to make the visitors adopt the human rights frame, for example through a *Human Rights School*. The second major frame, that of 'responsible motherhood' appeals to the Russian gender symbolism, which is meaningful for ordinary people. The main advantage of this stimulating analysis is that it allows one to take into account both the human rights and the motherhood dimension of the action.

This maintains the normative distinction between a mature social movement – defending rights – and an immature one that relies on traditions of patronage and dependence. Its two main problems is that it treats these two dimensions as separate while failing to explain their combination, and makes a normative distinction between the human rights frame, emphasized as a good support for collective action, and the responsible motherhood frame, supposed to be a remnant of old beliefs. In so doing, the analysis neglects all forms of common action that are not formulated in reference to general interest and impersonal citizenship.

This chapter will suggest an alternative approach to the *Committee of Soldiers' Mothers*, inspired by the conceptual tools of the French Pragmatic sociological school. The point is to show how personal concerns can be used as a basis for the construction of a community that is not validated solely by reference to civic principles. The most personal and the most public cognitive schemes are here combined to form a common action.

The pragmatic sociology approach in the analysis of collective action

The theory of cognitive formats – or *orders of worth* – developed by French pragmatic sociology, and particularly by Boltanski and Thévenot in their work *On Justification* (Boltanski and Thévenot 1991), offers a new insight into the analysis of collective action, overcoming the opposition between tradition and human rights, and between Russia and the West, as well as the apparent inadequacy of Western sociological concepts for the Russian case.

One of the central focuses in the work of Boltanski and Thévenot is the critique. Many social situations, some of which happen on the public scene, suppose a critique of the other and a dispute based on different principles of justice. The authors stress the plurality of conceptions of what is valuable and fair in society. For example, both the factory worker who considers that he should not be fired because he has been loyally working there since his youth, and the factory director who decides to fire him because it is necessary for the economic survival of the business, refer to different principles of justice. Each of them evaluates the other from the standpoint of a justice principle, being the basis for what Boltanski and Thévenot call 'worth'. Six of these are described in *On Justification* (Boltanski and Thévenot 1991: 200–62). The concept of industrial worth refers to what is technically rational; market worth values free market relations; the worth of fame esteems what is well known; the worth of inspiration refers to the value of spontaneous creation. The last two are the most useful for us: civic and domestic worth. Civic worth values the general interest of the community and the figure of the autonomous individual capable of overcoming his or her personal interests. The civic grammar, which is a set of practices and principles derived for the order of worth, appears in impersonal rules, legal texts, and the institutions that defend civil rights. Domestic worth places value on tradition and proximity relationships: its grammar emphasizes relatedness and mutual help. In a dispute, whatever its importance, the world is rearranged by the confrontation and combination of different conceptions of justice which create orders of worth. The expression of orders of worth appears in any social situation where coordination, agreement, and evaluation are requested, from the micro-social level of a dispute between two people, to the macro-social level of the principles guiding the organization of a country. The orders of worth support a particular vision of the community. Collective action is usually expected to be based on civic worth, as an action of individuals concerning an issue of general interest that is formulated in impersonal terms. On the other hand, domestic worth, with its personal relations and mutual dependence, is seen as an unsuitable basis for collective action.

In the description of the civic and the domestic orders of worth, the reader can certainly see similarities with the two dimensions of the *Soldiers' Mothers'* action, human rights and motherhood, described earlier. While the most prevalent collective action analysis would encounter difficulties in understanding the place of motherhood in the *CSM*'s action, pragmatic sociology would offer an accurate analysis of the combination of two orders of worth.

The pragmatic approach, respectful of the intentions and priorities of social actors, helps to propose another way to integrate Russian social realities into a generally valid analysis of protest and collective action. In the case of the *Soldiers' Mothers* this chapter will first show how a mother gets engaged in collective action in a proximity relationship, challenging the vision of a mobilization based on a shared political goal. Second, it will emphasize the inequality of partners in collective action, which is different from the common vision of social movements as associations of equal individuals. In the last part, the chapter will explain the path from personal concerns to collective action, describing the compromise between civic and domestic orders of worth built by the *Committee of Soldiers' Mothers of Russia*.

Engagement as a relationship between two mothers

Addressing the CSM *with a personal concern*

Up to 3,000 letters of complaint have been received by the Moscow office of the *CSM* every year since the beginning of the 1990s. The same number of soldiers or soldiers' relatives comes in person to the *CSM* with their request.

More than 75 per cent of the claimants who write to the *CSM* are mothers of soldiers, of former soldiers, or of conscripts-to-be. About 10 per cent are the young men themselves. Almost every one of these people addresses the *CSM* to find help and support in a difficult situation related to conscription. Criticizing the Army or expressing political support for the *Soldiers' Mothers* is rarely the main objective of the letter. This does not mean that general ideas or political positions are absent, but that general judgement is secondary in the intentions of the authors and derives from what is essential to them: their personal situation. Most of the time, people do not express a desire to participate in the *CSM*'s action or to be involved in political protest actions. During a five-year-long observation, only once did I see a visitor – an elderly man – come to the *CSM* and suggest the organization of a collective protest action.

From this point of view, the claimants represent a non-object for classical social science analysis of mobilization and participation. Described as beneficiaries of the *CSM*'s action, they are assumed to play a part in the movement different from the activists. The difference is not between egoistic and altruistic motivations, social science having overcome the idealistic vision of selfless involvement of activists (Gaxie 2005), but between the personal and the general as a basis for action. The claimants are supposed to be primarily concerned with their particular situation, while the activists are expected to follow general objectives, aimed at the defence of a whole social category. In becoming an activist, the claimant is supposed to leave behind his or her individual focus to act for a collective stake, reformulating his or her problem in general terms that other social actors can share and a movement they can join. In other words, s/he is expected to abandon the priorities of domestic worth and switch to civic worth-based action.

When a researcher or a journalist comes to the *Committee of Soldiers' Mothers'*, s/he presumes that s/he will find a non-governmental organization with volunteers and clients who are clearly separated. But a careful observation of the *CSM*'s everyday activities reveals a different situation.

Most of the *CSM*'s volunteers are mothers who came initially to present their son's case. We will see that their involvement does not necessarily suppose a redefinition of their action in general and impersonal terms. How should we analyse this participation in collective action?

Worrying together: a way of entering in collective action

'Hello, dear women, honourable soldiers' mothers' (Letter of a mother, 1993), so does a mother who has not received any letters from her soldier son for months address the *CSM*. 'A soldier's mother is writing to you with her pain and her hope' (ibid.). The majority of letters addressed to the *CSM* begin this way. The mother tries to establish a relationship, not between a claimant and a non-governmental organization but between mothers of soldiers with common experience and understanding: 'You, my unknown friends, help the mother, relieve if you can my painful heart's wound' (ibid.). The name of the organization implies that it is composed of soldiers' mothers and invites this kind of communication. The reader of the letter is supposed to share the mother's pain and to help her in the same way as a close friend would do. When it is a soldier that asks for the *CSM*'s help, he also appeals to women who should care for him as his own mother would do. A young soldier appeals to the *president* of the *NGO* as to a *relative*: 'Honourable president of the committee of soldiers' mothers! I write to you as to a mother' (Letter of a soldier, 1997). The motivation of the action attributed to the *CSM* is based on compassion and proximity. In other words, it refers to domestic worth. The primary link established between the claimants and the *CSM* is a common intimate experience, which does actually constitute a basis for engagement in collective action.

When a mother visits the *CSM* with her request, she usually spends time in the organization's office: preparing official documents, waiting for a phone call from a military official who would give her information about her son, coming back again and again to ask for advice. Often, she has nothing to do but wait, sometimes for hours. Gradually, the mother becomes familiar with the organization's functioning and begins to help the volunteers and the other visitors: she prepares tea, goes to the post office to send the *CSM*'s mail, and distributes the *CSM*'s printed forms to other visitors. Her motivation is the desire to help those women who currently help her. Later, she can herself advise some other mothers in a similar situation, feeling compassion for them and sharing her new knowledge with them. When her own case is solved, she can either stay for a while with the *Soldiers' Mothers*, continuing to help them, or return to her usual occupation. In the *Soldiers' Mothers* Moscow office there are always two or three women who choose to stay because they feel gratified by helping other mothers, provided that they can afford to do volunteer work because they are otherwise unemployed or very badly paid.[4] Sometimes, the volunteers also bring their relatives, most often sons or husbands, to the organization. Why should we describe this kind of occasional participation as collective action? Seen on the ground, the *Committee of Soldiers' Mothers* is mostly composed of such people for whom the boundaries between activist and beneficiary are blurred. The leaders of the movement also consider these mothers as members of the organization. Valentina Melnikova, the *CSM* leader, says:

> If a mother decides to come to the Committee, she must take part in her son's destiny, she must accompany us, she must learn with us. I often say:

here you are in the *Committee of Soldiers' Mothers*. You are a soldier's mother, so you are a part of it.

(Melnikova and Lebedev 2001: 93)

Ella Polyakova, the leader of the *Soldiers' Mothers* of St Petersburg organization, gives the same definition of membership: 'Every person who comes here not for the first time is a member of our organization. He/she can exchange experience with others' (Zdravomyslova 1999a). This configuration of action suggests an enlarged definition of the involvement in collective action, not only to episodic forms of mobilization, but also to a way of doing things together based on proximity relationships, 'often illegitimate or at least undervalued in social and political science' (Thévenot 2001: 271). Following Thévenot, the research outlined in this chapter focused on access to public space based on proximity attachments (Thévenot 2006).

Proximity engagement

Civic engagement, which has come to refer to the classical forms of idea-based activism performed by individuals in non-governmental organizations, is only one of the ways to participate in a social movement. Another way of being a part of common action is through *proximity engagement*, which consists in worrying and caring together. The concept of proximity, a direct relation between one person and another, does not restrict the engagement in common action to family relations or friendship, but designates all forms of commonizing[5] intimate relations and attachments. Are the mothers who address the *CSM* friends or relatives of the activists of the movement? Certainly not. Nevertheless, they expect the *CSM*'s members to be sensitive to a mother's concern for her son. They engage the *CSM*, and, at the same time, engage in common action. A mother writes to encourage the *CSM* to help her: 'I don't know what to do, I will pray God for you. Yes, I know how hard it is for you. But don't let one additional soul die' (Letter of a mother, 1992). The common experience expected by this mother creates precisely this person-to-person link that constitutes the basis for proximity engagement. When a mother enters into collective action, she expects to help some other mothers in their worries and grief, which is very different from an action aimed at the defence of soldiers' rights.

A common action in a dependence relationship

The mother as the weak

An important characteristic of proximity engagement is the inequality between partners in common action. Without it, one could have a naive vision of an idyllic collaboration between equal people closely tied by a close relationship, something that looks like mutual help between friends. Inequality and dependence are at the very heart of the domestic grammar that supports proximity engagement, because they emphasize the mutual obligations of the weak or the 'small' (children, weak persons, and animals) and the strong, or the 'great' (parents, powerful people). The mothers' engagement in collective action is based on the dependence of 'ordinary', isolated mothers, on the more powerful collective mother, namely, the *Committee of Soldiers' Mothers*. In their requests, the claimants define themselves as ignorant, weak, and distant from the political institutions. Indeed, most of the people addressing the *CSM* are in a fragile social position: single mothers, poor workers, and people living in small towns or the countryside are over-represented among the claimants. The point is that soldiers and their families come to believe in their own weakness when the military and public institutions exhibit their contempt for legal procedures – a situation often described by the term *bezzakoniye* ('lawlessness'). 'We live in a village, we don't know either the rules or our rights' (Letter of a mother, 2001), a mother writes, explaining that when she addresses the local authorities for information, she does not receive a answer: 'even if you read something in the newspaper and you come to the village council or elsewhere with this information, they will tell you: "that's only twaddle"' (ibid.). As a consequence, people tend to believe in the uselessness of their legal action, and conclude that they are in a situation where only the hierarchical positions of the social actors matter.

The *Soldiers' Mothers* as the great

In the meantime the *Soldiers' Mothers* are expected to be powerful, competent, and close to the political decision centres. For instance, a group of mothers whose sons are fighting in Chechnya argue: 'We are far from Moscow, we don't have the possibility to meet the important persons on whom our sons' destinies depend, plus we are not as highly positioned as you, the *Committee of Soldiers' Mothers*' (Collective letter, 2001). This presumed proximity of the *CSM* to political institutions is visible in the way people address the *Soldiers' Mothers* on envelopes: in one letter out of five, there is no destination details other than *Committee of Soldiers' Mothers of Russia*, Moscow. There are also strange addresses that clearly indicate that the *CSM* is assumed to be powerful in nature: 'The Kremlin', 'Red Square', 'The White House',[6] or even 'Ministry of Soldiers' Mothers of Russia'. This style of official designation of the *CSM* is not contradictory with the proximity relationship: for example, a mother who writes to the 'CSM, The State Duma'[7] addresses the *CSM*'s volunteers as mothers: 'All of you have children and you know what a child means to his parents and especially to his mother' (Letter of a mother, 1994).

A dependence relationship

In asking for the *CSM*'s help, people entrust their destiny to the care of the *Soldiers' Mothers*, abandoning their autonomy or, in other words, the confidence in their ability to defend themselves in society. A mother describes this path from autonomy to dependence very well. 'I never asked for anybody's help, as long as I could solve my problems by myself', she says in her letter (Letter of a mother, 2000). Explaining the situation, she adds that her soldier son had asked her to send him a small present for New Year's Eve. As she had no money, she decided to ask the local administration to pay her the social help they owed to the family. The head of the village, as well as the military officials, rejected her legally legitimate demand, and even laughed at her. 'I can't sleep after that and I cry every day, because I'm deeply offended' (ibid.). The abandonment of her autonomy is a deep wound for this mother who concludes: 'lawlessness and pain forced me to send you this letter' (ibid.). For other people, the renunciation of their autonomy is easier, as they have never believed anyway, since Soviet years, in their status of individuals provided with rights (Bogdanova 2006). The proximity engagement we previously described is then based on a dependence of a weak actor, the mother, on a stronger one, the *Soldiers' Mothers*. What kind of common action results from this engagement? Does it correspond to the idea, previously expressed by some researchers of the *Soldiers' Mothers'* movement, of a static gap between the leaders acting in a human rights frame and the mothers, unable to fit in this frame?

The observation of the interaction between the *CSM*'s volunteers and the claimants shows, to the contrary, a dynamic of access to the public space from the proximity attachments.

From a mother's personal concern to collective action

Accessing collective action through proximity relationship

Associations, Thévenot suggests, offer:

> very appropriate devices aimed at facilitating the transitions between proximity and public distance, and at contributing to the making of a public thing which lends care to personal attachments. They encourage the public access for human beings whose own attachments often prevent them from being considered as citizens without losing some of their dignity.
>
> (Thévenot 2001: 273)

For instance, social welfare institutions aim to transform the beneficiaries of their action into autonomous individuals. Indeed, taking into account the weakness of those social actors, the proximity relationship is necessary to support them in their access to autonomy, even if the compromise between proximity and public distance is difficult to maintain (Pattaroni 2005). These remarks concerning some west-European cases of social welfare associations are also relevant for the *Soldiers' Mothers* case. The *CSM*'s claimants, being socially fragile when confronted by the military, do not have the possibility of defending their rights by themselves. The *CSM* offers them an accessible way of engaging in common action, and guides them to autonomy by transposing their request into a format adapted to public action.

One must pay attention to the grammar in which action is formulated. Most often, as we have seen, the requests are based on domestic grammar, which emphasizes the personal relationship between a mother and a son, compassion for the weak, and mutual help. This format is not chosen because people are ignorant of the civic grammar, but because they consider the domestic grammar more relevant to their request.

For the *CSM*, the domestic grammar seems unsuitable for the action on the public scene requested in the soldiers' cases, for two reasons. The first reason is that a positive response to a compassion-based request, as the *CSM*'s leader argues, would be a fragile favour. 'A favour obtained by a charming smile, a tearful glance of a grieving woman, or an emotionally manipulative plea has no value: it does not engage anybody and can be withdrawn at any time' (Melnikova and Lebedev 2001: 16). On the contrary, a favourable decision based on law is more solid. The second reason is that the domestic worth seems less convenient for generalizing the claims: 'Everyone among us could have obtained favours for her own son in this way, but we could never have changed the general situation of soldiers' (ibid.).

Translating a personal concern into a civic format

For each personal request, the *CSM* translates the situation as formulated in terms of domestic grammar into civic grammar. For instance, while a mother wants her son back home because she is sick and lonely and cannot manage by herself, the *CSM*'s volunteers reformulate her request in legal terms. They define her family and health situation with regards to the law on military service, which allows parents in some particular conditions to have their sons released from their military obligation. When a mother comes to the *CSM*, the way she is received tends to orientate her towards a civic way of acting. First, she is asked to fill in a form with a set of questions. The volunteers begin the interaction by reading the form, asking for details from time to time. A goal is defined: contesting an irregular conscription, hospitalizing a sick soldier, releasing a deserter from his military obligation. The volunteer and the mother then try to find a legal way to achieve this goal. They search through the texts of laws, write official letters, and contact the authorities responsible. No space is left at that point for the expression of the mother's emotion or for compassion. The response to a mother's letter is more or less similar: ignoring the emotional part of the message, the *CSM*'s volunteer focuses on the facts that can be used in a legal request. In the second phase, the mother is taught how to act by herself. While initially it is the *CSM*'s volunteer who composes the official request, step by step the mother takes charge of her own case, with the *CSM* serving only to advise her.

At the same time, even if the civic grammar is explicitly emphasized, the domestic worth remains essential in the *CSM*'s work. First, because the personal concerns exposed in the requests – a mother worrying about her child's situation, or a soldier wanting to be closer to his elderly parents – are important to the organization. Besides, a soldier's well-being is always given priority over the mother's by the *CSM*, because the young boy is supposed to be weaker and to need care and support. When a soldier's situation does not fit into a convenient legal category, the volunteers try as much as they can to change the legal qualification of the facts, in order to make an action possible. For instance, in certain conditions, the *CSM* could propose that a soldier's parents file for divorce, if being single allows the mother to have her son back home, according to the law. The civic action, resorting to law and referring the matter to the courts, is mostly a tool meant to deliver the main objective, namely, to respond to a personal concern. Even if the official goal is to defend the visitor's rights, the action undertaken often combines it with another objective which is to restore a family's or a person's well-being.

Building a compromise

In their relationship with military officials, the *Soldiers' Mothers* also combine civic and domestic worth in order to build an action that would be accepted by them. Observing the way in which the *CSM*'s activists present a case to military institutions, one might incorrectly conclude that their actions rely on private relations with military officers. Actually, the *CSM* closely collaborates with some officers, especially the military prosecutors or the military doctors, precisely because they are particularly sensitive to the orders of worth the *Soldiers' Mothers* rely on. The military prosecutors, whose function is the control of legal affairs in the Army, are ready to support the *CSM* when it denounces irregular military decisions. The military doctors are, on the other hand, receptive to the *Soldiers' Mothers'* concern for a soldier's well-being. Nevertheless, the *CSM*'s relationship with some officers is cordial, but never private, which would mean a direct link between two persons without reference to a common good. In any interaction with military officials, common goods such as respect for the law or the well-being of a soldier are engaged and combined, forming a compromise between the domestic and civic orders of worth. As domestic worth is very present in the interaction between citizens and the State in Russia, and as civic worth is not always sufficient to address the public authorities (Bogdanova 2006), compromise between the two is almost always the only way to make collective action acceptable for the officials and to obtain a positive answer.

Access to the public space through domestic grammar, in a dependence relationship, is troublesome from the viewpoint of Western political science (which has actually migrated east in the last twenty years). The figure of the liberal individual, which seems to be missing in Russia, is not only a conceptual tool but first of all a political project for post-Soviet societies. It is closely associated with the ideas of democracy and justice, and opposed to the figure of the Soviet citizen dependent on the State. Nevertheless, a better understanding of the recent evolutions in Russia is possible if we pay special attention to forms of social regulation based on domestic grammar, which manage access to the public space in a different way than that described by the classical theories of collective action.

Conclusion

Civic and domestic orders of worth in collective action were presented here in relation to the case of the *Committee of Soldiers' Mothers of Russia*. The two dimensions had already been identified by researchers working on mobilization in post-Soviet Russia, but in a way that either stressed only one of these dimensions, or described them as separate. Both of these approaches referred to a normative model of a social movement and came to a conclusion as to the adequacy of the *CSM* in terms of that model, which allowed a judgement on the 'normality' or the 'specificity' of collective action in Russia. Usually, the presence of domestic worth in the *CSM*'s functioning was regarded as demonstrating the immaturity of the social movement.

This chapter points out that collective action can indeed be based on personal concerns. In elaborating a compromise between proximity attachments and civic action, the *CSM* allows access to the public space for people unable to fulfil the requirement of civic action. From this point of view, the *Soldiers' Mothers'* case is very similar to the problems encountered by social welfare institutions in Western countries. How can dependent persons gain access to individual autonomous action? From the viewpoint of Western societies, dependence and proximity attachments are conceptual anomalies that must be overcome in order to access the public scene. The *Soldiers' Mothers'* activity, on the contrary, shows how they can foster autonomy, which leads us to consider the importance of proximity in building the collective in contemporary societies.

Notes

1 Also designated here as the *CSM* and *Soldiers' Mothers*.
2 Five hundred and seventy-four letters sent to the Committee between 1991 and 2001 have been analysed from a qualitative and a quantitative point of view.
3 See Caiazza 2002; Colin Lebedev 2009; Danilova 2004; Daucé 1997, 2002; Elkner 2004; Hojer 2004; Lebedev 2006; Sperling 1999, 2003; Vallance 2000; Zawilski 2006; Zdravomyslova 1999a, 1999b, 2000, 2007. This list is far from being exhaustive.
4 In the 1990s, the non-payment (or late payment) of wages to employees was frequent in former Soviet administrations and factories.
5 'The verb "commonize", modelled on "publicize", is used to refer to the operation of making things common, shared' (Thévenot 2007: 11, footnote 3).
6 The Kremlin and Red Square in Moscow are the symbolic heart of political power in Russia. The Kremlin, situated on Red Square, is the Russian Federation's Presidential residence. The Moscow 'White House' is the Parliament Building.
7 The State Duma is one of the two chambers of the Russian Parliament.

Bibliography

Benford, R. and Snow, D. (2000) 'Framing processes and social movements: an overview and assessment', *Annual Review of Sociology*, 26: 611–39.
Bogdanova, E. (2006) 'Sovetsky opyt regulirovaniya pravovykh otnosheniy, ili "v ozhidanii zaboty"', *Zhurnal sotsiologii i sotsial'noy antropologii*, 1(34), vol. 9: 77–90.
Boltanski, L. and Thévenot, L. (1991) *De la justification: les économies de la grandeur*, Paris: Gallimard.

Caiazza, A. (2002) *Mothers and Soldiers: Gender, Citizenship, and Civil Society in Contemporary Russia*, New York: Routledge.

Colas, D. (ed.) (2002) *L'Europe post-communiste*, Paris: PUF.

Colin Lebedev, A. (2009) 'Du souci maternel à l'action en commun. Le Comité des mères de soldats de Russie et ses requérants, 1992–2001', unpublished thesis, Institut d'Etudes Politiques de Paris.

Danilova, N. (2004) 'Pravo materi soldata: instinkt zaboty ili grazhdansky dolg?', in S. Ushakin (ed.) *Semeynyye uzy: modeli dlya sborki*, 188–210, Moskva: NLO.

Daucé, F. (1997) 'Les mouvements de mères de soldats à la recherche d'une place dans la société russe', *Revue d'études comparatives Est-Ouest*, 2: 121–53.

——(2002) 'Les paradoxes de l'insoumission en Russie', *Courrier des Pays de l'Est*, 1022: 36–43.

Elkner, J. (2004) 'Dedovshchina and the Committee of Soldiers' Mothers under Gorbachev', *The Journal of Power Institutions In Post-Soviet Societies*, 1. Online. Available: http://pipss.revues.org/index243.html (accessed 29 March 2011).

Gaxie, D. (2005) 'Rétributions du militantisme et paradoxes de l'action collective', *Revue suisse de science politique*, 1/11: 157–88.

Hojer, M. (2004) 'Reforming Habitus, Reordering Meaningful Worlds: Soldiers' Mothers and Social Change in Postsocialist Russia', unpublished thesis, Institute of Anthropology, University of Copenhagen.

Kryshtanovskaya, O. (2005) *Anatomiya rossiyskoy elity*, Moskva: Zakharov.

Lebedev, A. (2006) 'The test of reality: understanding families' tolerance regarding mistreatment of conscripts in the Russian army', in F. Daucé and E. Sieca-Kozlowski (eds) *Dedovshchina in Post-Soviet Military: Hazing of Russian Army Conscripts in a Comparative Perspective*, 47–74, Stuttgart: Ibidem-Verlag.

Ledeneva, A. (1998) *Russia's Economy of Favours: Blat, Networking, and Informal Exchange*, Cambridge: Cambridge University Press.

——(2006) *How Russia Really Works: The Informal Practices that Shaped Post-Soviet Politics and Business*, Ithaca, NY: Cornell University Press.

Levada, Yu. (2000) *Ot mneniy k ponimaniyu. Sotsiologicheskiye ocherki 1993–2000*, Moskva: Moskovskaya shkola politicheskikh issledovaniy.

Melnikova, V. and Lebedev, A. (2001) *Les petits soldats: le combat des mères russes*, Paris: Bayard.

Pattaroni, L. (2005) 'Le *care* est-il institutionnalisable?', in P. Paperman and S. Laugier (eds) *Le souci des autres*, 177–203, Paris: Raisons Pratiques.

Snow, D., Rochford, E., Worden, S. and Benford, R. (1986) 'Frame alignment processes, micromobilization, and movement participation', *American Sociological Review*, 51: 464–81.

Sperling, V. (1999) *Organzing Women in Contemporary Russia: Engendering Transition*, Cambridge: Cambridge University Press.

——(2003) 'The last refuge of a scoundrel: patriotism, militarism and the Russian national idea', *Nations and Nationalism*, 9/2: 235–53.

Thévenot, L. (2001) 'S'associer pour composer une chose publique', in J.-N. Chopart, (ed.) *Actions associatives, solidarités et territoires*, 267–74, Saint-Etienne: Publications de l'Université de Saint-Etienne.

——(2006) *L'action au pluriel: sociologie des régimes d'engagement*, Paris: La Découverte.

——(2007) 'The plurality of cognitive formats and engagements: moving between the familiar and the public', *European Journal of Social Theory*, 10: 409–23.

Vallance, B. (2000) 'Russia's mothers: voices of change: Committee of Soldiers' Mothers of Russia', *Minerva: Quarterly Report on Women and the Military*, Fall–Winter. Online. Available: http://findarticles.com/p/articles/mi_m0EXI/is_2000_Fall-Winter/ai_73063468/ (accessed 29 March 2011).

Zawilski, V. (2006) 'Saving Russia's sons: the soldiers' mothers and the Russian–Chechen wars', in S. Webber and J. Mathers (eds) *Military and Society in Post-Soviet Russia*, 228–40, Manchester: Manchester University Press.

Zdravomyslova, E. (1999a) 'Peaceful initiatives: the Soldiers'Mothers Movement in Russia', in I. Breines and D. Gierycs (eds) *Towards a Women's Agenda for a Culture of Peace*, 165–80, Paris: Unesco Publishing. Online. Available: www.indepsocres.spb.ru/zdrav2.htm (accessed 29 March 2011)

——(1999b) 'Ot sotsialnoy problemy k kollektivnomu deystviyu: pravozashchitnaya organizatsiya "Soldatskiye materi"', in V. Kostushev (ed.) *Obshchestvennye dvizheniya v sovremennoy Rossii : ot sotsialnoy problemy k kollektivnomu deystviyu*, 51–64, Sankt-Peterburg: SPb Filial Instituta Sotsiologii RAN.

——(2000) 'Civic initiatives: Soldiers' Mothers Movement in Russia', in H. Patomaki (ed.) *Politics of Civil Society: A Global Perspective on Democratisation*, 29–42, Helsinki: NIDG Working Paper.

——(2007) 'Soldiers' Mothers fighting the military patriarchy: re-invention of responsible activist motherhood for human rights' struggle', in I. Lenz, C. Ullrich, and B. Fersch (eds) *Gender Orders Unbound? Globalisation, Restructuring and Reciprocity*, 207–26, Opladen/Farmington Hills: Barbara Budrich Publishers.

7 Opposition substitutes: reflections on the collective action in support of the European University at St Petersburg

Vadim Volkov

The spring semester of 2008 started at the European University at St Petersburg (EUSP) on 4 February. By that date the university was already under close attention from two Federal inspections that had visited it during the winter break. First, the Fire Safety Inspectorate conducted its regular annual check. In the previous ten years, fire inspectors registered minor violations, most of which were related to the layout and general condition of the nineteenth-century palace that has served as the EUSP's main and only premises since 1995, but none of them had ever had any administrative consequences. This time, on 18 January 2008, fire inspectors displayed an unusual zeal, registering fifty-two violations and stating that they would submit a request to shut down the university to the District Court. Three days later came the inspection by the Federal Registration Service. This agency has the authority potentially to liquidate the EUSP as a legal entity, should it find any major mismatch between the legal status of the EUSP and its de facto activities. This inspection was to last for over a month before producing its formal conclusion.

On 6 February, the Fire Safety Inspectorate submitted its report to the Dzerzhinsky Court of the Central city district, and on the next day, demonstrating unprecedented speed, the court ruled to stop all educational activities in the EUSP. Rushing to enforce the decision, the bailiffs appeared in the university on the following day, Friday 8 February. This was the end of the first week of the semester. Uniformed officials came during class hours, entering classrooms and demanding that all teaching be terminated. Elena Zdravomyslova, a professor of sociology, recalled that the bailiffs interrupted her class right when she was recounting the story of how the European Humanitarian University in Minsk had been closed down by the President of Belorussia Aleksandr Lukashenko. In one hour all lecture rooms and faculty offices were sealed. Students were requested to leave the building.

After that the university remained closed for forty-two days until 21 March. Students and faculty launched a civic campaign, enjoying wide support from the media and the international professional community. The closure of the EUSP became in effect a practical test for Russian civil society, which is usually portrayed as underdeveloped and passive. The episode can also serve as a case study of a particular repertoire of protest actions and mobilization techniques in the context of the mild authoritarian political conditions of the last years of Vladimir Putin's presidency. The case of the EUSP was related to a number of other cases of civic activism during the same period, such as the conflict between the city authorities and employees of a private hospital in Tarusa, in the Kaluga region near Moscow, and the protest movement against the building of the Gazprom tower in St Petersburg.[1] What united these cases was that they meant to be political but did not explicitly label themselves as such. The activists and communities that challenged the state authorities in these cases avoided being associated with political opposition. The phenomena may be called 'opposition substitutes'. This chapter looks at the activities in support of the EUSP that led to the political decision to reopen the university as an instance of opposition substitutes. The potential of civic mobilization for and the chances of success of these evidently political causes were higher if the substitute way of action was followed, that is, when their relation to politics and political opposition were understated or even denied. This was an element of the strategy used by civil society in Russia, which acknowledged the strong constraints and high risks of political action, yet did not refrain from the latter.

Why was the EUSP closed?

Even now, over a year after the events, many details are not clear. We do not know who gave the order to close the university and who coordinated the attack on the EUSP. But the reasons and the causes are fairly clear. Partly, they are related to what the EUSP was (and is), and, partly, to what it did. Founded in 1994 by the liberal Mayor of St Petersburg, Anatoly Sobchak, and a group of academics, the EUSP functions as a graduate college in the social sciences and humanities. Its mission is to promote international standards of research and education and gradually to change the overall style of the social sciences in Russia, which still bear the imprint of the Soviet ideological legacy and consequently remain rather backward. It is a non-state university, and the bulk of its funding until recently came from US foundations and various international research grants. By virtue of the many publications of its professors in English, the EUSP was better known abroad than at home, and has entered several international ratings.

Throughout the libertarian 1990s and even during Putin's first term in office as he proceeded to build what he coined the 'power vertical', the existence of an independent international university did not pose any problem for the authorities. While the Russian state was weak and could not subsidize education and science, many institutions and academic communities survived by applying for Western grants and participating in international projects. As the Russian state consolidated and hydrocarbon export revenues filled its coffers, the government became increasingly involved in regulating academia and the NGO sector. The so-called 'coloured' revolutions in Georgia and Ukraine in 2003–5 demonstrated the vulnerability of regimes as they went through elections and alerted the Kremlin to the role of Western-funded NGOs in monitoring, vote-counting, and other technologies that helped to dispute official results. In 2006–7, the Duma amended the law on NGOs, compelling them to renew their registration. State authorities exerted pressure on foreign NGOs and those Russian ones that received funding from abroad, accusing some of espionage against the country. The notion of 'sovereign democracy' popularized from 2006 onwards served as the ideological backup for the defensive and isolationist policies of the Kremlin. Although the EUSP was at no point involved in any civic or political activities, the general political shift of Putin's second term objectively moved it into the category of somewhat 'alien' organizations. As the 2007–8 electoral cycle approached (Duma elections were scheduled for December 2007, presidential ones for March 2008), the Kremlin and the ruling party, *United Russia*, were preparing to tighten control over the political field and to purge it of any organizations reminiscent of the 'orange' threat.

In the spring of 2007 the EUSP received a 683,000 euro two-year grant from the EU Commission to establish what became the Interregional Electoral Network of Assistance (IRENA). Having set up IRENA, its director and political science professor Grigory Golosov and his colleagues began to gather and process electoral statistics, and to conduct training for representatives of political parties and NGOs in legal and organizational aspects of electoral monitoring. Their activity did not remain unnoticed. In the end of June 2007, shortly after IRENA started to work, the *United Russia* party deputy Gadzhimet Safaraliyev alerted the Duma of EU interference in Russia's domestic politics. In an interview to a newspaper he claimed that the EUSP was an instrument of foreign interference, mentioning IRENA in connection with alleged preparations to dispute the results of the approaching elections. He requested the office of the Prosecutor General and the St Petersburg Committee for Higher Education to check whether the content of IRENA's activities matched the formal license and by-laws of the EUSP. The Prosecutor's office simply requested documents and, having received them, took no further action, while the educational committee recommended the EUSP and IRENA to reduce or stop the training of potential electoral observers. The university accepted the recommendation and reduced IRENA's activities to expert seminars and data analysis.

On 26 October Putin spoke at the EU–Russia summit in Mafra, Portugal where he mentioned the Kremlin's new initiative of creating institutes that would monitor elections and human rights in the USA and Europe in response to Western attention to Russian elections (Putin 2007). His aid Sergey Yastrzhembsky explained at the press conference that it could be taken that Putin's remarks applied to the EUSP, to which the EU had allocated 700,000 euros in order to monitor the approaching elections. The EUSP was invoked as a justification for the symmetric response by Russia in relation to the EU: you monitor our elections, we will monitor yours. Consciously or not, Yastrzhembsky distorted the facts, implying that the university was created wholly with EU money with the sole purpose of interfering in Russia's domestic affairs. Such a statement from an official of the Administration of the President was likely to have been perceived as a signal by lower officials to attack the university. On 21 November Putin spoke at a *United Russia* forum to boost electoral support for the ruling party, where he condemned opponents for trying to weaken the state. Having no support from the people, he concluded, the opponents of the ruling party were 'compelled to jackal at foreign embassies, knock at the door of foreign missions, counting for support from foreign funds and governments'. This was a clear message to the executive powers about the source of internal threats. In the context of electoral fever and alerts about the 'orange' threat, the EUSP as an independent institution with international ties and foreign funding could not but fall into the category of suspicious institutions. The IRENA project served to draw attention to the EUSP and triggered the attack. It is hard to say which group in the executive power structure ordered the inspections to find reasons to justify the closure, but the very fact that the city authorities were not aware of the campaign against the EUSP, as became clear from the public comments of the Governor, Valentina Matviyenko, indicates that it was managed by the Federal executive power structures, possibly the FSB, which, according to operational procedures, are independent from the regional authorities. The use of Federal controlling services, such as the Fire Safety Inspectorate, for political purposes was by then not a novelty at all. Technical and fiscal regulation could help to stop the activity of any organization without the need for any explicit reference to political causes. The Russian authorities could, and in this case evidently did, use purely administrative actions to put pressure on those they considered politically unreliable or dangerous.

Changing responses

The first reaction of the EUSP's administration to the visit of the inspectors was to seek an informal settlement with state authorities. The priority became to preserve the university at the expense of the project that had irritated the Kremlin. On 27 January 2008, after the first visits by the inspectors and almost two weeks before the closure, the EUSP's Academic Council made the decision to close the IRENA programme. This apparently did not stop the attack. After the court had ordered the closure, the EUSP, according to procedure, conducted a number of urgent fire safety improvements, submitted a report to the court and waited for the second decision. In the meantime, the rector's office decided to communicate directly with the Administration of the President, but the response was somewhat surprising: they claimed to have no relationship to the attack on the EUSP. The recourse to an informal compromise allowed a better control over the outcome, although the conditions of the compromise itself were not easy to predict. Informal compromise is always personal, and the problem in this case was that no one wished to represent the side of the authorities. At no point during the crisis did any official ever reveal any involvement, except for the fire inspectors and the city educational committee who denied that there was any political dimension to the case. Whoever orchestrated the attack against the EUSP took great care to hide the political reasons behind technical ones.

A week into the crisis, a coordination committee consisting of the rector, vice-rectors, and several heads of departments emerged in a process of collective decision making. Later, a student committee emerged as well, and the two bodies effectively made decisions and interacted in implementing them. The EUSP faculty decided to continue with the teaching programme of the spring semester and use alternative premises for teaching, which was referred to as 'individual consultations'. In anticipation of the second court hearing that was scheduled for 18 February, the coordination committee decided upon a backup plan that was to be followed in case attempts to reach an informal settlement failed and the court confirmed its earlier decision and keep the EUSP shut. Following the negative court decision, the St Petersburg committee for Science and Education sent a formal letter notifying the EUSP that its license for conducting educational activities had been suspended. Thus, it became clear that what the authorities wanted was not only to stop the IRENA project, but to close the EUSP. In this situation, the only way out was to try and foster a wide public campaign in support of the university.

But before this could be done, several more choices had to be made. Before going public, the EUSP had to decide how to explain the closing of the university, who to point at as the source of attack, how to justify its own actions, and so on. In other words, a strategy and a basic frame had to be worked out. Moreover, the degree of politicization and potential addressees of the public campaign had to be decided. The mass media, including the central newspaper *Kommersant*, started reporting about the EUSP case almost the day after it happened, but the shortage of information and the lack of any official commentaries prevented a wider discussion of this news item. While the choice of the strategy of the campaign was deliberate, the repertoire of actions formed as a result of improvisations, *ad hoc* opportunities and collective decision making by different support groups.

The EUSP's administration held a press conference in the House of Journalists on 19 February. Its aim was not only to draw public attention to the EUSP but also to set out the frame. In the theses written for the press conference by the author of this text, several major points about the origins and meaning of the conflict were suggested. Thus, it was explicitly stated that the issue of fire safety was irrelevant and only served as an instrument, or pretext, for closing the university. The real cause for the closure was the independent status of the EUSP and its international connections. The rector's remarks made at the press conference connected the EUSP's case with the general assault on civic freedoms in Russia on the eve of the presidential elections. Those who put pressure on the EUSP also meant to spoil the election campaign, stated the rector. The use of Federal inspections against the EUSP was an instance of broader administrative abuse against civil society that had to be actively resisted. Since it was possible that some shadowy business interests intended to expropriate the premises of the EUSP, a nice centrally located palace, a raiders' attack was also cited as a possible moving spring of the situation. The press conference was reported by three city TV channels, the *Echo Moscow* radio station, and a number of news web sites. The framing was an important part of the resistance campaign throughout. As no state authority ever responded in public to give the official view, the administration and supporters of the EUSP enjoyed the initiative, and their interpretation of events remained unchallenged.

While the official TV channels and the media outlets associated with the Kremlin ignored the EUSP case, all the independent media followed it closely. The Federal channels *NTV* and *REN-TV* reported the situation twice. Journalists called the university office on a regular basis to find out about upcoming activities and events. In private conversations some admitted that their policy was to keep the EUSP in the 'information field' as long as possible and not let the public forget about the case. Hence they demanded the creation of what can be called 'reportables' – some events or situations that could thereafter serve as news items to be reported. In fact, the journalists were aware of many episodes of the campaign at the design stage. The outcome was overwhelming: the conflict around EUSP was reflected in over 550 publications in the media over the period of one and a half months.

The repertoire of collective actions

The internet made a big difference. Professional web sites in social sciences, such as *polit.ru*, blogs, and internet newspapers (*fontanka.ru*, *zags.ru*, and *rosbalt.ru*) took the largest share of the job of publicizing the case of the EUSP and mobilizing support. The popular web site *polit.ru* created a special rubric dedicated to the EUSP, publishing interviews with faculty and updates on events. It published all the open letters of support from professional associations and institutions. Blogs proved a timely innovation. At least three major community blogs in support of the EUSP were created. The blog *Save_eu* (2008) was set up by students on 18 February and operated from St Petersburg. Its primary purpose was to inform the public and mobilize supporters. It collected all the information and media coverage about the crisis in a single web space and publicized all the actions in support of the university, including open letters. Not least, it served as a common ground for discussing the strategy and tactics of resistance. This became particularly relevant when, in March, a group of students called for street protests. They submitted a request to conduct a meeting to the city authorities and after the authorities had refused to sanction the meeting, called for taking the action out to the streets anyway. Nikita Okhotin, the Chairman of the Moscow division of *Memorial*, one of Russia's leading human rights organizations, published a letter in that blog suggesting that the consequences of such a decision needed to be carefully considered. The authorities, he argued, were waiting for the EUSP to cross the line and take part in non-sanctioned meetings. Once provoked, they would have a reason for closing the EUSP forever, accusing students of 'orange' extremism. In this case, wrote Okhotin, 'there will be no compromises and you will no longer study, because the university will be shut forever' (*Community* 2008). The post provoked over fifty comments. To more radically minded students a moderate strategy was unacceptable. Others suggested that in the absence of street actions the administration of the EUSP would prefer secret negotiations with the Kremlin and possibly choose to move the university to Helsinki. The journalist from the

Kommersant, Kira Dolinina, made by far the most convincing comment. When the academic community writes petitions, when students collect signatures, even when students conduct creative street actions, despite the political overtones present in the case from the very beginning, she argued, the news about the EUSP was presented in the media under the rubric 'society' or 'education' and under such classifiers they were put on the tables of officials in the Kremlin every morning. But if the support of the EUSP took the form of meetings dissolved by the police with people beaten or arrested, the case would be immediately transferred to the 'politics' section of the *Kommersant*, and this would mean a wholly different attitude. If the EUSP became a newsmaker in politics, it would inevitably and irreversibly be closed. The strategy, therefore, was to go ahead with protests but to avoid excessive politicization and open clashes with the authorities. This line of reasoning eventually prevailed over the hot heads calling for barricades.

Mikhail Gabovich at Princeton University created a blog in English where the EUSP's case was explained and updated for the international scholarly community (Gabovich 2008). It also served as a vehicle for collecting signatures. Daniel' Lur'ye, who worked with a group of internet specialists, originally from St Petersburg but at the time residing in Moscow, contacted the author of this chapter and suggested creating yet another blog (Lur'ye and Volkov 2008). Their main business was the creation and promotion of web sites. So their team offered volunteer help in disseminating information through the web. Thus another blog functionally equivalent to a web site was created. Besides concentrating all news on one site, the idea was to explain to the general public in the most clear and accessible manner why the EUSP had been closed, what had happened, and to give some idea of what could be done to support it. Finally, a great impact was made by the personal blog of Ilya Utekhin, the Head of the Anthropology department of the EUSP. He widely used the then new *YouTube* opportunities to transmit live pictures and interviews and created a kind of private internet TV (Utekhin 2008).

Professional communities and associations are an important part of civil society. Their mobilization was key to the success of the campaign. Russian and international associations of sociologists, political scientists, Slavic languages, ethnologists, as well as groups of scholars wrote letters of support, thirty-six overall, sending them to the authorities, or signed petitions through the internet. The web site *Ruthenia.net* (2008), linked to Tartu University, and the page set up by Alexey Yurchak and Michele Rivkin-Fish at *GoPetition* global site (Yurchak and Rivkin-Fish 2008) collected 2,298 and 3,808 signatures, respectively. It is no exaggeration to say that thousands of social scientists from all over the world joined the campaign. Another display of professional solidarity was the open letter by twenty-eight full members of the Russian Academy of Sciences to Putin and Medvedev, published on the pages of the *Kommersant*. Students collected over 600 signatures in the cafes of the city. All such letters and signatures were also sent to the office of the Governor of St Petersburg, for which, as it turned out, a separate storage room had to be reserved.

Since the authorities closed the university premises, the students' activity naturally moved into the streets or to alternative venues. Creative actions of resistance occupied a prominent place in the repertoire. Periodic debates over strategy, like the one described above, produced the general belief that any street actions should be framed as artistic rather than political. In that context, any non-sanctioned street action would inevitably have political significance even if the political agenda of the EUSP case remained understated. Being artistic rather than political in its explicit form, creative actions could achieve a great deal of effect without running the risk of repressive actions from the state. They constituted 'reportables' for the media and kept the spirits of the EUSP community high, especially during moments when prospects looked grim. In a way, this strategy was also followed by the movement against the Gazprom tower: it too used non-political means and language for making public statements that were political in nature (see below).

To begin with, the students performed a ceremony involving the laying of a fire hose at the monument of the founder of Russian science Mikhail Lomonosov. First, under the watchful eye of numerous cameras, the rolled up fire hose, which became the symbol of the standoff, was laid at the foundation of the monument. Then the participants unrolled it and, forming a line, solemnly carried it to the nearest waste bin. A few days later, students declared 'the week of the European University' in town, organizing public gatherings and a photo exhibition dedicated to the EUSP in one of the rock clubs. Students of ethnography wrote a play about the standoff between the firemen and the academic community. The play was stylized as a traditional folk carnival show usually staged during the Shrovetide (Pancake week). The witty script instantly became an internet hit. The actual show was then performed in the square near the university, and no incidents happened, despite fears of police intervention stirred by informal phone calls from the authorities advising the performers to refrain from street activity. Another creative idea emanating from the student milieu was the so-called 'street university' – weekly open-air lectures and seminars in the square in the Solyanoy lane close to the EUSP. The themes of lectures varied from the sociology of student protest movements to radical aesthetics, gender and revolutions, and the comparative analysis of student unions in Russia and the USA. At least four street-university sessions were run during the crisis, and a few more after that. The activists suggested turning it into a regular institution, but after the EUSP's classes reopened and professors naturally demanded that students fulfil the usual high academic requirements for the spring semester, the pool of street enthusiasts dwindled. Finally, the EUSP challenged the Firemen School to a football match under the slogan 'Play by the rules!' – and lost two to three.

The last action in the series, held in the main hall of the Palace of Architects, was a public event featuring prominent Russian intellectuals, such as the writer Dmitry Bykov, the journalist Andrey Konstantinov, the publicist Lev Lur'ye, the Director of the Hermitage Mikhail Piotrovsky, and the lead singer of the rock group *DDT*, Yury Shevchuk. Besides demonstrating support for the university, the implicit aim of the event was to link the EUSP case discursively with the more general protest agenda in St Petersburg and Russia, concerning issues such as abuse of the law, the destruction of the historical centre of St Petersburg, the corruption of the administration, civil rights, and so on. Thus the particular agenda of the EUSP was symbolically merged with a more universal civil agenda, strengthening both.

A few days later, the cumulative effect of the media coverage, petitions, and public actions drew attention from the Administration of the newly elected President. President Medvedev ordered that the situation be resolved, and the Federal services (presumably including the FSB) had to back down. The Fire Inspection submitted a positive report about safety improvements that had been made in the meantime, and on 21 March, the court reopened the university. A few days after that, the Registration service finished its inspection, finding no violations. The 21 March is now celebrated annually as 'EUSP Day'.

Opposition substitutes

Theories of social movements and concepts of contentious politics explain political change as a result of the mobilization and collective action of social groups against authority. In these struggles, political opportunities, resources, and ideologies matter a lot, because they allow the tipping of the balance of forces in favour of those who challenge the existing order (Tilly 2004; McAdam, Tarrow and Tilly 2001). This framework, however, does not accommodate all scenarios of resistance. In the conditions of high power asymmetries between opposing parties, the strategy of conflict tends to change from one of open head-on collision to more subtle and flexible forms. Michel de Certeau (1978) and James Scott (1986) have explored the tactics of consumers and weapons of the weak, stressing the benefits of improvization, mimicry, and local knowledge. Dominant orders, they argued, can be subverted by means of creative interpretations and practical usage of those very orders – of urban spaces, texts, laws, and so forth. Vaclav Havel's *Power of the Powerless* (1985) celebrates the non-violent creative forms of resistance of East-European intellectuals to oppressive regimes he called 'post-totalitarian'. The resistance of citizens consisted in revealing the lies and hypocrisy of the regime. They did so not in blunt and contentious forms but, rather, with the use of subtle artistic statements or, on the contrary, by grotesque manifestations of loyalty that in fact signified the opposite, yet did not give the authorities a legitimate chance to resort to repression. While the weapons of the weak theme stresses the tactics and guerrilla-like qualities of resistance, Havel ultimately refers to actions that undermine the ideological hegemony of state power and that eventually lead the authorities to relinquish political control and launch the process of political change whereby the opposition takes power – what is known as the 'velvet revolution'. At the same time, both phenomena describe the avoidance of explicit political articulation as being itself one of the major conditions of successful resistance: misrecognition and substitution should be viewed as deliberate and assertive.

A similar substitute way of action is discernable in the case of the EUSP and in some parallel cases in Russia. Putin's second term in office saw the strengthening of authoritarian features in domestic politics, expressed in the domination of the *United Russia* party combined with the reduction of the possibility of holding fair and competitive elections. Oil export revenues allowed a boost in private consumption and a reduction in people's incentives to participate in political life or to oppose the regime. Though few cases of open political repression were recorded, the pressure upon NGOs and opposition groups took the form of administrative and legal sanctions for reasons formally unrelated to politics. The Federal services, such as the Tax inspectorate or the Registration service, even the Sanitary control service, could effectively shut down any organization under a legal pretext. With the courts having no independence from the executive, the latter perfected the art of using laws and formal procedures for its own purposes – for extorting bribes or for political repression. The semblance of legality became the hallmark of Putin-style authoritarianism. All of these trends became more pronounced during the electoral cycle of 2008–9, as the Kremlin wanted to exclude any uncertainty about and during the transfer of power.

The political scientist Vladimir Gel'man (2005) has analysed the process whereby the political opposition in Russia was extinguished after 2004. This happened due to the closure of political opportunities and skilful institutional manipulation by the Kremlin administration combined with the promotion of the 'party of power' *United Russia*. Formally, political opposition in Russia does exist, being represented by the Communist and National-Bolshevik parties on the left flank, and the *Yabloko* party, the *Pravoye Delo*, the *Other Russia* and *Solidarity* movements on the liberal right. The real influence of the opposition is weak and not only because of its limited access to decision making and the mass media. The Communists are evidently on the decline curve, representing the older generation and social groups connected with agricultural labour. The leaders on the right flank, such as Kasparov or Nemtsov, command little sympathy even with opponents of the regime. Their popularity ratings have remained consistently low, even among the educated middle class. A significant proportion of the population, who did not support either Putin or the existing opposition, remained therefore unrepresented.

One possible explanation of the unexpectedly high support for the EUSP and the mobilization of civil society in its cause could be linked to its choice of frame and action strategy which appealed to those segments of the politically active population that were oppositionally minded yet unwilling to be explicitly identified with politics and political opposition. At a time when conditions meant that joining the political opposition carried risks, and when opposition parties and movements were either discredited or severely constrained by the lack of a positive agenda, the so-called opposition substitutes provided an alternative way of expressing political protest. By avoiding explicit involvement in politics but being pro-active, the EUSP and its supporters could avoid the risk of authoritarian repression and of being used by political forces that they genuinely did not support. Balancing on the fine line between the civil and the political, the movement had more chances of success, even though this tactic was sensitive to accusations of being hypocritical or even cowardly. In fact, it could not even be called asymmetrical. The state authorities' political attack masqueraded as a reasonable and proper concern for fire safety issues, and did not call things by their proper name, while the counter-actions of the EUSP were deliberately kept, to use Dolinina's definition, within the themes of 'society' and 'education', thus avoiding being reclassified into 'politics' and 'opposition'. In the clash of deliberate misrecognitions the EUSP won because the state was constrained in using its coercive and administrative powers. This underscores the importance of civil and cultural causes, be it education, architecture, medicine, or ecology, as powerful tools for mobilizing resistance in authoritarian conditions, provided that the logic of opposition substitutes is followed.

While the principal form of political opposition, that is, one that uses political rhetoric and calls for political action, may be extinct in Russia, oppositional civil movements that use the alternative tactics of political substitutes are certainly not. In this, one might see some continuity with the Soviet period or even with earlier patterns of protest movements that opposed the authorities on issues of ecology, architecture, the vision of history, education, and the like. Most recently, the substitute mode of action seems to have brought success to the civic movement against the Gazprom tower in St Petersburg. In November 2005 the state-controlled company Gazprom announced plans to build an over-four-hundred-metre high office building on the Neva embankment in downtown St Petersburg. Because the centre of the city is an organic architectural ensemble, which is mostly in a nineteenth-century classicist style and restricts the height of buildings to no more than five or six storeys, the erection of a modern sky-scraper would inevitably change not only the skyline, but the whole concept of the city. The top management of Gazprom unleashed a campaign to support its plans, arguing that the city should not remain a museum-town, but should modernize and enter the twenty-first century with a new image.

Prominent cultural and intellectual leaders of the city demanded either that the project be cancelled or that the tower be moved away from the historical centre. The civic movements *Zhivoy gorod* ('The living city'), *Okhtinskaya duga* ('The Okhta arch'), the NGO *Bellona*, the *Yabloko* party, and a number of other organizations started campaigning for the preservation of the architectural shape of St Petersburg. Given the huge role of Gazprom in international politics and its closeness to the political authorities, citizens could not fail to associate the construction project with the architectural expression of state power and its will to dominate society. Advancing a political cause, the movement, however, kept its agenda within the boundaries of architectural and civic matters, hence its wide support. Citizens were able to make political statements without using political discourse, while the authorities had no legitimate reasons for discrediting or suppressing the activism, as they routinely do with regard to overtly political opposition groups. A group of forty-four prominent academics and intellectuals signed a letter to President Medvedev, in which they claimed that the construction site contained valuable archaeological findings, such as a medieval Swedish fortress and a five-thousand-year-old Neolithic settlement. As public opinion polls indicated that there was widespread disapproval of the Gazprom project, and with an increasing number of negative comments being transmitted by the media, the tide began to turn. The leaders of the ruling party *United Russia* criticized the project at its party convention in St Petersburg in December 2009. While the fate of the Gazprom tower was still undecided at the time this chapter was being written, there are strong indications that the state authorities are ready to change their mind.

Notes

1 The private cardiological hospital was set up in the town of Tarusa, in the Kaluga region by a group of Russian medics and foreign businessmen, using charity donations and endowments. Soon after the hospital opened, local bureaucrats started inspections and threatened to close it, filing criminal charges of fraud. The Mayor of Tarusa, Yury Nakhrov, suspended the work of the hospital and demanded the resignation of its chief physician. After a public campaign that lasted several weeks and the personal intervention of the Governor of the Kaluga region, the Mayor had to resign, and the hospital resumed its work. See the story in *Moscow News*, no. 10, 13 March 2008. The Gazprom tower is discussed later in this chapter.

Bibliography

de Certeau, M. (1978) *The Practice of Everyday Life*, Berkeley: University of California Press.
Gabovich, M. (2008) *Save the European University at St Petersburg*. Online. Available: http:// euspb.blogspot.com/ (accessed 29 March 2011).
Gel'man, V. (2005) 'Political opposition in Russia: a dying species?' *Post-Soviet Affairs*, 21/3: 226–46.
Havel, V. (1985) *The Power of the Powerless: Citizens against the State in Central and Eastern Europe*, London: M.E. Sharpe.
Lur'ye, D. and Volkov, V. (2008) *Yevropeysky universitet v opasnosti*. Online. Available: http:// saveeu.blogspot.com (accessed 29 March 2011).
McAdam, D., Tarrow, S., and Tilly, Ch. (2001) *Dynamics of Contention*, Cambridge: Cambridge University Press.
Moscow News (2008), 10 (13 March). Online. Available: www.mnweekly.ru/national/ 20080313/55316772.html (accessed 15 August 2010).
Putin, V.V. (2007) 'Zayavleniye dlya pressy i otvety na voprosy po itogam XX sammita Rossiya – Yevrosoyuz', *Prezident Rossii*. Online. Available: www.president.kremlin.ru/ appears/2007/10/26/2205_type63377type63380_149679.shtml (accessed 29 March 2011).
Ruthenia.net (2008) 'Obrashcheniye v podderzhku Yevropeyskogo universiteta v Sankt-Peterburge' Online. Available: www.ruthenia.ru/euspb (accessed 31 December 2010).
Save_eu (2008) Online. Available: http://community.livejournal.com/save_eu/ (accessed 29 March 2011).
Scott, J. (1986) *Weapons of the Weak: Everyday Forms of Peasant Resistance*, New Haven, CT: Princeton University Press.
Tilly, Ch. (2004) *Social Movements, 1768–2004*, London: Paradigm Publishers.
Utekhin, I. (2008) *ethnomet.lifejournal*. Online. Available: http://ethnomet.livejournal.com (accessed 29 March 2011).
Yurchak, A. and Rivkin-Fish, M. (2008) 'Letter of support for European University at St Petersburg.' Online. Available: www.gopetition.com/petitions/european-university-in-st-petersburg.html (accessed 29 March 2011).

8 Political culture in Russia from a local perspective

Risto Alapuro and Markku Lonkila

A comparative perspective: how to move between the personal and the public

Political culture, broadly understood, is about public ways to pursue common ends.[1] Party politics, a constituent part of a representative political system, is only one manifestation of political culture in this sense, along with numerous other forms of joint action. Among those other forms of doing things together voluntary associations constitute a central element. In this chapter the question is, what we can learn about the particularity of Russian political culture by looking at the associational way of making things public, or, more precisely, at the way people acting in associations move from their personal attachments and concerns to demands which can be legitimated publicly and which therefore must have a degree of generality, appropriate in public discussion.

We hope that in examining this dimension at the micro level, we will be able to advance a hypothesis of a key aspect of Russian political culture vis-à-vis its counterparts in Western Europe. This is so because its particularity is usually traced precisely to the specific 'Russian' itinerary from familiar engagement to public engagement and the oscillation between the two (on the distinction, see Thévenot 2007: 416–21). According to a well-established but also somewhat stereotypical view, characteristic of Russian joint action, including associational life, is its familiar nature and the importance of personal loyalties. Associations and especially their cores are said to consist of friendship networks or more or less closed circles of trust; they have even been described as 'small private worlds' (Richter 2000: 5, cited in Evans 2002: 326). A stark contrast allegedly separates them from Western voluntary associations, usually portrayed as sites of civic activity, that is, as public actors par excellence, which champion the interests of different groups and lay claims to the state and other actors in civil society, of which they constitute the main part. In this stereotypical image the major difference between 'Russian' and 'Western' associational life lies in the sticking of the former to the level of personal concerns and attachments, whereas the latter reaches the public realm. It is true that more detailed analyses avoid this trap and give a more sophisticated picture of the nature of associational activity in Russia (see, e.g., Salmenniemi 2008). Yet we believe that an approach that explicitly focuses on the move between the two levels and thereby differs from various civil society based approaches helps specify the character of Russian political culture in relation to corresponding 'Western' understandings and styles of action.

The issue is studied through a comparison between two local associations in St Petersburg, Russia, and two corresponding associations in the Helsinki region, Finland. One pair consists of grass-roots diabetes associations, the other one of car drivers' associations. Diabetes is a widespread disease in both countries, and therefore the organization process provoked by it is presumably expressive of the mode of voluntary organization more generally, notably in the social sphere. Car drivers' associations constitute a prime example of associations that in modern societies gather people around material concerns. But it is to be noted that material considerations also permeate the diabetes associations in the form of medicines (insulin) and the instruments needed in their use.

Both instances of sustained collective action pursue common and at least in principle similar ends, and promote their cause especially vis-à-vis the state and the local authorities. In the former case at issue are patients' interests and in the latter case the interests of what customarily is called a consumer group.

To have an idea of the transition between familiar and public engagement, it is useful to look at the activist-level discourses and practices, because activists are located between rank-and-file members and the authorities. The burden of the 'rise in generality' or of making the cause public falls notably to them (cf. Doidy 2004: 64–69).[2]

The question is, first, what is this transition like in the Russian and the Finnish diabetes associations and the Russian and the Finnish car drivers' associations, and, second, what tentative conclusions can be made about the differences between the Russian and the Finnish cases more generally.

Diabetes association in St Petersburg

The *Kaplya Zhizni* ('Drop of Life') is a district-level diabetes association in St Petersburg, founded in 1998. In 2007 it had 217 members, mainly elderly women with modest resources, which is common in Russian diabetes associations. In its activity it combines, naturally enough, two aspects: the promotion of diabetics' interests and mutual help between those involved (for details, see Alapuro 2010).

In this case, as in patients' associations as a rule, the starting point for (joint) action is the eminently familiar, personal experience of an illness. It is inseparable from the particular conditions in which the diabetic lives and from his or her proximate relations with people close to him or her.

How does the 'rise in generality' from personal experience – which is shared by all members – to public engagement take place in the association? More precisely, how are the familiar form and the public form of engagement linked to each other or perhaps even fused, or how is public engagement based on the individual experience of diabetes?

An answer can be sought first by looking at the dimension of *care*, which is by definition an integral part of the diabetic's identity, an activity that, to cite a definition of care, includes everything we do to maintain and repair our 'world' in order to live in it as well as possible. 'That world includes our bodies, our selves, and our environment, all of which we seek to interweave in a complex, life-sustaining web' (Fisher and Tronto 1991: 40, cited in Tronto 1993: 103). Care is strongly present in the discourse of the chairperson of the *Drop of Life* interviewed for the study, as a dimension that regulates relations inside the association between activists and other members. Graphically the aspect of care appears in the answer to the question 'why in your opinion do people join the association?' The chairperson evokes *obshcheniye* and/or 'moral help' for people in distress. *Obshcheniye*, usually translated as 'intercourse', 'relations', or 'links' (*Oxford Russian-English Dictionary*, s. v.), implies 'a (mutual) contact or bond with other people or nature', for example (*Slovar' russkogo yazyka*, s.v.). *Svyatoye obshcheniye* means 'the partaking of the Communion' (*Tolkovy slovar' zhivogo velikorusskago yazyka Vladimira Dalya*, s.v.). The interviewee continues:[3]

> Sometimes people are heavy at heart and feel sad [*prikhodit toska*], well, all in all, are insulted, have had a quarrel, are in tears, [and then can] talk. Sometimes a conversation is more useful than a doctor or a medicine. You talk, you convince, you tell something, the person leaves smiling and satisfied.

At issue here are the particular needs of individual persons in relationship to those who are taking care of them. At the same time the description implies an *asymmetric* relationship between activists and those who are taken care of: the former provide (moral) help, talk to the latter, providing personal support and consolation. Activists are said to be people who have 'the desire of the soul' [*dusha*] for voluntary work. The term used to describe such people is *obshchestvenniki*. It goes back to the Soviet period and denotes persons who actively participate in social life, engaging in voluntary activity for the good of others (Colin Lebedev 2009: 335–36). One can say that their personal engagement, care, and public engagement as *obshchestvenniki* are intertwined in the activist's role, or, that a good part of their public engagement is based on their personal engagement. This is still more true because as diabetics they share the personal experience of diabetes.

But if the fusion of the personal and the public appears in the activists' conduct vis-à-vis rank-and-file members, it is also observable in their activity outside the association, in their public activity in the proper sense, in relation to the authorities. At this level they represent an association that has been created on the basis of the 'common interests' of those having diabetes (*Statutes* 1999: § 1.1). It is crucial in terms of common interests that the first item in the list of tasks is 'the acquisition of medical products and [products of] medical technology' (*Statutes* 1999: § 2.1). The importance of medicines, notably insulin, in this public activity means that the principal public activity is very closely tied to the very personal experience of every member, up to and including their corporal everyday and most intimate concerns. The 'rise in generality' is above all based on the right of the diabetics to medicines, which is guaranteed by law but not properly realized in practice. Here lies the principal legitimacy of the public activity of the association, its justification. Public action is justified by arguments of equality and solidarity, and a concern with the general interest – by virtue of the diabetics' rights as citizens to acquire medicines and related supplies. The point is that in the statutes there is a very direct and very concrete link from the personal everyday concerns and anxieties of diabetics to the general argument, put forward in public, a 'justifiable action engagement' based on civic solidarity (Thévenot 2007: 417–18).

The entanglement of the personal with the public also appears in the realization of the distribution of medicines and instruments to members of the association. These products are only to an insufficient degree distributed through impersonal procedures, that is, by public agencies such as health centres, following the stipulations formulated as rights of diabetics as citizens and aiming at reducing inequalities. Another principle, attentive to people's personal situations and familiar attachments in their local milieu, operates as well (cf. Thévenot 2007: 416, 420). The members of the association have access to medicines specifically as members of the *Drop of Life*, and some allocation practices are particularistic by nature. The distribution is carried out at various times organized by the authorities, and also made possible by donations from influential individuals, mostly politicians. The local administration organizes 'diabetes evenings' once a year in November. It lends money for the evening and for the acquisition of a package of diabetes supplies.

> Everybody is there, we invite everybody, all members of the association. And everybody agrees to participate with pleasure in them and looks forward to such evenings, because there is both a sense of togetherness [*obshcheniye*] and some kind of material support, even though [it is only] a small supply package worth 200 roubles, but anyway, for them, it means a lot.

Indicative of the social dimension in the connections between the association and the municipality are the tea hours held in the district twice a year. Also the administrative organs of the city district and its subunits have a major role. They invite members on (bus) excursions and to 'evenings, occasions which they organize', and especially to 'the day of diabetes', when they 'present us with diabetic foodstuffs'. 'We make them a request for the products, they make the purchase, we get [the products]'. Smaller contributions by the local administrative organs come in the form of gifts, such as small boxes of diabetic confectionary given to the oldest members on their birthdays. Moreover, successful appeals have been addressed to the chairman of a political party, *Spravedlivaya Rossiya* ('Just Russia'), and to deputies of the State Duma; one deputy has distributed a small sum of money to the members.

All this means that the engagement in the public domain includes different principles, the principle of equality or civic solidarity, but also a particular attention to member-diabetics and their personal situation. Moreover, in both senses it is the medicine that constitutes a close link between the personal and often very acute needs of individual diabetics and the principal public engagements of the association. This role of the medicine problem is exacerbated by the fact that the

Drop of Life, like many other patient organizations in Russia, is an organization mainly for *invalids*, that is, only for those diabetics whose illness has left them disabled, whose situation is most precarious, and who are therefore presumably in the greatest need of insulin and most at the mercy of the public health care system.[4]

Finally, the care attached to the issue of medicines also appears in the conceptions of two further aspects of public engagement, namely interest and representation. The *Drop of Life* sees itself very definitely as an organization of its members. Other diabetics in the district are not excluded, but their representation is not explicitly mentioned even in the statutes. The main public concern, the acquisition of medicines and equipment, presents itself above all in relation to the members.

Diabetes association in the Helsinki region

The Kirkkonummi and Siuntio section of the Diabetes association of the Helsinki region was founded in 1985, and in 2007 it had 278 members. As in St Petersburg, elderly women are overrepresented among the members, but their over-representation is much less marked, and the social composition of members is more varied.

Here too participation is based on personal experience of diabetes, but the move from the proximate and personal realm to the public one takes a different form. When the interviewed former secretary speaks of the relations inside the association, she does not primarily evoke moral help or consolation given to particular others in similar situations as was the case in St Petersburg, but 'peer support' as characteristic of the mutual connections between members and as the main form of internal activity. Personal experience is not lacking in her interview (and here as well there is presumably a factual asymmetry in the relation of activists to other members), but the discourse reveals a conception in which the common experience is based on the perceived similarity everybody shares as a diabetic, that is, an idea of their equality as bearers of the illness. Other activities stressed (along with the emotional aspect and the sharing of a common experience) are the instrumental exchange of knowledge in monthly get-togethers, like the importance of observing the temperature of the insulin before its use, and the distribution of 'information' and 'practical guidance' in the everyday treatment of the illness. In other words, here personal experience is accompanied, one could say, by arguments of equality and mutual solidarity. A form of engagement, namely civic solidarity characteristic of public action, appears here at the level of personal engagement.

The contrast to the St Petersburg case is heightened by the Helsinki interviewee's answer to the question about why people join the association. Unlike the answer to the same question in St Petersburg, she says nothing about giving consolation to people in distress (that is, about personal engagement) but refers to their common interests vis-à-vis the world outside the association (that is, to the civic form of public engagement):

[To join the association] is no impulse of the moment. The person reflects on whether he or she will join. In this kind of association for the disabled, the members think about whether and how they can profit from this. And those people [who do not join] don't understand that they should be members. As I see it, one should be a member to provide more weight for us.

Note that the acquisition of medicines is not mentioned here; it is not a problem because it is guaranteed by the public health care system. Moreover, it does not appear even indirectly in the characterization of the more intimate internal activity.

In conformity with the stress on the advancement of interests in the realm of public engagement, the conception of representation is broader in Helsinki. The association sees itself more definitely as representing all diabetics – following a 'categorical generality' typical of civic argumentation[5] – in its area of activity than does the St Petersburg association. The interests are given more weight and they are seen in a broader perspective, including not only the acquisition of medicines and supplies, but also health education and a healthy way of life. In terms of the association's relations with the municipal council, lobbying before decisions are taken is essential, as are attempts to exert pressure before elections when it comes to political parties. Likewise, the membership category is broader in Helsinki. It includes not only 'invalids' but anyone who has diabetes, and in principle even those who do not, if they share the aims of the organization.

In sum, in the two cases the relationship between the most familiar and personal realm and the realm of public engagement was different. It seems that in St Petersburg the stress on personal attachments and concerns, so prevalent in the association's internal activity, extended into public engagement along with the civic principles expressed in the statutes. Diabetics were helped both regularly and accidentally because they were recognized as members in particular need of the association. A part of public engagement was closely related to attachment to members' particular situations (e.g., special attention to the oldest members on their birthdays). In Helsinki, instead, even personal forms of engagement bore resemblance to a specific form of public engagement, namely justification through equality and the idea of categorical generality.

Obviously the central role given to the acquisition of medicines and the limitation of membership to invalids in St Petersburg is heavily influenced by differences in the material resources available in the two countries. Yet this disparity by no means invalidates the differences in the oscillation between the personal and the public in the two cases. It rather specifies a conception of associational activity – its character as a public institution and a site of joint action.

Car drivers' association in St Petersburg

Our example of a Russian car drivers' organization is the *Vserossiyskoye Obshchestvo Avtomobilistov* (*VOA*), a member of the *International Automobile Federation* (*Fédération Internationale de l'Automobile*, or *FIA*) whose predecessor was founded in 1973.[6] The

VOA has a four-tiered hierarchical structure which has remained practically intact from the Soviet era. Below the national level are the city-level chapters, which in St Petersburg are divided into eighteen subunits, or district chapters, corresponding to the eighteen administrative city districts. One of these is the object of our examination. It includes thirty-six 'primary organizations' (*pervichnyye organizatsii*, or *PO*), which constitute the lowest level in the structure of the *VOA*.

The *PO*s provide, in exchange for the membership fee, places for their members in garage parking areas (*garazhnyye stoyanki*) which cover an immense amount of land in the city. These areas often contain a great number of small garage huts built of metal sheets, concrete, or tiles. The parking areas are equipped with electricity and running water and in many cases car repair and washing services, and are guarded around the clock by paid staff. Like member organizations of the *FIA* in other countries, the *VOA* declares its task in its statutes as the promotion of the interests of car drivers and motoring in general. In practice, however, the main reason to join is the possibility of owning a garage, and the activities of the St Petersburg chapter have been focused mainly on providing parking and additional services (such as discounts for insurance and gasoline) for its members. The bulk of the running of the association is delegated to paid staff, who are expected to take care of the daily problems of the members.

The activity of the association thus concerns very tangible things: garages and cars. This kind of grounding of the *VOA* membership in concrete material objects includes a personal relationship to the immediate surroundings and familiar attachments with these surroundings, to use Laurent Thévenot's characterization of the regime of familiar engagement (2007: 416, 418). It directs the activities of the association towards its members and their garages, not towards all Russian car drivers, the general public, or abstract ideas concerning car driving.

The garages are indeed in several ways linked to the personal life of the *garazhniki* ('garage owners'): their ownership and neighbourhood ties at the garage parking areas not only go back a long way but are often passed down from generation to generation within a family. Moreover, the garages are used, in addition to keeping cars, also as an extra storage space – or extension of home – where all kinds of stuff that won't fit in the crowded apartments is stored.

A specific feature of our *VOA* district chapter is that it forms part of a nation-wide hierarchical organization inherited from the Soviet era. This structure marks the activities of all district chapters in the city, and shapes the rank-and-file members' opportunities to engage in public action. Another specific feature is that, due to the vast amount of land covered by the *VOA* parking areas, they have become an object of considerable commercial interest in St Petersburg. Consequently, defending them against new building projects has been one of the primary issues in the activity of the organization since 2006, when the so-called 'garage war' (*garazhnaya voyna*) broke out. This war forced the dormant Soviet era organization into a defensive struggle, only part of which was, however, waged through public debate.

The *causa belli* of the garage war was the beginning of the expropriation of some garage parking areas for building projects. The expropriations shook the financial foundations of the whole St Petersburg city chapter, which was based on the considerable amount of money paid as membership fees (and allegedly for illegal repair services in these areas), and its ex-chairman was killed for reasons most probably related to this war (Lonkila 2011).

In the interview, the chairman of the district chapter justifies the *VOA*'s stand in the garage war with various arguments, ranging from the efficiency of the *VOA* garage maintenance compared to alternative ways of organizing parking to the necessity of guaranteeing inexpensive means of keeping cars for common people and pensioners. Importantly, the chairman evokes images of the tradition of local parking areas and the idea that they are rooted in the city district, including the work of *druzhinniki* – the Soviet-era tradition of volunteers who monitor traffic and give lectures on traffic regulations and safety in local schools.

Though the *VOA*'s whole activity is deeply anchored in the garage parking areas, the move from familiar forms of engagement to public action takes place by delegating disputed matters to the *VOA* administration, which in turn prefers lobbying behind the scenes to engaging in public debate. Prior to the legislative assembly elections in St Petersburg and the national parliamentary elections in 2007, for example, the *VOA* promised to ask its members to support *United Russia*'s candidate in an obvious attempt to obtain in exchange the candidate's support for the association's interests. The actual struggle conducted by the administration seems thus to consist of making deals with the power vertical, rather than encouraging its rank-and-file members to engage in public action.[7]

Car drivers' association in Helsinki

Our Finnish case is the Helsinki chapter of the *Autoliitto*, the Finnish car drivers' association, which, like the *VOA* in Russia, is a member of the *FIA*. Its predecessor *Autoklubi* ('Auto club') was established in 1919 in Helsinki as an interest, service, and hobby association of private car drivers at a time when car ownership and driving were still rare in Finland.[8] As is the case with the *VOA*, in Helsinki a significant proportion of the *Autoliitto* members join to get benefits such as discounts on insurance and several other products, road service both at home and abroad, and a journal with ten annual issues.

The Helsinki chapter, the biggest of the *Autoliitto*'s chapters, is well integrated and connected to the national level to the extent that it is sometimes, unlike in the *VOA* case, difficult to distinguish the two. The activities of the *Autoliitto* vary from traffic safety to tourism and motor sports, but the most important goal of the organization according to the chair of the Helsinki chapter is 'to secure the freedom for responsible moving around'. This focus on an abstract issue concerning the rights of all car drivers is in stark contrast to the *VOA*'s struggle to defend the material property of its members – and simultaneously its own structure and revenues. Unlike the *VOA*, the *Autoliitto* is lobbying on behalf of the interests of *all* car drivers, not only those of the *Autoliitto* members, in, say, voicing its views regarding city planning.

The *Autoliitto* was created as a civil society organization, but it has good informal and formal contacts with the city administration: the traffic-planning manager of the city of Helsinki is a member of the traffic committee of the Helsinki chapter. This is different from the *VOA*. The St Petersburg city chapter also has strong ties with the city district administration, probably dating back to the Soviet era, but its ties with the top leadership of this five-million strong metropolis are much weaker and the chairman of the district chapter analysed above even claims to protect the garage owners of St Petersburg from the arbitrary measures of 'businessmen and the city administration'. It is notable that the *Autoliitto* uses general arguments at all levels, including the local – such slogans as 'the freedom for responsible moving around', concern everyone, not only the members of the *Autoliitto* chapter.

This stress on generality implies that even though the Helsinki section of the *Autoliitto* is a local association like our *VOA* district chapter, its attachment to the locality differs from that in St Petersburg. New members directly join the nation-wide *Autoliitto*, whereas in the *VOA* the members are locally anchored in a particular garage parking area, and thus with the particular *PO* administering the garage. Consequently the representative function of the *VOA* is more limited and at the same time more locally anchored than in the Finnish case.

Moreover, there is a marked difference between the categorization of the St Petersburg *VOA* members as an association of *garazhniki*, whose activities concern local garage parking areas, and the activities of the Finnish car drivers' (*autoilijat*) association which focuses on broader issues of 'freedom for responsible moving around'. The actions organized by the *Autoliitto*, for example, are open to everyone and are frequently directed to outsiders in order to make them understand the viewpoints of the organization and to gain new members. In St Petersburg, the main activities revolve instead around garage maintenance and are open only to members.

All in all it seems that the move from the personal to the public (and back) takes a different course in the two cases, stemming from a difference in the function of the car – the obvious key in the organization process – in St Petersburg and Helsinki. The car is certainly a personal matter with familiar attachments, even an extension of the person(ality) of many people everywhere. But the car has at least two different linkages to the public realm of engagement, exemplified by our cases: as an object in need of maintenance and protection and as a means of (free) moving around. The prevalence of the former function in St Petersburg goes back to the Soviet model of organization of private car driving, which was developed without a concomitant provision of an effective maintenance service or system of repair shops and without including the creation of private garages in the planning and building of housing. The prevalence of the latter function in Helsinki derives from the absence or the relative insignificance of both of these problems. Hence the *personal and free moving* as the key in the oscillation between the personal and the public in Helsinki, manifest in public as the advancement of moving at will for all drivers, with all its various repercussions. And hence the attachment to a *place* of maintenance and to a *locality* more generally (*druzhinniki*) in St Petersburg, made manifest in public as a defence of the control of these places. Both associations wage a struggle on behalf of the interests of car drivers, but in the *VOA*'s case, because of the localized attachments of *garazhniki*, the struggle is waged in the name of the members, whereas in Helsinki, where the issue is convenience and freedom in driving, the campaigns necessarily cover all car drivers, not only members of the *Autoliitto* chapter.

Conclusions

The 'rise in generality' took a different form in St Petersburg than in Helsinki. In the two Helsinki cases the move was in many ways strikingly similar. Public engagement or demands which can be legitimated publicly appeared at the local level, within the associations. In the diabetes association a form of mutual support – peer support together with arguments of equality and interest promotion – predominated in the discourse describing internal activities. This emphasis was in full conformity with the public discourse of civic solidarity prevalent in the association. In the Helsinki car drivers' association the penetration of the public form of engagement at the local level was similarly visible and clearly expressed in the *Autoliitto*'s slogan about 'responsible moving around'. In fact, the whole distinction between the local level and the national level is vague in the case of the *Autoliitto*, due to the character of its main activity. Tangible benefits negotiated nationally, such as insurance discounts and road service, provide the glue that gives cohesion at grass-roots level. Even the local level is permeated through and through by material interests and advantages, typical of consumer organizations more generally.

Compared with this picture the St Petersburg scene is different. In the diabetes association, the *Drop of Life*, personal engagement in the form of care prevailed not only in the internal discourse, but this engagement or attention to the particular needs of its members also marked relations with the main interlocutors, the administration and political parties. The contrast is reminiscent of what Olga Koveneva (forthcoming) observed between local environmental activists in Russia and France. Interestingly she found that Russian activists positioned themselves close to ordinary people – both in relation to the authorities and to higher-level associational structures. Local activists saw themselves as 'residents who live here', and maintained close relations to other local people and the environment. For example, they did not react to minor ecological offences by directing a heavy arsenal of ecological arguments at offenders but by talking and using everyday language to persuade them. In order to sensitize inhabitants to ecological problems, they preferred personal contacts to associational meetings, which made it easier to avoid an excessively abstract tone in their message. If there is a parallel here with the St Petersburg diabetes association, the French case in Koveneva's comparison resembles in certain respects the Helsinki diabetes association. In the French ecological movement, public engagement already appeared strongly at the local level. Small local tensions were immediately transformed into more general issues and treated in terms of reconciliation procedures and public representation.

As a consequence even new volunteers of the local group were able to challenge the authorities and specialists, to force them to justify their action from a civic point of view and to question their paternalism and their authority based on expertise.

The contrast between the *VOA* and *Autoliitto* is different to that between the *Drop of Life* in St Petersburg and the Kirkkonummi and Siuntio diabetes section in the Helsinki region. The *Autoliitto*'s activity, in representing the interests of driving and drivers in general, seems to be of a predominantly public nature starting from the level of proximate connections, and the rise in generality thus does not produce particular problems. In St Petersburg, by contrast, the daily activities of the rank-and-file members revolve around their personal engagement rooted in garage maintenance in small local communities, and the rise in generality consists of the defence of the localized interests of the members only. Therefore, when forced to defend its position in the garage war publicly, the members repeatedly evoke the link to the local, and largely personal, level through the defence of the garages. The link creates a tie between a material object incorporating a personal aspect (the particular garage in relation to its owner and to fellow owners in a parking area) and a public aspect (the defence of garages against encroachments by the city administration and business interests). It is no accident that the term used is *garazhnik*, or garage owner, not car driver, as in Helsinki (*autoilija*).

This is a peculiar mode of the rise in generality, which is not met in the Finnish associations. Here as well, as in the case of diabetes, personal engagement is more present at the local level than in the corresponding association in Helsinki, but here the move to public engagement does not involve a personal aspect (as was the case in the *Drop of Life*), but takes a radically public form through a socio-political conflict, provoked ultimately by the incompatibility between the Soviet legacy and the demands of the Russian type of market economy.

Interestingly in both Russian cases the move is incarnated in material objects in a way not found in the Finnish cases – in the insulin and the garages. In the corresponding Finnish cases the central role in the move – or the oscillation between the levels – is played by the promotion in the one case of diabetics' interests and in the other of services and other advantages that make driving more comfortable and less costly. Significantly, prominent demands that define the public image of the two Finnish associations, which are also relevant at the local level, include its campaigns for a healthy way of life and the 'freedom of responsible movement', respectively.

This last difference can apparently be traced to differences in the nature of the public sphere in the two cases (cf. Urban et al. 1997). Public engagement requires pursuing 'justifiable action', that is, evaluations which 'must be valid for a third party and characterized by generality and legitimacy' (Thévenot 2007: 417). In other words, they must involve the specification of worths that are held to be common goods in the society in question. But this kind of justifiable action seems to be much more present in the activities of the Helsinki association than in those of the St Petersburg association. The interests of all diabetics as citizens and the advancement of health policy more generally, or the right to move comfortably and at will for all drivers, are arguments based on civic equality and solidarity. They are put forward in a public discussion in which justifications are developed and used in pressure politics. Corresponding debates are not lacking in Russia either, but our data support the hypothesis that they are of a different character and that the public sphere more generally is also perhaps of a different character. It is clear that in the public form of engagement manifest in the relations of the *Drop of Life* to the authorities and politicians, the aspect of care functions as a common good more self-evidently than in Helsinki. It is also the case that the degree of generality in the demands is greater in both Helsinki cases. This may refer to differences in the structure of the public sphere – differences in whose formation the micro level of associational activity only constitutes the reverse of the macro level of state policy. In St Petersburg the conception of the diabetes association in a narrow way as an association for invalids and the definition of the main objective as a concern about access to insulin direct the attention to the circle of members and effectively foreclose or seriously limit evaluations characterized by 'generality', such as health policy in general,[9] which are relevant to the public discussion. Likewise in the case of the *VOA*, focusing its interest solely on the defence of its members' tangible benefits forecloses a public formulation of interests rising in generality to cover drivers and driving more broadly.

A hypothesis emerges, then, from our observations that the stereotypical image of Russian associational activity and of Russian political culture more generally as consisting of friendship networks and closed circles of trust could be fruitfully questioned by a perspective that focuses on the ways people in associations move from their personal attachments to demands which can be legitimated publicly. In this perspective it seems that in the trajectory from personal engagement to public engagement a specific tone can be observed in the Russian cases. Above all the presence and apparent legitimacy of care and trust should be noted; they count as the basis for justifiable public action more emphatically than is true in the Finnish cases. Also, limits in the functioning of the public sphere, it would appear, can be subject to analysis from the perspective of the move between the personal and the public. And finally, to put this claim in a broader context, we hope to have shown the fruitfulness of looking at such phenomena at close quarters, or of a micro perspective, in the study of political culture.

Notes

1 As one authoritative definition suggests: 'Political cultures are the sets of symbols and meanings or styles of action that organize political claims-making and opinion-forming, by individuals or collectives' (Lichterman and Cefaï 2006: 392).

2 The analysis is based on interviews with a central actor in the four cases (the chairperson and the former secretary of the association in St Petersburg and in Helsinki, respectively), on the rules and other documents of the four associations and on relevant information gathered from various sites on the Internet. The interviews were conducted and the reports prepared by Anastasiya Tsygankova in St Petersburg and by Sara Lamminmäki and Risto Alapuro in Helsinki. Material from the Internet was collected by Sylvi Nikitenkov, who also conducted additional telephone interviews. This chapter is part of a larger comparative study, in which interviews were conducted in four

associations (an environmental association, a car drivers' association, another consumer association, and a diabetes association) in four cities (St Petersburg, Helsinki, Tallinn, and Paris). The project is led by Risto Alapuro and Markku Lonkila and funded by the Academy of Finland.

3 Unless indicated otherwise, all quotations in this section are from the interview with the chairperson of the *Drop of Life*.

4 This restriction, which sets narrow limits to the conception of patients' organizations in Russia, is due to a tax exemption that the state grants to those associations of whose members at least 80 per cent are invalids or their legal representatives.

5 '[T]he civic qualification presupposes grasping people and things in a categorical generality that guarantees equality of treatment for all' (Thévenot 2007: 419).

6 The Soviet-time predecessor of the *VOA* was called *Vserossiyskoye Dobrovol'noye Obshchestvo Avtomotolyubiteley* (for other car drivers' organizations in Russia, see Lonkila 2011).

7 During the garage war many garage owners grew tired of the *VOA*'s inaction and competing *garazhniki* movements emerged (Lonkila 2011).

8 In the early 1920s, Finland had only 1,800 cars. The *Autoklubi* merged with competing associations in 1972 to form the *Autoliitto* (see 'Vuosisata suomalaista autoilua' 2007).

9 An example of the 'generality' in the Helsinki diabetes association is the use of the 'Current care recommendation' as a guide in justifying demands. Prepared for diabetics by a working group appointed by the Finnish Medical Society *Duodecim* and the Medical Advisory Board of the Finnish Diabetes Society, it is a guide to which one can appeal in dealings with the authorities. It was evoked by the interviewee from the Helsinki diabetes association.

Bibliography

Alapuro, R. (2010) 'Diabetes associations and political culture in St. Petersburg and Helsinki', in T. Huttunen and M. Ylikangas (eds), *Witnessing Change in Contemporary Russia*, 107–35, Helsinki: Kikimora Publications.

Colin Lebedev, A. (2009) 'Du souci maternel à l'action en commun: Le Comité des mères de soldats de Russie et ses requérants (1989–2001)', unpublished doctoral thesis, Institut d'Etudes Politiques de Paris.

Doidy, E. (2004) 'Une lecture inquiète de l'activité militante: épuisement et effondrement dans deux mobilisations contemporaines en France', *Modern & Contemporary France*, 12: 63–74.

Evans, A.B., Jr. (2002) 'Recent assessments of social organizations in Russia', *Demokratizatsiya*, 10: 322–42.

Fisher, B. and Tronto, J.C. (1991) 'Toward a feminist theory of caring', in E. Abel and M. Nelson (eds), *Circles of Care: Work and Identity in Workers' Lives*, 35–62, Albany: State University of New York Press.

Koveneva, O. (forthcoming) 'Vivre ensemble dans la nature et dans la ville: capacités et expériences de la mise en commun en France et en Russie'.

Lichterman, P. and Cefaï, D. (2006) 'The idea of political culture', in R.E. Goodin and Ch. Tilly (eds), *The Oxford Handbook of Contextual Political Analysis*, 392–414, Oxford: Oxford University Press.

Lonkila, M. (2011) 'Driving at democracy in Russia: protest activities of St. Petersburg car drivers' associations', *Europe–Asia Studies*, 63: 291–309.

The Oxford Russian-English Dictionary (1972) Oxford: Clarendon Press.

Richter, J. (2000) 'Citizens or professionals: evaluating Western assistance to Russian women's organizations', working paper, Carnegie Endowment for International Peace.

Salmenniemi, S. (2008) *Democratisation and Gender in Contemporary Russia*, London: Routledge.

Slovar' russkogo yazyka (1982) Moskva: Russky yazyk.

Statutes (1999) *Ustav regional'noy obshchestvennoy organizatsii invalidov 'Diabeticheskoye obshchestvo "Kaplya zhizni"'*, Sankt-Peterburg.

Thévenot, L. (2007) 'The plurality of cognitive formats and engagements: moving between the familiar and the public', *European Journal of Social Theory*, 10: 409–23.

Tolkovy slovar' zhivogo velikorusskago yazyka Vladimira Dalya (1905) Sankt-Peterburg/Moskva: Izdaniye T-va M. O. Vol'f.

Tronto, J.C. (1993) *Moral Boundaries: A Political Argument for an Ethic of Care*, New York/London: Routledge.

Urban, M., with Igrunov, V. and Mitrokhin, S. (1997) *The Rebirth of Politics in Russia*, Cambridge: Cambridge University Press.

'Vuosisata suomalaista autoilua' ('A century of motoring in Finland') (2007) Online. Available: www.stat.fi/tup/suomi90/lokakuu.html (accessed 29 March 2011).

9 Soviet modernity: the case of Soviet fashion

Jukka Gronow

Introduction

The main thesis of this chapter is that the 'experiment of building socialism' in the Soviet Union did, during its reign, which lasted over three generations, exert a homogenizing influence on Russian culture, as well as on the other former Soviet republics. It had a long-lasting effect on the everyday patterns of interaction, cultural practice, and taste preferences of ordinary people. The ideals guiding Soviet cultural policy were, at least after the 1920s, by no means taken from the radical and subversive revolutionary movements of the nineteenth century but rather presented, in a simplified and standardized manner, European classic humanistic learning. Richard Stites has characterized the doctrine of socialist realism, established in the 1930s and preserved more or less intact to the end of the Soviet Union, as follows:

> They canonized classical music, ballet, and architecture, realistic theatre, and didactic painting. At the same time they helped fashion a 'mass culture' of socialist realist fiction, state-sponsored folk lore, mass song, military bands, parades, movies and radio – accessible to all.
>
> (Stites 1992: 65)

Many of the basic rules of everyday aesthetics guiding the practices and choices of common aesthetics were an eclectic compilation of maxims from European philosophical aesthetics. This debt was hardly anywhere clearer than in fashion. As Soviet ideologists knew, rapid changes of fashion only served, by ageing the products artificially, the interests of profit making. Because it did not satisfy any real needs, fashion was an anomaly in socialism. It did not have any place in a rationally planned economy. On the other hand, as the Soviet authorities soon found out, they could not abolish fashion – it was almost like a natural force, particularly favoured by women. Therefore they simply had to learn to live with it. Under these circumstances, the best a citizen could do was not to be carried away by fashion but to try to preserve one's personal style, corresponding to one's own personality. This was the same advice given by the great cultural heroes of European modernity, such as Kant and Goethe, and repeated in books of etiquette and other popular instructions about how to dress both properly and beautifully. The fact that such an attitude was functional in terms of the needs of the planned economy – it helped to make changes of fashion moderate and less abrupt – made it particularly attractive to Soviet propagators of good taste.

Soviet modernity

Was the Soviet Union a modern society? This is the core question in the lively controversy that has been going on among historians of the Soviet Union and socialist Eastern Europe since the collapse of communism. On the one hand, the 'modernists', like Stephen Kotkin, the author of the famous work *The Magnetic Mountain* (1995), have emphasized that the building of socialism shared many of the tendencies and aspirations essential to the project of modernity, such as economic and scientific progress, educational achievements, urbanization, and so on (Kotkin 2001). In defence of the 'modernists' one could also argue that the Soviet Union had, in fact, all the main institutions of a modern society, from a parliament and economic market to trade unions, academies, and other institutions of higher learning. On the other hand, the 'neo-traditionalists', like Sheila Fitzpatrick (2000), have argued that, despite some of its seemingly modern features, the Soviet Union was more traditional than modern, pointing out, among others, the role of clientelism and the importance of ascribed social statuses, both ethnic and professional pseudo estates or clans, as well as the privileges and corruption following from them. Something essential was always lacking from these supposedly modern institutions: the right of free assembly from the parliament, market prices from the markets, the freedom to go on strike from the trade unions, and the freedom of learning from the academic institutions (Neidhart 2003).

The answer to this question undoubtedly depends on what one means by a modern society or modernity. As is usual in scientific disputes like this, the adversaries often talk about different things and thus their arguments, however well founded, fail to convince the other side. In a recent article that aptly summarized this dispute, Michael David-Fox (2006) suggested that we should pay more attention to the concrete forms of cultural transfer between the capitalist West and the socialist East and to the various ways in which social institutions were adapted and modified in their countries of destination. The social institution of fashion offers itself as an excellent case for study in this respect.

If we are to believe the great sociologist of modernity, Georg Simmel (1905), fashion, if anything, is essential to our experience of modernity with all its ambivalences. As Simmel claimed, fashion does not have to decide 'to be or not to be' since it both 'is and is not' at one and the same time. The very moment it conquers the scene it disappears and becomes totally obsolete. Fashion is fleeting, changing, and contingent. There are no 'real' reasons why something becomes fashionable or is in fashion. Things could just as well be otherwise. At the same time fashion exercises its grip on us as an external social force, which we have to take into account and learn to live with. According to Simmel, fashion teaches us, among other things, to tolerate and live with the experience of perpetual change typical of modernity (cf. Marshall Berman's 1983 book *All That Is Solid Melts into Air*, whose title paraphrases Marx and Engels' *Communist Manifesto*).

The Soviet authorities copied often quite openly and without reservations, but always selectively, many of the basic social institutions and organizations from what they thought to be the most advanced countries in the West. This process had already started in Lenin's and Stalin's times and continued long into the Brezhnev era. In fashion, Parisian *haute couture* and Christian Dior in particular acted as the absolute points of reference and excellence after the Second World War (Zakharova 2004, 2010). In culinary culture, for instance, it is not as easy to name any such single point of reference, but it is quite clear that French and continental *haute cuisine* was the main source of inspiration for Soviet specialists too, even though at the same time the example of standardized and mass pro- duced American fast food and snack bars (*amerikanki*) attracted Soviet planners (Gronow and Zhuravlev, forthcoming). After all, Soviet luxury was ideally there for the people, everything was mass produced in millions of copies and available to all from the very start (Gronow 2003). This was the main challenge facing Soviet fashion designers too.

The Soviet fashion system

By the end of the 1960s, the Soviet Union had many impressive accomplishments to show in the area of scientific technological progress. Even the leading powers of the West looked with envy and admiration at its sputniks and cosmonauts. At the same time, the economic growth of the country was quite impressive, and its leaders', Nikita Khrushchev's in particular, pompous talks about overcoming the production levels of the USA in many basic industrial products and food stuffs, meat included, did not seem all that farfetched (Hanson 2003). It is less generally known that at the same time the Soviet Union made major investments in fashion design (Zhuravlev and Gronow 2005). To promote fashion and improve the standard of clothing was an essential part of the general policy of improving the standards of material culture in the Soviet Union. The Soviet Union certainly never enjoyed a high reputation among the world of *haute couture*. Its standardized, industrially mass-produced clothes had quite a bad reputation both among Soviet consumers and foreign visitors. If anything, Soviet citizens were for the most part unsatisfied with the domestic supply of clothing. To for- eign visitors, fashion in the streets of Moscow, not to mention smaller provincial towns or the countryside, looked rather dull, uniform, and grey.[1]

At the same time, the Soviet Union had one of the world's largest organizations of fashion design, all planned, financed, and supported by the state. All in all, four huge, parallel organizations existed side by side in the country from the 1960s. The four ministries, those of light industry, trade, local industry, and everyday services, all had their own extensive fashion design organizations which in turn had their own units on every administrative level from the central, or *All-Union*, to the Republican, from the regional to the local. Thousands of professional and well- educated designers worked in these Soviet institutions of fashion design. They designed, according to annual plans, thousands of new fashionable clothes and accessories for industrial mass production, for fashion shows and for the smaller and bigger fashion ateliers, as well as clothes patterns to be sewn at home.

By the mid 1960s, these institutes of fashion design had certainly accomplished a lot to be proud of. They promoted Soviet fashion and Soviet culture of dress by increasing the variety of industrially produced clothes and dresses as well as by their quite spectacular fashion shows, which were well received both at home and abroad. Thus, Soviet fashion contributed to the Soviet effort in the peaceful competition between the two world systems, socialism and capitalism. As became obvious during the 1970s, not even the intensified efforts put into fashion and fashion design could overcome the inherent rigidity of economic and bureaucratic limitations of the planned economy.

The reason for the discrepancy between the *input* and *output* of the Soviet system of fashion is an interesting one. The problem was quite well known to Soviet fashion experts and economic planners. Various and repeated suggestions were made to solve it. Serious shortages, problems with quality, and the limited variety of designs regularly on sale in Soviet shops certainly did not plague the fashion industry of the USSR alone. They were common in most fields of Soviet 'light' or consumer goods industry from food to private cars (see, for example, Osokina 1998; Gronow 2003; and Siegelbaum 2008). However, these problems probably plagued the clothes industry more than many other fields of consumption. The rapid, seasonal change of fashion did not, after all, fit into the system of a planned economy. After the short period of the Cultural revolution of the 1920s with its attempts to create anti-fashion and its radical demands for abolishing all fashion as an unnecessary and dangerous bourgeois remnant alien to socialist society, no one seriously suggested any longer that the authorities and economic planners should totally neglect or try to do away with the social mechanism of fashion. It was, on the contrary, more or less taken for granted.[2] Clothes designers and producers as well as their customers simply had to learn to live and cope with it.[3] The promotion of good taste and the proper dress code was an important part of this coping strategy.

Soviet ideals of good taste

In the immediate post-war decades, both the Soviet media and the professionals of fashion design saw it as their important task to propagate fashion thereby cultivating the taste of Soviet citizens. Articles and press reports published in numerous fashion journals, women's magazines, and central and local newspapers propagated fashionable designs, gave advice about new trends in fashion, answered general questions concerning how to dress properly, and discussed the important problems of the role and nature of fashion under socialism and in the Soviet Union in particular. Despite the fact that some ideologists obviously still thought that fashion, with its rapid and as such irrational changes of style which only lead to the artificial ageing of clothes, did not really belong to socialism and a centrally planned economy, there seemed to reign a general consensus that, at least for the time being, the socialist planned economy had to learn to live with fashion. Even if one wanted to, it could not be totally suppressed, only modified and moderated, to suit the planned economy better. In practice, Soviet fashion was ideally a slowed-down fashion, functional, practical, and as inconspicuous as possible. It was believed that it should avoid any kind of extravagance and unnecessary whims in its creations. In cultivating her or his taste the Soviet consumer should follow the rule of the golden mean and prefer a proper fit rather than running after all the caprices of fashion. Above all, she or he should learn to adapt fashionable creations to his or her own personal style and needs.

In practice the advice given by fashion designers and consultants to the ordinary consumer was quite simple: try to avoid extremes and any abrupt changes! Respect the classical rules of harmony and proportion in every aspect of your appearance! Let us take some typical examples from the fashion pages of the popular local press. E.G. Solov'yeva (1963) wrote in the local Chelyabinsk based youth newspaper that:

> the very word fashion is used among us in another meaning than in the West. If one dresses fashionably in the West that means that one attempts to draw to oneself the attention of those surrounding one. With us fashion means above all the culture of dress, the high standard of aesthetic taste. The main traits of our fashion are simplicity and comfort. We are against all kinds of extravagancy and exaggeration in clothing, against the love of form for the sake of form alone.

In the same spirit the author of the article '*Odevat'sya so vkusom*' ('How to dress with taste') declared that:

> we call caprices of fashion all kinds of strange exaggerations and deviances from the generally accepted norms. These should be avoided by all means in dress … Such caprices of fashion will pass away rapidly, as quite unnecessary and contingent, since they do not follow the demands of beauty and practicality. Instead the basic and generally accepted lines will stay.
>
> (*Zaporozhskaya Pravda*, 19 August 1960)

A local fashion designer from Cherkessk, A. Tikhonov (1960), summarized this view quite concisely: 'One should follow fashion but one should also remember that beauty is above all modest and does not demand too much attention'.

Soviet fashion was moderate in another respect too: it was never sexually provocative and thus respected the rules of common decency. Warnings against the wearing in public of low-necked dresses or too daring, sleeveless summer gowns were commonly heard both in the fashion columns of the popular Soviet press and in the more professional fashion journals. The question of women's trousers, widely regarded as threatening common decency by blurring the traditional borders between the male and the female sexes was one of the big issues of the 1960s.[4] In many ways, similar moral and aesthetic worries and questions were also raised at this time in the popular press and women's magazines of the West. The mini skirt, which entered the Soviet world of fashion after a couple of years 'delay', caused a moral panic in the Western world of fashion. The big difference between them, in addition to the relative slowness of Soviet fashion, was that the sexuality of fashion was not openly confronted or discussed in the Soviet Union.[5] Everyone seemed to know without saying what was proper and what not, what was allowed to be presented, what not. Soviet fashion models learned never to adopt any sexually provocative poses in their photo sessions. Lingerie, underwear, and more daring beach fashion such as bikinis were simply never shown on the pages of women's journals or at fashion shows.

The other big difference in the public image of Soviet fashion compared to its Western counterpart was the absence of commercial advertisements and promotions on the pages of journals and magazines. Soviet fashion journals and other publications openly promoted the designs of particular fashion houses and their fashion designers by presenting them to their readers as examples of the latest fashion and good taste and thus worth buying and wearing. Many fashion designers and models became real Soviet celebrities too. Most of the designs were, however, totally beyond the reach of ordinary readers. In the best case, they could dream of sewing themselves a copy by following the pattern of a fashionable dress attached to a journal as best they could with the resources at their disposal. Therefore, there was certainly some truth in the claims of Soviet fashion theoreticians that Soviet fashion, in contrast to its Western counterpart, did not have to appeal to the 'base and lower instincts of man' with the sole purpose of seducing him or her to buy the dress or piece of cloth advertised or put on sale. Instead, Soviet fashion designers and their customers more often faced another kind of a dilemma: what was the purpose and use of designing and propagating new, beautiful, and fashionable clothes if they were not on sale anywhere? The other side of the coin was the question of what should be done with all the millions of those industrially produced clothes which were a far cry from the creations shown on the journals' pages and which the customers only bought if there was absolutely nothing better available to them. This dilemma was discussed all the time and various solutions offered to it both among Soviet experts and in the Soviet press – without much practical effect. The standard suggestion was to allow the production and sale of 'small series' in fashion houses and in their own shops (such shops known as *boutiques* in the West were called in Russian *firmennye magaziny*) (Lordkipanidze 1974). This idea remained largely a suggestion since it did not really fit into the general outline of the centrally planned economy.

The informalization of the Soviet dress code and petit-bourgeois taste

An important change or at least reorientation took place in the Soviet discourse on fashion sometime during the 1960s. Instead of moralizing about spontaneous fashion, which supposedly corrupted Soviet youth by misleading it with Western ideals and idols, the Soviet gate keepers of common morality and decency started increasingly to warn their readers not to draw too hasty and simple a conclusion about the moral character of a person based only on his or her dress and general appearance. A young man who looked like the notorious *stilyagi*[6] because of his exaggerated dress could just as well be following the latest 'official' Soviet fashion copied from the pages of the Moscow *Zhurnal mod* or another popular fashion journal. What was even more important, despite the fact that he might be dressed in a quite exaggerated manner thus breaking the rules of good taste, he did not necessarily have to be a total good-for-nothing or a lazy drunkard. Quite the contrary, as experience showed, the *stilyagi* could just as well turn out to be quite excellent workers and honest members of the *Komsomol* Youth League.[7]

The worrying examples of *stilyagi* vehemently and repeatedly discussed in the Soviet press had their female counterparts. In the case of women, the rules of decency were, however, more openly to do with sex, concerning the questions of too revealing dresses or overstepping the traditional borders between the male and female dress (the case of women's trousers). In both respects, Soviet rules of decency and proper dressing gradually became more liberal during the 1960s. What is even more interesting, the previous strict prohibitions, which were actually enforced in the streets with the help of the local people's militia, gradually gave way to more flexible instructions allowing, and expecting from, the individual more freedom in deciding what was appropriate, given the circumstances and the company in question. External social control thus gave way to internal self-control. One could therefore speak about processes of informalization and individualization even in the Soviet Union resembling similar developments almost at the same time in the capitalist West initiated by and often associated with the youth revolution of the 1960s (Wouters 2007). Just like Soviet fashion, this Soviet process of informalization was, however, moderate and slow compared to the West.

Soviet ideologists of fashion continuously warned their audiences and readers of the danger of getting carried away by all kinds of caprices of fashion which, if adopted, would only lead to unnecessary extravagancies with the sole purpose of showing off, distinguishing oneself from one's peers. To let oneself be seduced in this way by the commodities of material culture was, in the opinion of these experts, a typical sign and harmful remnant of a petit-bourgeois mentality (*meshchanstvo*), which should be rooted out from socialist society and culture where higher spiritual goals and values reigned sovereign instead. Paradoxically, if we are to believe historical and empirical studies about the taste of different social classes and groups in European bourgeois society, the very advice and attitudes concerning fashion, style, and proper conduct, which these Soviet experts recommended, followed as a matter of fact the typical petit-bourgeois disposition towards the new consumer culture (Bourdieu 1984: 352). Members of the petite bourgeoisie were by no means generally disposed towards indulgence or extravagance, nor were they inclined to experiment with novelties or easily seduced by the 'caprices' of fashion. The first disposition was typical of – if anyone – the new economic elites, the second of the new upwardly mobile cultural elites of bourgeois society. The petite bourgeoisie appreciated, on the contrary, precisely the values propagated by Soviet experts on taste and fashion: in its work it valued order, rigour, and care, in its everyday aesthetics, austere and traditional values. According to Bourdieu, the new professional executive class or lower civil servants in the France of 1960s preferred 'sober and correct' clothes (1984: 351–52). In other words, the Soviet, socialist aesthetics of dress – and consumption in general – was nothing more than the loyal image of the petit-bourgeois mentality! It repeatedly and dutifully repeated the warning common to the European humanistic tradition of not resigning to fashion's temptation. One should instead always try to preserve one's personal style, that is, to protect one's real inner self against all such external social forces like fashion.

Conclusions

The highest principle in the minds of the Soviet experts and propagandists that should have guided both Soviet fashion design and their customers' taste in selecting their clothes properly was the principle of harmony. The post-war Soviet ideology of fashion was thus basically inspired by the European ideals of *Bildung* personified in such European cultural heroes as Kant and Schiller. It could however just as easily refer to its own Russian cultural tradition and its own cultural idols like Pushkin or Chekhov. Had not Pushkin contrasted Yevgeny Onegin's London dandyism with Tatyana's natural beauty and modesty? Had not Chekhov let one of his main characters, doctor Astrov, formulate the very maxim which then became the leading principle of the Soviet cultural policy, fashion included: 'In a human being everything should be beautiful: his face, and dress, and the spirit, and the thoughts'?

   If one, however, had to name one classical source that better than anyone else acted as an ideal for Soviet aesthetics and the etiquette of fashion, it would without doubt be Jean-Jacques Rousseau, who in describing the taste of the main character in his *Julie, or New Heloise*, expressed in a concise form the basic contradiction between on the one hand extravagancy and fashion and on the other hand good taste and modesty which became the golden rule of Soviet fashion. For Julie, novelty is not a temptation but rather a reason to reject things since it gives them value which is not genuine:

> As the law of the mode is inconstant and ruinous, so hers [Julie's] is economical and durable. What good taste once approves of is forever fine; if it is rarely stylish, on the other hand it is never ridiculous, and in modest simplicity from the compatibility of elements it derives sure and unalterable rules, which remain when the modes have past.
>
> (Rousseau 1997 [1761]: 450)

Soviet fashion was in many ways a good example of the dual and ambivalent nature of Soviet modernity. On the one hand, the Soviet authorities actively promoted fashion and invested a lot of resources in the establishment and development of the basic social institutions of fashion design, following the example of the most famous Parisian fashion houses. They took for granted that Soviet citizens, and women in particular, had a right to and needed new fashionable clothes which allowed them to express their own style and individuality better. On the other hand, fashion was an anomaly in socialist society since its contingent and eternally changing nature did not at all fit into the basic principles of the centrally planned economy, which promised to satisfy only the 'rational' or basic needs of the human being and not all his/her personal whims. Therefore, Soviet women and men were expected above all to exercise moderation in their choice of clothes as in all the other fields of individual consumption.

At the same time, we can observe interesting processes of informalization and individualization in the Soviet clothes culture almost parallel, possibly with a small delay, to their Western 'bourgeois' counterparts. First, the strict traditional line dividing masculine and feminine dress codes gradually eroded during the 1960s and 1970s. Women wearing trousers were no longer an anomaly. Second, a crucial change in the everyday moral discourse took place with the recognition that one could not and should not draw any straightforward and hasty conclusions about a person's character and inner self from their outward appearance. In other words, one's dress was no longer regarded as a straightforward sign of one's social standing and personal worth as it had been in the 'old world'. People could thus have multiple roles and even identities.

What has all this to do with cultural and social developments in the present state of post-Soviet societies?

In his interesting study based on observations and interviews with people from various conservative or nationalistic organizations in the city of Barnaul, *The Patriotism of Despair*, Serguei Oushakine argued that the ordinary citizens' reactions – and the traumas associated with them – to the rapid economic and social transformation reflected the fact that 'people had difficulty accepting monetized social exchanges when those exchanges were not accompanied by the expected symbolic context' (2008: 27). The previous relationships, familiar from the Soviet system of economic exchange, between the pecuniary exchange and ethical assumptions had been seriously disrupted. Previously:

> money and monetary exchanges were viewed as part of a larger, non-monetized, symbolic system rather than as a form of activity opposed to this system. The balance between the individual and the collective was achieved through maintaining a particular form of relationship between the short-term sphere of politico-economic exchanges and the long-term sphere of morality.
>
> (Oushakine 2008: 23)

One could, admittedly with some reservations, apply the same kind of reasoning to the transformation in the role of fashion in the post-Soviet moral economy. The system of fashion under socialism was typically embedded in a wider moral discourse about rational needs and the ideal Soviet type of personality, which in many ways restricted and moderated the impact of fashion. At the same time, the principal incompatibility of fashion with the planned economy threatened to challenge the moral order of the socialist society. In this respect fashion resembled monetary relations which, at least in the minds of the authorities, constantly threatened to get out of hand and begin a life of their own, thus changing the priorities of the economic order (concretely in the figure of a black market speculator and other illegal private entrepreneur).

Under the new conditions of the market economy fashion has been given free reign to act on its own, following its own economic and social logic. The democratization and individualization of fashion, essential to the project of modernity, were strongly moderated and restricted under socialism. Therefore it is quite understandable that a person's appearance has, under the present conditions of increasing social inequality and uncertainty about status, become once again more closely associated with the economic and social status of that individual. In present day Russia, the social role of fashion thus resembles, to a certain extent, traditional societies or early modernity more than is the case in the West. Post-Soviet societies are notorious for their conspicuous consumption, which has produced rather easily recognizable stereotypes of clothing, 'uniforms', signalling quite directly both the economic status as well as the 'clan' adherence of their wearers. Fashion is, just as it was under socialism, embedded in the wider moral–economic order of the post-socialist society which hinders its further individualization and democratization.

Notes

1 For an interesting photo-report on the 'street fashion' in Moscow, see Levashova (1971) in whose opinion Moscovites dressed better and much more fashionably than the rest of the country.

2 In the collection of essays edited by V.I. Tolstykh (1973) with the characteristic title, *Moda: za i protiv* ('Fashion: for and against'), the majority of the contributors were definitely 'for fashion' even though some of them also expressed highly critical opinions about the frivolity of fashion.

3 The economist Braverman's article 'Moda glazami ekonomista' ('Fashion through the eyes of an economist'), published in 1963, made a sober attempt to analyse the phenomenon of fashion in its relation to the planned economy. According to Braverman, it would be totally impossible for the socialist economy to clothe the whole population according to the latest fashion. The promise to satisfy all the needs of man inherent in communism only concerned the so-called rational needs. Obviously the need to dress fashionably was not rational. If Braverman's position was more or less typical of its time, A. Levashova and I. Gordon's article '*Moda i ekonomika*' ('Fashion and economics') published in *Pravda* almost ten years later (1971) categorically declared that the wish to dress fashionably was totally legitimate even under socialism. The fact that the article was published in the central organ of the Communist Party gave additional weight to its opinion.

4 As late as 1964 the Soviet state TV and broadcasting company had an official policy of forbidding women to wear trousers at work (Vasil'yev 2006: 324).

5 In this respect it followed the general Soviet attitude towards sexuality (Kon 1993).

6 Originally, *stilyagi* referred to the youth fashion of the early 1950s with extremely narrow black trousers and high-pointed black shoes, which the Soviet authorities claimed to be a dangerous imitation of the capitalist West. Gradually it became a generic name for all deviations from the proper dress code associated with the style of the Soviet male youth.

7 G. Aksel'rod's (1959) article '*O vkusakh nado sporit*'!' ('One should dispute about the matters of taste!') is an excellent example of Soviet investigative journalism, which typically used concrete cases to discuss problematic ethical issues. In the end, the author leaves his case open and cannot really decide whether the local youth with their exaggerated fashionable dress and taste for Western art and jazz music should be morally condemned or not. These very same youngsters proved to be exemplary workmen with very good and civilized manners. They did not even drink or harass women!

Bibliography

Aksel'rod, G. (1959) 'O vkusakh nado sporit'!' ('One should dispute about the matters of taste!'), *Kazakhstanskaya Pravda*, 31 March.

Berman, M. (1983) *All That Is Solid Melts into Air: The Experience of Modernity*, New York: Simon and Schuster.

Bourdieu, P. (1984) *Distinction: A Social Critique of the Judgement of Taste*, Cambridge, MA: Harvard University Press.

Braverman, A. (1963) 'Moda glazami ekonomista' ('Fashion through the eyes of an economist'), *Dekorativnoye iskusstvo SSSR*, 10 (1963): 12–13.

David-Fox, M. (2006) 'Multiple modernities vs. neo-traditionalism: on recent debates in Russian and Soviet history', *Jahrbücher für Geschichte Osteuropas*, 54: 535–55.

Fitzpatrick, S. (2000) 'Introduction', in S. Fitzpatrick (ed.) *Stalinism: New Directions*, London/New York: Routledge.

Gronow, J. (2003) *Caviar with Champagne: The Common Luxury and the Ideals of Good Life in Stalin's Russia*, London/New York: Berg.

Gronow, J. and Zhuravlev, S. (forthcoming) 'The book about healthy and tasty food: the establishment of Soviet *haute cuisine*', in J. Strong (ed.) *Educating Tastes*, Lincoln, NE: University of Nebraska Press.

Hanson, Ph. (2003) *The Rise and Fall of the Soviet Economy: An Economic History of the USSR from 1945*, Harlow: Longman.

Kon, I.S. (1993) *Sex and the Russian Society*, Bloomington: Indiana University Press.

Kotkin, S. (1995) *The Magnetic Mountain: Stalinism as Civilization*, Berkeley: University of California Press.

——(2001) 'Modern times: the Soviet Union and the interwar conjecture', *Kritika: Explorations in Russian and Eurasian History*, 2/1: 111–64.

Levashova, A.A. (1971) 'Moskvichi na ulitse' ('Moscovites in the streets'), *Dekorativnoye iskusstvo SSSR*, 1/158: 41–45.

Levashova, A. and Gordon, I. (1971) 'Moda i ekonomika' ('Fashion and economy'), *Pravda*, 9 May.

Lordkipanidze, N. (1974) 'Terpelivo idti k tseli' ('Go to the goal with patience'), An interview with A.A. Levashova and V.V. Chertovskaya. *Nedelya*, 7 April.

Neidhart, Ch. (2003) *Russia's Carnival: The Smells, Sights and Sounds of Transition*, Lanham, MD: Rowman & Littlefield Publishers.

'Odevat'sya so vkusom' ('How to dress with taste') (1960), *Zaporozhskaya Pravda*, 19 August.

Osokina, E. (1998) *Everyday Stalinism: The Politics of Shortages and Famine in the Soviet Union, 1928–1941*, Armonk, NY: M.E. Sharpe.

Oushakine, S.A. (2008) *The Patriotism of Despair: Nation, War and Loss in Russia*, Ithaca/London: Cornell University Press.

Rousseau, J.-J. (1997) *Julie, or New Heloise: Letters of Two Lovers Who Live in Small Town at the Foot of the Alps*, Ph. Stewart and J. Vacher (trans.), Hannover, NH: University Press of New England.

Siegelbaum, L. (2008) *Cars for Comrades: The Life of the Soviet Automobile*, Ithaca/London: Cornell University Press.

Simmel, G. (1905) *Philosophie der Mode*, Berlin: Pan.

Solov'yeva, E.G. (1963) 'Devushkam polezno znat' ('What the girls should know'), *Komsomolets*, 10 March.

Stites, R. (1992) *Russian Popular Culture: Entertainment and Society since 1900*, Cambridge: Cambridge University Press.

Tikhonov, A. (1960) 'Krasivoye – znachit skromnoye' ('Beautiful means modest'), *Leninskoye znamya*, 22 July.

Tolstykh, V.I. (ed.) (1973) *Moda: za i protiv*, Moskva: Iskusstvo.

Vasil'yev, A. (2006) *Russkaya moda*, Moskva: Slovo.

Wouters, G. (2007) *Informalization: Manners and Emotions since 1890*, London: Sage.

Zakharova, L.V. (2004) 'Kazhdoy sovetskoy zhenshchine – plat'ye ot Diora! Frantsuzskoye vliyaniye v sovetskoy mode 1950–60-kh gg.', in *Sotsial'naya istoriya: Yezhegodnik*, 4 (2001/2002): 347–53.

——(2010) 'Dior in Moscow: a taste for luxury in Soviet fashion under N.S.Khrushchev', in S. Read and D. Crowley (eds), *Socialist Luxuries*, DeKalb, IL: Northern University Press.

Zhuravlev, S.V. and Gronow, J. (2005) 'Krasota pod kontrolem gosudarstva: osobennosti i etapy stanovleniya sovetskoy mody', *The Soviet and Post-Soviet Review*, 32/1: 1–90.

Part III

Culture

This section examines the perpetual process of self-definition and striving for conceptual self-understanding, so characteristic of the Russian cultural tradition in relation to Western culture. Foreign elements are not only translated into Russian equivalents, but at the same time transformed into something completely new, lacking the initial connection both to the Own and the Alien, a new that can be regarded as the 'Third', the synthetic level of meaning arising from cultural juxtapositions. For this reason the adoption of the foreign structures and their gradual transformation into something that is considered 'Own', and specifically Russian, is a fruitful starting point for the study of Russian culture in particular. The history of the process can be traced back to earlier periods in Russian history, but the issues involved have gained new topicality as a result of recent social upheavals.

The notions of truth, utopia, and revolution are among the terms that may occur in a number of different contexts; they admit of several interpretations, and this makes them particularly interesting in the Russian context. They involve contact and cross-breeding between the Western and Russian traditions, whereby the relationship between the Own and the Alien is highlighted. The 'truth as it is' propounded by the Russian realists almost always includes a specific understanding of 'what the truth should be like'; this notion, for its part, is a fundamental tenet of socialist realism. In Russian postmodernism, the denial of one truth, reality, or great tale is not as self-evident as it is in the West. Utopia is one of the fundamental concepts of Russian culture; it has been interpreted in particular ways in the context of revolutionary doctrine and, subsequently, of Soviet reality, but it also exerts a strong influence on the post-socialist and postmodernist interpretation of reality. Revolution, on the other hand, is much more than a concrete political concept. Russian cultural history may be examined as a continual series of upheavals, where a phenomenon or a trend that was once perceived as new and innovative comes to be rejected as outmoded and reactionary. It usually then recedes to the periphery of culture and later returns to the forefront at a new stage in history.

Russian culture is approached from various angles in the six chapters, but the assimilation and appropriation of the Own and the Alien is shared by all of them. The issues examined encompass over a thousand years of Russian culture, from folklore to the contemporary uses of the Internet. None of the chapters are devoted to a single art form, but strive to unite different fields of culture. The point of view varies from general overviews to entirely novel scientific endeavours.

The chapter by Boris Gasparov offers a comparative analysis of features of poetic language, imagery, and rhetoric in two major traditions of folk epic poetry: Finnish (related to the *Kalevala*) and Russian (*byliny*), which coexisted for centuries in close conjunction in East Karelia. The conclusion is that while direct points of influence between the two traditions are scarce (primarily because of the language barrier), their ways of poetic symbolization, deeply rooted in their discourses, show a fundamental kinship. This means that both epics, arising from a scanty, secluded, and marginalized environment, strive to create a world of magnificence and formidable power. The situation is not unlike that of Homer's epic memories of a world of magnificent richness – memories retained in an environment totally alien to them, in the depth of Greece's dark ages.

In Chapter 11, Tomi Huttunen discusses autogenesis as a special trait pertaining to Russian culture. The notion of autogenesis – the idea of spontaneous and rootless formations in culture – is essential in discussing Russian avant-garde artists' and theorists' way of defining their position in relation to (a) European influences and (b) the previous cultural tradition. It is evident that in human culture nothing is born out of nothing, by itself, but everything exists in a historical continuum of tradition and intellectual communication. Suggesting the existence of autogenetic, spontaneous formations and self-creation in culture therefore seems absurd. Nevertheless, autogenesis as a declaration is very often emphasized in Russian culture, especially by those representing abruptness and unexpectedness.

The chapter by Gennady Obatnin dwells upon the history of one aesthetical and social notion, *poshlost'*. Usually translated into English as 'banality' or 'triviality', with further implications of 'carnality', this concept has aroused the special interest of Western visitors to Russia. When approaching the study of the concept of *poshlost'*, one is confronted with two important factors. For a native of the Russian language and culture, there is nothing about this term that demands conceptualization or any other form of defamiliarizing critique. The need for such distance only arises in the context of an external point of view. A common theme in discussions of *poshlost'* is the impossibility of preserving the word's semantic fullness when translating it into foreign languages. Description of the concept cannot be organized through analogies with other cultures and languages. It is precisely for this reason that *poshlost'* is logically placed among those terms that form the basis for a specific piece of the Russian conceptual picture of the world.

Evgenii Bershtein approaches the Russian religious philosophy of the early twentieth century (Rozanov, Florensky, Berdyayev) from a rather exceptional point of view. The terms in which today's Russian intellectuals tend to conceptualize homosexuality may strike a Western observer as pre-modern. However, these terms are rooted in a number of specific modern and modernist philosophical ideas that preoccupied the Russian intelligentsia in the *fin de siècle*. By accounting for the intellectual roots of today's ideological discussions, we can

reach a better understanding of the cultural specificity of the attitudes to (homo)
sexuality common among post-Soviet Russia's educated elite.

Chapter 14, by Sergei Shtyrkov, examines how the religious nationalists in
Northern Ossetia have had to copy many of the main traits of the dominant
religion that they oppose, while at the same time aiming to construct a system of
faith going beyond the restrictions of the modern Western conception of religion.
Religion is closely bound up with the concept of nationhood in the social consciousness of contemporary Russia, and a nationalistic discourse penetrates Russian
religious life.

Ilya Utekhin's chapter explores the Russians' use of the Internet as an integral
part of contemporary culture. The use of the Internet for social networking began
later in Russia than in the West, and its first manifestation was active blogging,
especially on the *LiveJournal* platform, which remains popular, but has been
overshadowed lately by social networking sites analogous to *Classmates* and *Facebook*.
The chapter relates these Russian forms of social networking to their Western
counterparts.

10 *Spiritus loci*: two East Karelian folklore epic traditions

Boris Gasparov

One region – two poetic cultures

It is well known that the epicentre of both Finnish and Russian folk epic poetry, upon its discovery in the nineteenth century, turned out to be situated in two closely adjacent parts of a fairly compact region, comprising a Northern part of the Olonets province (*guberniya*) (Northern Onezhye) and a Western part of the Arkhangel'sk *guberniya* (Viena Karelia).[1] The Romantic consciousness treasures the national folk epic as the most elevated and presumably most 'authentic' expression of the national spirit; in this respect, the magnificently archaic and solemn discourse of both Finnish-Karelian runes and Russian folk epic poems (*bylinas*) did not fail to inspire the public imagination. They sounded like a voice from the primordial past, a time when either nation's most fundamental spiritual features had presumably been born. It was a matter of no small surprise, then, that these crucial testimonies to the 'organic' depth of the national tradition were to be found in a marginal, ethnically and linguistically mixed habitat, while what each nation's heartland could show in this respect were their scattered echoes at best.[2]

The situation looked particularly intriguing from the Finnish side. After all, the cradle of Kalevalan poetry[3] not only belonged to Russia administratively but had some of its crucial cultural features related to the Russian habitat. First among them was the Orthodox faith, common to all the inhabitants of the region. All the singers of the runes were Orthodox, as is evidenced, among other things, by the names many of them were given when they were baptized, such as Arhippa, Ontrei, Iivana, Mihkaili, Olonja, and so on. As records show, many of them were descendants of migrants from the West, who had moved eastward in the sixteenth and seventeenth centuries to escape pressures from the Lutheran church.[4] Yet many Russian inhabitants of the region had moved there to escape religious persecution as well: they were *Old Believers* who had found a refuge in the far North. In the 1830s, the time of Lönnrot's expeditions, the Old Believers' communities, both Karelian and Russian, still lived practically undisturbed side by side with members of the Orthodox parish, or 'mir' (*mierolaiset*).[5] Later, during the severe persecutions of the 1850s, when many Old Believers, their monasteries (*sketes*) and places of worship destroyed,[6] were compelled to bow, at least officially, to the Orthodox church, families still remained confessionally mixed: women tended to keep the Old Faith, while men might have felt stronger motivations to convert.[7] Many if not all singers of Kalevalan songs were either Old Believers or belonged to families with Old Believer connections (Pentikäinen and Raudalainen 1999: 48). Likewise, according to A. Gil'ferding, *bylinas* were equally popular among Old Believers and members of the mainstream Orthodox community.[8]

Another cause for the migration, from the West and South alike, was economic. The traditional cut-and-burn agriculture by which inhabitants of this unyielding environment used to support themselves (in addition to fishing and hunting) had been banned since the seventeenth century by the Swedish administration (Siikala 2002b: 41; Karhu 1994: 59), and began to be banned in the nineteenth century by the Russian one.[9] The ban pushed people into ever more remote and inaccessible areas where it could not be easily enforced.

The cultural 'chronotope' of the region can be characterized as a curious mixture of strong adherence to tradition, on the one hand, and a resistant, even defiant attitude toward the world outside, on the other; and by an economic 'backwardness' that in fact needed to be maintained as the only realistic means of survival under extremely inhospitable conditions. The traditional economy together with religious conservatism worked as forces of preservation that allowed the epic poetic tradition to stay alive in all its archaic magnificence.[10] Moreover, it might have been the dire state of agriculture that contributed, paradoxically, to the thriving of the poetic tradition: it absolved the local peasant from 'crushing' (to use Gil'ferding's word) agricultural labour, which sapped all the energies of his counterpart in more productive areas, and by the same token encouraged alternative occupations, such as fishing, hunting, and various crafts, that were less monotonous and physically taxing.[11] The two principal ingredients of the peculiar spiritual climate of the region – resistance to external pressures and traditionalism – were succinctly formulated by Gil'ferding as 'freedom and backwater conditions' (*svoboda i glush'*) (Gil'ferding 1871/1983: 24).

Despite the fact that the two major folk epic cultures coexisted for centuries side by side in a very similar material and spiritual environment, there are few signs of their awareness of, let alone influence on, each other. The linguistic barrier proved to be too high to allow a meaningful cultural cross-pollination, despite the common denominator of the Orthodox church service.[12] To be sure, the language of Kalevalan poetry featured a number of borrowed East Slavic words, usually in a well-assimilated form (many of which subsequently entered the Finnish literary language via Lönnrot's *Kalevala*), but they testify to practical contacts more than to a deeper cultural influence. Attempts to find signs of linguistic cross-breeding in terms of syntax and rhetoric have proved to be inconclusive so far.[13] On the other hand, the presence of words of Germanic origin in the poetic language of the runes,[14] as well as the abundance of seafaring situations in their stories, seem to point to their connection to Ostrobothnia (Siikala 2002a: 175).

The same can be said about the subject matter of the epic 'stories'. Although some common motifs in Finnish and Russian folk songs were noted already in the nineteenth and early twentieth centuries (Krohn 1885; Mansikka 1906, 1907), few instances of direct borrowing have been discovered so far and belong to the margins of each nation's folk epic corpus.[15] Paradoxically, it was the conservative predisposition and the spirit of independence that both communities of the region shared that had prevented them from entering into a more active cultural intercourse.

Both folk epic traditions reflect memories going back to the Middle Ages. In the case of *bylinas*, it was the time of Kievan Rus' and the Tatar invasion; vague as *bylinas*' references to Prince Vladimir and his court are, they contain some tangible details of the Southern steppe landscape that could not have found their way to the North other than by memory transmission. Likewise, stories about adventurous maritime expeditions and battles in Kalevalan runes reflect memories of the era of the Vikings and the Crusades. On the other hand, both epic traditions bear traces of a more ancient cultural layer, perhaps going far back in time. In the case of *bylinas*, it consists of vestiges of pre-Christian East Slavic mythology and pagan deities and rites. As to the runes, their cosmogony myth shows a tangible kinship with South Asian mythology (Siikala 2002a; Haavio 1952), while many instances of magic and sorcery point to the culture of sub-Arctic Siberian shamanism (Comparetti 1892; Siikala 2002a).

Although the co-presence of these layers in *bylinas* and runes is undeniable,[16] a great deal depends on which one of them is highlighted by one or another scholar. Emphasizing the historical background draws the folk epos more closely to the national tradition and its observable historical past. From this perspective, the two epic traditions part company, in terms of their origins: one points to pre-Mongol Kiev, the other to the Baltic shores; their present situation comes across as secondary – the last vestige of their past glory, preserved due to the remoteness and seclusion of their location. In contradistinction to this, foregrounding the mythological element includes the epics in a context that is much more extensive with regard to both space and time – so extensive in fact that its maintenance indicates a more active role of the *locus* and its inhabitants in shaping those extremely distant echoes into magnificently elaborate epic tales. By the same token, it suggests a certain degree of commonality between the two traditions – at least, a commonality of spirit stemming from identical environmental and similar cultural–economic conditions.

In this regard, the first half of the twentieth century could be called a time of 'separation', when attempts to connect the folk epic directly with the national historical past definitely gained the upper hand,[17] sometimes to the point of vulgar literalness. In works by Rybakov and his followers, *bylinas* were treated as a documentary supplement to Kievan Chronicles, whose imagery allowed him to come to far-reaching conclusions about Kievan material and political culture.[18] Propp's voice, urging caution and emphasizing the creative nature of epic stories (Propp 1958/99),[19] sounded lonely at the time.[20] On the Finnish side, the historical approach also remained dominant for several decades, after the classical works by Kaarle Krohn early in the century (Krohn 1924).[21] A strong stance against the predominant tide, somewhat reminiscent of Propp's contemporary opposition in Russia, was taken by Haavio (1952) in his elaborate attempt to reclaim the mythological background of the runes. In works by Finnish scholars of the last twenty years one can see a new rapprochement with Lönnrot's original view, according to which the runes, while reflecting numerous archaic themes and motifs, attained their epic 'duration' relatively recently, perhaps no earlier than the eighteenth century.[22]

Emphasizing the pre-Christian genealogy of the epics highlights their spiritual, magic, and mystical aspect, while a historical approach casts them into reminiscent echoes of documented military and courteous exploits of the past. By the same token, the two approaches enhance or reduce, respectively, the role of the Karelian locus vis-à-vis the national mainland. Thus, in the 'history vs myth' controversy the origin of the epics and their interpretation are closely entangled. The question of whether the epic stories, both Russian and Finnish, had originated in the Middle Ages in a different environment, and migrated to the East Karelian region later, or were primarily the achievement of migrants to the region, who transformed vestiges of the memories they had brought with them into an epic discourse, is at the same time a question about the nature of these epic stories: are they memories of heroic deeds or expressions of a world view?

It should be reiterated once again that whatever the story of how they found themselves in the Karelian–North-Western Russian locus, the Kalevalan and Russian folk epics, while coexisting in the region, remained, with minor exceptions,[23] largely independent from, even unaware of, each other. Given the sensitivity of questions of kinship and provenance, due to the sad history of the twentieth century, it looks almost like a blessing that so few signs of their relationship are visible. This opens the way for a comparative analysis free from 'accursed questions' of influence and origin. In this respect, the differences between the two poetic discourses may prove to be as illuminating as the similarities. Moreover, sometimes, overtly different features, when looked upon without any claim of genealogical kinship, reveal deeply ingrained similarities. It is the search for such deeply rooted parallels between the two epic discourses, which owe more to the commonality of their habitat than to any direct intercourse, that constitutes the goal of this chapter.

The stories and the discourses

The Russians 'discovered' their Northern folk epics – at least, on a major scale – much later than the Finns; when the first volume of P. Rybnikov's collection appeared in 1861 (Rybnikov 1861–67),[24] it was met with some incredulity.[25] The decisive breakthrough occurred some ten years later, when A. Gil'ferding published his monumental *Onezhskiye byliny* (Gil'ferding 1871–73). By that time, grandiloquent Romantic visions of the first half of the century gave way to the 'positivist' spirit of precise recordkeeping.[26] No attempt was made on the Russian side to congregate separate epic stories into a super-narrative, even though singers tended to perform songs as a cycle of a sort, united by the figure of the central hero.[27] But if compared, irrespective of the question of influence, the stories told in Kalevalan runes and *bylinas* exhibit more than a few parallels.

In particular, the cycle about Dobrynya brushes on many points with Kalevalan runes of the Lemminkäinen–Ahti–Kaukomieli cycle (three related figures converged into one in Lönnrot's *Kalevala*). Like his Kalevalan counterpart, Dobrynya departs for a military campaign, abandoning his wife and ignoring his mother's advice; specifically, Dobrynya's mother admonishes him about the mortal dangers of the 'Bloat-river' (*Puchay-reka*), which can be seen as a Russian counterpart of the Tuonela. Dobrynya's exhibition of defiant bravery is mixed with a hint at his sexual adventures: he swims in the river naked, evoking protests from local maidens.[28] Eventually, the news of his body being torn apart in the river by the vicious serpent reaches his mother and wife. In the rune, it is Lemminkäinen's mother who fetches pieces of his body from the stormy Tuonela and then restores and revives it; in the *bylina*, the rumour of Dobrynya's death proves to be false. As it turns out, he escaped the attack by crossing the turbulent Bloat-river in one stroke, and then killed the serpent on the shore.

Another pair of heroes whose features bear certain personological and narrative similarities to each other are 'the old Cossack Il'ya Muromets' (*staroy kozak Il'ya Muromets*) and 'sturdy old Väinämöinen' (*vaka vanha Väinämöinen*). Particularly significant is the motif of their 'late emergence' as epic heroes: Il'ya remained paralysed for thirty years, which he spent lying on the stove, until one day he suddenly emerged from this embryonic state as a warrior of extraordinary strength; likewise, Väinämöinen, after a prolonged confinement in his mother's womb, was born as an old sage. The constitutional 'elderness' of both heroes seems to weigh on their deportment and affect their destiny, in particular, their relationships with women. Il'ya's extraordinary strength, even by the standards of *bylina* warriors, is often emphasized; a similar motif may be implied in Väinämöinen's name, even though his main power is that of a magician and singer.[29] Finally, the motif of Il'ya's killing of his daughter by slashing her breast finds a parallel in Väinämöinen having nearly slashed a fish he caught, the fish being in fact his would-be bride who had turned into a maiden-salmon.

Despite all these and some other parallels, the gist of the narrative in *bylinas* and runes is different. The two contrasting principles on which the worlds of the Kalevalan runes and the *bylinas* are founded can be called 'magical' and 'legendary', respectively.

The predominant driving force of the Kalevalan epos is that of magic power, which manifests itself primarily as the power of words uttered in the manner of incantations. The runes (particularly of the Sampo cycle) do feature adventurous expeditions and battles traditional for the heroic epos. Yet the heroes' victories and defeats are contingent not so much on their physical might and martial prowess as on their command of spiritual forces.[30] The world of the *Kalevala* is moved by clashes between competing magic skills.

In contradistinction to this, Northern *bylinas* adhere to a more conventional scale of epic values. Their heroes are bestowed with a superhuman, larger-than-life physical strength and courage, which makes them invincible in combat. Their feats, with almost no exception, are those of a warrior, epically magnified. Words serve them, at most, for teasing the enemy and exhorting the combatants.

The heroes of the *Kalevala* take their power from secret magic forces that underlie their world. The *bylina* heroes also live in a world beyond ordinary human conditions, yet there is nothing secret in it. It is a world of miraculous phenomenology, so to speak – a real world projected to superhuman proportions. What the *bylina* depicts is a hyperbolic reality, but a reality nevertheless, only magnified into dimensions inspiring an awesome vision of a legendary primordial universe.[31] Mikula the ploughman handles a 'little plough' that a hundred warriors are unable to move from its place; Il'ya's single stroke cuts a 'street-wide' pass in the mass of the enemy, whose number is beyond count; the whistle of the evil Brigand Nightingale causes church tops to fall down and people to drop dead. The hero's combat club weighs a 'hundred poods' (one and a half tons), his horse (or otherwise, his reins of pure silk) cost 'five hundred roubles', and so on.

The *bylinas* depict a magnificent world of a legendary past that is no more. It is a world of mind-boggling splendour, abundance, and power; even its evil characters are bestowed with supreme strength and daring spirit, even its drunken brawls achieve 'Homeric' dimensions. Yet unlike Homer's epos, whose grandeur is clad in innumerable magnificently tangible details, the splendour of the *bylina* world is rather vague. The story-teller has little to say about Prince Vladimir's feasts, beyond mentioning the superabundance of food and drink. Yet atmospherically, the *bylina* conveys the sense of wonderment and awe, whose effect is further enhanced by the implicit contrast with the impoverished real-life context in which it is sung.[32]

Interestingly enough, while the world in general as depicted in *bylinas* achieves miraculous proportions, their narrative is almost totally devoid of a magical or religious element.[33] The *bylinas* quite often refer to the Christian faith, which its heroes defend against the 'pagans', but these references are purely formulaic; in this sense they are radically different from folk religious songs.[34] Neither sorcery nor magic play any significant role in *bylinas*. This attitude is captured in the figure of one of the *bylinas'* heroes, Vasily Buslayev, who *ne verit ni v son, ni v chokh, ni v ptichy gray* ('believes neither in dreams, nor in sneezing [as an omen], nor in birds' crowing'). Fantastic evil creatures, like the huge serpent that attacked Dobrynya, have in fact nothing supernatural in them beyond their superior strength. The depiction of Tatars as devilish forces has a rich tradition in Russian literature, from *Zadonshchina* to Lomonosov's odes; yet the token 'Tatars' in *bylinas* have nothing to show as far as their belonging to a netherworld is concerned, except the infiniteness of their number. This is a world of phenomena, with no metaphysical or magical super-reality underlying it; the world of *bylinas* is a super-reality in itself, plainly manifest in all its larger-than-life proportions.

The world of the *Kalevala* is different. People and things in the runes, with a few exceptions, adhere to ordinary proportions; there is nothing supernatural in their overt physical appearance. Occasionally the epic hyperbola takes place in depictions of nature (for instance, the oak that grew up to heaven and cast its shadow over the whole world), but usually the heroes' material conditions of life adhere to the realities of a Northern peasant household, while the heroes, at least in their external appearance, seem to be perfectly fitting to that modest habitat. There is nothing in the household of the *Kalevala*'s heroes that would inspire awe as a vision of a legendary larger-than-life magnificence. Even if the narrator occasionally refers to 'these wretched times of a stale bread-crust' (*tällä inhalla iällä, katovalla kannikalla*), in a presumed contrast to the splendour of the past, the primordial world he depicts does not strike one with its abundance either. Likewise, the primordial heroes, while showing great skills as hunters, marksmen, and artisans, do not exceed human dimensions too liberally in exercising those skills.

The supernatural element in the *Kalevala* is for the most part not phenomenological but metaphysical; it is a secret world of magic forces lurking behind its modest, even subdued surface. Every object – be it an animal, a plough-field, an axe, iron, beer, or honey – is charged with a magic force that gives it an ability either to give help or to inflict harm. The access to a phenomenon's hidden essence, from which comes its helpful or hurtful potential, lies in a magic word or words that reveal its 'origin' (*synty*). The hero's power to transform the world and to prevail on his adversaries comes from his knowledge of those secret words that make the respective objects bow to the hero's command. By the same token, failure to know the proper word fatally leads to defeat. Väinämöinen is unable to stop blood gushing from a wound he inflicted on himself with an axe, because he does not know the ultimate word of 'origin' for iron; Lemminkäinen is struck down on the Tuonela shore, because he cannot remember the magic word given to him by his mother; Joukahainen is defeated by Väinämöinen, because the latter's words prove to be 'older', that is, closer to the original word or term for certain things.

The contest between the heroes is a contest of their magic powers stemming from the depth of their knowledge of underlying essences. Väinämöinen tramples Joukahainen down into the swamp by his singing: he literally 'sings' his opponent into the ground. In purely physical terms, the 'singing' (or whistling) of the *bylina*'s Brigand Nightingale results in a similar effect: it makes the earth tremble, and people fall dead or near-dead. Yet what produces this effect is in the latter case the sheer physical power of the sound, while in the former, it is the magic power of words uttered by Väinämöinen. The difference is that between hyperbolic super-reality and trans-reality, between the superior material force and the force beyond the material.

The same relation can be seen between the depictions of Lemminkäinen's death and Dobrynya's near-death in the river. To begin with, the dangers of the 'Bloat-river' come solely from its violent tide. The physically violent character of Tuonela is also indicated by the reference to its waterfalls, yet its dangers are mystical rather than phenomenal: it is the river of death; no one can survive approaching it without the defence provided by the knowledge of magic words. In his fatal moment, Lemminkäinen realizes that he did not listen to his mother attentively enough: now he can remember only two of the three words she had conveyed to him, which means that he is doomed. Dobrynya, like Lemminkäinen, finds himself disarmed when he is attacked by the serpent, but what he is missing is not proper words but physical means of combat; he eventually disposes of the serpent by striking him with a 'little hat' (weighing forty poods) he found on the shore. Dobrynya's opponent is a creature of supernatural size and might; but his power is straightforward, which allows Dobrynya to win the fight simply by swimming faster and striking stronger. On the other hand, there is nothing remarkable in the appearance of Lemminkäinen's adversary: he is a 'wet-hat herdsman, a blind old man of Pohjola' (*märkähattu karjanpaimen, ukko Pohjolan sokea*); yet Lemminkäinen is defenceless against the evil influence he exudes. Interestingly enough, the motif of a 'hat' appears in both stories. In the case of Dobrynya, it is the incredible weight of the hat that helps him in combat; in Lemminkäinen's story, the 'wet hat' of his adversary makes his outward appearance especially pathetic, yet it is possibly the magic power of the hat that makes Lemminkäinen helpless against him.[35]

The difference between the two epic narrative modes is particularly manifest in the way they treat powerful female figures. Both epics feature women of great power, capable of posing a formidable challenge to the male hero.[36] In the world of the *Kalevala*, where power emanates from the spiritual element, it comes across as natural that female witchcraft (that of the mistress of Pohjola) proves to be more than a good match for male magic. In *bylinas*, however, witchcraft does not thrive; the sorceress Marinka, despite her temporary triumph over 'hundreds' of warriors, is soundly defeated as soon as she meets a truly mighty opponent – Dobrynya. For a woman in a *bylina*, to match a male hero means to be equal to him in physical strength and valour; hence the emergence in *bylinas* of a Russian folk counterpart of the Amazons – the *polyanitsas*, or female *bogatyr's*. In full agreement with the *bylina*'s values, the *polyanitsa* comes out as superhumanly big and strong as the male heroes with whom or against whom she is fighting.[37]

The difference in the overall narrative modalities of each epic tradition becomes manifest in terms of their poetic discourses.

The rhetorical devices of bylinas

Rhetorical devices favoured in *bylinas* are aimed at the 'enlargement' of the narrative space. There is a strong tendency to 'stretch out' every element of the discourse – from the rendition of the story in general to single poetic lines, and even single words – to increase its duration, thus slowing down its pace. The resulting discourse exudes epic grandeur while loosening connections between separate elements. The feeling is like that of the plough field cultivated by Mikula Selyaninovich, which is so large that one's voice cannot be heard from its other end. This is a spacious narrative world, in which single elements do not stay in close contact, and, as a consequence, are not involved in an intense relation with each other.

To begin with, words – particularly those central for the meaning of a phrase or a period – tend to be extended into the longest shape possible. In the case of verbs, this effect is achieved by adding prefixes (often more than one) and by the preferential usage of the imperfective aspect: *pokhvastayet* rather than *khvastayet* 'boast'; *pozabrasyval* rather than *zabrosil* or brosil.

> Стал Владимир *повыспрашивать*:
> 'А давно ли ты *повыехал* из Муромля?'
> ('Vladimir was asking: Did you leave Murom a long time ago?')
>   (Trofim G. Ryabinin, *About Il'ya of Murom*)

The prefix *po-* in the example is purely ornamental; semantically, it is disposable, as indicated by another version of the line in the same story where it is removed: *Стал Владимир-князь выспрашивать*. Indeed, the addition of an *Aktionsart* prefix often does not change the empirical content of the situation described in any tangible way. Yet on a symbolic level, it makes the situation appear magnified, as it were, above the average experiential level. By the same token, it increases the physical length, and thus slows down the tempo of the discourse itself:

> А плеча-то его да *испростреляны*,
> Голова-то его да *испроломана*.
> ('His shoulders have been shot through, his skull broken')
>
> (Petr L. Kalinin, *Dobrynya Nikitich*)

The same can be said about the excessive use of the imperfective or 'hyper-imperfective' (*khazhivali, skazyvali,* etc.) forms. Semantically, it seems superfluous if not counter-intuitive, as attested by frequent cases when the perfective and imperfective aspect are used indiscriminately in parallel constructions:

> Вси на пиру да напивалися [Imperfective],
> Вси на пиру да поросхвастались [Perfective].
> ('All present at the feast got drunk // got into boasting')
>
> (Aksin'ya K. Fomina, *Il'ya Muromets*)

> Сама повыпустила [Perfective] скорых послов,
> Садилась-то [Imperfective] на стулья на дубовыи
> ('She dismissed the fast messengers, and sat herself on oak chairs')
>
> (Fomina, ibid.)

Again, the excessive use of the imperfective aspect works as a symbolic device on both the semantic and the phonetic level. Semantically, it makes the action described less of an 'event', dissolves it in a durational vagueness, as it were. At the same time, the frequent usage of imperfective forms, which are usually longer than their perfective counterparts, results in extending the physical length of poetic lines.

With the nouns, the same purpose is served by frequent use of diminutives, which often appear hand in hand with extended verbal forms:

> Да не могут они сошки с земельки повыдернути,
> Из омешиков земельки повытряхнуть.
> ('They cannot pull the little plough out of [little] earth, [and] to clean little blades from [little] earth')
>
> (Ryabinin, *Vol'ga and Mikula*)

As in the case of verbal *Aktionsarten*, the addition of diminutive affixes is often not semantically motivated. There are cases when the diminutive and the basic form of a word are used as full synonyms: *пированьицо почестен пир* ('a little feast, an honourable feast'). Diminutive forms by no means 'diminish' the scale of the phenomena described. If anything, diminutives make the hyperbolic scale of events look even more impressive, as if suggesting the possibility of something even more grandiose:

> Он скорешенько ставал да на резвы *ножки*,
> Кунью *шубоньку* накинул на одно *плечико*,
> То он *шапочку* соболью на одно *ушко*.
>
> ('He stood up promptly on his little fast feet, put his little marten coat on his little shoulder, put his little sabre hat over his little ear')
>
> (Vasily P. Shchegolenok, *Dobrynya and the Serpent*)

The splendour of the hero's marten coat and sabre, as well as his own physical prowess, instead of being diminished by persistent diminutives, seems to be enhanced by them – as if the described reality were so magnificent that only its symbolic diminishing made it perceivable on a human scale.

Like imperfective verbal forms, abundant diminutive nouns provide a symbolic 'softening' effect on the discourse in general, making it more soft-spoken and circumspect. The effect of making the discourse less definitive, of slowing down its pace, goes along with the extension of the physical length of key words and as a result, of entire lines. The physical lengthening, provided by nominal diminutive forms, verbal prefixes, and imperfective suffixes, symbolically expresses the epically magnified narrative space and narrative duration. The slowed down tempo and symbolic 'spaciousness' of the narrative bestows on it an epic magnificence (Gasparov 1995).

In addition to the morphological means of discourse extension described above, a number of syntactic devices is employed towards the same end. Typically, the syntactic carcass of a sentence is extended by the addition of monosyllabic particles and demonstrative pronouns, and by the repeated use of prepositions in parallel nominal constructions:

> *Как* у *той ли то* у грязи-*то* у Черноей,
> *Да* у *той ли* у березы *у* покляпые,
> *Да* у *той ли* речки *у* Смородины,
> У *того* креста *у* Левонидова.
>
> ('As it happened at that Black Soil, near that battered birch tree, at that small river Smorodina, near that Leonide Cross')
>
> (Ryabinin, *Il'ya and the Nightingale*)

The extension of a phrase can also be achieved by means of an appositive reduplication of a verb, a noun, or an adjective:

> Стал Вольга *ростеть матереть*
> ('Vol'ga began growing up-maturing')

Щукой рыбою ходить Вольги во синих морях,
птицей соколом летать Вольги под оболоки
('Like a pike the fish would Vol'ga move in blue seas, like a falcon the bird would he fly near clouds')

(Ryabinin, *Vol'ga and Mikula*)

Нагнано-то силушки *черным черно*
('It has become darkly dark from the summoned [enemy's] little forces')

(Ryabinin, *Il'ya and Kalin the Tsar*)

(The use of the diminutive *silushka* – literally 'little force' – seems to contradict the hyperbolic meaning, yet it contributes to the hyperbola by symbolically amplifying the description on the discourse level.)

The discourse amplification achieves its climax when expanded expressions are coupled in parallel constructions. In such cases, not only is a single line protracted but the narrative pace of a larger segment of the text is slowed down by a chain of parallel expressions, each abundant with the means of amplification described above:

А орет в поли ратой, понукиваёт,
А у ратая-то сошка поскрипываёт,
Да по камешкам омешики прочиркивают.
('The ploughman is ploughing his field, nudging his horse, his plough slightly squeaking, its little blades chirping when striking little stones')

(Ryabinin, *Vol'ga and Mikula*)

The principal effect is, once again, that of amplifying the narrative – making it more elaborate and circumspect – as if a single snapshot of a situation would not be enough for accessing its scope. At the same time, the parallel construction did not make relations between adjacent segments intense, because of their excessive length. Instead of moving forward, the story lingers on the closely paraphrased dimensions of a situation.

The slowing-down effect becomes particularly pronounced when the end of one of the parallel lines is repeated at the beginning of the next one. This narrative formula, which can be described as A–B // B–C, is employed in *bylinas* with exceeding frequency:

Прямоезжая дорожка заколодела,
Заколодела дорожка, замуравела.
('The straight little road has become impassable, the little road has become impassable, grown with weeds')

(Ryabinin, *Il'ya and the Nightingale*)

Он по городу Крякову погуливает,
Он погуливаё а й похаживаё.
Сам крепку думу подумываё.

('He is strolling along the city of Kryakov [casually], he is strolling along and walking along [casually], while thinking [casually] his grave thought')
(Shchegolenok, *Il'ya's Early Deeds*)

Sometimes this device is repeated several times in a row, creating an extreme durational effect:

Кладывают на коней оны исподнички,
На исподнички оны войлочки,
На войлочко оны седёлышко,
Да седёлышко оны черкальское.
('They put on their horses' little girths, on top of the little girths little felts, on top of the little felts a little saddle, the little saddle the Circassian one')
(Shchegolenok, *Dyuk*)

To summarize: the rhetorical devices of *bylinas* symbolically create a narrative space whose 'chronotope' is characterized by large panoramic expanses and a slow and smooth progress. Its elements are 'comfortably' accommodated vis-à-vis each other in an expansive setting, whereby they tend to be attached to each other loosely, avoiding too tight connections. This is a narrative world that is wide open, epically unhurried and circumspect. The properties of its discourse are homomorphous to those of the Southern steppe landscape – albeit totally alien to the real-life environment in which the epic tradition has been maintained – that provides the scene for the deeds of the *bylinas'* heroes. The total alienation of the *bylinas'* chronotope from the real-life experience of the singers and their audience only further enhanced the characteristic proportions of the stories.

The rhetorical devices of the **Kalevala**

The rhetoric of the *Kalevala*, by contrast, is directed toward emphasizing relations between adjacent elements. Within a phrase, words are tightly knit by sound repetitions; within a line, they are squeezed by the trochaic metre, which is superimposed over varied word lengths and vowel lengths.[38] The Kalevalan epic discourse is permeated with what is usually (and rather imprecisely) called 'alliteration', that is, repetitions of sound clusters in close conjunction. Adjacent words do not just follow each other – their phonetic shapes overlap, making them merge in symbiotic interconnections. This is a discourse whose elements are constantly grouping and regrouping through the forces of mutual attraction.

The study of the rich poetic texture of the *Kalevala* and related folk runes has so far remained almost exclusively confined to the domain of formal 'poetics'. There is no question that to proponents of 'grammar of poetry', keen on exploring various figures of versification, alliteration, and parallelism, the Finnish epic presents a highly gratifying object of analysis. Yet studies of this kind, while offering detailed formal classifications and statistics,[39] leave aside the question of how these features may be related to the spiritual values they express – while works concentrating on those spiritual values largely leave aside the formal features of the epic's poetic discourse. Under this compartmentalized formal approach, the ubiquitous sound repetitions in the Kalevalan discourse amount to no more than a mnemonic device – a 'code of memorialisation' facilitating shamanist incantations (Siikala 2002a: 36; see also Kuusi 1994c: 41).

My contention is that a purely formal approach to the sound texture of the *Kalevala* results in its misrepresentation even on a technical ground. The term 'alliteration', automatically borrowed from the arsenal of formal poetics, is plainly misleading as a reference to Kalevalan sound repetitions. It unduly draws attention to the repetition of consonants, a feature that is indeed characteristic of Germanic verse but has little to do with Finnish runes (Sadeniemi 1951: 94).[40] The predominant pattern of sound repetition both in the *Kalevala* and in the runes involves a CV combination, although truncated versions, with either a sole consonant or a sole vowel repeated, as well as expanded patterns involving more than two sounds, are also possible.[41] I venture to suggest that all the talk about 'alliterations' in the *Kalevala* reflects a lingering influence of the Germanic-Scandinavian example, despite its evident incompatibility with the case in hand. It should be stated in unequivocal terms that the governing principle of sound repetitions in the *Kalevala* is syllabic rather than consonantal.

Even more important, however, is the fact that these sound repetitions are always directly correlated with meaning. In an overwhelming majority of cases, sound echoes occur between two (occasionally three) words that are syntactically and semantically related: they either belong to the same phrase or constitute syntactic parallels in adjacent phrases. Both intra-phrasal and parallel inter-phrasal phonic links occur in a tight conjunction, almost always within the space of a single eight-foot line:

> Ei tiedä e*mo* po*lo*inen eikä ka*nt*aja ka*ta*la,
> missä *lii*kkuvi *li*hansa, *viere*vi oma *vere*nsä,
> kä*vi*kö *käp*ymäkeä, ka*ne*rvista ka*ng*asmaata,
> vai *me*ni *me*ren selällä, *la*kki*p*äillä *la*inehilla.'
> ('For the poor mother does not know, the wretched one who carried him,
> where his flesh is moving, his blood turning,
> whether he walked by a pine mountain, a heather field,
> or moved over the sea, on waves with capped heads')
>
> (The *Kalevala*, rune 15)

Phonic correlations in the Kalevalan discourse work in two opposite yet interconnected ways. On the one hand, the presence of a repetition highlights a semantic link between related words. On the other, a correlation rarely appears in isolation; typically, a correlated word couple is confronted with another word couple (usually in the following phrase), linked by another sound repetition, in such a way that the two couples are cast into a certain opposition to each other. The predominant pattern of sound repetition in the *Kalevala* and related folk poetry can be described by a formula: A'–A" // B'–B", whereby the oppositional phonetic pattern of repetition (A vs B) manifests a contrastive relation between the 'A' and 'B'.

For example, if one word couple features the repetition of an *a* or *e*, the other one might have a repeated *u* or *i*; repetition of a *k* in one phrase would lead to a repeated *p* in the other, and so on. As to the meaning, the opposed word couples represent either different members of a larger class of phenomena (different kinds of plants or animals, plain vs mountainous terrain, day vs night, etc.), or synonymic alternatives, which in this context signify different aspects of the same phenomenon:[42]

> Lauloi *pä*ivät *pää*tyksen, *yht*ysen *yö*t saneli.
> ('He sang the succession of days, expressed in words the accumulation of nights')
>
> (The *Kalevala*, rune 3)

The emergence of contrastive sound patterns *pä-* and *y-* as phonic attributes of respective phrases highlights the opposition between 'day' and 'night'.

> *Sa*nat *suu*ssani *su*lavat, *puhe*'et *puto*elevat.
> ('Words are melting in my mouth, expressions precipitate')
>
> (The *Kalevala*, rune 1)

Sanat and *puheet* are near synonymous as metonymic indications of 'speaking'. Their contrastive relation as two different aspects of poetic speech is underscored by contrastive patterns of phonic correlation for the respective phrases: *sa-* vs *pu-*.

The correlation between two instances of sound repetition is often reinforced by an ellipsis, which makes the connection between the contrasted couples more tight:

> Alku *rau*an *ruo*stehesta, vasken *ka*nta *ka*lliosta
> ('The origin of iron is from rust, of copper from a cliff's foot')
>
> (The *Kalevala*, rune 3)

Another often used means of bringing the related couples even more closely together is that of concluding each of them with the same grammatical ending, in a kind of 'grammatical rhyme' (*sulavat ... putoelevat; ruostehesta ... kalliosta*, etc.).

The binary structure of repetitions underscores their semiotic rather than poetically ornamental character. As for the purely phonetic status of such repetitions, it appears to be of secondary importance; both the degree of precision and the number of repeated sounds are varied. For instance, it is not rare to observe 'imprecise' repetitions featuring related but not identical sounds, such as *m* and *n* (*emo poloinen*), *a* (or *ai*) and *ä* (*mätäs on märkä maita vanhin*), *au* and *uo* (*alku rauan ruostehesta*), and so on.

So far we have considered phonic correlations in the *Kalevala*. In this respect, authentic folk runes exhibit much similarity with, but also some difference from,

Lönnrot's epic. In the *Kalevala*, the web of phonic links and contrasts is nearly total. In its folkloric sources, phonically correlated lines are interspersed with occasional 'plain' segments of a purely narrative character. Here, the uncorrelated lines, while still in a minority in the overall narrative, have a distinct role to play. They usually introduce a character or an action that triggers the story whose progress then is underlain by correlations.[43]

> Üks' on vanha Väinämöini,
>   Toine on nuori Jougahaini,
>   Ajettihpa vassakkaha
>   *Selv*ällä meren *sel*ällä
>   Vaingo *suu*ren *suo*n selällä,
>   *Kaun*ehella *kan*gahalla.[44]
> ('One is old Väinämöinen, the other young Joukahainen. And so, they ran against each other over the bright surface of the sea, over the perilous depth of a swamp, over a beautiful cape').

The three last lines, indicating alternative locations in which the collision between the heroes occur, feature a sound pattern that is identical with that regularly employed in the *Kalevala*. However, the first three lines in this example feature something that is exceedingly rare in Lönnrot's narrative: namely, a whole segment without any pertinent phonic correlations.

The discourse of the *Kalevala* and of Kalevalan runes, permeated with phonic correlations, presents a picture of a world whose phenomena – from aspects of the natural environment to items of material life, to human thoughts and feelings – are intertwined in manifold, constantly restructuring interconnections. Each element of the world appears in manifold constellations established by phonic links, as if in a flickering light that allows snapshots from different angles. A wet stone glistening in the sun turns out to be 'multicoloured' (*kirjava*) in one semiotic incarnation, as *kivi*, yet 'shining' (*paistavainen*) in another, as *paasi*: *Kivi oli kirjava selällä, paasi kullan paistavainen*. When it slips down into the water, its two incarnations behave differently, each according to phonic links attracted by their respective signifiers: *kivi* 'tumbles' into the 'water' (*kilahti kivi vetehen*), while *paasi* 'escapes' to the 'bottom' (*paasi pohjahan pakeni*). When Väinämöinen pleads to be born, to experience the world, the character of that would-be experience varies in regard to different elements of the universe. Each object to be perceived is accommodated according to a link between its signifier and that of a particular kind of perception: Väinämöinen would 'look' at the moon in the sky (*kuuta taivon katsomahan*), 'marvel' at the sun (*päiveä ihoamahan*), 'learn' the Plough (*otavasta oppimahan*) and 'watch' the stars (*tähtiä tähyämähän*).

Stark-Arola (1989) describes the world of shamanist magic as a world permeated by forces of 'sympathy and contagion'; each phenomenon is 'charged with power' that enables it to 'act' upon another phenomenal body. This metaphysical model of the world is incarnated in the *Kalevala*'s discourse. All described phenomena pose as semiotic 'werewolves': their notional 'souls' assume varied phonic 'bodies', each behaving differently due to the power of attraction it attains by its phonic correlation with other words. By uttering a certain word, the narrator triggers its potential connection with certain other phenomena; the choice of a word structures the picture of the world in a certain way.[45] He symbolically creates the world by singing, precisely the way Väinämöinen does. The presence of phonic correlations, by revealing kinships and contrasts between verbal incarnations of certain ideas, gives their connection an ontological inevitability – as if those connections were sealed by a magic power.

The effect of the magical 'power of the word' is particularly striking in the famous description of the flow of inspired poetic speech at the poem's opening:

> Sanat suussani sulavat, puheet putoelevat,
> Kielelleni kerkiävät, hampahilleni hajoovat.
> ('Words are melting in my mouth, expressions precipitate, they hurry to my tongue, scatter over my teeth')
>
> (The *Kalevala*, rune 1)

Phonic correlations bring forth an intrinsic connection between various items of speech and the singer's particular speech organs. Words (*sanat*) melt (*sulavat*) in the singer's mouth (*suu*), while speeches, or utterances (*puheet*), precipitate (*putoelevat*); they both hurry (*kerkiävät*) to his tongue (*kielelle*), and scatter (*hajoovat*) over the teeth (*hampahille*). One is given to understand that the singer's mouth, tongue, and teeth have magical 'special relations' with words and expressions, which gives him power over them – the same way as a magician who knows the secret words of the 'origin' (that is, the essence) of iron or honey, of the swamp or the river, is able to subdue those substances, making them act according to his will.

The shaman's spiritual power consists in knowing the metaphysical essences of all the phenomena – their 'origin' (*synty*).[46] This knowledge is secret – it is hidden under the surface of things, which betrays no clue to their essence to the uninitiated. Phonic correlations in the Kalevalan discourse can be viewed as a poetic recreation of that magic power. A link between unrelated words, suggested by the effect of a sound echo, works as a clue to the essential qualities of the signified phenomena. By the sheer means of putting words together in a certain way, something is revealed about the world that would not otherwise be apparent. The poetic device of phonic correlations works as a tool by which the secret 'magic' power of words is brought forth, with the narrator posing as a rhetorical counterpart of a sage-magician *tietäjä*.

Things are being fitted together in innumerable different ways, exposed from different sides. Various connections surface in the flow of poetic speech, only to give way to new ones, as if in unceasing trials in a quest for the ultimate match that would eventually reveal the word's mystical 'origin'. The *tietäjä*, bestowed with magical knowledge, makes repeated spiritual trips to the trans-experiential world,[47] bringing in various revelations about the things, until the ultimate word of 'origin' is found. This is what the *Kalevala* does in terms of linguistic signs whose signifiers reveal their meaning by being arranged in ever new constellations by means of phonic links. The fundamental tension of the *Kalevala* narrative, underlying its heroes' deeds and adventures, is a struggle to conquer the world by means of word power. It is the supreme command of words, manifested in the agility with which they are put in ever new constellations, that gives the epic hero – and symbolically, the epic's singer – the power to create, to destroy and to transform.

Conclusion: two distinct yet kindred epic voices

The respective discourses of Russian *bylinas* and Finnish-Karelian runes turn out to be as different as the world visions projected by their epic traditions. The Kalevalan discourse is built on interconnections that encapsulate the narrative story in a dense web of juxtapositional and contrapositional links. The narrative pace is extremely tense: every image instantly attracts another one, each correlation calls for another as its opposition or periphrastic alternative. This is a dynamic world, whose phenomena are involved in a whirlwind of unceasing commotion; the reader/listener is compelled constantly to shift his or her attention from one image to another according to their links, making the overall picture 'flicker' in ever-changing constellations. It is a world in which nothing is taken for granted, nothing is open to a straightforward and steady vision; a world through which one proceeds by constantly changing the direction of one's eyes. One's view is constantly being obstructed by a kaleidoscope of images in which certain phenomena momentarily come together only immediately to evoke an alternative or a whole series of alternatives. It is indeed a magic world in which what one sees always presents itself as a hint at or a clue to something else. The epic struggle of the Kalevalan heroes and its narrator alike is the struggle to conquer this shifting world metaphysically: arresting its werewolf-like phenomena by getting to their essential 'origin'. The crucial weapons with which they are armed in this struggle are words; they put words together, trying them out in various constellations, in search of the definitive magic formula.

The world of the Russian *bylina* is fundamentally different. It is a world of steady, straight-faced panoramic views. As a real-life phenomenon, the image of an 'open field' (*chisto pole*), often evoked as the locus of *bylina*'s actions, is totally alien to the habitat in which *bylinas*' singers and audience live.[48] But as a narrative reality, it is crucial for establishing the panoramic perspective on the events and phenomena described.[49] Everything is so 'big' in the *bylina* that it could be appraised by the eye only with a far-reaching perspective. All rhetorical devices are aimed at creating an extensive narrative space that is fitting for the panoramic proportions of the narrated world. Key words are set as widely apart from each other as possible, due to their expansion by over-abundant affixes and intermediary particles, always ready to be inserted to lengthen the pace of a line.

The difference between the two epic traditions can be seen in the way each of them treats the phenomena of repetition and parallelism. Although Kalevalan runes employ parallelism to some extent, its usage is overshadowed by far by phonic correlations between single words. *Bylinas*, by contrast, use parallel constructions with exceeding frequency, while exhibiting an almost total indifference to sound repetitions on the micro-level of word stems. At first glance, the two devices are similar: both provide an effect of rhythmical recurrence, that pivotal category of Jakobsonian 'grammar of poetry'. Yet their effect on the discourse at large is quite different, if not opposite. Sound repetitions between closely juxtaposed words enhance their interconnection. An abundance of such repetitions makes the discourse appear tightly woven, permeated with forces of attraction. The discourse literally 'jumps' from one element to the next, creating the effect of phenomena piling up and superimposing themselves on each another. Contrary to this, repetitions and parallelisms in *bylinas* operate with larger units – entire lines and sentences, or even larger narrative segments. The links established by such parallelisms gain little in the intensity of the discourse: the large scope of such linked units makes their interconnection rather loose. Their primary effect is that of expanding and slowing down the narrative's progress through repetitions and paraphrases.

The narrator of the *Kalevala* does everything to obstruct a clear view, in order to make tangible the presence of the metaphysical, spiritual, and magic element lurking behind the depicted world; the pace of its imagery and its verse is throbbing with tension. The narrator of a *bylina*, on the contrary, does everything to open up the view, making the audience see the depicted world face to face – in short, creating conditions under which that world, improbable though it may seem, evokes the unquestioning trust of the audience. Paradoxically, the obstructed view, constant expectations of something lurking behind something else, the sense of proceeding in tense steps on a convoluted path – the narrative strategies that bestow the discourse of the runes with magic power and metaphysical intensity – all reflect real-life conditions of the habitat in which epic actions take place; while *bylinas*, with their straight-faced claim of veracity that jumps over the head of everyday experience, create a fictional space of infinite expanses and eternal summer that puts actual physical conditions aside, or rather, soars over them.

The relation between the two epic worlds is captured in the names by which each epic tradition is known to its adherents: the 'runes' and the 'starinas' (*stariny*: the term by which *bylinas* are referred to by the region's inhabitants), that is, 'secret' tales[50] and 'ancient' tales. Their respective spiritual quests are for the metaphysical world, co-present with and hidden behind the physical reality, and for the ideal primordial world, whose vestiges exist solely in the epic memory.

As often happens, outlining an opposition allows one to perceive a common denominator that underlines its poles. In our case, this common denominator seems to be the intense involvement with the transcendent that is characteristic of both epic traditions. Both are engaged in building an epic picture of the world, whose scope of characters and events transcends the empirical here-and-now. They arrive at such a picture by different paths: either by saturating the world as one sees it with magic synergy, or by providing a telescopic distancing of vision that delegates the described world into primordial times where things, impossible by quotidian standards, were just natural. The *bylina* imports the miracle into the world, so to speak, while the *Kalevala* pushes the world into mystery and magic.

Arising from a scanty, secluded, and marginalized environment, both epics strive to create a world of magnificence and formidable power. The situation is not unlike that of Homer's epic memories of a world of magnificent richness, memories retained in an environment totally alien to them, in the depth of Greece's dark ages. Perhaps it was a compelling need for a similar kind of transcending spiritual energy that gave such force to the two folk poetic voices from East Karelia.

Notes

1 Cf. for instance the meticulous cartography of the geographic distribution of particular *bylina* stories in Dmitriyeva (1975), on the one hand, and detailed maps of Lönnrot's expeditions in Karhu (1996), on the other, which show the astonishing degree of the geographic overlap between the two folklore traditions.

2 In Propp's words:

> The Karelian-Finnish epos, like the Russian one, lost its presence nation-wide. It remained only in some secluded places – natural preservation parks, as it were. Russians lost their epos in the South and in central regions, but had preserved it in the North. Finland lost its epos, although its clear and unequivocal traces remained, while in Karelia it has been preserved.
>
> (Propp 1976: 313–14)

3 Coined by Lönnrot as the name of the epic land, the word 'Kalevala' has become associated not only with his composition but with folk runes in general that constituted its base. In this chapter, I will speak of the 'Kalevalan epos' and 'Kalevalan poetry' in reference both to the *Kalevala* and the folk runes. Whenever the distinction between the two needs to be made, it will be explicitly pointed out.

4 Yevseyev (1957–60: I, 327–28) even suggests that in the medieval epoch Swedes persecuted singers, while the Russians only made them pay some 'taxes'; this helped the development and preservation of the folklore tradition on Russian territory. He cites early mentions of song performers in *Pistsovyye knigi* going back to the late sixteenth and early seventeenth centuries. In a similar vein, Chernyakova (1998: 12–13) cites the severe persecution of sorcery (the 'witch hunt') in Western Europe in the seventeenth century – a trend that was relatively mild in Scandinavia but still took place – as one of the driving forces of this migration.

5 For detailed accounts of Lönnrot's impressions of Old Believers' faith and communities, see Pentikäinen (1999b: 124 ff.) and Karhu (1996: 70–72). The latter particularly emphasizes the absence of religious fanaticism in the region, which Lönnrot viewed with approval, even though he expressed a vintage Enlightenment attitude toward the Old Believers' conservative customs and their alienation from modernity (the very features that allowed both epic traditions to stay alive).

6 The wave of persecution was universal. Mel'nikov-Pechersky (who himself, as a state official, zealously pursued the policy at that time) later left a dramatic account of it in his epopee *On the Mountains*. Likewise, Gil'ferding described the devastation of the Old Believers' culture in the Olonets district, which he witnessed in the early 1870s:

> the same picture almost in every village: everywhere chapels falling apart and sealed off by an order from Petersburg; graveyards with barred gates, strictly forbidden to be entered … everywhere this kind, friendly, gentle population of hard-working Vygozero people is deprived of the comfort of religion!
>
> (Gil'ferding 1871/1983: 24)

7 Characteristic is the story of Iivana and Olonja Nikitin, the father and the aunt of a prolific early twentieth-century singer of runes, Marina Takalo: Iivana, who was Orthodox, strictly forbade singing at home, while his sister, who kept the Old Faith, taught Marina old songs when she was a child; later Marina also belonged to the Old Believer community (Pentikäinen 1971: 365–66).

8 Gil'ferding's predecessor P. Rybnikov, whose expeditions in the late 1860s pioneered the discovery of epic folk poetry in the North, was convinced that all epic singers belonged to the Orthodox church, while Old Believers banished the singing. Yet Gil'-ferding, who retraced his steps a few years later, found *bylinas* being performed by Old Believers and Orthodox parishioners alike. According to Gil'ferding, this curious contradiction in their findings might be due to the fact that Rybnikov's official position made Old Believers mistrust him (Gil'ferding 1871/1983: 27–28).

9 Gil'ferding, convinced that the traditional cut-and-burn agriculture offered the only possibility for a minimally productive economy in the area, given the poor quality of the soil, lamented the devastating economic consequences of the forest preservation policy (1871/1983: 22–23).

10 Virtanen and DuBois (2000: 47) speak about the 'Byzantine' religious conservatism of the Orthodox Old Believer community as the principle force of cultural preservation, while according to Pentikäinen (1999b: 128), it was the spirit of opposition both to the official church and to the administrative pressures in the Northern communities that made possible the survival of vestiges of pre-Christian shamanistic culture.

11 Gil'ferding (1871/1983: 22 and 32) and Grigor'yev (1904: 141) make a similar point, citing the 'involuntary leisure' (*nevol'ny dosug*) of the Northern economy as a factor in preserving cultural memory. As for Lönnrot, he had an opposite view: convinced that agriculture constituted the backbone not only of a nation's economy but of its spirit as well, he lamented what he perceived as a neglectful attitude to land cultivation in the area (Karhu 1996: 52). Lönnrot's position was essentially Romantic, while his Russian counterparts, who spoke some thirty to fifty years after him, reflected more differentiated positivist environmental concerns.

12 Apparently Karelians knew little Russian; at any rate, the *bylinas* remained virtually unknown among the Finno-Ugric population (Skaftymov 1924: 141). By the same token, Russian Orthodox clergy had little knowledge of Karelian-Finnish (Virtanen and DuBois 2000: 46). Still, one should not underestimate the potential impact of the constant presence of Church Slavonic in the church service.

13 Yevseyev (1957–60: II, 300–28) pointed to such features in the Kalevalan poetic language as the postpositive placement of attributes (*Laiha poika Lappalainen*) and an occasional use of locative words (*ala* etc.) as prepositions, both features contradicting standard Finnish, as signs of Russian influence. Oinas (1969: 153–54) argues, however, that such inversions reflect the peculiar conditions of the poetic usage of language, and might arise spontaneously, in connection with metrical considerations; Laugaste (1955: 139) finds similar features of inverted word order in Estonian lyrical folk poetry.

14 Some words of Germanic origin, such as *muna*, *portti*, and so on, are quite prominent in the Kalevalan language (Ruoppila 1967: 65–71; Turunen 1979: 15), which seems to suggest the Western provenance of the epic tradition. Other authors, however, see a possible explanation in the fact that Germanic words had been brought into the area by early migrants and later used in the runes, which took their shape later in the new area (Siikala 2002b: 42; Yevseyev 1957–60: I, 215).

15 For instance, the parallels in Finnish folklore with the *bylina* of Vavila and the jesters (*skomorokhi*), which are rare and deteriorating (Haavio 1967; Oinas 1985c).

16 To this effect, Matti Kuusi (1994a) has built a panoramic picture that comprises all the different layers of cultural memory in terms of a historical succession, while Putilov (1988b) speaks of 'cosmogonic', 'magic', 'heroic', and 'Christian' motifs as universal stages in the development of the European folk epic.

17 Kirkinen (1987: 94) expressed this attitude in the sharpest of terms: 'Finnish intellectuals, in their struggle against tsarist Russia and against what they perceived as the Oriental totalitarian system, searched in the West for the foundations of their land's identity.'

18 See in particular Rybakov (1948). Cf. also numerous attempts to link *bylinas*' principal characters to historical figures: Dobrynya as 'a prominent actor of the [Kievan] epoch' (Plisetsky 1962: 222), Alesha Popovich as the double of an Aleksandr Popovich mentioned in the Chronicles (Likhachev 1949: 24), and so on.

19 See also the direct polemics between Propp and Rubakov in the 1960s: Propp (1962); Rybakov (1961).

20 Cf. a later description of the atmosphere of the ideologically charged polemics of the time in Azbelev (1982); Azbelev's stance is similar to that of many Finnish scholars of the last several decades.

21 An early stage of the controversy is succinctly described in Comparetti (1892), while its later development (in particular, the shift of Krohn's position toward an emphatic historical approach) is discussed in Haavio (1952); cf. also Kirkinen (1987).

22 Pentikäinen (1999a: 88); Siikala (2002b: 42). For a similar argument about *bylinas*, see Azbelev (1982: 32–33).

23 Among the few features of possible cross-pollination between the two traditions, the rhetorical device of negative parallelism – widespread in Russian folk poetry, and occasionally employed in the runes – can be cited (Oinas 1985b).

24 About sporadic earlier attempts at collecting Northern folk poetry (the 'Russian Iceland'), see Bazanov (1947).

25 As Pypin noted in his historical survey, 'the first impression among scholars all around the world was surprise followed by bewilderment and even suspicions'. When Sreznevsky was commissioned to write a review of Rybnikov's collection, he felt it necessary to make enquiries among Olonets intellectuals, to check the veracity of Rybnikov's work; they fully confirmed the authenticity of the collection (Pypin 1890–92: II, 63). See also Gruzinsky (1909: xiv).

26 In his essay, Gruzinsky pointedly emphasized Rybnikov's virtual obsession with the precision of the recording; however, Gil'ferding found even Rybnikov's method insufficiently precise (Gruzinsky 1909: xlvi–xlvii). According to Gruzinsky, Rubnikov's and Gil'ferding's 'positivism' and Lönnrot's 'romanticism' could both be seen as expressions of a 'national idea', each in its own way. Propp (1949/2002: 125) concurs, adding that even the early Slavophile folkloristic tradition of the 1830s and 40s (P. Kireyevsky's song collection) laid the emphasis on the collective of all the available variants without converging them into a unified version.

27 Grigor'yev (1904: xiv) even noted a tendency among the singers to arrange songs about the various deeds of a hero in a plausible chronological order. He considered this trend to be recent, perhaps emerging in the nineteenth century.

28 In general, sexual references in the *Kalevala* are much more explicit; Oinas (1985a: 45) considers this to be a reflection of chivalrous culture from the time of the Vikings.

29 Haavio (1952: 22) cited as one of possible etymologies of Väinämöinen's name the word *väin* (*väen*) 'powerful'.

30 'In 1892, the Italian scholar Domenico Comparetti stated that a hero of the Kalevala runes was more likely to be a shamanistic sage than a swordsman' (Pentikäinen 1999a: 177). While magic power and skills are quite obvious in the case of Väinämöinen (cf. also Haavio 1952: 4) and Ilmarinen, they are in fact no less pronounced in Lemminkäinen (Siikala 2002a: 301).

31 According to Gil'ferding, both the performers and their listeners 'have an unconditional faith in the miracles depicted in a *bylina*'. When asked how such events could have ever happened, they reply that 'the matter is very simple: in old times people were not at all like they are now'; this literal faith is characteristic of what Gil'ferding calls an 'epic world view' (*epicheskoye mirosozertsaniye*) (Gil'ferding 1871/1983: 25–26).

32 Novikov (2000: 47) notes an interesting detail of *bylinas'* narratives: they rarely mention winter, snow, snowstorms, and so on; the 'eternal summer' reigning in *bylinas* poses a marked contrast to runes, whose narrative abounds with pictures of harsh weather conditions.

33 Assertions to the contrary, which began to appear in recent years, treat the texts too liberally (see, e.g., Barlen 1993).

34 The difference was emphasized by Gil'ferding, who found out that *bylinas* and folk spiritual incantations (*duhovny stikh*) are performed by different people who, moreover, belong to different social strata of Northern peasant society. Performers of spiritual songs were professionals: they made their living by travelling through villages, receiving alms for their performance; performers of *bylinas* were ordinary peasants (often relatively well-to-do, by local standards) who sang in their leisure time (except, of course, when they sang to a collector for money). The two groups usually had little knowledge of each other's repertoire; occasional attempts by performers of spiritual verses to imitate the singing of epics turned out to be 'most ridiculous' (Gil'ferding 1871/1983: 30). Half a century later, however, Skaftymov (1924: 140) cited evidence of the contamination between the two genres – perhaps a result of the deterioration of the tradition.

35 On the magic function of a shaman's hat, cf. Siikala (2002a: 117).

36 Some scholars find in these features a vestige of a matriarchate.

37 'In the northern part of the Olonets district ... every peasant would tell you that in old times heroic deeds by men and women were equally matched, and that one used to the men *bogatyr's*, and the women *polyanitsas*. I heard this dozens of times' (Gil'ferding 1871/1983: 42).

38 For a detailed description of the complex relation between the trochaic tetrametre of the runes and varied word length employed in each line (and also, different vowel lengths falling on strong and weak metric positions), see Sadeniemi (1951). On the historical development of these complications of the trochaic metre, see Kuusi (1994c).

39 See in particular the following fundamental investigations of the Kalevalan metre and 'alliterations': Sadeniemi (1951); Leino (1994). On the history of the Kalevalan metre, see Kuusi (1994c); Korhonen (1994).

40 The distinction was drawn most unequivocally in Yevseyev (1968: 3), whose agenda, however, was to highlight the alleged Russian influence in this feature over the alleged Germanic one.

41 In order to keep this phenomenon under the habitual 'alliteration' label, Sadeniemi had to resort to an artificial distinction between the alliterations 'one' and 'two' – the first purely consonantal, the second also involving a vowel; according to Sadeniemi's statistics, 'alliteration two' (which is, strictly speaking, not an alliteration at all) constitutes a large majority of cases: its ratio to 'alliteration one' can be 2:1, or in some cases, even 3:1 (Sadeniemi 1951: 79–99). Precisely where the repetitions of vowels or of more elaborate sound clusters stand in Sadeniemi's description remains unclear.

42 Some examples of coupling sound repetitions into opposing pairs are cited in Yevseyev 1957–60: II, 119–20), without, however, any semantic analysis of this pattern.

43 Yevseyev (1957–60: II, 137–41) noted that in runes sound repetitions are less intense than in Lönnrote's *Kalevala*. He also suggested that patterns of sound repetition should be studied in connection with narrated 'topics', without indicating, however, how the sound repetition and the meaning could be connected.

44 A rune recorded in 1872 from Miihkaline Simana (SKVR 1, no. 144).

45 Cf. a point made in Virtanen and DuBois (2000: 93): words in the *Kalevala* are not arbitrary signs but bodies subject to magic manipulation.

46 According to Comparetti (1892: 25–26), the 'word' of origin (*synty*) of the harmful or helpful phenomenon, by which the 'knowledgeable' healer (*tietäjä*) enacts his magical help, means in fact 'speech' (in the sense of *epos*), that is, a magical incantation. For instance, there exist 'words' for making beer (*oluen sanat*), for making a snake harmless

(*käärmeen luomoomasanat*), and so on. (cf. also examples of incantations of water and fire in Stark-Arola (1989)).
47 About the spiritual subtext of the *Kalevala*'s heroes' journeys, see Kuusi (1994b: 69); Siikala (2002a: 73).
48 Gil'ferding found compelling words to describe the total artificiality of bylinas' chronotope, in regard to the actual condition of their creators and audience's habitat:

> We do not pay attention to the fact that preserving details of the natural environment of the Dnieper region is a miracle of people's memory ... Has an Onega peasant ever seen an oak? He is as familiar with an oak as you, my readers, are with something like the banana tree ... Has he seen even once in his lifetime 'a free and clear expanse' (*razdol'noye chistoye pole*)? No: a field as an open expanse that could be galloped through is a notion entirely alien to his experience; for the fields that he has seen are small, and usually surrounded by the forest.
>
> (Gil'ferding 1871/1983: 41)

49 About the expansive character of the 'epic space', see Putilov (1988a: 18–32).
50 The original meaning of *runa* (adopted into Finnish from Germanic) is 'secret'; thus, *runoilijat* are 'singers of secret words' (Siikala 2002a: 279–80).

Bibliography

Azbelev, S.N. (1982) *Istorizm bylin i spetsifika fol'klora*, Leningrad: Nauka.

Barlen, D. (1993) *Russkiye byliny v svete taynovedeniya*, Kaluga: Dukhovnoye poznaniye.

Bazanov, V.G. (1947) *Narodnaya slovesnost' Karelii*, Pertozavodsk: Izdatel'stvo Karelo-Finskoy SSR.

Chernyakova, I.A. (1998) *O chem ne rasskazal Elias Lönnrot: k istorii kraya, gde okazalis' sokhraneny i zapisany epicheskiye pesni drevnego naroda*, Petrozavodsk: Izdatel'stvo Petrozavodskogo universiteta.

Comparetti, D. (1892) *Der Kalevala oder die traditionelle Poesie der Finnen*, Halle: Max Niemeyer.

Dmitriyeva, S.I. (1975) *Geograficheskoye rasprostraneniye russkikh bylin*, Moskva: Nauka.

Gasparov, B.M. (1995) 'Epicheskaya predikatsiya (Ob upotreblenii glagol'nykh form v fol'klornykh epicheskikh tekstakh)', *Russian Linguistics*, 19/1: 1–23.

Gil'ferding, A.F. (1871–73) *Onezhskiye byliny, zapisannyye A. F. Gil'ferdingom letom 1871 goda*, 1–3, Sankt-Peterburg: Akademiya nauk.

——(1871[1983]) 'Olonetskaya guberniya i yeye narodnye rapsody', in *Onezhskiye byliny*, 21–67, Arkhangel'sk: Russky Sever.

Grigor'yev, A.D. (1904) *Arkhangel'skiye byliny i istoriheskiye pesni*, 1, Moskva: Akademiya Nauk.

Gruzinsky, A.E. (1909) 'P. N. Rybnikov', in *Pesni, sobrannyye Rybnikovym*, tom. 1, 2-e izd., Moskva: Sotrudnik shkol.

Haavio, M. (1952) *Väinämöinen: Eternal Sage*, Helsinki: Suomalainen tiedeakatemia.

——(1967) *Suomalainen mytologia*, Porvoo: W. Søderstrøm.

Karhu, E.G. (1994) *Karel'sky i ingermanlandsky fol'klor v istoricheskom osveshchenii*, Sankt-Peterburg: Nauka.

——(1996) *Elias Lönnrot. Zhizn' i tvorchestvo*, Petrozavodsk: Karelia.

Kirkinen, H. (1987) 'La poésie kalévaléenne: histoire ou mythe?', in H. Kirkinen and J. Perrot (eds) *Le monde kalévaléen en France et en Finlande: avec un regard sur la tradition populaire et l'épopée bretonnes: actes du colloque tenue à Paris et à Riec-sur-Belon du 13 au 16 mars 1985*, 89–102, Paris: A.D.E.F.O. /Helsinki: Suomalaisen Kirjallisuuden Seura.

Korhonen, M. (1994) 'The early history of the Kalevala's metre', in A.-L. Siikala (ed.) *Songs beyond the Kalevala: Transformations of Oral Poetry*, 75–87, Studia Fennica, Folkloristica, 2, Helsinki: Suomalaisen Kirjallisuuden Seura.

Krohn, J. (1885) *Suomalaisen kirjallisuuden historia*, 1: *Kalevala*, Helsinki: Weilin & Göös.

Krohn, K. (1924) *Kalevalastudien: Einleitung*, FF Communications, 53, Helsinki: Suomalainen Tiedeakatemia.

Kuusi, M. (1994a) 'The five stylistic periods of ancient Kalevala epic', in M. Kuusi (ed.) *Mind and Form in Folklore*, 37–49, Studia Fennica, Folkloristica, 3, Helsinki: Suomalaisen Kirjallisuuden Seura.

——(1994b) 'Considerations of poetic epic', in M. Kuusi (ed.) *Mind and Form in Folklore*, 66–78, Studia Fennica, Folkloristica, 3, Helsinki: Suomalaisen Kirjallisuuden Seura.

——(1994c) 'Questions of Kalevala metre', in A.-L. Siikala (ed.) *Songs beyond the Kalevala: Transformations of Oral Poetry*, 41–55, Studia Fennica. Folkloristica, 2, Helsinki: Suomalaisen Kirjallisuuden Seura.

Laugaste, E. (1955) 'Arhailised jooned eesti rahvalaulude keeles', *Tartu Riikliku Ülikooli Toimetised*, 38: 15–37.

Leino, P. (1994) 'The Kalevala metre and its development', in A.-L. Siikala (ed.) *Songs beyond the Kalevala: Transformations of Oral Poetry*, 56–74, Studia Fennica, Folkloristica, 2, Helsinki: Suomalaisen Kirjallisuuden Seura.

Likhachev, D.S. (1949) 'Letopisnyye svidetel'stva ob Aleksandre Popoviche', *Trudy Otdela Drevnerusskoy Literatury*, 7, Moskva/Leningrad: Izdatel'stvo AN SSSR.

Mansikka, V.J. (1906) 'Das Lied von Ogoi und Havatitsa', *Finnisch-ugrische Forschungen*, 6: 40–65.

——(1907) 'Alesha Popovich i Ivan Godinovich v Finlyandii', *Etnograficheskoye obozreniye*, 3: 38–39.

Novikov, Yu.A. (2000) *Skazitel' i bylinnaya traditsiya*, Sankt-Peterburg: Dmitry Bulanin.

Oinas, F.J. (1969) 'The problem of Russian word order influence on the word order of the Kalevalan-Finnish epic' in F.J. Oinas (ed.) *Studies in Finnish-Slavic Folklore Relations*, 151–59, Helsinki: Suomalainen Tiedeakatemia.

——(1985a) 'The Finnic epic', in F.J. Oinas (ed.) *Studies in Finnic Folklore: An Homage to the Kalevala*, 32–68, Helsinki: Suomalaisen Kirjallisuuden Seura.

——(1985b) 'Negative parallelism in Karelian-Finnish folklore', in F.J. Oinas (ed.) *Studies in Finnic Folklore: An Homage to the Kalevala*, 146–53, Helsinki: Suomalaisen Kirjallisuuden Seura.

——(1985c) 'Lemminkäinen and Vavilo', in F. J. Oinas (ed.) *Studies in Finnic Folklore: An Homage to the Kalevala*, 115–30, Helsinki: Suomalaisen Kirjallisuuden Seura.

Pentikäinen, J. (1971) *Marina Takalon uskonto*, Helsinki: Suomalaisen Kirjallisuuden Seura.

——(1999a) *Kalevala Mythology*, 2nd edn, Bloomington: Indiana University Press.

——(1999b) 'Old Believers: summary. The religio-cultural manifestations of Russian peripheries', in J. Pentikäinen (ed.) *'Silent as Waters We Live': Old Believers in Russia and Abroad – Cultural Encounter with the Finno-Ugrians*, 126–28, Studia Fennica, Folkloristica, 6, Helsinki: Suomalaisen Kirjallisuuden Seura.

Pentikäinen, J. and Raudalainen, T. (1999) 'Old belief among the Uralic people', in J. Pentikäinen (ed.) *'Silent as Waters We Live': Old Believers in Russia and Abroad – Cultural Encounter with the Finno-Ugrians*, 40–54, Studia Fennica, Folkloristica, 6, Helsinki: Suomalaisen Kirjallisuuden Seura.

Plisetsky, M.M. (1962) *Istorizm russkikh bylin*, Moskva: Vysshaya shkola.

Propp, V.Ya. (1949[2002]) 'Kalevala v svete fol'klora', in V. Ya. Propp, *Fol'klor, literatura, istoriya*, 120–36, Moskva: Labirint.

——(1958[1999]) *Russky geroichesky epos*, Moskva: Labirint.

——(1962) 'Ob istorizme russkogo eposa', *Russkaya literatura*, 2: 98–111.

——(1976) *Fol'klor i deystvitelnost'*, Moskva: Nauka.

Putilov, B.N. (1988a) *Geroichesky epos i deystvitel'nost'*, Leningrad: Nauka.

——(1988b) 'Puti rekonstruktsii arkhaicheskikh form slavyanskogo geroicheskogo eposa', *X Mezhdunarodny s"ezd slavistov. Istoriya, kul'tura, etnografiya i fol'klor slavyanskikh narodov*, 301–14, Moskva: Nauka.

Pypin, A.N. (1890–92) *Istoriya russkoy etnografii*, 1–4, Sankt-Peterburg: Akademiya Nauk.

Ruoppila, V. (1967) *Kalevala ja kansankieli*, Helsinki: Suomalaisten Kirjallisuuden Seura.

Rybakov, B.A. (1948) *Istoriya kul'tury Drevney Rusi*, 1: *Domongol'sky period*, Moskva/Leningrad: Izdatel'stvo AN SSSR.

——(1961) 'Istorichesky vzglyad na russkiye byliny', *Istoriya SSSR*, 5: 141–66 and 6: 80–96.

Rybnikov, P.N. (1861–67) *Pesni, sobrannyye P. N. Rybnikovym*, chasti 1–4, Moskva: Tipografiya A. Semena.

Sadeniemi, M. (1951) *Die Metrik des Kalevala-Verses*, Helsinki: Suomalainen Tiedeakatemia, FF Communications, 139.

Siikala, A.-L. (ed.) (1994) *Songs beyond the Kalevala: Transformations of Oral Poetry*, Studia Fennica. Folkloristica, 2, Helsinki: Suomalaisen Kirjallisuuden Seura.

——(2002a) *Mythic Images and Shamanism: A Perspective on Kalevala Poetry*, FF Communications, 280, Helsinki: Suomalainen Tiedeakatemia.

——(2002b): 'The singer ideal and the enrichment of poetic culture: why did the ingredients for the Kalevala come from Viena Karelia?', in L. Honko, (ed.) *The Kalevala and the World's Traditional Epics*, 26–43, Studia Fennica, Folkloristika, 12, Helsinki: Finnish Literary Society.

Skaftymov, A.P. (1924) *Poetika i genezis russkikh bylin. Ocherki*, Moskva/Saratov: V.Z. Yaksanov; reprinted The Hague: Mouton, 1970.

SKVR (1908) *Suomen kansan vanhat runot*, 1–2. *Vienan Läänin Runot*, Helsinki: Suomalaisen Kirjallisuuden Seura.

Stark-Arola, L. (1989) 'The dynamic body in traditional Finnish-Karelian thought: *väki, vihat, nenä*, and *luonto*', in A.-L. Siikala (ed.) *Studies in Oral Narrative*, 67–103, Studia Fennica, 33, Helsinki: Suomalaisen Kirjallisuuden Seura.

Turunen, A. (1979) *Kalevalan sanat ja niiden taustat*, Lappeenranta: Karjalaisen kultuurin edistämissäätiö.

Virtanen, L. and DuBois, Th.A. (2000) *Finnish Folklore*, Studia Fennica, Folkloristica, 9, Helsinki: Suomalaisen Kirjallisuuden Seura.

Yevseyev, V.Ya. (1957–60) *Istoricheskiye osnovy karelo-finskogo eposa*, 1–2, Moskva/Leningrad: Izdatel'stvo AN SSSR.

——(1968) *Karel'sky fol'klor v istoricheskom osveshchenii*, Leningrad: Nauka.

11 Autogenesis in Russian culture: an approach to the avant-garde

Tomi Huttunen

> *Смотраны написанные худогом, создадут передею природы.*
> 'Seens written by an arter will create a redressing of nature'
> (Velimir Khlebnikov, *Victory over the Sun*, in Janecek (1996: 228))

It is evident that in human culture nothing is born out of nothing, by itself, but everything exists in a historical continuum of tradition and intellectual communication. Thus in culture all new, even the most creative, spontaneous phenomena (innovative texts) are eventually considered in relationship to a tradition. Suggesting the existence of autogenetic, spontaneous formations and self-creation in culture therefore seems absurd. Nevertheless, autogenesis as a declaration is very often emphasized in Russian culture, especially by those representing abruptness and unexpectedness. More generally, the question of autogenesis in culture could be translated into a dialogue between *creation* and *evolution* and their often paradoxical interaction in cultural history. These are of course phenomena raised rather in theology and natural science than cultural studies.[1] However, my approach to autogenesis is that of cultural semiotics, also close to new cultural anthropology.[2] In this chapter autogenesis will be treated as the ultimate expression of unpredictability, considered typical for the history of Russian culture. The empirical material comes mainly from Russian avant-garde literature, from phenomena that especially declare their independence, unexpectedness, and discontinuity. My aim is not to give an overall picture of autogenesis in Russian culture here, but to provide an introduction to the subject, concentrating on two avant-garde cases which I consider illustrative and interesting for the further development of cultural theory.

From self-understanding to self-creation

In terms of Yury Lotman's semiotics, the history of Russian culture is often seen as a paradoxical continuum of revolutions, upheavals, and rebellions, a kind of paradoxical succession of explosions. In other words, the history of Russian culture repeats itself by producing unpredictable new phenomena, received by the contemporary representatives of culture as eschatological revolutions. The study of this intriguing dialogue between unpredictable discontinuity and predictable continuity was based on the interpretations related to the so-called binary system of Russian culture. As final statements on this subject, Lotman's last two works – *Culture and Explosion* (Lotman 1992, in English: 2009) and *Unpredictable Mechanisms of Culture* (Lotman 2010), the latter published posthumously, concentrate on the processes of predictability/unpredictability and continuity/spontaneity and their interaction.

From today's point of view it is evident that Yuri Lotman was a 'combinator' of twentieth-century Russian theory, innovatively synthesizing his predecessors' thinking into a general and – as he himself thought – universal theory of culture, whose applicability in studying specifics of Russian culture has been proved many times. Lotman's notion of the 'semiosphere' from the early 1980s (Lotman 1984; in English: 2005) emphasized, among other things, an objective and external viewpoint to *cultural self-understanding*, to the way representatives of a certain culture define themselves.[3] The notion of a dialogue, a central feature in Mikhail Bakhtin's theory as well, became extremely important for Lotman (2005: 218): 'Consciousness is impossible without communication. In this sense it can be said that dialogue precedes language and generates the language.' His 'dialogo-centric' theory of the semiosphere emphasizes the idea that in culture there are no pre-existing components, except for the dialogue (Lotman, Torop and Kull 2004; see also Kull 2005: 179 and Torop 2009: xxxii). Eventually, this dialogo-centrism was taken to another level and developed further in the book *Universe of the Mind*, where Lotman (1990: 143–44) underlined that 'The need for dialogue, the dialogic situation, precedes both real dialogue and even the existence of a language in which to conduct it: the semiotic situation precedes the instruments of semiosis.'

While discussing his post-structuralist theory of the semiosphere – the dynamic cultural space of constant dialogue, intellectual interaction, and communication – Lotman turned to the famous Soviet cosmist, the theorist of ecology, biosphere, and noosphere, Vladimir Vernadsky.[4] Lotman introduced the term as a continuum of cultural communication, which draws from the essential assumption that absolutely nothing in culture is created out of nothing – on the contrary, everything is related to other formations and to the whole culture. In a letter to his colleague Boris Uspensky, Lotman wrote (1997: 629–30):

> I am reading Vernadsky and … I am stunned by one of his statements. You know … my opinion that a text can exist (it can socially be recognized as a text) only if it is preceded by another text, and that any developed culture should be preceded by another developed culture. And now I find Vernadsky's thought, deeply founded on the experience of exploring cosmic geology, that life can arise only from living, that it is preceded by life … Only the *semiotic sphere* makes a message a message. Only the existence of mind explains the existence of mind.
>
> (trans. in Kull 2005: 178)

Thus, as a conclusion Lotman made one of the general definitions of the semiosphere: it is a continuum of texts. A semiotic definition of culture means constant interactivity and intertextuality, and the space surrounding all intellectual activity presupposes the dialogic situation. Intersemiotic and intertextual features are thus taken as part of the culture's essential being, not as specific or exceptional phenomena.

In his last books Lotman was trying to synthesize his earlier findings by concentrating on two features of historical cultural progress: gradual (predictable) and explosive (unpredictable) processes.[5] This time he turned to another theoretician, the physical chemist and Nobel laureate Ilya Prigogine, whose studies on stability and instability inspired Lotman's theory of cultural unpredictability.[6] The gradual processes of motivated predictability in culture meant for Lotman something that is obvious, understood with certainty and inescapably received by consumers – it meant processuality, continuity, and the logical evolution of consistency (Lotman 1992: 17–18). Against the background of Lotman's general theory, these gradual processes should be understood as neutral dialogue from the point of view of cultural history, since he was mainly interested in cultural formations that would revolt against norms, even against understanding. This was obvious in his theory of the semiosphere, where he had described the asymmetry of semiotic space as an altering dialogue and interaction between weakly structured dynamic peripheries and strongly structured static centres (Lotman 1990: 127–30). In his last work he was looking for a general theory opposed to neutral, accepted and understood communication – he suggested the category of explosions, unexpected eschatological changes in culture, unpredictability as the object of science.

Based on his definition of the two different cultural processes, Lotman ended up by classifying different cultural formations as either binary or ternary, treating Russian culture as a binary (unpredictable) system and something opposed to the Western European system of ternary (predictable) structures (Lotman 1992: 266–70). Lotman was approaching the question of autogenesis in Russian culture from this same perspective, and Prigogine explicitly discussed self-organization as an argument that would develop Vernadsky's ideas in a new direction: 'The early appearance of life is certainly an argument in favour of the idea that life is the result of spontaneous self-organization that occurs whenever conditions for it permit' (Prigogine and Stengers 1984: 176).

From Chaadaev to the avant-garde

One of Lotman's favourite examples was the philosopher Petr Chaadaev. In nineteenth-century Russian culture, the question of autogenesis played a significant role in the discussion of Russianness, due to Chaadaev's *Philosophical Letters*.[7] In his search for a Russian geopolitical self-definition in relation to Europe, he declared that Russian culture was autogenetic, born by itself. According to him, Russians did not have any wise men of old. Russia existed outside of temporality, and its geopolitical existence between East and West meant non-belonging:

> We have never advanced along with other people; we are not related to any of the great human families; we belong neither to the West nor to the East, and we possess the traditions of neither. Placed, as it were, outside of the times, we have not been affected by the universal education of mankind. This admirable interconnection of human ideas throughout the passing centuries, this history of the human spirit which led men to the position which they occupy in the rest of the world today, had no effect upon us … Every nation has its period of stormy agitation, of passionate restlessness, of activity without conscious motivation … We, on the other hand, have nothing like that. First, a brutal barbarism, then crude superstition, after that fierce, degrading foreign domination by strangers whose spirit was later inherited by the nation – that is the sad history of our youth … Glance over all the centuries through which we have lived, all the land which we cover, you will find not one endearing object of remembrance, not one venerable monument which might evoke powerfully bygone eras and might vividly and picturesquely depict them again for you. We live only in the narrowest kind of present without a past and without a future in the midst of a shallow calm.
>
> (Chaadaev 1991: 20–21)

Thus, according to Chaadaev, the whole of Russia was born out of itself. For him, Russia was outside the European community, independently formed, rootless, and indeed an 'orphan'. Europe lives in time, says Chaadaev, while Russia lives only in space, outside of time. The autogenetic emergence of Russia lead into spatial and social non-belonging: 'In our houses we seem to be camping; in our families we look like strangers; in our cities we look like nomads' (Chaadaev 1991: 20). This extra-temporality and rootless non-belonging is defined as a definite lack of family unity among Russians, 'who have come into the world like illegitimate children without a heritage … Each one of us must try individually to mend the rift broken within the family' (ibid.: 22). This results in unpredictability in Russian history. Everything in Russian culture – starting from the adaptation of Christianity in 988 – was imported and imitated from foreign sources and transformed, falsified into something new, Russian. On the one hand, Russia was born out of nothing, and, on the other hand, it was compiled out of false foreign sources. Thus Chaadaev's idea of an autogenetic Russia is once again a paradox: something opposed to the synthetic ideas about Russia combining in itself the West and the East, but also another aspect of this synthesis. 'Russianness' as a specific trait in world history is emphasized in both of these theorems.

Apart from the self-reflective definitions of Russia's specific appearance in world history, unpredictable motifs of autogenesis can be found in several individual phenomena, important to Russian cultural history. First of all, the subject of rootless unpredictability is closely related not only to Chaadaev's philosophy, but also to his own 'artistic' behaviour and appearance. Lotman – in several studies dedicated to the dynamics of fashion in culture – concentrates on the philosopher's appearance as a Russian dandy, a creator of new fashion. While discussing Chaadaev, Lotman turned to Chaadaev's friend, the poet Aleksandr Pushkin.

Both Chaadaev and Pushkin represent autogenetic explosions of culture for Lotman. It is worth noting that the same year Chaadaev wrote the first of his *Philosophical Letters* (in 1836), Pushkin wrote the poem *Ya pamyatnik sebe vozdvig ner-ukovorny* ('I have built a monument to myself') about an autogenetic statue and about a lyrical subject, who is indeed a maximalist and imagines being praised among the different nations, hailed in different languages. This poem was Push-kin's version of an ancient story about a poet declaring himself to be the irre-placeable, the greatest poet of his times.[8] However, in Pushkin's version the statue is 'not made by hands' (*nerukotvorny*), instead it is something that arises from within itself. Obviously, Pushkin was referring in this poem to a certain source in the Russian iconographic tradition, which flourished in Novgorod during the thir-teenth century. One of the major motifs developed from the Byzantine tradition by the Novgorod school was the motif of *Spas Nerukotvorny* ('Holy Mandylion').[9] The story of Mandylion is essentially about an autogenetic image of Christ. The icon is, typically, of the Novgorod school of iconography, exceptionally expressive and dynamic in its simplicity – at the same time it is one of the images related to the legend about the emergence of the first icons.

It is precisely through the primitively simple, yet expressive iconographic tradition of *Spas* that a logical way of relating the question of autogenesis to the aesthetics of Russian avant-garde painting may be found. The most striking likeness with this particular tradition can be seen in the work of the Futurist David Burlyuk. In 1917 Burlyuk, who declared himself 'the father of Russian Futurism', painted a portrait of the Futurist poet Vasily Kamensky (who was called the 'mother' of Russian Futurism) – a portrait which was very reminiscent of *Spas*. More generally, the influence of traditional icon painting on Russian avant-garde art was enor-mous. Even Kazimir Malevich called his *Black Square on White Canvas* (1915) 'the icon of icons', and the Suprematists generally used icons as their source of inspiration. Analogous intertextual pairs to *Spas* and *Portrait of Kamensky* are easy to find from the avant-garde art of the early twentieth century (Spira 2008: 46, 56).[10] One of the most famous examples is Vasily Kandinsky's treatment of the tradition of *St George* (1911), which already in its title referred to the famous Novgorod tradition of St George. Kandinsky managed to illustrate his art theory and the idea of 'improvisation' with the help of this modernization of the icon tradition.

The Futurist David Burlyuk's intertextual treatment of Vasily Kamensky's portrait refers not so much to the Christ-likeness of the Futurist poet, but rather to Russian culture's general auto-communicative need for self-references and to the Futurists' way of declaring themselves as a self-emerged, spontaneous appear-ance without any possible connection with Filippo Tommaso Marinetti's Italian Futurism, even though the Marinettian manifestos (1909) had been published years before the first Russian Futurists' declarations.[11] An interesting detail in this context is Marinetti's visit to Russia in 1914, when his manifestos became well known to Russian colleagues, and even new translations by the poet Vadim Shershenevich appeared exclusively for this event. However, the translator Shershenevich was the only poet from the Futurist group who met Marinetti at the railway station in Moscow. Apart from rejecting the Italians and Marinetti, the Russian Futurists wanted to reject everything that they had learned from their own culture. In 1913 they signed the famous declaration *A Slap in the Face of the Public Taste*. Symptomatically enough, it was titled *Unexpected*.

> To the readers of our New First Unexpected.
>
> *We* alone are the *face* of *our* Time. Through us the horn of time blows in the art of the word.
>
> The past is too tight. The Academy and Pushkin are less intelligible than hieroglyphics.
>
> Throw Pushkin, Dostoyevsky, Tolstoy, etc., etc. overboard from the Ship of Modernity.
>
> He who does not forget his *first* love will not recognize his last …
>
> And if *for the time being* the filthy stigmas of your 'Common sense' and 'good taste' are still present in our lines, these same lines *for the first time* already glimmer with the Summer Lightning of the New Coming Beauty of the Self-sufficient (self-centred) Word.
>
> (Burlyuk in Lawton 1988: 51–52. Italics original)

This kind of declaration of autogenetic rootlessness was typical of the Russian avant-garde. Poets, painters, film-makers, and theatre workers were all eager to declare themselves the newest, the most innovative, independent, and impressive artists of the time. It is symptomatic of how Sergey Eisenstein, for example, formulated the emergence of Soviet avant-garde cinema, as if there was not cinematic art in Russia before montage films:

> We came to cinema as something not yet existent. We came upon no ready-built city; there were no squares, no streets laid out, not even little crooked lanes or blind alleys such as we may find in the cinematropolis of our day. We came like Bedouins or gold-seekers to a place with unimaginably great possibilities, only a small section of which has even now been developed.
>
> (Eisenstein 1965: 3)

The predecessors, the Symbolists, were rejected just as aggressively as Western European influences, though both were inevitable sources for Russian avant-garde writers. This is one of the most obvious reasons why the avant-garde artists would turn to the idea of autogenesis. Declaring themselves self-created also meant rejection of the tradition. Nevertheless, autogenesis in the Russian avant-garde is very often related to the image of Christ, as we can see in the way icons were reproduced, even though it clearly belongs to the rejected world of the old and is an essential part of the old culture's language. However, the Christian motif of autogenesis is related not only to the *image* of Christ, and thus to the paradoxical rejection of previous tradition, but also to the emergence of language according to the Bible. In fact, while studying the Russianness of the Russian avant-garde it is of great importance that the autogenesis in the Bible is rooted in the question of the emergence of language. The main Biblical source for autogenesis is based on the basic notions of language in the *Book of Genesis* and in the *Gospel according to St John*.

For Russian avant-garde literature, an author, or her/his protagonist, was supposed to institutionalize a new beginning in the world – s/he should be represented as an 'innovator' or as a 'thirteenth apostle', as in Vladimir Mayakovsky's famous long poem *Oblako v shtanakh* ('A Cloud in Trousers', 1913). An avant-garde author was supposed to be Another Adam (see Kruchenykh in Lawton 1988: 67 and Kruchenykh 1928: 17). Adam saw the world like a child and thus named the animals in his own manner, while the authoritative author (God the Creator) remained silent and watched how Man would complete his first semiotic act (Gen. 2.19–20). Language, according to the *Book of Genesis*, emerged along with the act of naming the animals – the text preceded the language.[12] As a semiotic act, this possibility that had been given to Adam was intriguing for Russian post-Symbolists, especially the Acmeists, who also called themselves the Adamists. In the Bible, the idea of linguistic autogenesis was further emphasized in the *Gospel according to John*, especially in the prologue, also called the *Hymn to the Word* (Gr. Λόγος), which introduces the conception that Jesus Christ is the Word: 'In the beginning was the Word, and the Word was with God, and the Word was God' (John 1.1).

According to John, the Word, which had participated in the creation, in fact gave birth to itself. It was not created or given birth to, it existed before the world was created, and it was realized by being 'made flesh' (John 1.14). However, even though the Word was God, it was not understood by people. Christ as Logos remained misunderstood. The divine, autogenetic word was born out of itself and was received with confusion. The hymn to Logos is obviously an autogenetic motif, but at the same time we can speak of a word being difficult to understand as an expression of an unknown language, which the people in their 'darkness' (Gr. σκοτία) did not 'comprehend' (Gr. κατέλαβεν). Theologically, the idea of the people not comprehending the Logos was soon – ever since Origen (c. 185– 254) – considered very problematic, even though the idea is further emphasized in the Gospel itself.

In fact, this autogenetic perception of Jesus Christ is much more evident in the apocryphal texts, especially in the Gnostic *Secret Book of John*, which was written in the late second century. There Christ is called the 'Self-Generated' or 'Autogenes' and defined as an active participant in world creation, pre-existing in the same way as the Holy Spirit: 'And the Word followed the Will. For through the Word, Christ, the divine Self-Generated created the All' (*The Apocryphon of John* II.7.9–11 in Waldstein and Wisse 1995: 45).

Obviously, the interpretation of Logos in the *Secret Book of John* (as well as in the prologue in John) is related to the Stoic philosopher Heraclitus' idea of Logos, which is the cosmic word (source and fundamental order) behind everything in the world, the ratio, not understood by the people. Eventually, all these sources emphasize the same idea that the word is an autogenetic expression that creates its own language while being pronounced as part of a speech act (or incarnation).

This is why it cannot be understood as spoken. The main paradox is that an autogenetic word should not, on the one hand, be drawn back to any pre-existent information in the culture of its origin, otherwise it would not be a *creation* of ultimate unpredictability. On the other hand, it should be semantically justified in order to be at least potentially interpreted.

Case 1: declaration of Russianness in *Dyr bul shchyl*

The Futurist manifesto *A Slap in the Face of the Public Taste* ended with 'the New Coming Beauty of the Self-sufficient (self-centred) Word', which was especially studied by Velimir Khlebnikov and Aleksey Kruchenykh. Together they published a manifesto called *Slovo kak takovoye* ('The Word as Such') in 1912, and Khlebnikov separately studied the essence of the *samovitoye slovo* ('self-sufficient word'). These two Futurist poets were searching for a literary means of expression that was independent and free from the burden of previous usage. According to Mayakovsky, Khlebnikov's 'self-sufficient word' was 'an independent force, organizing material of the feelings and thoughts' (Mayakovsky 1978: XII, 24). The Futurist word, completely free from everyday life and usage, was to become the main subject of their poetry, and the immediate contact with Christian terminology seemed inevitable at each turn in its definition. Attempting to defend the Futurists and their experiments, Viktor Shklovsky wrote a theoretical study on the Futurist word with the title *Voskresheniye slova* ('Resurrection of the Word', 1914), hailing the Futurists' way of bringing dead words back to the life with the help of new vehicles:

> And now, today, when the artist wishes to deal with living form and with the living, not the dead, word, and wishes to give the word features, he has broken it down and mangled it up. The 'arbitrary' and 'derived' words of the Futurists have been born. They either create the new word from an old root (Khlebnikov, Guro, Kamensky, Gnedov) or split it up by rhyme, like Mayakovsky, or give it incorrect stress by use of the rhythm of verse (Kruchenykh). New, living words are created. The ancient diamonds of words recover their former brilliance. This new language is incomprehensible, difficult, and cannot be read like the *Stock Exchange Bulletin*. It is not even like Russian, but we have become too used to setting up comprehensibility as a necessary requirement of poetic language. The history of art shows us that (at least very often) the language of poetry is not a comprehensible language, but a semi-comprehensible one.
>
> (Shklovsky 1973: 46)

Aleksey Kruchenykh's poem *Dyr bul shchyl*, considered a highly programmatic and experimental text, is one of the most famous and most analysed texts in Russian avant-garde literature of the first half of the twentieth century. It is one of the symbols of the Russian avant-garde in general. It is well known to anyone interested in Russian literature of that time. It has been said that the text was already in the 1920s far more famous than its author (Kruchenykh 1996: 17), who, in fact, has remained relatively unknown among the general public, especially outside Russia.[13] The reasons for this are to be found in the astonishing combination of nonsense and familiarity of the poem, experienced by Russian readers:

Дыр бул щыл
убешщур
скум
вы со бу
р л эз

The poem was first published in Kruchenykh's almanac titled *Pomada* ('Pomade', January 1913), which was a booklet made with a technique the Futurists called 'self-writing' (*samopis'mo*), meaning lithographic printing (Janecek 1984: 69–71). The poem is closely related to Kruchenykh's declaration of the 'Word as Such', which followed the poem in the spring of 1913. Kruchenykh's and Khlebnikov's studies resulted in one of the peculiarities of Russian avant-garde literature, the notion of *zaum'* (trans-rational word and language). The above text has been an intriguing and endless puzzle and challenge for many Russian and foreign scholars. Nikolay Bogomolov (2005, 172–92) has presented these different approaches exhaustively, which is why I shall concentrate only on the aspects of 'autogenesis' and 'Russianness' in relation to Kruchenykh's experiment. At the same time, I shall have to return to the question of *zaum'*, to a discussion which Bogomolov deliberately and understandably ignores because of the heterogeneity of its treatment by literary scholars.

In several auto-commentaries on the text, Kruchenykh has pointed out that the poem is both essentially trans-rational (*zaumnoye*), and essentially Russian (Kruchenykh 2001: 412). In the declaration of the 'Word as Such' he wrote: 'as a matter of fact, in this five-line poem there is more of the Russian national spirit than in all of Pushkin' (Brodsky et al. 1929: 80). Of course, the name of Pushkin is no coincidence here – Pushkin was one of the Russian writers to be thrown out from the 'steamship of contemporary literature', according to *A Slap in the Face of Public Taste*. Following Kruchenykh's auto-commentaries, the poem could be read as a 'declaration of Russianness'. The painter David Burlyuk had asked Kruchenykh to write a poem made of 'unknown words'. And Kruchenykh answered him with *Dyr bul shchyl* (Khardzhiyev 2006: 390). The poem was considered by the author also from the point of view of its possible translation. He criticized Ilya Ehrenburg's attempts to translate the poem into French by referring to the famous dictionary of Russian literary language, which claimed that only the writers Ivan Krylov and Aleksandr Griboyedov were writing in Russian. Meanwhile, Pushkin's language was half-French. Kruchenykh himself was trying to deliver the phonetic sound system of Russian language. One of the essential features of an autogenetic Russian text is that it could not be translated into any other language.

Apart from being 'essentially Russian', the poem *Dyr bul shchyl* was also declared to be a 'text in its own language'. Kruchenykh's original task was to write a poem in a previously unknown language, so that readers would not comprehend it. This would further become the plain idea of *zaum'*, trans-rational language, which was originally driven by foreign sources, such as Cubism and Abstractionism in the visual arts. For Kruchenykh it meant the absolute freedom of the poet (2001: 415). *Dyr bul shchyl* was not meant to be understood. Today we can say that in this the author has succeeded, since the process of interpreting the text seems endless. Whatever the 'final' interpretation of this poem would be, it is obvious that a *new*, previously non-existing language was meant to be created on its basis. And, paradoxically, this non-existing language was essentially Russian. By 1917–18 Kruchenykh's *zaum'* texts would include foreign Georgian and Armenian elements, but that already signalled a different phase in the history of the avant-garde and requires a different treatment too (see Janecek 1996).

Case 2: the Imaginists imitating autogenesis

In 1920, the Imaginist poet Vadim Shershenevich wrote a poem about the lyric subject being born out of himself, meaning maximum creativity in his power, but which leads to the logical conclusion that he is also going to finish his life himself. The image of Christ is once again present in this poem as a point of comparison for the autogenetic poet:

> Oh Lord! In front of you I am quiet,
> You are just as tired and repulsive!
> Since you could not save yourself,
> you sure will save me, won't you?
> Who could ease the heart in my chest? ...
> I was born from my virgin self,
> and I shall kill myself too, of course!
> (Shershenevich 2000 [1920]: 217. Translation mine)

The author had been a Symbolist and a Futurist before appearing as one of the leaders of a new poetic group, the Russian Imaginists[14] that began their activity right after the October Revolution. The Imaginists were not Futurists; on the contrary, they aggressively attacked the Futurists in their manifestos. However, they received significant support from the Bolshevik party, especially the Soviet People's Commissar of Enlightenment Anatoly Lunacharsky. It seems that the Bolsheviks were ready to support the Imaginists for at least three reasons: (1) Futurism was not supposed to become too influential in the difficult post-revolutionary years – it was convenient to have an opposition;[15] (2) Imaginist poet Ryurik Ivnev was one of the (very few) first poets to have joined the new party in power and declared his faithfulness to Lunacharsky himself, and he appeared in the position of Lunacharsky's secretary;[16] and (3) both Lunacharsky and Trotsky seemed to be keen on Imaginist poet Sergey Yesenin's oeuvre. Thus the Imaginists were given exceptional privileges, such as their own publishing house, a journal, cafés, film theatre, and so on.

The poet Shershenevich was a polyglot. He had translated Marinetti's Italian manifestos into Russian in 1914, a collection of poems by Jules Laforgue from French, and he was a great fan of Walt Whitman's poetry. Apart from these biographical details, it was obvious that the Russian Imaginists had heard of the Anglo-American Imagists, or Vorticists (Ezra Pound, T.E. Hulme, T.S. Eliot, Hilda Doolittle) – if not from elsewhere, they must have known Ezra Pound from Zinaida Vengerova's interview, an article called 'English Futurists' (*Angliyskiye futuristy*), which was published in 1915 in the Futurists' anthology *Strelets* ('Sagittarius').[17] Nevertheless, Russian specialists studying the Imaginists today are still looking for arguments against these influences. In public, the Imaginists emphasized that they were 'self-made', had nothing to do with either the Futurists, or the English Imagists. They also rejected the Symbolists (Bal'mont, Bryusov, and Blok), although their poetry was greatly under their influence. Shershenevich's poem shows that this position of epigonic rejection influenced Imaginist poetry also.

For the Imaginists, autogenesis is clearly a motif emphasizing their rootlessness and non-belonging in the surrounding reality, especially the contemporary city: Sergey Yesenin's constructed authorial image was '*the last* poet of the village', while Anatoly Mariengof's key image was '*the only* dandy of the republic'. However, they were lacking originality – in their declarations of cultural autogenesis, the Imaginists were acting as the Futurists' imitators, representatives of '*arrière garde*' rather than avant-garde. Thus, the notion of *poshlost'* was often coined as a definition in relation to the group.[18]

Yesenin and Mariengof, who lived together for some time in the early 1920s and kept dedicating poetic anthologies and plays to each other, emphasized catachrestic motifs related to autogenesis via their lyric subjects. Obviously, simulation of homosexuality became part of their everyday life theatre. For Mariengof, a repeating image of the lyric subject is a variety of non-acceptance of new-born children by their real parents: *nedonosok* ('premature infant'), *vykidysh* ('dead embryo'), *priyemysh* ('adopted child') or other representations of non-belonging: *inostranets* ('foreigner'), *chuzhoy* ('alien') and so on – someone not belonging to, or separated from, the family unity. Especially illustrative in this respect are Mariengof's verses from a poem that was written in 1922:

> In my country
> I am like an adopted child,
> To fame–
> A non-beloved son ...
> My fellow citizens, what do I do
> With your love or hatred.
> In a glass of beer in vain is wheezing
> The lovely foam of misleading praise.
> O fate, I am looking at your empty pools
> And I feel:
> My hair is getting grey.
>
> (Mariengof 2005 [1922]: 321. Translation mine)

This poem, which was not published until 2005, clearly reflects the poet's frustration over the revolution, which had meant so many privileges and so much fame ('the lovely foam of misleading praise') for the Imaginists. Mariengof's poem also introduces the image of a foreigner: 'Oh, friends, our land denies her motherhood. / Let us be aliens in our own country.' In 1924 Sergey Yesenin, it seems, answered Mariengof with his well-known poem *Soviet Rus'*. To the lines 'In my country / I am like an adopted child' Yesenin replied: 'In my country I am like a foreigner'. More generally, this poem by Yesenin should be revised in the context of Mariengof's poems of 1922 about frustration. If Mariengof writes in 1922: 'what do I do with your love or hatred', Yesenin replies: 'other young men are singing other songs'. Both of these poems were dedicated to the same question of the lyric subject appearing as an 'alien' in the Soviet Russia of the New Economic Policy period. Mariengof's hero is an 'adopted child'; he is no longer beloved by the reading public. And after returning to his home country, Yesenin's hero realized that his fellow-citizens were speaking in a foreign language and that he himself had become superficial: 'O Mother Russia, how ridiculous I have become! / ... The language of my fellow-citizens became alien to me, / In my country I am like a foreigner.'

Aging ('my hair is getting grey') in Mariengof's poem is related to the subject of frustration, but it was a constant dreadful tragedy for the poet, who was nicknamed 'the only dandy of the republic' by the theatre director Vsevolod Meyerhold. In fact, the grammar of dandyism – as a means of absenting oneself from the surrounding reality – seemed an essential act for the young poets Mariengof and Yesenin during these years. They bought themselves top hats in order to highlight their non-belonging to the everyday life of Moscow's and Petrograd's citizens. Once again, this was not original, because the Futurists had posed in photographs with top hats years earlier. Nevertheless, these 'arbitrarily found' top hats became vital in their theatre of everyday life. As anachronistic symbols they were meant to be misunderstood by their fellow-citizens, whose 'love or hatred' was of no importance to these arrogant poets. The Imaginists did not want to be taken as themselves, but as foreigners, this seems to have been of significance for their self-definition. It appears the top hats were not arbitrary symbols of the Imaginists' everyday life, but a way of absenting oneself from past and future at the same time. The Imaginists' paradox in relation to the autogenetic avant-garde is as follows: even though they emphasized their autonomous (Russian) emergence and sovereignty, independence from foreign sources (French, Italian, or English), they were treated as foreigners themselves, and eventually they ended up cultivating their own alienated origin.

Towards understanding autogenesis

Spontaneous formations, unexpected phenomena and declarations of autogenetic independence, as well as the alienated rootlessness of non-belonging, were typical phenomena in Russian avant-garde literature and culture. The avant-gardists were searching for the ultimate unpredictability, which leads to the interaction between genuine unpredictability and its imitations. This is crucial for the development of the language in culture. The above case studies of Kruchenykh's notion of *zaum'* and the Imaginists' self-alienation were meant to serve as examples in discussing the unpredictable and predictable in the history of Russian avant-garde.

Evidently, in his semiotic theory, Yury Lotman was moving towards studying autogenetic phenomena in Russian culture.[19] In his last works he was discussing how the unpredictable mechanisms of culture were in a complex antithetic dialogue with predictability. This asymmetric dialogue is one of the presuppositions for cultural and intellectual activity in a semiotic understanding of human societies. In the transition to a new culture, the unpredictable mechanisms are hardly ever the only visible or noticeable dimension, because we can decipher simultaneous predictable processes at different levels of the culture. The semiotic processes of understanding differ crucially between these phenomena. In fact, the ability of the audience to understand the first experiments of such avant-garde poets as Velimir Khlebnikov or Aleksey Kruchenykh required a cooling down of the explosive, unpredictable event, and its turning into a predictable process. Nevertheless, this does not mean that these works would not be celebrated by critics, scholars or cultural institutions. In fact, they often should be, since in the case of a cultural text this process of cooling down produces new phenomena, which are crucial for the audience's correct understanding: translations, criticism, adaptations, and other kinds of meta-texts of the original. Russian Imaginists were considered imitators and *poshlost'* among the Futurists, who thought of themselves as genuine innovators. Imitations of a genuine innovation (an artistic or cultural text, for example), always represent a more predictable and gradual process.

Studying autogenetic phenomena in culture thus means an attempt to describe the indescribable, that is, to predict ultimate unpredictability in culture. In order to make preliminary conclusions about autogenesis in relation to Lotman's theory of predictability/unpredictability, I shall turn to the following diagram, describing the semiotic process of gradual understanding in the case of a phenomenon, declaring its own unpredictability and its own autogenetic origin. An unexpected, spontaneously formed, theoretically incomprehensible phenomenon – a 'genuinely innovative' artistic text in culture, for example – is transformed into a gradual, predictable process and appears in a dialogue with more predictable processes (see Figure 11.1).

An artistic text, for example, which is not understood by the contemporary readers/recipients, is described as a spontaneous appearance at a certain moment of time. Its autogenetic nature relies on the fact that it has no language. Here it is shown as the vertical arrow in the middle of the diagram (1). This unexpected phenomenon is followed in time by different meta-communicative (meta-textual) processes or practices of culture (2–6), such as immediate criticism, analyses, or translations – all these processes represent the act of gradually relating the spontaneous phenomenon to its contemporary culture. They could also be characterized as ways of interpreting, attempts to understand the phenomenon. They are more stable, structured, and predictable in the cultural context of the event.

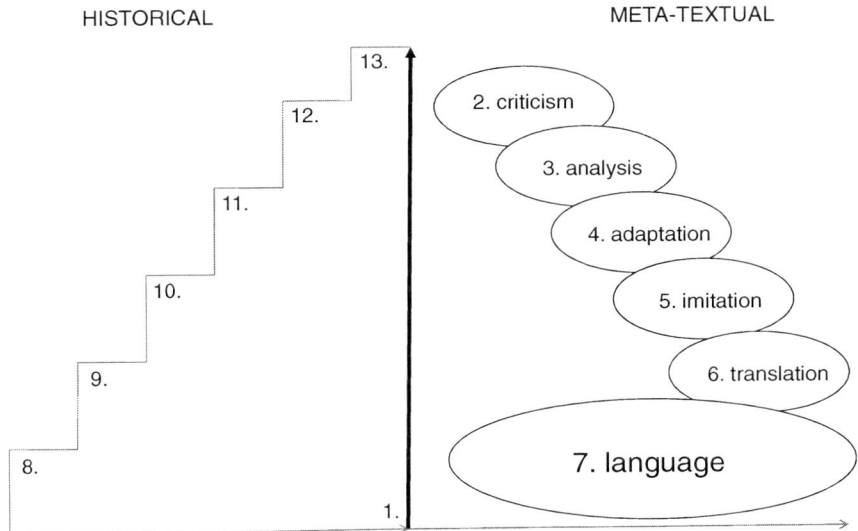

Figure 11.1 Diagram describing the semiotics of an autogenetic phenomenon in culture

Typical of the semiosphere's activity, these meta-textual processes appear in the form of a dialogue between cultural languages. At the same time, these meta-textual processes lead eventually to the formation of the *language* of the phenomenon (1), which was originally unknown, since it did not have a language in the culture. So, the result is its structuration (7). Only this kind of emergence of language makes it possible for contemporaries to reconstruct certain historical causalities (8–13), leading to understanding the incomprehensible, predicting the non-predictable, knowing the unknown.

After an autogenetic phenomenon, in all its ultimate unpredictability, has turned into a gradual, predictable process in culture (achieved its own language with the help of meta-texts and other languages), it is possible for the recipients to begin, on the one hand, to understand the phenomenon and, on the other hand, to start reconstructing the causalities behind it, and thus its historical framing becomes possible. In other words, after the explosion has changed into a more gradual process, people are able to decipher certain causalities behind it, processes leading to it. This is the case with wider cultural, historical and even political explosions as well as revolutionary phenomena. For contemporaries they are eschatological, but for future generations they are understandable phenomena with their own laws of causality. Suddenly something that had seemingly happened by chance, unexpectedly, appears as the only possible choice. The unpredictability comes to be replaced by predictable regularity.

The question of autogenesis in relation to Russianness leaves us eventually with a series of intriguing puzzles, therefore it is probably better to phrase these final arguments as questions: should Russian culture – in the spirit of Chaadaev's philosophy and following the direction supposed here of Lotman's semiotics – be understood as a genuinely autogenetic formation, which would then explain much of its unpredictability and constant problematic attention towards Western Europe? Should this self-generated rootlessness and alienation then be considered as sources for the much discussed itinerant features of Russianness, or are we merely dealing with a series of autogenetic simulations? Finally, should autogenesis be treated as a specifically Russian feature in the Russian avant-garde, whose relationship with Western European culture was very actively discussed and considered problematic by the representatives of different avant-garde 'isms'?

Notes

1 The question of autogenesis is essentially interdisciplinary. The approaches in different disciplines offer much variety. In theology (exegetics), autogenetic phenomena are usually associated with the study of the *Book of Genesis* and the essence of Jesus Christ as the 'Divine Logos' (the *Gospel according to St John*), and this aspect will be discussed further in this chapter in relation to avant-garde culture. The philosopher Heraclitus' idea of a self-emerging Logos is often juxtaposed with the Johannian prologue also called the *Hymn to Logos*. In different cultures and religious traditions there is, however, a great variety of autogenetic divine creatures. In evolutionary biology (Csanyi and Kampis 1985) and thermodynamics (Prigogine 1989; Prigogine and Stengers 1984), autogenetic mechanisms are connected with replicative systems and self-organization of existing material, with patterns or structures that arise without an external agent imposing them (Heylighen 2001). In the general system theory, self-creation is what makes a system autonomous: the differentiation of a sub-system within a macro system with the help of extracting elements that are vital for its functioning (Luhmann 1986). An autonomous system can be visualized as a whole in creative dialogue with itself. In social psychology, in turn, the early self-organization of the human self has been discussed in terms of autogenesis (Schwalbe 2007).

2 See Mikhail Yampol'sky's (2009) novel treatment of the innovation potential (and self-organization) in society in the hundredth issue of the journal *Novoye Literaturnoye Obozreniye*. The article is part of a manifesto by the journal, a declaration of a new paradigm in Russian studies: New Cultural Anthropology.

3 In the early theses of the Tartu-Moscow School, Lotman and his colleagues described the internal view on cultural self-understanding, which relied on the interaction between 'culture' (what is included in the concept) and 'non-culture' (what is excluded), the latter meaning a surrounding, mirror-like 'sub-consciousness' of the former (see Ivanov et al. 1998).

4 It is worth noting that Lotman had rather unexpected sources of inspiration. He would rely in his works on the aesthetics of the scientist-theologian Pavel Florensky, who was generally considered a very important source in Soviet semiotics; film director Sergey Eisenstein's theory of montage was also of great importance; and the phenomenologist Gustav Shpet is one of the figures that should be studied today as an important point of departure for the semiotic theory of Russian culture.

5 Torop (2009: xxvii) emphasizes the distinction between static and dynamic aspects of culture in earlier Lotman and its significance in discussing the theory of unpredictability.

6 One of Prigogine's central arguments was that instability had not been studied in science, because it was generally and ideologically denied (Prigogine 1989).

7 On Chaadaev's philosophy and paradoxes more generally, see Vesa Oittinen's chapter in the current volume.

8 The source of inspiration for Pushkin's poem and its epigraph *Exegi monumentum* was Horace's ode III.30 *To Melpomen*, which had been translated by M.V. Lomonosov in 1747 and adapted by G.R. Derzhavin in his poem *A monument* (1795). Pushkin's poem was not published until his death in 1837, and only in 1881 in its original form.

9 According to Lotman (1998: 536–37), the fact that Pushkin emphasizes the self-emergence of the statue underlines the artificial essence of cultural 'signs of memory' in general. See also Voytekhovich (2000: 228).

10 See V. Chekrygin's *Portrait of Tatlin* (1913), or M. Larionov's *Self-portrait* (1910–12), for example.

11 Marinetti visited Russia in 1914, and many of the Russian Futurist writers felt that he had not understood what was happening in Russia (Markov 1968: 147–68; Janecek 1984: 21).

12 Lotman was in fact considering this same phenomenon in his later semiotics; see Mikhail Lotman's treatment of the philosophical bases of his father's theory (Lotman 1995).

13 Kruchenykh is one of the 'resurrected' Russian avant-garde poets, whose oeuvre is nowadays actively studied (see, for example, the special issued dedicated to him: *Russian Literature* 65/1–3 (2009)). For more on this 'Bogeyman of Russian literature', see, for example: McVay 1976.

14 Apart from Shershenevich, the group included such poets as Sergey Yesenin, Anatoly Mariengof, Ryurik Ivnev, Ivan Gruzinov and Aleksandr Kusikov, the playwright Nikolay Erdman, and the painters Georgy Yakulov and Boris Erdman.

15 This becomes obvious from I.A. Yakovlev's notion (addressed to Stalin) about the poetic groups that were considered close to the Bolsheviks. Right after naming the proletarian writers and the Futurists (Mayakovsky, Aseyev and Bobrov), Yakovlev listed the names of the Imaginist poets Mariengof, Yesenin, Shershenevich and Kusikov (see Artizov and Naumov 1999: 39).

16 See Anatoly Lunacharsky's letter from 1920 to Valery Bryusov, regarding the publication of Ryurik Ivnev's poetry (Bogomolov 2004: 299). Imaginist Ivnev had, for a time at least, become 'untouchable' in Soviet literature.

17 In a private letter, Sergey Yesenin openly confessed that they had taken the name of the group from Vengerova's article, and only changed it a little for their own purposes (see Yesenin 1995–2002: VI, 126).

18 On various interpretations of *poshlost'* in Russian culture, see Gennady Obatnin's chapter in the current volume.

19 Mikhail Lotman (1995) has noted that he found a collection of non-published articles by his father titled *Samovozrastayushchy Logos* ('Self-emerging Logos'), referring most obviously to Heraclitian and Johannian treatment of Logos.

Bibliography

Artizov, A. and Naumov, O. (eds) (1999) *Vlast' i khudozhestvennaya intelligentsiya. Dokumenty 1917–1953*, Moskva: Demokratiya.

Bogomolov, N.A. (2004) *Ot Pushkina do Kibirova. Stat'i o russkoy poezii*, Moskva: Novoye Literaturnoye Obozreniye.

——(2005) '"Dyr bul shchyl" v kontekste epokhi', *Novoye Literaturnoye Obozreniye*, 72: 172–92.

Brodsky, N.L. and Eimermacher, K. (eds) (1929) *Literaturnyye manifesty ot simvolizma k Oktyabryu*. Moskva: Federatsiya.

Chaadaev, P. (1991) *Philosophical Works of Peter Chaadaev*. Dordrecht: Kluwer Academic Publishers.

Csanyi, V. and Kampis, G. (1985) 'Autogenesis: the evolution of replicative systems', *Journal of Theoretical Biology*, 114/2: 303–21.

Eisenstein, S. (1965) *Film Form: essays in film theory*, Cleveland, OH: Meridian Books.

Heylighen, F. (2001) 'The Science of Self-Organization and Adaptivity.' Online. Available: http://pespmc1.vub.ac.be/papers/EOLSS-Self-Organiz.pdf (accessed 29 March 2011).

Ivanov, V.V., Lotman, Yu.M., Pyatigorsky, A.M., Toporov, V.N. and Uspensky, B.A. (1998) *Tezisy k semioticheskomu izucheniyu kul'tur. Theses on the Semiotic Study of Cultures. Kultuurisemiootika teesid*, 33–60, Tartu: University of Tartu.

Janecek, G. (1984) *The Look of Russian Literature. Avant-Garde Visual Experiments 1900–1930*, Princeton, NJ: Princeton University Press.

——(1996) *Zaum: The Transrational Poetry of Russian Futurism*, San Diego, CA: State University Press.

Khardzhiyev, N.I. (2006) *Ot Mayakovskogo do Kruchenykh: izbrannyye raboty o russkom futurizme*, Moskva: Gileya.

Kruchenykh, A. (1928) *15 let russkogo futurizma*, Moskva: Izdatel'stvo Vserossiyskogo Soyuza Poetov.

——(1996) 'Avtobiografiya dichayshego', in R. Duganov (ed.) *Nash vykhod: K istorii russkogo futurizma*, Moskva: Literaturno-khudozhestvennoye agentstvo 'RA'.

——(2001) *Stikhotvoreniya, poemy, romany, opera*, Sankt-Peterburg: Akademichesky proyekt.

Kull, K. (2005) 'Semiosphere and a dual ecology: Paradoxes of communication', *Sign Systems Studies*, 33/1: 175–89.

Lawton, A. (ed.) (1988) *Russian Futurism through Its Manifestoes, 1912–1928*, Ithaca/London: Cornell University Press.

Lotman, M. (1995) 'Za tekstom: zametki o filosofskom fone tartuskoy semiotiki (stat'ya pervaya)', *Lotmanovsky sbornik*, 1: 214–22.

Lotman, M., Torop, P. and Kull, K. (2004) 'Dialogue and identity', in V. Puronas and V. Skirgailiene (ed.) *Globalization, Europe and Regional Identity*, 143–55, Vilnius: Lithuanian Academy of Sciences.

Lotman, Yu.M. (1984) 'O semiosfere', *Izbrannyye stat'i*, 11–24, Tallinn: Aleksandra.

——(1990) *Universe of the Mind*, London: I.B. Tauris.

——(1992) *Kul'tura i vzryv*, Moskva: Gnosis.

——(1997) *Pis'ma. 1940–1993*, B.F. Yegorov (ed.), Moskva: Yazyki russkoy kul'tury.

——(1998) 'Sobesednik v tret'yem litse', *Vvedeniye v khram*, 536–37, Moskva: Yazyki russkoy kul'tury.

——(2005) 'On the Semiosphere', *Sign Systems Studies*, 33/1: 205–29.

——(2009) *Culture and Explosion*, W. Clark (trans.), M. Grishakova (ed.), Berlin/New York: Mouton de Gruyter.

——(2010) *Nepredskazuyemyye mekhanizmy kul'tury*, Tallinn: Tallinn University Press.

Luhmann, N. (1986) 'The autopoiesis of social systems', in F. Geyer and J. van der Zouwen, *Sociocybernetic Paradoxes: Observation, Control and Evolution of Self-steering Systems*, 172–92, London: Sage.

McVay, G. (1976) 'Alexei Kruchenykh: The Bogeyman of Russian literature', *Russian Literature Triquarterly*, 13: 571–90.

Mariengof, A. (2005) 'V moyey strane ... ', *Voprosy literatury*, 5: 321.

Markov, V. (1968) *Russian Futurism: A History*, Berkeley: University of California Press.

Mayakovsky, V. (1978) *Sobraniye sochineniy v 12-i tt.*, Moskva: Pravda.

Prigogine, I. (1989) 'The philosophy of instability', *Futures*, 21/4: 396–400.

Prigogine, I. and Stengers, I. (1984) *Order out of Chaos: Man's New Dialogue with Nature*, Toronto: Bantam Books.

Schwalbe, M.L. (2007) 'The Autogenesis of the Self', *Journal for the Theory of Social Behaviour*, 21/3: 269–95.

Shershenevich, V. (2000) *Stikhotvoreniya i poemy*, Sankt-Peterburg: Akademichesky proyekt.

Shklovsky, V. (1973) 'The Resurrection of the Word', in S. Bann and J.E. Bowlt (ed.) *Russian Formalism: A Collection of Articles and Texts in Translation*, 41–47, Edinburgh: Scottish Academic Press.

Spira, A. (2008) *The Avant-Garde Icon: Russian Avant-Garde Art and the Icon Painting Tradition*. Aldershot: Lund Humphries.

Torop, P. (2005) 'Semiosphere and/as the object of semiotics of culture', *Sign Systems Studies*, 33/1: 169–83.

——(2009) 'Lotmanian Explosion', in M. Grishakova (ed.) *Lotman, J. Culture and Explosion*, xxvii–xxxix, Berlin/New York: Mouton de Gruyter.

Voytekhovich, R. (2000) 'O goratsianskom pretekste "Ya pamyatnik sebe vozdvig nerukotvorny … "', *Pushkinskiye chteniya v Tartu*, 2: 228–34.

Waldstein, M. and Wisse, F. (eds) (1995) *The Apocryphon of John: synopsis of Nag Hammadi codices II,1; III,1; and IV,1 with BG 8502,2*, Leiden: Brill.

Yampol'sky, M. (2009) 'Innovatsionny potentsial i struktura obshchestva', *Novoye Literaturnoye Obozreniye*, 100: 35–44.

Yesenin, S. (1995–2002) *Polnoye sobraniye sochineniy v 7-i tomakh*. Moskva: Nauka-Golos.

12 Two hundred years of *poshlost'*: a historical sketch of the concept

Gennady Obatnin

When approaching the study of the concept *poshlost'* ('vulgarity, philistinism'), one is confronted with two important factors. First, for a native of the Russian language and culture, there is nothing about this term that demands conceptualization or any other form of defamiliarizing critique. For confirmation of this fact one can cite the opinion of a popular rock musician and talk-show host Andrey Makarevich. In his autobiography, Makarevich muses:

> Since the definition of *poshlost'* is perfectly known to all but at the same time is completely subjective, every one of us thinks he sees and senses *poshlost'* clearly, but in fact sees it absolutely in his own way and in different things.
>
> (Makarevich 2008: 81)

The musician conducted a survey among his friends and offered a number of answers to the question of how *poshlost'* can be defined. The filmmaker Ivan Dykhovichny referred him to Nabokov; another filmmaker, Dmitry Svetozarov, suggested that it is 'something to do with form' (and not content); the actress Yuliya Rutberg responded by saying that *poshlost'* 'is always overkill' and 'too much'; the singer Alena Sviridova said that it is 'the inorganic'; a certain A. Romanov generalized to say that *poshlost'* is 'among one's innermost feelings'; the prose writer Yuz Aleshkovsky sent Makarevich a full letter (which cannot comfortably be quoted due to its vulgar language); and the rock musician Boris Grebenshchikov offered an entirely subjective formulation: '*Poshlost'* is fear of rejecting your habitual vision of the world even when you are sick of it yourself' (Makarevich 2008: 82–84). The same quality of being recognizable, but escaping definition is characteristic of what society calls 'bad taste' (cf. Eco 1989: 180).

The need for such distance only arises in the context of an external point of view. A common theme in discussions of *poshlost'* is the impossibility of preserving the word's semantic fullness when translating it into foreign languages.[1] Vladimir Nabokov insisted on the word's absence in languages other than Russian, and apparently, were it not for him, the concept would not have found its way into the class of terms essential for describing the mentality of the Russian people, once again showing how important the role of individuals can be in an informational vacuum (Nabokov 1944: 63).[2] Description of the concept cannot be organized through analogies with other cultures and languages, as, for example, when developing themes like 'Russian eroticism' or 'Russian democracy'. It is precisely for this reason that *poshlost'* is logically placed among those terms that form the basis for a specific piece of the Russian conceptual picture of the world.[3] This leads to a second a priori consideration important in the description of such a concept: only analysis of its evolution reveals unfamiliar aspects of its meaning.[4] Anything that a thoughtful native speaker of Russian could say about *poshlost'*, relying only on his own linguistic and cultural competence, would be too obvious to occupy anyone's interest. As a rule dictionaries of the modern language only help formulate things, without adding anything at the level of meaning.[5] It is unusual or unclear usages of the word, for example, or certain cultural actors' excessive attention towards it, arising from personal interest or external circumstances, that draw the literary historian to study such a word. The former can be found in abundance in the history of this concept, and the latter direct our focus to its critical moments, when its meaning underwent transformations.

The historical side of things, most extensively presented by Viktor Vinogradov in a 1947 article, confirms our sense of the Russian term's originality. According to Vinogradov, the verbal adjective *poshly* (from *poyti*, 'to go') 'originates in prehistoric antiquity' and is used in surviving examples of seventeenth-century mercantile language in the sense of 'practiced since olden times, usual, normal'.[6] Towards the end of the seventeenth century and the beginning of the eighteenth, the word acquires a negative connotation – 'low in quality, utterly ordinary, trifling' – which is logical for the era of Peter I's transformations and for the inheritors of his ideology. Vinogradov dates a renewal of interest in the word to the end of the eighteenth century and the beginning of the nineteenth, although he refers to an 1847 dictionary, which features all three definitions: 'ordinary/ trifling, low/unsophisticated, and long-standing/time-honoured'.[7] Here we also come across the interesting problem of fixed collocations with the adjective *poshly* – the appearance of the phrase *poshly durak* ('simple fool') can be found in the *Russian National Corpus*, primarily among writers from the first half of the nineteenth century (Zagoskin, Narezhny, Gertsen, Belinsky, and others, twenty-three cases in all), and indeed today this expression intuitively strikes one as outdated.[8] The fixed expression *poshly fars* ('vulgar farce') sounds just as stylized, in all likelihood belonging to the age of modernism with its amateur theatres (the corpus gives Kuprin's 1905 'The Duel' as the first example).[9]

According to Vinogradov, the revival of interest in the word *poshly* followed a rise of interest in Russian history at the turn of the eighteenth and nineteenth centuries, and it is then that the abstract noun *poshlost'* appears. The abstraction of a given quality and attribution of additional features to the resulting noun is a process which can be observed in other cases of language change. For example, if Michel de Certeau is to be believed, this is precisely how the concept of 'mysticism' (*la mystique*) took shape, albeit over a much longer period of time (Certeau 1992: 76–82). Vinogradov cites the famous quotation from *Selected Passages from Correspondence with Friends*, where Gogol' relates how Pushkin characterized his gift as a writer: 'He would always tell me that no other writer had ever possessed such a gift for exhibiting the stark *poshlost'* of life, for outlining with such style the *poshlost'* of *poshly* people' (1843). According to Gogol', in *Dead Souls*, it was precisely 'the *poshlost'* of everything that scared the reader so much': 'They would have forgiven me if I had exhibited portraits of evil fiends, but for *poshlost'* I could not be forgiven' (Gogol' 1898: 94).[10] As Gogol' insisted, the same design produced the characters in the first part of his novel, which 'had to be pure *poshlost'*' (Gogol' 1898: 96). He abstracted from whole personalities particular features he found in his acquaintances and in himself, and conferred them upon his characters.

It should come as no surprise that a Gogol' scholar as well known as Vasily Gippius collected all instances of the author's use of the word *poshlost'*, perhaps planning to write a separate work on the subject. The scholar's archive contains several pages listed under the title 'Gogol's Usage of the Word *Poshlost'*'. One also finds a reference to the use of the word *poshly* in the Novgorod dialect to refer to a merchant who is 'in' on a deal. On the back of an envelope with a stamp dated 27 November 1935, one finds the first attempts at a generalized definition: 'Features lacking in any obvious signs of quality – (inertia), but harmful, i.e. inert in the sense of requiring resistance'(Gippius 1935: 6). From the perspective of how the theme will develop in this chapter, it is also important to note Gippius' mention of Vladimir Odoyevsky's story, 'Princess Zizi', in which one of the narrators says, 'It is well-known that the most *poshly* thoughts are the most elevated, and, vice versa, the most elevated are the most *poshly*' (Odoyevsky 2006: 61). Odoyevsky's story, published in 1839, deals with an important theme for its time – what will be the fate of high moral principles, associated with an out-moded romanticism, as capitalism rises and the class of businessmen with their particular form of morality grows? In different ways, this problem confronts each of the story's characters, including the two narrators and especially the heroine, who is forced to sublimate a passion for her sister's husband into an exaggerated virtue. The words of Byron about hating life and holding the human race in contempt sound ridiculous in the mouth of a hack poet. High ethical principles, now no more than a phrase, enter the sphere of *poshlost'* – this is the sense of the quoted passage.

Vinogradov's observations can be confirmed by material in the *Russian National Corpus*: Vissarion Belinsky's review of *Woe from Wit* (1839), Valerian Maykov's review of a collection of poems by Aleksey Kol'tsov,[11] and again Gogol's *Selected Passages*, while in poetry the first case is Nikolay Yazykov's epistle *To P.V. Kireyevsky* (1835). Thus *poshlost'* separates itself from the adjective *poshly* in the middle of the 1830s and does not belong to the epoch of romanticism, as might have been previously assumed, but heralds the following stage in the evolution of literary tastes. Significantly, the adjective *poshly* appears in the poetic corpus at least thirty years earlier, in Ivan Dmitriyev's poem *The Broken Violin* (1805). One finds the first appearance of the adjective in a work of prose at the same time in Ekaterina Dashkova's *Notes*, while Vinogradov cites as early an example as Trediakovsky (Vinogradov 1999: 532). Pushkin's comment, however, is related to the mature Gogol', who had become Belinsky's ideal model, almost a kind of banner to which the critic remained loyal even when the author himself had changed direction. Vinogradov, intentionally or not, does not connect the birth of this concept with either romantic or realist aesthetics in any way, however, and dryly indicates the appearance of other forms derived from the same adjective in the middle of the nineteenth century: *poshlyak* ('a vulgar person'), *poshlyatina* ('vulgar stuff'), and *oposhlit'sya* ('to descend into vulgarity'), among others. He entirely ignores the second half of the nineteenth century and the beginning of the twentieth, leaving space for this study to explore. Indeed, looking ahead, we may say that, after the age of realism, modernism is the second critical epoch in the history of the concept of *poshlost'*.

Like every fashionable word, *poshlost'* began to acquire different shades of meaning, accommodating the most diverse contexts, finally becoming an entirely bleached out concept.[12] Still, it is possible to say that the emerging aesthetics of Russian realism, which laid the foundation for the contemporary understanding of the word, actualized its pejorative meanings of the ordinary, low-class, and unsophisticated, completely forgetting the Old Russian meaning.[13] This shift was connected to two problems that had troubled Belinsky. The first was how the new art, in its attempts to capture a genuine popular spirit, could avoid descending into a low-class aesthetic. Belinsky hoped to cultivate a new déclassé, eventually intellectual mass reader, whose recent emergence he noted and applauded. Evidently, this was when the social meaning of *poshlost'* was actualized, having lain dormant through the famously socially turbulent Petrine era. Belinsky brought the word *poshlost'* closer to the aristocratic Anglicism, *vul'garnost'* ('vulgarity').[14]

To understand Belinsky's idea more clearly, let us consider his review of *Woe from Wit* (1839), in which one finds fairly unusual contexts for the words *poshly* and *poshlost'* from the perspective of contemporary usage. The review effectively demonstrates the direction of Belinsky's thought at the time. The critic confidently defends the new aesthetic lying at the foundation of Russian realism:

> Being prone to dreams in the nineteenth century is just as ridiculous, *poshly*, and mawkish as being sentimental. *Reality* – this is the by-word and slogan of our age, reality in everything – in beliefs, in science, in art, and in life. This brave and mighty age will not suffer anything false, artificially weak, or diffuse, but loves only what is powerful, strong, substantial … today's poetry is a *poetry of reality*.

For Belinsky, 1839 was a time of Hegelianism, when 'the word "reality" meant everything that is the world of visibility and the world of spirituality, the world of facts and the world of ideas', 'spirit revealing itself to itself is *reality*; just as everything private, everything contingent, everything irrational is *ghostliness*, the opposite of reality, all that merely *seems*, but does not *exist*.' Later he repeats this idea: 'Reality is positive living; ghostliness is its negation' (Belinsky 1948: 465, 469, 671). Describing the quarrel between Gogol's Ivan Ivanovich and Ivan Nikiforovich, Belinsky remarks paradoxically: 'There were two neighbours and friends, joined to one another by the bonds of mutual *poshlost'*, habit, and idleness' (Belinsky 1948: 475). These 'bonds of mutual *poshlost'*' (recall the idiom, 'bonds of mutual love') naturally reflect the attachment of both Ivans to the ghostly world; in the famous final lines of the story Gogol' laments their unawareness of the existence of real life. This same idea, the idea of the negation of life, the idea of ghostliness, according to Belinsky, is expressed in Gogol's *Inspector General* (Belinsky 1948: 485). And it is the same meaning of *poshlost'* that the critic invokes in his analysis of Griboyedov's comedy, characterizing the world of Famusov and Moscow high society. When Famusov raves about Moscow, Belinsky even calls it 'the lyrical enthusiasm of *poshlost'*' (Belinsky 1948: 506, 507). Chatsky's love for someone so inconsequential as Sof'ya is implausible, ghostly, and has nothing in common with reality. This is why 'Chatsky's love is so *poshly*, because it is not necessary for its own sake, but only for the plot of the comedy', writes Belinsky (1948: 515). It is also in this exact sense that the poet Nikolay Nekrasov used the word after the critic's death: 'Only with a *poshly* toast / Can we respond to his bright ideas' (Belinsky 1853) – meaning that instead of actualizing Belinsky's ideas in deeds, we can only raise our glasses to him.

The second problem that troubled the theorists of the new, realist art was closely connected to the first. Just like Bakunin and Gertsen, Belinsky was concerned about the future historical development of Russia. As convinced socialists, these 'men of the forties' actively debated how to achieve the paradise on earth for which they yearned. One obstacle was the need to progress through the historical stage of a bourgeois republic. In the introduction to *On the Development of Revolutionary Ideas in Russia* (written in 1853, later than the main text), Gertsen describes his impressions of the road out of Russia, where, upon entering the Livonian province, he stops and stays with some Baltic Germans:

> They are deeply offended by our recklessness, our habits, our neglect for the standards of decency, the way we boast about our half-barbaric, half-perverse passions. To us they are deadly boring with their bourgeois pedantry, marked by purism and the irreproachable *poshlost'* of their behaviour.
>
> (Gertsen 1956: 143)[15]

An unauthorized German translation in a journal was the first publication of Gertsen's composition, while in 1851 the author himself participated in the work's appearance in French in a separate edition, which became the model for subsequent re-issuings. The quotation above is from a Russian translation of 1861, which was produced by a group of Moscow students with whom Gertsen had no connection. The original reads: ' ... *par leur conduite irréprochablement mesquine.*' The last word means 'petty, stingy, meager' (Gertsen 1956: 15). Typically, *poshly* is translated into French as *vulgaire, trivial, banal, plat*; while *poshlost'*, in the metaphorical meaning of 'dirtiness' (*sal'nost'*, from the Fr. *sal*, 'dirty'), is translated as *platitude* (cf. the expression *ploskaya shutka*, 'a bad [lit. flat] joke').[16] Thus, it is in the works of Gertsen and Bakunin – authors driven by their specific biographies to adapt Russian terminology to the language of European socialism and communism – that a close link arises between *poshlost'* and *meshchanstvo* ('petty bourgeois values').[17] Moreover, it is not impossible that precisely at this time, as a result of such translations, the clear borrowing from French of the metaphor 'flat' in the meaning of 'indecent' enters the semantic field of *poshlost'* and gradually, towards the beginning of the twentieth century, assumes within it a central place.

Gertsen makes his idea clear in the same work in a passage devoted to the animosity between Russians and Germans, part of a survey of Russian history. After the reign of Peter I, Germans received such attention from the Russian government that they became, on the one hand, the most loyal subjects of the Russian empire, inundating its chancelleries and ministries, while on the other hand they became completely separate from the ethnic Russians: 'The Russian government finds in German officers and officials exactly what it needs: the accuracy and dispassion of a machine, the silence of deaf-mutes, and the stoicism of obedience under any circumstances, diligently working, never tiring' (Gertsen 1956: 179).

There is a natural thread of association running from these comments to the German character of tsarist rule in Russia – Germano-Byzantine, as Gertsen refers to it later in the same book. This is why in *From the Other Shore* (1850), Gertsen's first book written abroad, he speaks of Russia's 'bourgeois autocracy' (Gertsen 1956: 17). It was not, as is sometimes thought, Bakunin who invented the idea of the tsar 'of German decent' in his famous speech of 29 November 1847 at the banquet celebrating the anniversary of the Polish Uprising. The Decembrists Aleksandr Bestuzhev (Marlinsky) and Kondraty Ryleyev had already co-authored an agitational song in the beginning of the 1820s, in which the first lines introduced this theme: 'Our tsar – a Russian German – / Wears a tight-fitting uniform. / Hey, hey, tsar! Hey, hey, tsar! / The Orthodox sovereign!' (Gusev 1965: 332).[18]

In this way, towards the middle of the nineteenth century, the concept of *poshlost'* (*poshly*) took on the qualities that would determine its subsequent place in the culture. Acquiring a broad, almost abstract character, easily incorporating almost any negative connotation, the word was associated at this stage of its existence with German everyday culture, which was standing in the way of Russia's path to socialism.

*

Russian cultural consciousness would continue to be involved with this constellation of ideas during the second important period in the history of *poshlost'*: the turn of nineteenth and twentieth centuries. Here one can identify two tendencies in the term's development: one that continues and another that transforms the semantic inheritance that accompanied it into the epoch of modernism.[19] Naturally, analysis of concrete cases of the word's use will not reveal pure reflections of one meaning or another, but only predominating tendencies. The most obvious and therefore interesting case in this regard is that of Anton Chekhov, who not only spoke critically about *poshlost'* on numerous occasions, but whose reputation as a writer was shaped in relation to the concept. In 1904 Chekhov's death itself provoked a discussion of the theme of *poshlost'*. Maksim Gor'ky was among those who remembered the arrival in St Petersburg of Chekhov's body after his death in Germany. Because of confusion over the telegrams, the deceased writer was only met by a very small crowd of mourners and the body was transported in a red commercial car with a sign that read, 'oyster section'. Gor'ky called it an act of revenge by the *poshlost'* with which Chekhov had struggled all his life ('*Poshlost'* always found in him a harsh and cutting judge … His enemy was *poshlost'*). The only difference was that he remembered the car as green: 'To me the dirty-green stain of that car is like the giant, triumphant smile of *poshlost'* standing over an exhausted enemy' (Gor'ky 1921: 30, 34, 36).

In the same year, Merezhkovsky published an article by his wife Zinaida Gippius in their journal, *The New Path*, titled, 'On *Poshlost'*'. The famous symbolist author used almost the same words as Belinsky, only in place of the Hegelian term *reality*, she used what was for her a more natural term, *being*:

> For *poshlost'* is not a manifestation of life, but of non-life. *Poshlost'* (we shall establish the conceptual content of this word without subtracting from its root negative meaning of repelling the living) *poshlost'* is the immobility, the inertia, the dead point, the anti-being at the very heart of the world.
>
> (Gippius 1908: 215–16)

Needless to say, the basic idea Gippius expresses here is a fine example of her creative collaboration with her husband, Dmitry Merezhkovsky – so close is it to the conception of his book *The Approaching Boor* (1906), about the boorishness the writer identified in European *meshchanstvo*, or in his book, *Gogol' and the Devil*, published at the same time. Traces of a shared metaphorical logic can be found in Gippius' famous poetic declaration in the poem *Everything Around*, which develops the symbolic imagery of a grey, petty, and thus devilish world.

Originally called 'More on *Poshlost'*', Gippius' article was a response to the article, 'On *Poshlost'*', written by the prose writer Yury Dyagilev (1878–1957, the younger brother of the famous art historian and entrepreneur Sergey Dyagilev) and published in *The New Path* under the pseudonym of Yury Chereda. Quoting Dostoevsky and Chekhov extensively, Dyagilev claimed that Russia was witnessing a shift from one type of *poshlost'* to another:

> The middle zone is widening, conceiving of new and unheard-of forms. The old, naïve *poshlost'* of something called serfdom, the twilight-hour *poshlost'* known and loved by all, is departing, being erased, and something new, as of yet unseen, utterly voluptuous and intricate, is occupying its territory and expanding it, and we have no power to deal with it. Instead of manual *poshlost'*, we have a *poshlost'* that is machine-driven, able to produce in a single minute thousands of new, intricate patterns and variations, as in a factory.
>
> (Chereda 1904: 233)

Gippius argues against Dyagilev's juxtaposition of Dostoevsky and Chekhov, claiming that Dostoevsky was aware of these crevasses from which death blows; 'indeed, he called *poshlost'* a devil' (Gippius 1908: 216). It is no accident that the devil in *The Brothers Karamazov* wants to be reincarnated as a merchant's wife, weighing 110 kilos. Dostoevsky, in Gippius' opinion, was a prophet, horrified by the 'sinkhole' of *poshlost'*, while Chekhov was 'a slave upon whom ten talents and great trust had been bestowed, but who did not live up to that trust' (Krayny 1904: 243). Gippius concludes the passage in which she criticizes the opinion of Dyagilev with this last phrase, accusing her opponent of mistaking the trifles of life for *poshlost'*. 'A man, after all, who curses life *now*, does not really curse life, but only its unnatural immobility, inertia, and the devil-*poshlost'*; he struggles not with life, but with its enemy, in the name of life' (Krayny 1904: 219).

It is appropriate to see Father Pavel Florensky as the direct ideological descendent of this position. In 1914 Vasily Rozanov published his controversial essay, 'The Tactile and Olfactory Attitude of the Jews to Blood', and, apparently without asking the author, included under the pseudonym Ω a private letter from Florensky, dated 23 October 1913. The letter begins in a very characteristic manner:

> That is precisely the problem, dear Vasily Vasil'yevich – in the past years the Russian people have been given a real test, and they are failing it again and again. ... I will never come to terms with the fact that the Russian people and the Russian church can tolerate and endure *poshlost'*.

Before completing this quotation, it is worth pausing to consider a related fragment from the seventh letter, entitled 'Sin', of what is likely Florensky's most famous work, *The Pillar and Ground of the Truth*, written not long before the letter to Rozanov, and in which the meaning Florensky attributed to *poshlost'* appears in greater relief. In this passage, Florensky writes of the Devil Mephistopheles, who, because of 'a preponderance of reason', 'does everything in a flat and *poshly* manner': 'The Devil Mephistopheles, as Reason Incarnate, is also *Poshlost'* Incarnate; that is why he can only perceive stupidity around him.' Florensky adds two notes to this deeply anti-Kantian passage, in the first of which he names Flaubert (as the author of *Bouvard and Pécuchet*) and Saltykov-Shchedrin as authors expressing a feeling for life as stupidity. But his scope is even greater: 'Evolutionism, historicism, mechanism etc. – these are nothing but individual cases of a general method of transforming life into something inanimate, *poshly*, and stupid' (Floresnky 1914: 179, 702–3).

With this in mind, Florensky's subsequent enumeration of the different features of *poshlost'* in his letter to Rozanov can be read as signs of the Devil in public life. The decadence and stagnation in political life after the revolution of 1905–7, the achievement and subsequent loss of autonomy by the universities, the Muscovite Orthodox Church's condemnation of the monastic theological movement on Mt Athos ('church positivism'), and the victory of the lawyers in the fabricated, anti-Semitic 'Beylis affair' – all this he considered a manifestation of *poshlost'*. 'A kind of sticky grey mud is oozing everywhere', Floresnky exclaimed, employing the characteristic colour symbolism discussed above (Rozanov 1914: 200). Florensky ends the passage in characteristic fashion: 'Is this not *the end of the world?*' Sergiy Bulgakov shared Florensky's point of view, following his friend and teacher in claiming that the nature of evil is nothing, absence, non-being: '*Poshlost'* is the seedy underbelly of the demonic' (Bulgakov 1999: 170).

As is well known, it is often the case that those who develop other people's ideas take them further than the teachers who first inspired them. A deeper look at Merezhkovsky's writings reveals traces of a different attitude to *poshlost'*, one that superficially recalls the discussion of Odoyevsky's 'Princess Zizi' above. Gippius also makes a distinction in her response to Dyagilev between *poshlost'* and the quotidian trifles of life. The prose writer, Ieronim Yasinsky, whom Gippius knew well, tells a story in his memoirs about how the young Gippius, upon arriving in St Petersburg with her husband, would receive guests 'lying on the carpet in the living room, playing cards, or appearing with a toy duck in her hands. The duck was meant to symbolize the couple's separation from one another, since they considered sexual relations in marriage to be a form of *poshlost'*' (Yasinsky 1926: 255).[20] However, the end of Merezhkovsky's narrative poem, *Family Idyll* (1890), directly proclaims the holiness within quotidian *poshlost'*:

> two or three people is enough sometimes
> For love, that great and holy thing that all possess,
> To shine, eternal, in the midst of quotidian *poshlost'*,
> Like a glimpse into another world, like a glimpse of blue sky!
>
> (Merezhkovsky 2000: 370).

The author is clearly suggesting the words of Christ that 'where two or three are gathered together in my name, there am I in the midst of them.' This allusion acquires a special meaning if one takes into account the Merezhkovskys' subsequent domestic experiments, such as their *ménage à trois* with journalist Dmitry Filosofov, which they treated as the basis for a new Church. In the introduction to the 'Family Idyll' Merezhkovsky declares what he has written to be true and not invented, and he attacks the literary norms of novellas and novels with their 'unnecessary fictions and convoluted intrigues' (Merezhkovsky 2000: 358). In fact, all the people the poet describes are relatives of his wife – her mother, sister, aunt, and nanny. The poet lives with them at their dacha outside Moscow, and their life is quite prosaic, as is his own domestic life with its linens, ironing, tubs, and pots, and it is only the appearance of love that saves them from the 'degeneracy, *poshlost'*, and prose of our days'. For example, Aunt Nadya, an old woman in a bedraggled housecoat who has gone to seed, sincerely loves her ancient mother, and Merezhkovsky concludes: 'Even here, even in this deeply prosaic *poshlost'*, / There is one wounded, there is love, there is warmth and light!' (Merezhkovsky 2000: 361). The last but one section of the poem, a lengthy apostrophe to *The Reader*, which accuses him of leading an entirely unheroic life, brings us back to experience that thin boundary between life and literature around which the poem is constructed.

One can say that the path of uncovering the holy within *poshlost'* is its own kind of heroic path. This line of thinking can be found not only in the works of Merezhkovsky, but also in those of his close comrade, poet Fedor Sologub. In as early a work as the novel *Bad Dreams* (1895), this logic can be traced throughout the dialogue between the protagonist, Login, and his beloved. Login is alarmed by the thought that they will live 'an ordinary life, just like everyone else'. They will marry, start a family, he will get upset and then 'crawl to her with kisses': 'Tender names, so *poshly*. And what will you call me? Vasya, Vasen'ka? And the squeal of children and the smell – all this will happen to us, too. The horror of *poshlost*!' To this his girlfriend Anna replies, 'No, even on the well-trodden path, one can meet the unexpected, things most people despise, but we crave' (Sologub 1990: 237).

Thus, what at first seemed to be an isolated polemic between Gippius and Dyagilev in fact touched upon one of the most important themes for the new generation of young writers and artists, essential for understanding the mood they shared. It is worth noting that like the 1830s, the beginning of the twentieth century was a time of social transformations. Russia was becoming an industrial country. A new consumer had entered the market, including the market for art, and his or her tastes, like those of the early bourgeois, required conceptualization. It is not irrelevant that the specific tradition of socialist thought saw the proletariat as the principle agent of history.

In 1906, a professor of St Petersburg University, the folklorist and literary critic Yevgeny Anichkov (1866–1937), released a brochure entitled *Art and the Socialist Order*. The author began his text with the following example: a Muscovite industrialist is transporting printed cotton textiles from Moscow to Turkestan. To achieve success, he first has to adapt his product to the tastes of his buyers, and only then, after he has made them dependent on him, that is, after he has destroyed all local cottage industry, he begins to dictate his own taste (Anichkov 1906: 12).[21] The worker does not sing folk songs, and the petty bourgeois is even more aesthetically impoverished than he. As Anichkov argued, we look on things with the eyes of a tradesman; it is the price that interests us, and, as for aesthetics, it is enough to know if something is fashionable: 'I mean fashion in the serious sense, and not the *poshly* one' (Anichkov 1906: 14). It is outside class interests, outside capitalism that the real art of our time will develop – 'here will one encounter real taste'. Collectivism strives for a 'human, all-too-human' ideal (a reference to the title of Nietzsche's book); first and foremost, collectivism is practical. This, Anichkov notes, is why Merezhkovsky named his ideal, 'the approaching boor'. But, the author writes, stringing together still more quotations from Nietzsche's *Thus Spoke Zarathustra*, man is not only a 'blonde beast', but also something that 'must be overcome': 'The beauty that has been destroyed by capitalist production must be reborn. … an *aesthetics of consumption* will rise and pour forth' (Anichkov 1906: 16, 29, 30).

A year after Gippius' polemic with Dyagilev, the journal *Questions of Life* published a story by the second-tier modernist Mark Krinitsky (Mikhail Samygin, 1874–1952) under the title, 'Poshlost'' (1905, 1912). The ironically depicted protagonist, who goes by the name of Khryapin, separates everything into what is and is not *poshlost*:

> Khryapin had an organic intolerance for what he called *poshlost*'. Never thinking too deeply about the meaning of this word, in his mind he divided all objects and actions into those that are *poshly* and those that are not *poshly*.

Interestingly, amateur plays feature among the *poshly* things (cf. '*poshly* farce'):

> So: serving as an official in some chamber, living in a dacha outside of Moscow, drinking the expected glass of vodka before lunch, playing whist every day on the terrace, taking part in amateur plays at the dacha – all this he considered *poshly*. By contrast, being a writer, spending the summer in Finland or Switzerland, drinking expensive wine, playing chess, and assuming a critical attitude to amateur plays at the dacha were not *poshly* to him.
>
> (Krinitsky 1905: 118)

Khryapin has an affair with one Tat'yana Aleksandrovna Kol'china, the incarnation of *poshlost'*, but falls in love with her because of her erotic eyes. Khryapin's musings recall the line of thinking Merezhkovsky pursues in his 'Family Idyll':

> Someone came up with the word *poshlost'* ... *Poshlost'*, as such, does not exist ... There is sin, misfortune, suffering, but not *poshlost'*. There is something oppressive, frightening, nameless, in which we get entangled and try to fight our way out like a fly in a spider's web. But there is no *poshlost'*. To evaluate a phenomenon as *poshlost'* is only possible when observing it indifferently and superficially from outside.
>
> (Krinitsky 1905: 132)

As he comes to believe, much like Anichkov, the justification for *poshlost'* can be found in the title of a the above-mentioned book by Nietzsche *Human, All Too Human*: 'for too long we have laughed at the human, punished the human, and is it not time, finally, to study it?'

The critics of Russian modernism did not let this turn of thought go unnoticed. Russian literary modernism, among its various thematic innovations, introduced erotic frankness to literature. Perceived as *poshlost'*, this frankness could supplant everything the modernists did in the eyes of a hostile reader, at the same time attracting unjustified accusations of a lack of moral scruples. This is particularly apparent in the play *Madame* Poshlost',[22] written by the famous actor of St Petersburg's Aleksandrinsky Theatre, Nikolay Khodotov. The play is about the fate of a young writer named Vladimir, who comes to St Petersburg from the provincial town of Petrozavodsk to study in the university, but soon realizes he is meant to be a writer. In the beginning of his career he has to choose appropriate company and learn how to conduct himself like a writer. Consequently, the author surrounds himself with two groups of people, those giving good and bad advice. The play's title attunes the viewer or reader to every utterance of the word *poshlost'*, making the text a kind of idiosyncratic guide to the word's semantics, although here I will only mention what is vital in its meaning. Strikingly, both groups of characters are fully convinced of the *poshlost'* of life – its pettiness, dirt, and so on – but there is a marked difference between the tough realists, who praise the good old days before the appearance of 'neuro-vultures' (*nervyatniki*,[23] a word used by the protagonists' father, the provincial doctor, Dobrynov) and the new, unprincipled writers. This difference lies in the realists' rejection of *poshlost'* while the new writers are prepared to plunge into it with pleasure. The decadent critic Stal'sky defends this position:

> And what is everyday life [*byt*] anyway? Everyday life is something that renders one's precious spiritual passions *poshly*. It demands a certain, agreed measure of real form, which puts a brake on the flight of human thought – and thought should be bright and instantaneous, like the zigzag of lightening. The literature of the past was only a pale, sapless copy of that zigzag, while the literature of the future will be that lightening itself.
>
> (Khodotov 1909: 30, 31)

Gavrilo Gavrilovich Gavrilov, an old and for that reason talented writer, although he ranks among the decadents, formulates a similar idea, using words almost identical to those of Khryapin in Krinitsky's story:

> And what is *poshlost'* anyway? Everything is *poshlost'*, depending on how you look at it. For a writer, *poshlost'* is essential – it is his sixth sense; he has to bathe himself fully in *poshlyatina* in order to know the price of beauty and to get a feeling for what he loves and hates … Yes, in the end, even in *poshlost'* itself there is great beauty!
>
> (ibid.: 38)

Aleksandr Blok's famous poem, *The Stranger*, has a twin, also written in the St Petersburg dacha region, Shuvalovo-Ozerki,[24] and referred to by its first line, *Ladies there show off the fashions*. This poem much more frankly depicts the tavern (not a restaurant, as in *The Stranger*), in which the main character meets the Stranger. Like a good bourgeois, he is drinking large steins of beer, not wine, and his companion's profession is more clearly marked – she does not hide the 'enchanting distance' of German romanticism under her veil, but 'a face with thin features'. All the same he asks the question:

> Amidst all this mysterious *poshlost'*
> Tell me, what should I do with you –
> So unique and unrepeatable,
> Like the smoky-blue evening?

After *The Stranger*, the restaurant will appear in the work of Blok's imitators numerous times as a site for mystical encounters. For example, the second-rate symbolist poet Nikolay Poyarkov mixes motifs from Blok and Bal'mont in his poem *In the Restaurant*: 'I came here to lose myself for a moment / In the nightmare of *poshly* hubbub. / To break the stubborn chains of woe, / To weave aromatic flowers into a wreath' (Poyarkov 1908: 105).

The logic of finding the holy within *poshlost'*, or, in other words, the logic of 'mystical *poshlost'*', can also be found in the project of 'transforming everyday life', which brought together diverse artistic and literary groups in the 1910s. It is clear that towards the beginning of the twentieth century *poshlost'* became associated with specific objects and things. For example, lilacs were considered *poshly*. Not for nothing was it that the first part of the collection, *The Loudly Boiling Chalice* (1913), by the poet Igor' Severyanin, whose name would become a symbol of *poshlost'*, was called *Lilac of my Soul*. Lilac also appears in many of Severyanin's poems as a metonym for spring and youth, and one poem even features 'lilac ice cream'. Lilac found its way into Russian poetry from the depths of mass literature, first of all from the culture of the romance, and more specifically, from the poem by Vsevolod Krestovsky, *Under a fragrant branch of lilac ...* (1857) (for more on this topic, see Belousov 1992: 321–22). These associations were alive both in the beginning of the twentieth century, when the romance of third-rate poet, Mikhail Gal'perin (1882–1944), *A Branch of Lilac*, was popular, and in the period's contemporary reception. For example, in 2007, the filmmaker Pavel Lungin released a film by the same name, the plot of which is based on the biographical legend that the pianist and composer Sergey Rakhmaninov received a branch of lilac as a gift from a stranger after every one of his performances.

However, not only concrete objects were called *poshly*, but whole artistic styles as well. The first of these must be mentioned, if only briefly, to be thorough: that is the so-called *style russe*, the 'pseudo-Russian' or, as it was ironically named, 'rooster' style (referring to the popular figure of a supposedly folk ornament) 'gravitating toward a poorly understood idea of "Russianness"', (Makovsky 2000a: 479) in other words, the odious stylization of officialdom, which was already known in courtly practices during the reign of Catherine II, but survived until the aesthetic whims of Russification under Alexander III. The activity of the art studios in Talashkino and Abramtsevo was associated with this style, as was the work of the artists in the so-called 'Mamontov Circle', which included the merchant and patron of the arts Savva Mamontov, who gave his name to the circle, another patron princess Mariya Tenisheva, the artists Mikhail Vrubel' and Mikhail Nesterov, the theorist Adrian Prakhov, and so on. In the beginning of the twentieth century, as prominent a sculptor as Sergey Konenkov defined himself in opposition to this style. In his novel *Satan*, Georgy Chulkov describes the typical interior of an apartment of one of the leaders of this anti-Semitic, pogromist circle:

> Konstantin Makovsky's *Beauty* was hanging on the wall; the furniture was done in a pseudo-Russian style with roosters and other official emblems; and, naturally, in front of the table there stood an armchair with a curved back, on which the proverb was carved: 'Slow and steady wins the race.'
>
> (Chulkov 1915: 40)[25]

Of course, this style was perceived as *poshlost'* by a particular segment of the artistic intelligentsia, for example, by Il'ya Repin. It is interesting that, Repin, who gained in popularity during the epoch of 'socialist realism', later became himself an example of kitsch for Umberto Eco (Eco 1989: 186).

Another style associated with *poshlost'* was that of German industrial design. The culture of everyday life changed dramatically with the introduction of the telephone, electricity, and other technical innovations at the turn of the century. The cosy life of the nineteenth century was left behind, as a movement began towards modernism and later the avant-garde, constructivism (cf. the name of their journal – *The Object*), functionalism, and so on. Maksimilian Voloshin complained that the invention of the phonograph at the end of the nineteenth century was premature, since mankind was not yet ready for it: 'This is the source of that sharp tinge of *poshlost'* that always accompanies gramophones' (Voloshin 2007: 105). Of course, French, German, and English material cultures each had their own distinct semantic haloes. If the French were perceived as seekers of luxury (the word *chic* itself became fashionable in its Russian derivative, *shikarny*), then German pragmatism was opposed to them, expressing itself through solid, industrially produced, unlovely things.[26]

One particular tendency in the resistance of German *poshlost'* stands out in Russian artistic life of the turn of the century. This is related first of all to the journals *Years Gone By* and, in part, *Apollo*, which collected the relics of Russian gentry culture, the art of the age of neoclassicism, Biedermeier, and the empire style (cf. Makovsky 2000b: 213). In 1905, Sergey Dyagilev organized an exhibition of Russian portraits that made him famous and was itself filled with hitherto unknown names. Three years later the art historian Baron Nikolay Vrangel' organized the 'Russian Rooms' exhibition, in which the interiors of manor houses were displayed. Along with the art historians and critics Sergey Makovsky and Aleksandr Trubnikov, Vrangel' wrote descriptions of several famous Russian estates, including that of the infamous state official, Arakcheyev, known as 'Gruziny'.[27] The art historian, regional ethnographer, and artist German Lukomsky travelled to numerous provincial Russian manors on assignment with *Years Gone By*, and he noted how the landowners had done significant harm to their houses between 1860 and 1900. The peasants, freed from serfdom, had turned their backs on the manor; manor-life was revolutionized by the factory; and the landowners themselves, giving in to the stream of 'crude, mechanical, stamp-press production', lost the capacity to judge beauty and craftsmanship, having become infected with 'low "Berlin" fashions' (Lukomsky 1923: 83).[28] Later on Lukomsky clarifies his meaning: 'alongside relics of the past, wonderful furniture made from Karelian birch, they would place a lamp made in Berlin, cast in iron, in a rococo style, with a scalloped silk lampshade' (Lukomsky 1923: 87). He was also always very sceptical about the structures built by the bourgeoisie before the First World War, which he called 'utterly banal and *poshly*' (Lukomsky 1923: 78).

Only about Things, a book written by Sergey Gorny (Otsup) in emigration, is devoted entirely to the nostalgic description of everyday life at the beginning of the century, and *poshly* German things occupy an important place in it. In the chapter titled 'Fringe', for example, one finds a description of the following decorative object:

The wooden cross-section of a birch tree, complete with bark and clumps of moss to make it look more natural, and Schwarzwald has been drawn on the face (probably a picture was simply glued on, with a few strokes of oil paint added here and there; the edges of the paper where it was glued were completely smeared over with paint, so they wouldn't be visible).

(Gorny 1937: 12)[29]

The well-known Soviet children's artist, Vladimir Konashevich, identified the middle of the nineteenth century as the moment this form of daily culture was born, when the 'simple and austere' decor of rooms gave way to interiors 'in which soft, fully upholstered and quilted furniture, decorated with fringe and tassels' was placed around the room in 'whimsical and unexpected' ways, and 'all sorts of decorations and different types of knick-knacks were piled on the fireplace and the innumerable bookcases, shelves, and tables, and the doors and windows were assiduously curtained off with blinds and drapes' (Konashevich 1968: 31).[30] Konashevich never mentions the words 'empire style', nor does he explicitly connect the interiors he is describing with 1890s women's fashion, the style of which is based on a principle of 'caprice' in his opinion. However, when one considers his descriptions closely, it makes sense that the search for a new style of artistic modernism would logically turn to European Biedermeier.[31]

Jukka Gronow has posed the question of why today one perceives the everyday material culture of Victorian England as kitsch. At the foundation of this idea lies the idea that kitsch borrows and popularizes the practices of elite culture. In one way or another, everyone who has studied kitsch has written about this fact (for example, Eco or Greenberg). Gronow's definition is no exception, although it is distinguished from its predecessors by its economy: kitsch is 'a cheap, mass-produced copy of some original object or model which was considered elegant' (Gronow 1997: 42).[32] Aside from this, in his opinion, kitsch is associated with the charismatic life of the upper classes, what, one might add, the *nouveaux riches* of Munich hoped to achieve in the middle of the nineteenth century. Kitsch, a more familiar concept for European cultural consciousness, touches on the social aspect of *poshlost'*: its commonness. However, the interpretation of *poshlost'* as something *fake, a mass-produced copy, a grotesque parody* or *stylization*, which forms the basis for the approaches of Boym and Stodolsky, is fairly marginal and rare. Nevertheless, some everyday objects that are often associated with kitsch have been and continue to be called *poshly* in Russian.

In the first place, this concerns those same knick-knacks that typically filled up the space of a European room at the end of the nineteenth century. At the beginning of the twentieth century, an interest in porcelain objects arose among the circle of artists associated with the *World of Art* movement as well as the above-mentioned journals *Years Gone By* and *Apollo*.[33] The famous modernist artist Konstantin Somov had already cast figures in porcelain such as his *Masked Lady*, *The Lovers*, and many others, while another artist from the same circle, Yevgeny Lansere, had planned the group composition, *The Round Dance*. Somov was a passionate collector of small porcelain figures, both Russian and Chinese, and a special publication was released describing his collection, the oldest pieces of which dated to the eighteenth century (Somov 1913).[34] However, the true flowering of decorative porcelain sculpture took place during the first years of Soviet rule, with the efforts of Natal'ya Dan'ko and Sergey Chekhonin, who worked as artists in the First State Porcelain Factory (formerly the Imperial Porcelain Factory, for more details, see Farmakovsky (1924: 82–97)). In the 1920s, Dan'ko created her famous porcelain figures, *Hooligans*, the flirtatious *Police Woman*, as well as portraits of all the leaders of the international proletariat, of Anna Akhmatova, and of Vsevolod Meyerkhol'd with his wife. Chekhonin founded an entire stylistic current of avant-garde design in the 1920s with his so-called 'agit-porcelain' – everyday dishes with avant-garde, revolutionary symbols. Nikolay Suyetin, an artist and sculptor who had studied with Kazimir Malevich, began to work at the Lomonosov Porcelain Factory in 1932, where he created the *Tractor* tea tray, and before that, in 1930, the composition, *Peasant Women* (Andreyeva 1975: 280–83). It is exceedingly important for our topic to note that the creators of this style of art and design clearly recognized the ideological context with which porcelain was associated. Natal'ya Dan'ko's sister Yelena, a poet, wrote:

> Of all the methods through which one may take control of the artistic legacy of the past, *meshchanstvo* perfectly mastered only one – the method of making something utterly *poshly* … In the language of artists and art critics, the word 'porcelain' sounds like a synonym for *poshlost'*.
>
> (Dan'ko 1936: 139, 140, 142)

Dan'ko wrote that although antique porcelain was becoming increasingly fashionable, the court of Nikolas II kept up the demand for lamps, Easter eggs, and so on: 'The poverty of taste among the last autocrats was legendary' (Dan'ko 1936: 143). Thus, *poshlost'* entered a new cultural and historical phase of its existence, acquiring connotations associated with the Soviet and the avant-garde.[35]

*

In the above-mentioned book about Gogol', which Nabokov wrote for his American students, several pages are devoted to an explanation of *poshlost'*. Possibly out of concern for accessibility as well as a desire to imprint the sound of the unfamiliar word in the students' minds (and not without his usual love for puns), Nabokov suggested transcribing the word as *poshlust*:

> I find it preferable to transcribe that fat brute of a word thus: *poshlust* – which renders in a somewhat adequate manner the dull sound of the second, neutral 'o.' Inversely the first 'o' is as big as the plop of an elephant falling into a muddy pond and as round as the bosom of a bathing beauty on a German picture postcard.
>
> (Nabokov 1944: 63)

All the component parts of this definition, which seems more concentrated on 'lust' than on 'posh', are familiar to us: the weight of the material world (cf. the motif of inertia and Dostoevsky's '110-kilo merchant's wife'), the filth of eroticism, and even the association with things German, which had a special significance for Nabokov, not only because of the rise of Nazism in Germany and the murder of his father in Berlin in 1922, but also because of the rejection of his country of exile, so common for émigrés. Concerning the German associations, he makes his point more concretely later on in the book: 'Germany had always seemed to us a country where *poshlust*, instead of being mocked, was one of the essential parts of the national spirit, habits, traditions and general atmosphere', and the state of war with Germany at the time these lines were written would not have disturbed him (Nabokov 1944: 64–65). It can be noted that in this passage, in which the author hopes for the annihilation of Germany 'to the last beer-mug and the last forget-me-not', the flower referred to apparently comes from the poem by J.W. Goethe, *Das Blümlein Wunderschön*, the hero of which is an imprisoned knight who converses with flowers – a rose, a lily, a carnation, and a violet – but subsequently forsakes them in favour of a forget-me-not. The name of Goethe, as the author of the *poshly Faust*, appears in the preceding paragraph of Nabokov's text. Goethe's poem was translated into Russian by S.P. Shevyrev, the ideological leader of the group of Germanophile *lyubomudry*, with whom Gogol' collaborated (a letter to him was included in *Selected Passages from Correspondence with Friends*). At the same time, while taking aim at Germans in general and Goethe in particular, Nabokov hit upon a topos of European sentimentalist literature. Mikhail Lermontov's poem *Forget-Me-Not* (1830) is an adaptation of August von Platen's *Vergissmeinnicht*, and it is possible that Nabokov also knew the ballad dedicated to this flower by Charles Millevoye, *La fleur du souvenir* (1815) and its Russian translation by Vasily L. Pushkin (1815).

However, there is another moment in the description of Chichikov's *poshlost'* which is quite recognizable: 'Chichikov himself is merely the ill-paid representative of the Devil, a travelling salesman form Hades, "our Mr. Chichikov" as the Satan & Co. firm may be imagined calling their easy-going, healthy-looking but inwardly shivering and rotting agent' (Nabokov 1944: 73).

Besides the tradition of Belinsky and Gippius, Nabokov's *poshlost'* is also located in another context, that of Soviet culture. Sergey Davydov, who has collected all the examples from world literature Nabokov associates with *poshlost'* in the collection *Strong Opinions*, begins the list with the author's four most unbeloved 'doctors': Freud, Zhivago, Schweitzer, and Castro (Davydov 1995: 630). Herbert Gold recalls how when Nabokov was leaving Cornell, he gave him his copy of Pasternak's novel with comments in the margins: 'stupidity!', 'poshlost!', 'foolishness!', 'idiocy!' The memoirist also once saw Vera Nabokov place a copy of Nabokov's *Lolita* on top of the Nobel Prize-winning novel in a bookstore (Gold 1984: 58). In fact, for the young heroes of Pasternak's novel, *poshlost'* plays quite an important role, appearing any time the topic of sex is raised; indeed both themes are equally important in Pasternak's writing.[36] It seems that, as an avant-gardist, finding art within banality was not alien to him either:

The downpour's shoots stick in the mud in bunches
And long, long before the dawn

> They scribble their acrostics down from the roofs
> Blowing bubbles into rhymes.
> Poetry, when under the tap is
> A truism …
>
> ('Poetry')

The 'bunches' referred to here are clearly bunches of lilac, which have made their way into Pasternak's poem precisely because of their banality,[37] a kind of parallel to the truism that figures in the last stanza. Nabokov himself refers to *poshlost'* so often and, at times, for such different reasons, that it is only necessary to mention a few specific themes. One should be addressed, if only briefly, because it echoes in an interesting way the opinion of another émigré poet, Marina Tsvetayeva. In the lecture 'Philistines and Philistinism' (1950), which coincides in several places with the text of the corresponding passage from the book on Gogol', Nabokov declares that a *poshly* person is not interested in literature but 'is trained to read magazines' (Nabokov 1981: 311). In her famous poem, *Readers of Newspapers*, the substitution of a *poshly* newspaper for literature inspires a seething hatred in Tsvetayeva (1935).

Soviet *poshlost'* held a special significance for Nabokov, and he refers to it in the conclusion of his lecture. From the perspective of the social history of Russian culture, this form of *poshlost'* appeared with the 'Stalin Revolution' (and the beginning of the five-year plans in 1928), when the Soviet *meshchanin* took the place of the New Man and his communist morality (cf. Gronow 2003: 1–16, 145–47; for observations on Soviet kitsch's copying of the everyday culture of the pre-revolutionary nobility, see ibid.: 33–36). When Clement Greenberg links socialist realism with kitsch in the above-mentioned essay, there seems to be more than just an interesting parallel with Nabokov; perhaps it was one of his sources of inspiration (if so, *poshlost'* would be a direct correlate of kitsch).[38] The situation remains ambiguous, however, since even as those in power basked in the courtly luxury of an Asiatic empire, the Soviet regime also zealously struggled against *poshlost'* in the name of the socialist future. A subtle play on these contradictions can be found in a poem by Nikolay Oleynikov, *The Ungrateful Shareholder* (1932, published in 1964):

> When they handed out the sugar and soap,
> He started going after herring and groats.
> … A typical *poshlost'* reigned
> In his rather small brain.
>
> (Oleynikov 2000: 115)

The hero of this poem, a shareholder in a consumer cooperative (*Potrebkooperatsiya*), behaves in an un-Soviet manner, or more precisely, in a way befitting not a communist, but a *meshchanin*. However, the irony of the poem lies in the fact that the *poshly* person is demanding only the simplest, most basic things, essential for life, while to call these modest desires *poshlost'* is to echo the severe judgements pronounced on bourgeois forms of behaviour under the old regime.

It is clear that Vladimir Mayakovsky fell into this trap of double standards. As an avant-gardist, he was already interested in the struggle with things in the 1910s, in their rebellion and in the world of machines.[39] However, as is well known, towards the end of the 1920s, Mayakovsky, like many other writers, created a number of works about the return of *meshchanstvo*, now in a Soviet wrapping. The heroine of his satirical play *The Bathhouse* utters a phrase that became a popular saying (though it sounds somewhat like a calque from the French) – 'make it pretty for me!' In the poem *Let's Have an Elegant Life* (1927), the poet mocks the behaviour of aesthetes, so out of place in a country of workers, and he mentions among other things their characteristic marking – a specially grown-out and manicured fingernail on the little finger (which one can see, for example, on the well-known photograph of one of the Russian formalists, Boris Eykhenbaum, which was taken by the famous portrait photographer, Moisey Nappel'baum); the 'poet from the people', Nikolay Klyuev, also had such a fingernail (see, for example, Krandiyevskaya-Tolstaya 1977: 194):

> ... All the little fingers
> > have two-feet long nails.

Such a Soviet aesthete loves chasing after women:

> ... and talking *poshlost'*
> > about lilies
> > > in a drippy tongue,

and reading Kalinnikov's *Holy Relics* in the VD clinic's queue. (Mayakovsky 1958b: 38).[40] However, it was not so much the return of bourgeois values that worried the poet, but, as with Belinsky, the related shifts in poetry that might occur as it changed to serve the new reader. Naturally, Mayakovsky was developing a theme here that had been important to him since the beginning of the new regime – the theme of the renewal of poetry for the needs of the new world. In his avant-garde manner, Mayakovsky also saw the creation of new rhymes as a source of renewal in poetry. In 1923, in a poem titled *The First of May*, he called the rhyming of words that were naturally assonant in the language a form of *poshlost'*:

> Poets
> > are a cunning bunch.
> A verse?
> > If you please.
> > > Just give them a bit of rhyme.
> There has been no greater *poshlost'*
> Spoken,
> > than about May.

> (Mayakovsky 1958a: 42)

The émigré philosopher, theologian, music teacher, and critic, Vladimir Il'in (1891–1974), writing under the pseudonym P. Sazanovich, and espousing views close to those of the Eurasianists, also noticed this shift. The occasion of his article, 'Poshlost'', was an agitational drawing in the Soviet satirical journal, *Crocodile*, where an old peasant couple is shown walking into a school that has been constructed out of a church, and a Communist Youth League member waits for them at the threshold. Noting that these peasants more closely resemble Slavophile paysans of the Socialist Revolutionary Party, I'lin keenly refers to the economic 'relaxation of requirements in the case of non-existent cattle' in Soviet domestic politics. The government emptied out the *Torgsin* shops and gave the people back their Christmas trees.[41] According to Il'in, the Soviet people is in fact the petite bourgeoisie, or, more accurately, the *'petit goujat'*, the petty boor, Pavel Ivanovich Chichikov, only in a new formation: 'a bourgeois-socialist and a free mason'. '"The Soviet people" (this expression was invented by "Chichikov") is starving, while the "man of average means" does not notice – there is abundance and an overflowing sea around him' (Sazanovich 1936b: 2).[42] In an article that appeared two weeks after the one quoted above, now on the destruction of the proletarian myth and proletarian consciousness, I'lin noted: 'Among the innumerable plagues of the proletariat, one can be noted as especially characteristic: the typical bad taste and *poshlost'* of bourgeois *meshchanstvo*' (Sazanovich 1936c: 2). The title of the next in this series of articles by Il'in, 'Empire and Freedom', reveals the ideological context in which these attacks on *poshlost'* must be understood. *Poshlost'* is the antipode of the romantic image of the empire's 'blossoming complexity' (Konstantin Leont'yev), whose law is that of 'realized freedom', an idealization of 'the will to greatness and expansion' (Sazanovich 1936a: 2). It is no accident that Il'in includes among the ideological ancestors of Bolshevism all the utopian reformers: populists, Westernizers, and Slavophiles alike. Of course, this intellectual tradition held the *meshchanin*, the bourgeois, and the proletarian all in contempt – each as social agents of *poshlost'*.

As one approaches the present, the subsequent fate of the concept of *poshlost'*, simultaneously a symbol of both the Soviet and the anti-Soviet, becomes increasingly difficult to describe using the methods of the history of language, literature, culture, and society. Leaving this history to the future researcher, I will note the relevance of the concept to critical moments in Soviet history – the epoch of the 'thaw' (perception of the *stilyagi* (youth interested in Western fashions) as representatives of *meshchanstvo* and *poshlost'*), and in the time of 'perestroyka'.[43] But, in any case, it should by now be clear that any definition of *poshlost'* can only create more material for study – the ever-open meaning of this term is clarified only by analysing the full history of its usage. Not to explain this concept, but to study it, as one studies a foreign language, has been the object of this chapter.

Authorized translation by Jonathan B. Platt.

Notes

1 Despite its surface resemblance to an historical study and its specific discoveries, which are not uninteresting, Svetlana Boym's work on the concept of *poshlost'* must also be considered speculative (see Boym 1994: 41–66; and also the more extensive version in the Russian edition: Boym 2002: 60–92).

2 Herbert Gold professed that the concept has 'now become almost a part of American literary criticism' (Gold 1984: 48). For an attempt to identify the qualities of *poshlost'* in one of Nabokov's novels, in which the characters' behaviour realizes the proverb that 'love is blind', see Mckenna (2007: 247–50). Admittedly, the analysis does not employ Nabokov's own connotations for the term (about which more below), though it does treat it as a specifically Russian concept.

3 Among this class of terms can be included, for example, the concept of *narodnost'* ('nationality') in the semantically bleached form it acquired in Russian culture beginning with Romanticism. This term has attracted the attention of specialists in the epoch numerous times (first of all Tynyanov and Lotman); among the most recent works is the article by Knight (2000: 41–64).

4 The absence of such analysis is the only general criticism one can raise with regard to the interesting work by Zaliznyak et al. (2005: 182–90). In order to enliven their explication, the authors wittily suggest that to judge something *poshlost'* is itself an example of *poshlost'*.

5 Anna Wierzbicka shares this conviction, claiming that even after reading Nabokov's explanations, let alone dictionary definitions, her Australian students still had no idea what *poshlost'* meant (Vezhbitska 2002: 9). Nabokov himself insists on the insufficiency of simple English translations of the word and does not refrain from attacking one of the dictionaries from his day (Nabokov 1944: 64).

6 A more complete version of the article, taken from the manuscript, was published as part of Vinogradov's *History of Words* (Vinogradov 1999: 531–33).

7 V.M. Vompersky briefly considers how Vasily Trediakovsky began to use the concept of 'good' and 'bad' taste, making it one of 'the central stylistic categories of his theory' (Vompersky 1988: 122). He points out that the metaphorical meaning of the word already existed in the 1730s; Antiokh Kantemir remarked in a note to the first edition of his second satire that the word comes from the speech of dandies, and it is also found in German–Russian and French–Russian dictionaries. In the rhetoric of Feofan Prokopovich, low or simple style still did not refer to anything objectionable; the pejorative connotation appeared only in the last quarter of the eighteenth century (ibid.: 90).

8 For a clearer explication of this expression, one may recall Lermontov's *Hero of Our Time* (1841) and the scene of the duel in which Grushnitsky's second is infuriated when he agrees to Pechorin's request to reload: 'Die then, like a *poshly* fool!', that is, like an absolute fool, in the most ordinary manner.

9 A description of the amateur theatrical circles which were widespread in Lesnoye, a well-known country spot outside St Petersburg, can be found in the memoirs of Nikolay Khodotov, the famous actor from the Aleksandrinsky Theatre (Khodotov 1932: 43–46). When Humbert Humbert, the protagonist of Nabokov's *Lolita*, uses this expression (in the author's own Russian translation of the novel) to characterize his own life, he takes it from the everyday life of this epoch, with which Nabokov's childhood coincided.

10 The derivational logic here is similar to that followed by Osip Mandel'shtam when he celebrated the 'goldfinchiness' (*shcheglovitost'yu*) of the goldfinch in his well-known poem, *My goldfinch, I throw back my head …* (1936), which of course also recalls the surname of the minister Shcheglovitov.

11 Here among other things one finds reference to a popular French romantic maxim from the 1830s, which, on the whole, provides the outline for the thought Odoyevsky's character expresses: *le beau c'est le laid* ('beauty is ugliness'; Maykov 1985: 71, 73, 99).

12 Something similar seems to have occurred not too long ago in the Russian language with the word *glamur* ('glamour').

13 Nevertheless, all three linguists mentioned above refer to the observation of Korney Chukovsky that in the 1860s *poshlost'* became associated with stagnation and devotion to old ways (Zaliznyak et al. 2005: 187). Obviously this reflects a resurfacing of the obsolete meaning of the word.

14 For a discussion of how this convergence occurred in the second half of the nineteenth century and the role of the English language in the appearance of the derogatory meaning, see Frolova (2003: 108, 115). In a semantic experiment, attempting to translate *poshlost'* adequately into simple, universal words, Anna Wierzbicka essentially preserves only one component: he who speaks of *poshlost'* knows something better than others (Vezhbitska 2002: 9).

15 See also the essential work on Gertsen's German associations, Herrman (1998: 905–12).

16 Cf. the opinion of a famous entertainer, who earned his living from his ability to tell jokes: 'One of the greatest enemies of humour is *poshlost*'' (Alekseyev 1972: 296).

17 A letter of Bakunin to a well-known socialist Georg Herwegh, written in Brussels at the end of December 1847, contains a story about the 'Democratic Society', whose work was being disturbed by the Germans, Karl Marx in particular: 'themselves are dyed-in-the-wool bourgeois'. In a letter of 8 December 1848 he is even more cutting: 'A bourgeois is never attractive, but a German bourgeois combines baseness with amiability' (Bakunin 1935: 282, 367; unfortunately, the publishers did not consider it necessary to print the original letters, which were written in German). The Russian word *meshchanstvo* comes from the word *meshchanin*, which meant 'city-dweller' in a social class sense, as indicated in a person's passport (much like *bourgeois* or *Bürger*). However, as an ideological and at times even philosophical construct, the word was of course used in a wider sense, not only in Russia, but in Europe as well (see Vihavainen 2006). In his discussion of the *poshlost'* Vihavainen relies on the above-mentioned work by Svetlana Boym (Vihavainen 2006: 18–21). As is well known, the proletariat, now seen as the primary agent of historical progress, has nothing except its chains.

18 Although the song was only published in 1859 in *The Polar Star*, according to Aleksandra Smirnova-Rosset, Pushkin sang it every time he visited Tsarskoye selo (Gusev 1965: 1008).

19 It appears that the old meaning of the word survived only in dictionaries, cf: 'Properly speaking, *poshly* (in the literal sense) refers to what has long since passed (*poshlo*), then to what is worn out, tiresome, colourless (because past its bloom), tasteless – sometimes indecent, rude' (Mikhel'son [1902]: 107).

20 I am consciously casting aside any analysis of Gippius' behaviour; the poet declared a number of times and in a variety of ways her desire to transgress sexual and familial norms.

21 Here one may note the proximity of *poshlost'* to kitsch, which, according to Clement Greenberg, 'is a product of the industrial revolution', and furnishes yesterday's peasants, who have now become the 'new urban masses', with an 'ersatz culture' (Greenberg 1986: 12).

22 In the introductory remarks to his own memoirs, Khodotov clearly designates his stage credo as 'Shchepkin-esque realism', adding Meyerkhol'd's biomechanics to the list of acting techniques he finds unacceptable (Khodotov 1932: 27–29).

23 The word is clearly a combination of *nervny* ('nervous') and *stervyatnik* ('vulture').

24 According to the contemporary poet and critic Aleksandr Skidan, Blok loved trips to Shuvalovo precisely because 'there the feeling of the world's mysterious *poshlost'*, which he loved, was especially strong' (Skidan 2005: 370). Of course, in Blok's work there are other cases in which he uses the word *poshlost'*, and some of them are easily recognized. For example, he remarks in the article 'A Knight-Monk', dedicated to the anniversary of Vladimir Solov'yev's death: 'There's something horrid about jubilee days. It's so easy to celebrate the *poshlost'* that goes by the name of *oblivion*' (Blok 1982: 448). This recalls the troubled lines from Nekrasov's 'Belinsky', quoted above.

25 At Makovsky's funeral in 1915 the Black Hundreds organized a demonstration that ended in a riot.

26 The book, *The Power of Money* (*La règne de l'argent*, Russian translation, St Petersburg, 1900), by prominent essayist Anatole Leroy-Beaulieu (1842–1912), is a polemical composition on the mercantilism of contemporary society. The author connects the

power of money characteristic of society to the spread of democracy, the development of banks, and the speculation and excitement of playing the stock market. For this reason, Thorstein Veblen's classic work, *The Theory of the Leisure Class* (1899) can be seen as a reflection on the feverish accumulation and consumption which seized the world on the eve of the new century. According to the author, the appearance and emergence of the social institution of individual property, on the basis of which lies competition, was originally not connected to providing for the basic needs of existence (Veblen 1934: 26–27). Jukka Gronow justly writes that the cutting edge of Veblen's criticism of 'conspicuous consumption' is directed at American *nouveaux riches* of the turn of the century (Gronow 1997: 38).

27 For more on this practice and on the mood of this circle, see Obatnin (2004), and also the memoirs: Makovsky (2000a: 472–73).

28 Protest against the economic expansion of Germany also occurred in Europe at the turn of the century. For example, it was starkly expressed in a book by the British journalist Edward Williams, *Made in Germany* (1897), the title of which was used to denote all mass-produced goods (including literature).

29 I am grateful to Albin Konechny for pointing out this source to me.

30 I am obliged to Kseniya A. Kumpan for directing me to this source.

31 By the way, the term Biedermeier itself was introduced in 1891 by Welheml Heinrich Riehl to designate the style of the 1820s and 1830s, and it was picked up by Georg Böttischer in 1894 and in the next year by Fritz Minkus. The resurrection of Biedermeier at the turn of the century began as a struggle with the style of 'historicism', and was connected with the name of Henry van de Velde. Hartwig Fischel in 1901 wrote a programmatic article, 'Biedermeier as a Model' (see Himmelheber 1989: 11, 44–46).

32 For a discussion of the conceptual interrelationship between kitsch and *poshlost'*, see Stodolsky (1998). I would like to take this opportunity to thank the author for allowing me to read his work.

33 It should be noted that the existing intellectual tradition of treating kitsch as one of the masks of modern culture is based predominantly on the texts and practices of European culture (Calinescu 1987: 225–29).

34 A catalogue was also published by one of the figures in this circle: Troynitsky (1911). L. Andreyeva connects the interest of the *World of Art* circle in porcelain to the enthusiasm for ceramics in the Mamontov Circle at the end of the 1880s as well as to Vrubel' and the desire 'to overcome the *poshly* banality of factory goods' (Andreyeva 1975: 17).

35 This is a supplement to the thoughts of Clement Greenberg who, in his classic leftist essay of 1939, opposed the two artistic styles named in his title, avant-garde and kitsch (Greenberg 1986: 11, 13–17). Umberto Eco admitted that the avant-garde culture contemporary with him, Pop Art, often 'borrows its own stylemes from Kitsch' (Eco 1989: 215).

36 Of course, just being interested in this is already *poshly* for Nabokov. In an interview with Herbert Gold for *Paris Review*, Nabokov again mentioned the persistent image of the love serenade, which he unambiguously associated with *poshlost'*. Gold himself later admitted, recalling his talks with Nabokov, that he was on close terms with almost no one: 'But I think his definition of "*poshlost*" expresses a kind of suspicion that he had of easy expression of emotion' (Gold 1984: 48). However, one must agree with the scholar who wrote that 'overcoming traditional sexual barriers' in Pasternak's work leads in the final analysis to 'deeper penetration into the tragic mystery of being' (cf. Aucouturier 1992: 112).

37 And, it is possible, also because of their connection with the theme of love, always hovering near in his poetry, cf. 'the moist labyrinth / Of warmed trees, lilac, and passion' from the poem, *Marburg*, or the universe 'seething with white howls' from the poem, *The Definition of Creativity*. On Nabokov's poetic quarrel with these poems of Pasternak, see Pirogovskaya (2007: 86).

38 Greenberg's essay is in large part directed against the kitsch he associates with all forms of academic art, the symbol of which, for him as for Eco, is Repin, as contrasted with

Picasso (Greenberg 1986: 14–16). On the eve of the Second World War Greenberg is naturally interested in state support of kitsch in the countries under totalitarian regimes – Germany, Italy, and Russia – each of which had a place in the history of the avant-garde (expressionism, futurism, and Russian cinema of the 1920s) as in the history of socialism. According to Greenberg, it was the inability of these regimes to raise the cultural level of the masses, combined with the avant-garde's unsuitability as effective propaganda, which led to the resulting situation (Greenberg 1986: 20). The possible connection of Nabokov's idea with Hermann Broch's essay *Kitsch* (1933), about which Boym writes (the passage is an addition to the Russian edition: Boym (2002: 62), seems less convincing.

39 For a description of the tradition of analysing this theme in the poet's work, see Klanderud (1996: 37–39).

40 The three-volume novel by Iosif Kalinnikov (1890–1934), *Holy Relics* (1925–27), which depicts the debauched life in monasteries in a naturalistic manner, was judged pornographic and removed from Soviet libraries.

41 The quotation is a reference to the allowance for peasants to keep domestic cattle as personal property, even though, as Il'in hints, at that moment all cattle had been destroyed in the collective farms. *Torgsin* was a state organization whose shops accepted valuables or hard currency as forms of payment. Taking advantage of a monopoly in the domestic market, *Torgsin* mercilessly plundered the country's population. On the adventures of the Christmas tree, which was forbidden in the first years of Soviet power as a religious throwback, see Dushechkina (2002: 227–96).

42 In another place, Il'in explained what he saw as the signs of the death of modern culture: 'We are choking in the shallow mud of *poshly* people who deny tragedy! … *Poshlost*' knows neither fear, nor pity' (Il'in 1929: 28).

43 For an analysis of *poshlost*' as it appears in the female prose of everyday life by Tat'yana Tolstaya and L'yudmila Petrushevskaya, see Ivanova (1991: 214–15).

Bibliography

Alekseyev, A.G. (1972) *Ser'yeznoye i smeshnoye. Polveka v teatre i na estrade*, Moskva: Iskusstvo.

Andreyeva, L. (1975) *Sovetsky farfor, 1920–1930*, Moskva: Sovetsky khudozhnik.

Anichkov, Ye. (1906) *Iskusstvo i sotsialistichesky stroy*, Sankt-Peterburg: Yakor'.

Aucouturier, M. (1992) 'Pol i "poshlost"'. Tema pola u Pasternaka', in L. Heller (ed.) *Amour et érotisme dans la littérature russe du XXe siècle*, Bern/New York: Peter Lang.

Bakunin, M.A. (1935) *Sobraniye sochineniy i pisem, 1828–1876*, vol. 3, Moskva: Izdatel'stvo Vsesoyuznogo obshchestva politkatorzhan i ssyl'no-poselentsev.

Belinsky, V.G. (1948) '"Gore ot uma." Komediya v 4-kh deystviyach', in V.G. Belinsky, *Sobraniye sochineniy v 3-kh tt.*, vol. 1, Moskva: Goslitizdat.

Belousov, A. (1992) 'Akklimatizatsiya sireni v russkoy poezii', in *Sbornik statey k 70-letiyu prof. Yu.M. Lotmana*, 311–22, Tartu: Tartusky universitet.

Blok, A. (1982) *Sobraniye sochineniy v 6-ti tt.*, vol. 5, Leningrad: Khudozhestvennaya literatura.

Boym, S. (1994) *Common Places: Mythologies of Everyday Life in Russia*, Cambridge, MA: Harvard University Press.

——(2002) *Obshchiye mesta: mifologiya povsednevnoy zhizni*, Moskva: Novoye literaturnoye obozreniye.

Bulgakov, S. (1999) *Svet nevecherny: Sozertsaniya i umozreniya*, Moskva/Sankt-Peterburg: Iskusstvo & Inapress.

Calinescu, M. (1987) *Five Faces of Modernity: Modernism, Avant-Garde, Decadence, Kitsch, Postmodernism*, Durham, NC: Duke University Press.

Certeau, M. de (1992) *The Mystic Fable*, vol. 1, Chicago: University of Chicago Press.

Chereda, Yu. (1904) 'O poshlosti', *Novyi put'*, Aprel': 228–38.

Chulkov, G. (1915) *Satana: Roman*, Moskva: Zhatva.

Dan'ko, Ye. (1936) 'Zametki o kul'ture farfora', *Literaturny sovremennik*, 1: 130–51.

Davydov, S. (1995) 'Poshlost'', in V.E. Aleksandrov (ed.) *The Garland Companion to Vladimir Nabokov*, 628–32, New York: Garland.

Dushechkina, Ye. (2002) *Russkaya yelka: istoriya, mifologiya, literatura*, Sankt-Peterburg: Norint.

Eco, U. (1989) 'The structure of bad taste', in U. Eco, *The Open Work*, trans. Anna Concogni, 180–217, Cambridge, MA: Harvard University Press.

Farmakovsky, M.V. (1924) 'Skul'ptura gosudarstvennogo farforovogo zavoda', in E.F. Gollerbakh and M.V. Farmakovsky (eds) *Russky khudozhestvenny farfor*, 82–97, Leningrad: Gosudarstvennoe izdatel'stvo.

Floresnky, P. (1914) *Stolp i utverzhdeniye istiny. Opyt pravoslavnoy teoditsei v dvenadtsati pis'makh*, Moskva: Put'.

Frolova, O.Ye. (2003) 'Vul'garny ili poshly', *Russky yazyk v nauchnom osveshchenii*, 1(5): 106–23.

Gippius, V. (1935) *Poshlost' v slovoupotreblenii Gogolya*, unpublished notes, Institute of Russian Literature, Manuscript Division, fund 47, inventory 1, file 131.

Gippius, Z. (1908) *Literaturny dnevnik*, Sankt-Peterburg: M.V. Pirozhkov.

Gertsen, A.I. (1956) *O razvitii revolyutsionnykh idey v Rossi*, in *Sobraniye Sochineniy v 30-ti, tt.*, vol. 7, Moskva: Akademiya Nauk SSSR.

Gogol', N. (1898) *Sochineniya*, 14 izdaniye, Sankt-Peterburg: Izdaniye A.F. Marksa.

Gold, H. (1984) 'Nabokov remembered: a slight case of poshlost'', in G. Gibian and S. J. Parker (eds) *The Achievements of Vladimir Nabokov: Essays, studies, reminiscences, and stories from The Cornell Nabokov Festival*, 45–59, Ithaca, NY: Cornell University.

Gor'ky, M. (1921) *Vospominaniya*, Berlin: Kniga.

Gorny, S. (1937) *Tol'ko o veshchakh*, Berlin: Petropolis.

Greenberg, C. (1986) 'Avant-garde and kitsch', in C. Greenberg, *The Collected Essays and Criticism*, vol. 1, 5–22, Chicago: The University of Chicago Press.

Gronow, J. (1997) *The Sociology of Taste*, London: Routledge.

——(2003) *Caviar with Champagne: Common Luxury and the Ideals of the Good Life in Stalin's Russia*, Oxford: Berg.

Gusev, V.E. (ed.) (1965) *Pesni i romansy russkikh poetov*, Moskva: Sovetsky pisatel'.

Herrman, D. (1998) 'Aleksandr Herzens Probleme mit den Deutschen', in D. Herrman and A.L. Ospovat (eds) *Deutsche und Deutschland aus russischer Sicht. 19. Jahrhundert: Von der Jahrhundertswende bis zu den Reformen Alexanders II*, 873–937, München: Wilhelm Fink.

Himmelheber, G. (1989) *Biedermeier, 1815–1835*, Munich: Prestel.

Il'in, V.N. (1929) *Ateizm i gibel' kul'tury*, Paris/Varshava: Dobro.

Ivanova, N. (1991) 'Neopalimy golubok (Poshlost' kak estetichesky fenomen)', *Znamya*, 8: 211–23.

Knight, N. (2000) 'Ethnicity, nationality and the masses: *narodnost'* and modernity in imperial Russia', in D.L. Hoffmann and Y. Kotsonis (eds) *Russian Modernity: Politics, Knowledge, Practices*, 41–64, London/New York: Macmillan Press.

Khodotov, N. (1909) *Gospozha poshlost'*, Sankt-Peterburg: tip. Glavn. upr. udelov.

Khodotov, N.N. (1932) *Blizkoye-dalekoye*, Moskva-Leningrad: Academia.

Klanderud, P.A. (1996) 'Maiakovskii's myth of man, things and the city: from *poshlost'* to the promised land', *The Russian Review*, 55: 37–54.

Konashevich, V.M. (1968) *O sebe i svoyem dele. Vospominaniya, stat'i, pis'ma*, Moskva: Detskaya literatura.

Krandiyevskaya-Tolstaya, N. (1977) *Vospominaniya*, Leningrad: Lenizdat.

Krayny, A. (1904) 'Yesche o poshlosti', *Novy put'*, Aprel': 238–43.

Krinitsky, M. (1905) 'Poshlost", *Voprosy zhizni*, 4–5: 118–33.

Lukomsky, G.K. (1923) *Staryye gody*, Berlin: E.A. Gutnov.

Makarevich, A. (2008) *'Sam ovtsa': avtobiograficheskaya proza*, Moskva: Zakharov.

Makovsky, S. (1958) *Polnoye sobraniye sochineniy v 13-ti tt.*, vol. 8, Moskva: Gos. izd. khudozhestv. literatury.

——(2000a) *Na Parnase serebryanogo veka*, Moskva: Izdatel'sky dom 'XXI vek – Soglasiye'.

——(2000b) *Portrety sovremennikov*, Moskva: Izdatel'sky dom 'XXI vek – Soglasiye'.

Mayakovsky, V.V. (1958a) *Polnoye sobraniye sochineniy v 13-ti tt.*, vol. 5, Moskva: Gos. izd. khudozhestv. literatury.

Maykov, V. (1985) *Literaturnaya kritika*, Leningrad: Khud. literatura.

McKenna, K.J. (2007) *'Poshlost'*, Hegelian syllogism, and the proverb: a paremiological approach to Vladimir Nabokov's *Laughter in the Dark*, *Proverbium: Yearbook of International Proverb Scholarship*, 24: 245–60.

Merezhkovsky, D.S. (2000) *Stikhotvoreniya i poemy*, Sankt-Peterburg: Akademichesky proyekt.

Mikhel'son, M.I. (1902) *Russkaya mysl' i rech'. Svoye i chuzhoye. Opyt russkoy frazeologii. Sbornik obraznykh slov i inoskazaniy*, vol. 2, Sankt-Peterburg: Akademiya nauk.

Nabokov, V. (1944) *Nikolai Gogol*, Norfolk: New Directions Books.

——(1981) *Lectures on Russian Literature*, London: Weidenfeld and Nicolson.

Obatnin, G. (2004) 'Iz istorii obshchestvennykh nastroeniy: passeisty', *Novy mir iskusstva*, 3/38: 9–15.

Odoyevsky, V. (2006) *Povesti i rasskazy*, Part 2. Online. Available: www.imwerden.de (accessed 29 March 2011).

Oleynikov, N. (2000) *Stikhotvoreniya i poemy*, Sankt-Peterburg: Akademichesky proyekt.

Pirogovskaya, M. (2007) 'abba abba ccd ede: ob odnoy partii Vladimira Nabokova', *Novoye literaturnoye obozreniye*, 86: 169–81.

Poyarkov, N. (1908) *Stikhotvoreniya*, Moskva: I.N. Kholchev i Ko.

Rozanov, V.V. (1914) *Osyazatel'noye i obonyatel'noye otnosheniye yevreyev k krovi*, Sankt-Peterburg: izd. A.S. Suvorina.

The Russian National Corpus (2003–10). Online. Available: www.ruscorpora.ru (accessed 29 March 2011).

Sazanovich, P. (1936a) 'Imperiya i svoboda', *Vozrozhdeniye*, 3898, 4 February: 2.

——(1936b) 'Poshlost'', *Vozrozhdeniye*, 3874, 11 January: 2.

——(1936c) 'Proletariat', *Vozrozhdeniye*, 3884, 21 January: 2.

Skidan, A. (2005) 'Krasnoye smeshcheniye', in L. Zubova and V. Kuritsyn (eds) *Stikhi v Peterburge. Poeticheskaya antologiya*, 366–72, Sankt-Peterburg: Platforma.

Sologub, F. (1990) *Tyazhelyye sny: Roman. Rasskazy*, Leningrad: Hudozhestvennaya literatura.

Somov, K. (1913) *Farfor iz sobraniya K. A. Somova*, Sankt-Peterburg: Sirius.

Stodolsky, I. (1998) *The Structure of Distaste: Poshlost and Kitsch as Structural Terms of Derision*, unpublished PhD dissertation, University of London, Birkbeck College.

Troynitsky, S. (1911) *Galereya farfora Imperatorskogo Ermitazha*, Sankt-Peterburg: Sirius.

Veblen, T. (1934) *The Theory of the Leisure Class: An Economic Study of Institutions*, New York: Modern library.

Vezhbitska, A. (2002) 'Russkiye kul'turnyye skripty i ikh otrazheniye v yazyke', *Russky yazyk v nauchnom osveshchenii*, 2/4: 6–34.

Vihavainen, T. (2006) *The Inner Adversary: The Struggle against Philistinism as a Moral Mission of the Russian Intelligentsia*, Washington: New Academia Publishing, LLC.

Vinogradov, V. (1999) *Istoriya slov*, Moskva: Institut russkogo yazyka RAN.

Voloshin, M. (2007) 'Pol' Verlen. Stikhi, izbrannyye i perevedennyye F. Sologubom', in
  M. Voloshin *Sobraniye sochineniy*, vol. 6, kniga 1, 102–10, Moskva: Ellis Lak.
Vompersky, V.M. (1988) *Ritoriki v Rossii XVII – XVIII vv.*, Moskva: Nauka.
Yasinsky, I. (1926) *Roman moyey zhizni. Kniga vospominaniy*, Moskva/Leningrad: Gosizdat.
Zaliznyak, A.A., Levontina, I.B., and Shmelev, A.D. (2005) 'O poshlosti i proze zhizni', in
  A.A. Zaliznyak, I.B. Levontina, and A.D. Shmelev, *Klyuchevyye idei russkoy yazykovoy kartiny
  mira*, 182–90, Moskva: Yazyki slavayanskoj kul'tury.

13 The notion of universal bisexuality in Russian religious philosophy

Evgenii Bershtein

Introduction

Homosexuality and bisexuality have been a sensational and hotly discussed topic in the post-Soviet media. The tenor of these discussions proves that despite its decriminalization in 1993, homosexuality has remained a controversial and problematic issue for the Russian public. Addressing this topic, contemporary Russian policy-makers, journalists, writers, and scholars find themselves having to consider religious taboos, scientific explanations, philosophical interpretations, and moral judgements attached to same-sex love. Moreover, the debate that is taking place today is shaped and informed not only (and not so much) by the social and political vocabulary produced by the gay movement in the West, but also by the interpretations developed around the notion of homosexuality in Russia in the early twentieth century. At that time, important religious thinkers, such as Vasily Rozanov, Pavel Florensky, Nikolay Berdyayev, and Sergey Bulgakov, examined the spiritual meaning of same-sex love. As Brian Baer has noted:

> the enduring figure of the spiritual homosexual suggests at least one way in which homosexuality in Russia today is imagined: not as an 'otherness' but rather as the very embodiment of traditional Russian values, underscoring the complex relationship that obtains between local and increasingly global discourses on the subject of homosexuality.
>
> (Baer 2009: 93–94)

The terms in which today's Russian intellectuals tend to conceptualize homosexuality may strike a Western observer as pre-modern. However, these terms are rooted in a number of specific modern and modernist philosophical ideas that preoccupied the Russian intelligentsia in the *fin de siècle*. The present chapter addresses the sexual theories developed by the Silver Age philosophers, to whose authority participants in today's debates frequently appeal. I believe that accounting for the intellectual roots of today's ideological discussions helps to create a better understanding of the cultural specificity of the attitudes to (homo)sexuality common among post-Soviet Russia's educated elite. In that spirit, I offer a study of the three uses of a single sexual motif that gained prominence in Russia a hundred years ago, regained its role in the post-Soviet sexual discourses, and remains significant even today.

Bisexuality (*dvupolost'*) in Weininger and Rozanov

My investigation begins in the period between 1906 and the years of the First World War, when the debate of the 'sexual question' (*polovoy vopros*) in Russian society coincided and overlapped with increasingly prominent modernist trends in literature and the arts.[1] The understanding of sexuality as both a crucial aspect of human existence and an all-important field for exploration became a character-istically modern artistic and journalist phenomenon. Among the multiplicity of new voices that addressed sexual themes at the time, the most expressive and provocative one belonged to Vasily Vasil'yevich Rozanov (1856–1919). A widely read author, Rozanov articulated the modern preoccupation with sexuality in an idiosyncratic and strikingly lyrical literary manner. His contemplation of sexuality led Rozanov to critique the official Orthodox church (and Christianity as a whole), state institutions as well as various social and intellectual movements in Russia. The theme of sex also gave him material for building his peculiar, unsys-tematic metaphysics. Although leading figures of the Silver Age acknowledged their intellectual debt to Rozanov as a philosopher of sex, the mechanisms of his influence have not yet been studied in detail.

In this chapter, I will examine the ways in which one ideological motif developed and advocated by Rozanov (although not 'invented' by him) generated con-sequential philosophical and theological responses from three major Russian thinkers who came from the Symbolist intellectual background, namely, Pavel Florensky, Nikolay Berdyayev, and Sergey Bulgakov. The motif in question is Rozanov's notion of universal bisexuality (*dvupolost'*), that is, the idea that every human being is a combination of masculine and feminine elements. With his trademark stylistic brilliance, Rozanov presented this concept in his 1911 *Lyudi lunnogo sveta: metafizika khristianstva* ('People of the Moonlight: Metaphysics of Christianity', Rozanov 1990a) and returned to it in many subsequent works.

In *People of the Moonlight*, Rozanov employed the idea of bisexuality to explain what he named 'spiritual sodomy', that is, certain people's lack of sexual desire for the opposite sex, and the role of this lack in religion and culture. Rozanov claimed that a small but enormously influential part of humanity – 'spiritual sodomites', 'people of the moonlight', or the 'third sex' – experienced (often unconsciously) predominantly same-sex desire. According to Rozanov, though largely failing to act on their desire, 'spiritual sodomites' feel the same aversion to the heterosexual act as that which the 'normal' person feels towards the *actus sodomicus*. Excluded from reproductive existence and the satisfaction it provides, people of the moonlight sublimate their inverted sexuality in spiritual, cultural, and political activity. Rozanov credits them, for instance, with creating Christianity and the ascetic Christian civilization. At the same time he accuses them of suppressing natural heterosexual expression: spiritual sodomites fill the universe with their animosity toward procreation and the world of biological reproduction.

According to Rozanov, Christianity is sodomitic inasmuch as it ignores the sexual, reproductive core of being. Rozanov sees the sexual division not only as the most fundamental feature of human ontology but also as part and parcel of divinity: 'there are two Gods – His *masculine* side and the *feminine* one' (*Dva Boga* – muzhskaya *storona ego, i storona* – zhenskaya) (Rozanov 1990a: 31, Rozanov makes this significant remark only in passing, which is typical of his rhetorical strategy).

In Rozanov's view, the omnipresent and culturally prominent 'third sex' possesses a peculiar psychological and sometimes biological constitution. While the feminine and masculine elements coexist in every person, a person of the moonlight is distinguished by a stronger presence of the opposite sex in his or her psyche and possibly body. The moonlight person is not necessarily a strongly effeminate male or masculinized female. Between such extremes as the virile man and the man-maiden (*muzhedeva*) stands a continuum of men, in whom the degree of heterosexual desire progressively decreases and the degree of sodomitic inclination progressively increases.

Rozanov's notion of gender/sex fluidity and his vision of homosexually inclined people as a separate intermediate gender/sex (*trety pol*) were not of his own making: they reflected authoritative contemporary opinions in the emerging medical field of sexual psychopathology. Books by this field's leading authors, such as Richard Krafft-Ebing, Iwan Bloch, August Forel, and Magnus Hirschfeld, were translated into Russian and read widely by the intelligentsia in the period between the revolution of 1905 and the onset of the First World War.[2] The reading public absorbed these works within the framework of the 'sexual question' that dominated the Russian print media at a time when the newspaper *Novoye vremya* ('New Time'), for which Rozanov was a leading author, diagnosed all of Russian society as experiencing an epidemic of 'sexual psychopathy' (I.I.V. 1908). In *People of the Moonlight*, Rozanov generously quoted case studies of sexual pathology, borrowing from classic works of early sexual science, such as Krafft-Ebing's *Psychopathia Sexualis*, as well as confessions of contemporary Russians. He subjected these biographic narratives to philosophical analysis, and by doing so acted both as a modernist thinker and a journalist, producing a metaphysical interpretation of this highly sensational material.

Formulating his theoretical views on sexuality, Rozanov drew on many sources and contexts, though none as important as the ideological trend dubbed, by Nikolay Berdyayev, as *veyningerianstvo* (the Weininger movement, or even the Weininger mania) (Berdyayev 1909: 104). In this respect, Rozanov's interest dovetailed the popular mania for Otto Weininger's best-selling *Sex and Character: A Principled Study* (1903; 1908, the first complete Russian translation).[3] Not only were Weininger's ideas a likely source for parts of Rozanov's theory, but they also conditioned the Russian reception of Rozanov's notion of 'people of the moonlight'.

Between 1908 and 1914, Weininger's *Sex and Character* was required reading for every self-respecting educated Russian. As new translations and printings of it continued to come out, the very discussion of the book became an industry. In the capitals and provincial cities, scholars lectured on Weininger; pedagogical, medical, and philosophical analyses of his ideas filled periodicals and pamphlets; and the humour magazine *Satirikon* satirized the spread of *veyningerianstvo*. 'Everywhere is Weininger, Weininger, Weininger', the critic Korney Chukovsky declared in January 1909 (Chukovsky 1909: 7).

In *Sex and Character*, Weininger attempted to construct a philosophical anthropology based on sexual categories. Boldly mixing scientific and metaphysical arguments with popular beliefs and the results of his personal introspection, he saw sex as a psychological and metaphysical element that defined every human being. Writing before the scientific discovery of sex hormones, Weininger claimed that every person was bisexual, that is, had elements characteristic of the ideal masculine and feminine types. Translating Weininger's sexual terminology into the language of today, one can say that his feminine and masculine archetypes are the categories of 'gender', 'sex', and 'sexual orientation', understood as a unity. Weininger sees his 'ideal types' as always coexisting in the human world. No one is an absolute man or an absolute woman, he claims, but each individual person is located somewhere on the continuum running between these two poles. Mutual attraction takes place not between biological males and females, but between their masculine and feminine elements: the manlier a given biological male, the more feminine is the partner that he desires, and vice versa. Biological women in whom the male element exceeds fifty per cent tend to be lesbian, or they seek effeminate male partners. Weininger proposed a mathematical formula for his 'law of sexual attraction'. According to this formula, sexual attraction was highest in those couples in which the combined totals for femininity and masculinity reached one hundred per cent.

Weininger arrived at the definition of his ideal types in a speculative manner, and his view of the feminine type was fiercely negative. According to him, W (that is, the absolute woman) is amoral and antisocial, she lacks a self, her life is much less conscious than a man's, and she cannot act as an autonomous subject or possess genius. Her whole being is defined by sexuality and built around the sex act. Unlike the man, the woman experiences continuous and overwhelming sexual desire but she does not know love. Love is a spiritual state, and the woman has no access to the realm of spirit. The woman's 'ugly' body is designed for the purposes of procreation, and being a slave to her body, she only strives to belong to man. Socially, two functions come naturally to her: that of a mother and that of a prostitute. The man created the family and monogamy, while the woman cannot control her desire for the penis.

The sexological part of Weininger's book reflected a scientific trend of the time.[4] His opinion that male homosexuality was often, if not always, caused by physiological and psychological effeminization was common in *fin-de-siècle* European medical science: it was shared by Richard Krafft-Ebing – Weininger's professor at Vienna University – whose *Psychopathia Sexualis* laid the foundation of the scientific study of sexual deviation. It was also supported by Dr Magnus Hirschfeld, the leading early advocate of homosexual rights, who popularized the term 'the third sex' to designate those who had female souls trapped within their male bodies. However, Weininger's book had a number of distinctive features, such as his strikingly personal intonation; his premonition of the coming collapse of culture, caused by its loss of masculine creative ability; his sexually based anti-Semitism (he regarded Jewish men as effeminate); and his peculiar mystical discourse supplanted with mathematical equations and examples taken from the natural sciences. In addition, important for the book's history and its success was the fate of the author, who committed a theatrical, staged suicide soon after the publication of his work, at the age of twenty-three.

Rozanov's model of fluid gender/sex and Weininger's calculus of desire had many similarities (see Laura Engelstein's brilliant comparative analysis of the two theories in her *Keys to Happiness* (1992: 310–33)). Yet the social and philosophical prescriptions that Weininger and Rozanov drew from their analyses differed dramatically. While Rozanov advocated the sexualization of culture (he famously demanded that sex be sanctified by placing the marital bed in the church), Weininger saw abstinence as the only path to salvation of civilization and the spirit (Rozanov 1990b: 100–3). Weininger believed passionately that masculinity was threatened in the modern world: becoming effeminate, men not only stopped feeling natural disgust at coitus, but also started defining themselves through sex, an entirely feminine feature. Weininger's call for the masculinization of culture found no sympathy in Rozanov, who described it as merely the symptom of the Austrian writer's own 'sodomitic' nature (Rozanov 1990b: 98–99). It is necessary to note that despite the fact that the cultural prescriptions suggested by Weininger and Rozanov pointed in opposite directions, contemporaries perceived the two thinkers' models of sexuality as 'related by blood' (*rodstvennye*), to use Pavel Florensky's expression (Florensky 1990b: 281). More often than not, Russian opponents of Rozanov also had to address Weininger's speculations.

The concept of bisexuality (*dvupolost'*) as presented by Weininger and Rozanov cannot be seen simply as a modification of the visions of androgyny that Symbolist culture borrowed from Platonic, Gnostic, and Christian mystical sources.[5] While images of the androgyne – mythological, philosophical, or (in the thinking of Vladimir Solov'yev) prophetic – referred either to the primordial, mythological past or the post-apocalyptic future of transfigured flesh, the phenomenon of universal bisexuality was understood as a scientifically observed reality of the current human condition. Androgyny revealed itself to mystical philosophers; bisexuality to medics and social scientists. Despite multiple exchanges that took place between the mystical and scientific discourses of the time, the notions of androgyny and bisexuality did not merge: each retained its own distinct epistemological function and set of connotations.

Case study one: Pavel Florensky and people of the moonlight

Pavel Aleksandrovich Florensky (1882–1937), the Russian theologian, philosopher, art theoretician, and scientist, studied Weininger's book with great attention. In the endnotes to his main work, he even compared its two different Russian translations with the German original.[6] Florensky's own extensive comments on gender and sexuality, specifically those on mechanisms of same-sex desire, were influenced by both Weininger and Rozanov (the latter was Florensky's friend and correspondent).[7] Moreover, his views contained a cohesive theory of same-sex love, which was both critical of his predecessors' models and derivative from them. I will argue that Florensky's sexual theory helps illuminate some crucial ideas in *Stolp i utverzhdeniye Istiny* ('The Pillar and Ground of the Truth', 1914), his seminal theological work written in 1906–14.

In 1909, Florensky had just finished his degree at the Moscow Spiritual Academy and began teaching courses in the history of philosophy in his *alma mater*. That year his friend Aleksandr Yel'chaninov, who had known Florensky since their Tiflis childhood and remained close to him in Moscow, made several entries in his diary. In these entries, he recorded his conversations with Florensky about the latter's 'indifference to ladies and his frequent infatuations with young men':

> The conversation was long, and I only remember the main points. We talked again about Pavlusha's indifference to ladies and his frequent infatuations with young men; we struggled with explanations for a long time, and only at the end P[avel] came across the following hypothesis. Man seeks for himself an object which is passive enough to accept his energy. For most men, such an object will be women. There are men whose nature is hypo-masculine, who seek their complements in masculine men. However, there are hyper-masculine men, for whom the feminine is too weak, just as a pillow is too weak for a steel knife. Such men seek and love either simply men or hypo-men.
> (cited in Keydan 1997: 201–2)

Yel'chaninov made this entry on 7 July 1909. Around that time the Russian press was full of heated discussions about Weininger's book; its Russian translation had just hit the shops several months earlier and become a major bestseller. Not that the erudite Florensky needed a Russian translation to read Weininger's famous work. However, its wide popularity precisely at that time made it the immediate intellectual background against which Florensky built his own polemical theory of same-sex love. Moreover, he applied this theory to himself.

As noted by Yel'chaninov, Florensky claimed that along with the model of male same-sex attraction, recognized in science and described by Weininger, there is another model, in which same-sex desire was caused by one's hyper-masculinity. He repeated and developed this idea in his 1913 *addenda* to the second edition of Rozanov's *People of the Moonlight*. In his commentary to Rozanov's work, Florensky (or the Anonymous, introduced by Rozanov as 'a person competent in such matters') politely noted 'the profound correctness' of Rozanov's theory and proceeded to attack it, along with Weininger's, as insufficient (Florensky 1990b: 281). Florensky suggests his own 'theses' on the subject, and notes that he is convinced of their 'unshakeability' (*v nepokolebimosti kotorykh ya uveren*) (ibid.). He claims that along with the inferior type of same-sex attraction, typical of effeminate 'psychopaths', there is a superior type, characteristic of hyper-masculine men and races (as was the case with the Ancient Greeks). While 'the third sex' is doomed to eternal wretchedness, the superior type is actually gifted with genius and 'incessant satisfaction'. Florensky names Oscar Wilde as an 'appalling example' that fits well with Rozanov's collection of the 'third sex', and opposes him to Goethe, Socrates, and Plato, who exemplify the genius that is always both hyper-masculine and bisexual at the same time (Florensky 1990b: 281–82). As for Rozanov's central point, the sodomite character of Christian asceticism, Florensky acknowledges that 'the conditions of everyday life' often drive those 'who are incapable of marriage' into monasteries but argues that Christianity 'elevates' one above sexuality (*pol*) and 'distracts' from sexuality, doing so by 'the songs of paradise but not in the least by intermediate [sexual] forms. A true monk does not become a woman, but he ceases being a man' (ibid.: 284).

Florensky's theory of same-sex attraction based on hyper-masculinity has a parallel (and possibly a source) in the works of the French scholar Marc-André Raffalovich. Raffalovich was a prolific author on the subject and, in the 1890s and 1900s, the leading contributor to *Archive d'anthropologie criminelle*, a scientific periodical that had become at the time a major European forum for the discussion of sexual deviation. In his 1896 book *Uranisme et unisexualité: étude sur différentes manifestations de l'instinct sexuel* ('Uranianism and Unisexuality: A Study of the Different Manifestations of the Sexual Instinct'). Raffalovich claimed the existence of the superior type of male inverts (or 'Uranians', a synonymous, although more poetic term): they are more masculine than 'normal' men and for this reason abhor femininity. The sexual attraction that these 'superior inverts' experience is rooted in the principle of similarity, not difference:

> *Les invertis ne se contentent pas du tout de la vieille explication de l'âme féminine dans un corps masculin. Certains sont plus masculins que les hommes habituels, et se sentent portés vers leur propre sexe en raison de la ressemblance. Ils disent qu'ils méprisent trop les femmes pour être efféminés.*
>
> (Raffalovich 1896: 15)[8]

Raffalovich presents the superior type of Uranians as a respectable alternative to the criminal urban subculture of inverts: the superior type have a more generalized and more controllable sexuality, they can remain chaste and sublimate their sexuality into religion and art ('*le génie le plus sensuel, le plus sexuel, peut toujours se reprendre après s'être abandonné*' (ibid.: 27)).[9] Raffalovich names Goethe, Michelangelo, and Shakespeare as examples of men of genius who belonged to this superior type of Uranian. Oscar Wilde, to whom Raffalovich devotes a spiteful, although informative chapter, represents the base and criminal type of the effeminate 'invert'. In contrast to him and to other immoral effeminate inverts, Raffalovich's 'unisexuals' of the superior type are not inclined to practice anal or oral sex (cf. Oscar Wilde who, as Raffalovich writes, '*pratiquait la succion pénienne et payait des galopins qui se laissaient adorer de cette façon*' (ibid.: 119n)). They find sexual satisfaction in platonic love and virtuous friendship-passion ('*l'amitié passion virtueuse*' (ibid.: 121)). Raffalovich devotes a large section of his book to friendship, noticing how difficult it is to differentiate between platonic love and 'virtuous friendship-passion'. The boundary between the two (as well as between the platonic and the physical) is extremely fine: for example, kissing the beloved as well as sleeping in his embraces in the same bed is 'the physical goal of platonic love, according to Plato', says Raffalovich (*'Coucher dans le lit de l'aimé, avec caresses, mais sans actes sexuels, est le but physique de l'amour platonique selon Platon'* (ibid.: 120n)).

The life story of André Raffalovich sheds interesting light on the image of the 'superior type' of Uranian, which he sketched so sympathetically in his book.[10] Raffalovich was born in Paris in 1864 to a fabulously wealthy family of Jewish bankers, natives of Odessa. Raised in France, he settled in London in 1884 and began a literary career as a novelist and poet of Decadent persuasion. He also hosted a literary salon in his fashionable home, where dandies and men of art dined lavishly, and where Oscar Wilde made frequent appearances. In London's high artistic society Raffalovich was seen as somewhat of a *parvenu*; this judgement was reflected in Wilde's famous *bon mot* about 'poor André', who 'came to London with the intention to open a *salon*, and ... succeeded in opening a saloon' (quoted in Ellmann 1987: 392).[11] By 1892, Wilde's personal relationship with Raffalovich was already so hostile that Wilde refused 'to sit next to him in the hairdressing establishment in Bond Street which they both patronized', citing as the reason his former friend's ugly looks (Ellmann 1987: 392).

This relationship was not helped by the fact that at that time Raffalovich developed an intimate friendship with the young and extraordinarily good-looking poet John Gray, a literary protégé of Wilde and possibly his former lover. Wilde himself pronounced Gray, who wrote and published homoerotic Decadent poems, including one entitled *Passing the Love of Women*, the model for his Dorian Gray. The friendship between Gray and Raffalovich turned into a lifelong relationship. In February 1896 (several months after Oscar Wilde's scandalous trials and spectacular fall), Raffalovich followed his friend into the Catholic Church. In 1898 Raffalovich entered the Dominican Third Order under the name Brother Sebastian. John Gray was ordained a priest in 1901. Together they moved to Edinburgh where Raffalovich funded the construction of St Peter's cathedral. Father John Gray became the First Parish priest of St Peter's. The two spent a long life by each other's side in a chaste union. They died only days apart in 1934.

Raffalovich continued to publish scientific articles on male homosexuality for many years after his conversion. The idealized image of the 'hyper-masculine' Uranian whose respectable life is given up to religion, art, science, and to that special kind of chaste male friendship, is clearly autobiographical. Together, Raffalovich's life story and his writings represent an attempt to create a respectable homophile identity that would be different from the emerging gay identity symbolized by the effeminate, flashy, immoral, and wretched Oscar Wilde.

Wilde's fate had direct relevance for Florensky as well. In the 1900s Florensky's emotional life focused on a series of passionate friendships with young men. The intensity of his friendship with Vasily Giatsintov is described in Yel'chaninov's diary:

> He has a lot of tenderness, devotion, love ... If he falls in love with someone, he will give away everything for this friendship, he wants to involve his friend

in all the details of his life, and he enters wholeheartedly into his life and interests; he will abandon his business, his acquaintances, urgent matters if his time is needed (or he thinks that it is needed) by his friend. He eats from the same cup with Vasen'ka [Giatsinov]; he will never sit down for lunch without him, even if the latter is not coming till the evening; he goes to talk to his [i.e., Giatsintov's] doctor; helps him write a paper, in general he [that is, Florensky] gives him [i.e., Giatsintov] 'neither rest nor time'.

(Keydan 1997: 212)

Living together with an intimate male friend in a chaste and family-like way seemed to be the established pattern of life for Florensky in the 1900s. This pattern ended in a crisis at the end of the decade, when Florensky had to face a choice between his long-time intention to take monastic vows and the call to the priesthood which, in the Orthodox tradition, required marriage. We do not know many details about Florensky's spiritual crisis of 1908–10 but we do know that his friends communicated intense worries about his well-being in their correspondence. Around this time he was reported to break into desperate loud crying during a service at the monastery Zosimova Pustyn' (Berdyayev 1949: 212). The January 1910 entry in Yel'chaninov's diary reveals Florensky's torments:

He [Florensky] replies to all reasoning with the same: 'I want real love; I only understand life together; without "together," I don't want even to be saved. I am not rebelling, I am not protesting, I simply have no taste for either living or saving my soul while I am alone. If others attempt to save me, I will not protest; but I myself don't want it'.

(Keydan 1997: 222)

The above passage reflects Florensky's difficult dilemma, as his *dukhovnik* ('spiritual mentor') Bishop Antony Florensov insisted that he abandon the idea of taking monastic vows and advised that he marry instead. Florensky obeyed: in the summer of 1910 he married Anna Mikhaylovna Giatsintova, the sister of his friend Vasily Giatsintov. 'This happened ascetically ... without any romantic element', Sergey Bulgakov reported in a private letter (Keydan 1997: 284). 'Through joyful quietness, deep sadness transpires in him', Vladimir Ern described the newlywed Florensky (Keydan 1997: 278). In April 1911 Florensky was admitted to the priesthood.

The Pillar and Ground of the Truth was written over a long period of time – between 1906 and 1914. *The Pillar* is composed of twelve letters, many of which are full of almost painful and overtly erotic tenderness. Most of the letters are addressed to an anonymous male friend (likely, a cross between Vasily Giatsintov and Florensky's previous 'friendship-passion', Sergey Troitsky (who died in 1910)) (Trubachev 1990: 828–31). The book reaches its emotional culmination in the eleventh letter, deemed the most important and the most controversial by critics. The letter is entitled 'Friendship'. To use the expression of Sergey Bulgakov, Florensky writes in this letter about the 'burning thirst' (*raspalennaya zhazhda*) for friendship (Bulgakov (1997: 693), note the erotic connotations of the Russian adjective used by Bulgakov). He argues that a pair of male friends, in love with each other, is the minimal unit, the molecule of the Christian community, 'just as the family was this kind of molecule for the pagan community' (Florensky 1997: 301). The task of this and any true friendship is the 'mutual penetration of personalities' (*'vzaimnoye proniknoveniye lichnostey'*) (Florensky 1997: 447). 'Marriage is "two in one flesh," while friendship is two in one soul' (*'brak yest' 'dva v plot' yedinu', druzhba zhe – dva v dushu yedinu'*) (Florensky 1997: 455).

Florensky's voice is both lyrical and dramatic as he argues for the mystical and ontological role of male friendship in a Christian community. He draws on examples from the Old and New Testaments, the Church Fathers, Plato, Schiller, the Orthodox liturgy of adelphopoiesis (*chin bratotvoreniya*), and (his favourite device) linguistic etymologies. To convey the supreme meaning of male friend-ship, he not only uses the words 'friendship' and 'love' (also 'friends' and 'lovers' (*lyubyashchiye*)) interchangeably, but also employs bold sexual imagery. Florensky's male couples are ascetic. However, there is one act, somewhat physical, that is allowed to them. This act is kissing. Just as Raffalovich was convinced of the admissibility of kissing on the lips, Florensky makes a similar point and defends it with an etymological proof:

> the very word for 'kiss' in Russian (*potseluy*) is close to the Russian word for 'whole' (*tsely*), and the Russian verb for 'to kiss' (*tselovat'sya*) signifies that friends are brought to a state of wholeness (*tsel'nost'*) or unity. A kiss is a spiritual unification of the persons kissing.
>
> (Florensky 1997: 316)

Florensky's theology was 'not scholastic but experiential', as Nikolay Berdyayev noted in *Samopoznaniye* (published in English as *Dream and Reality: An Essay in Autobiography*). Some readers who could not relate to Florensky's individual emo-tional experience responded negatively to *The Pillar*. Berdyayev added: 'In him [Florensky], Plato's ideas acquired an almost sexual character. His theologizing was erotic. This was new in Russia' (Berdyayev 1949: 173–74). The same Berdyayev, in the review entitled 'Stylized Orthodoxy', sharply rebuked Florensky for his treatment of friendship, saying that he 'Orthodoxizes the classical emotions' (*opravoslavlivayet antichnyye chuvstva*) (Berdyayev 1996: 282). 'The book by the priest Pavel Florensky is a document of the soul that is running away from itself' (*dokument dushi ot sebya ubegayushchey*), concluded Berdyayev (1996: 283). Georgy Florovsky, a historian of Russian Orthodox thought, echoed this judgement when he accused *The Pillar* of containing 'the dark sediment of erotic temptation' (*mut' eroticheskogo soblazna*) (Florovsky 1983: 498).

Florensky and Raffalovich, two deeply religious aesthetes, saw the explanation of their sexuality in their own hyper-masculine nature. Raffalovich limited himself to the creation of a socially respectable homophile identity. Florensky's treatment of friendship pursued a task which was as personal as that of Raffalovich, but vastly more ambitious. In *The Pillar*, he ontologized his experience of same-sex love. Florensky's utopian ideal of an Orthodox community composed of chaste, loving male couples shared common traits with a similar trend in European Catholic Decadence that manifested itself in Raffalovich's life and work. Yet it differed sharply from the model of tragic homosexual desire posited by the Russian Symbolists. The Symbolists commonly saw the inverted and wretched Oscar Wilde as a saint, martyred for his love and art (Bershtein 2010). As Vyacheslav Ivanov put it in 1909: 'the whole life of the noble singer and humble martyr of Reading Gaol has turned into the religion of a universal Golgotha' (Ivanov 1994: 164).[12] Florensky (and Raffalovich) had little sympathy for Wilde's sorrowful fate: he interpreted the British writer's Decadent Golgotha as resulting from his defective sexual constitution.[13] It is in contrast to this kind of constitution that Florensky developed the alternative ideal of same-sex love, modifying the bisexual model of gender and sexual desire. Florensky's ideal Orthodox community looked very much like a male monastery where the mutual desire of masculine monks translated into Platonic friendships and shared spirituality. Purified of physical sexuality and women's presence, this imagined community promised erotic intensity, spiritual comfort, and social respectability to its members, all in the service of God.

Case study two: the gender of the Russian soul

The second 'moonlight' episode that I will examine stemmed from Rozanov's proclivity to present his theories performatively. More specifically, Rozanov produced a form of narrative that enacted the theoretical premise of universal bisexuality in the figure of the narrator. This playful adoption by Rozanov of the Weiningerian view of the human psyche triggered a curiously formulated rebuttal from Nikolay Berdyayev, which contained one of the most memorable metaphors generated by Russian religious philosophy. A look into the rhetorical mechanism of this debate reveals how the Weiningerian notion of universal bisexuality was employed in social and political polemics.

In January 1916 Nikolay Berdyayev published a scathing critique of Rozanov in the newspaper *Birzhevyye vedomosti*. He entitled his essay '*O "vechno bab'yem" v russkoy dushe*' ('On the "Eternal *Bab'ye*" in the Russian Soul') where the untranslatable *bab'ye* stands for coarse and even evil femininity and thus puns on Eternal Feminine. Berdyayev took aim at Rozanov's 1915 book *The War of 1914 and the Russian Revival* (*Voyna 1914 goda i russkoye vozrozhdeniye*) as well as Rozanov's literary output as a whole. In the final chapter of his book, published earlier as a newspaper column, Rozanov described the storm of erotic desire that overtook him at the site of a squadron of mounted soldiers riding in the street: 'A strange thing happened: the exaggerated *masculinity* of what was before me changed the structure of my constitution, as it were, and threw it away, transforming it into a feminine one' (Rozanov 2000a: 339). Rozanov depicted his feeling as 'a purely feminine sensation of the lack of will, of obedience and the insatiable desire to "be near for a while", to see, to keep her eyes glued to him ... Certainly, it was the beginning of a girl's infatuation' (ibid.). He concludes patriotically: 'the essence of the army is that it turns us all into women – weak, trembling, air-embracing women. Some experience this more, some less, but everyone does *to some extent'* (no *skol'ko-nibud'* – kazhdy) (ibid.). In Rozanov's model, the proportion of the feminine to masculine in an individual is not constant: it fluctuates depending on the situation; he shows the feminine element taking over in himself at the moment of patriotic ecstasy.

In his response, Berdyayev rejects this model. Instead, he suggests a particular quality of the Russian national psyche – '*vechno bab'ye'* – one disturbing expression of which he found in Rozanov. In his view, Rozanov had *always* been distinguished by the '*bab'ye'* that deprives him of a self, makes it impossible for him to function as an autonomous subject, and ties him down to the natural, biological, and intuitive at the expense of the intellectual, individual, and active. Berdyayev accuses Rozanov of *always* being irresistibly attracted to and aroused by power – be it the power of the state, revolution, Decadence, political reaction, or war. Rozanov's shifting opinions are merely the infatuations of his feminine soul that is devoid of a firm core and self. Most importantly, Berdyayev claims that this feature of Rozanov's sexual constitution directly reflects a particular defect of the Russian national psyche: it lacks masculinity. This defect threatens catastrophic consequences for the Russian people who need to forge 'masculinity' and the 'active spirit' in order to 'create life in a manly way' (*muzhestvenno tvorit' zhizn'*) (Berdyayev 1995: 51).

Berdyayev, a leading proponent of Weininger's work in Russia, uses definitions of the feminine straight out of *Sex and Character*.[14] In *Smysl tvorchestva* ('The Meaning of the Creative Act'), Berdyayev energetically embraced Weininger's understanding of the feminine element as completely sexual and biological and therefore opposed to creativity. In '*O "vechno bab'yem"*', he applies Weiningerian concepts to the analysis of Russian patriotic frenzy, expressed by Rozanov's text and manifest in society as a whole. In his analysis, he finds the forms of Russian wartime patriotism to be feminine and therefore entirely sexual and biological; as such, they receive Berdyayev's unambiguous condemnation.

Rozanov had the last word in this literary duel, although it is unlikely that Berdyayev was aware of it. In *Posledniye list'ya. 1916 god* ('The Final Leaves, 1916'), never published during his lifetime, Rozanov included a record of his trip to the public baths on a fine July day of 1916 (Rozanov 2000b: 177–79). Vasily Vasil'yevich went to the bathhouse on Basseynaya Street where he was served by a seventeen-year-old bathhouse attendant (*banshchik*) Ivan. Ivan was distinguished by a powerful youthful physique and an unusually large sexual organ. With much pleasure, Rozanov reports that as Ivan was washing him (that is massaging his prostrate body with soap), Ivan's enormous member was touching his body, hanging over his eyes and capturing all his attention. Almost obsessively, Rozanov describes the boy's penis in the finest of detail: it was slightly engorged and touched on Vasily Vasil'yevich's cheek, causing both pleasurable sensations and fantasies of how this penis could bring 'seven maidens' great joy. In his characteristic combination of pornographic description and metaphysical reflection, Rozanov suggests that a penis of such size has great value; it is a thing of 'exceptional beauty'. Before Rozanov ordered a second washing, he read to himself a line from *The Song of Songs*: 'Oh, my beloved!' (*O, moy vozlyublenny*) – the very line that he quoted at the end of his army essay in *The War of 1914*. Rozanov had told us that the *banshchik* Ivan was about to be conscripted into the army and almost certainly killed. The boy was practically a soldier.

Rozanov's bathhouse entry clearly develops the very motifs from his earlier army essay that so outraged Berdyayev. There is good reason to think that Rozanov wrote it with Berdyayev in mind and intended it to be polemical. In *The Final Leaves. 1916*, the bathhouse entry (dated 17 July) is preceded by a passage devoted to Berdyayev (dated 16 July). In this passage, Rozanov ridicules Berdyayev as 'a Frenchman from Algeria' who is understandably 'out of place' ('*ne na meste*') among the Russian public (Rozanov 2000b: 176). The two entries link Rozanov's feminine and patriotic infatuation with the soon-to-be soldier's powerful masculinity to his ironic contempt for Berdyayev's awkward lack of national spiritual roots.

The scene with the young *banshchik* had solid literary and scientific pretexts. Medical researchers of sexual pathology – most notably Vladislav Merzheyevsky and Veniamin Tarnovsky, whose books on sexual deviance Rozanov read and quoted – depicted young St Petersburg bathhouse attendants (*banshchiki*) as an informal guild of male prostitutes (Merzheyevsky 1878: 208–9, Tarnovsky 1885: 70–71). Rozanov's acquaintance the poet Mikhail Kuzmin created quite a scandal by portraying St Petersburg bathhouses as institutions of commercial homosexual sex in his novel *Kryl'ya* ('Wings', 1906). When Rozanov reviewed *Kryl'ya* in 1907, he attacked Kuzmin for his tastelessly naturalistic depiction of homosexual commerce: 'Hadrian and Antinous would probably throw up from the disgusting bathhouse attendant Boris [sic!] and the bathhouse adventures: can it be that the ancients liked *that*?!!' ('*Adriana i Antinoya veroyatno stoshnilo by ot omerzitel'nogo banchshchika Borisa i bannykh priklyucheniy: neuzheli drevniye eto lyubili?!!*') (Maestro [Rozanov] 1907: 56). Later *Novoye vremya*, for which Rozanov wrote, was among many newspapers that fumed over Kuzmin's representation of *banshchiki* as male prostitutes.[15] While we find references to sexual activities taking place in public bathhouses in the diaries of many homosexual artists of the *fin de siècle* (Pyotr Tchaykovsky, Konstantin Romanov, and Mikhail Kuzmin – to name just a few), it took the happily married procreationist Vasily Vasil'yevich Rozanov to reverse his previous judgement and produce the graphic report on precisely how the interaction between bathhouse attendants and their customers took place. I suggest that Rozanov's bathhouse entry should be read at two intertextual levels: while Berdyayev is sharply rebuked for refusing to accept the (bi)sexual roots of patriotic feelings, Kuzmin receives a belated homage for his daring in introducing the theme of homosexuality into Russian letters.

Case study three: Father Sergius Bulgakov on the bisexuality of God

Sergey Nikolayevich Bulgakov, Florensky's and Berdyayev's philosophical ally and friend, met a remarkable fate. A prominent political economist and writer, Bulgakov became a priest in 1918 and was exiled abroad by the Bolshevik authorities in 1922. After a brief stay in Constantinople, and a period of work in Prague, Father Sergius Bulgakov settled in Paris, where he helped establish the only Russian Orthodox Theological Institute in Western Europe. The St Sergius Institute provided Bulgakov with an outlet for developing and spreading his own controversial theological system – Sophiology.

It took Bulgakov some twenty years (from the mid-1910s into the 1930s) and several thousand pages to develop his sophiological teaching. Summarizing it in a few paragraphs cannot do justice to a doctrine that included highly technical treatments of the most complex issues in Christian dogmatics.[16] What has become clear with recent publications of Bulgakov's diaries, letters, and unfinished manuscripts is the fact that the themes of bisexuality and sexual division in the creation was continuously on Bulgakov's mind as he refined his theory.

As early as 1912 Bulgakov briefly discusses Weininger's and Rozanov's views on sexuality while analysing Tolstoy's posthumously published works (Bulgakov 1912: 86–87). The same year he wrote to Rozanov, suggesting that *People of the Moonlight* was 'the most central and significant' of the latter's works (Kolerov 1992: 153). It is in response to this book that Bulgakov develops the idea that was to become exceptionally important for him: 'Equating sex [*pol*] and sexuality [*seksual'nost'*] is completely false because sexuality is only an expression of sex [*pol*], in a certain sense its sickly mask [*v izvestnom smysle yego boleznennaya maska*]' (Keydan 1997: 423). In *Svet nevecherny* ('Unfading Light', 1917) his first major theological treatise, Bulgakov repeats this thought almost verbatim. He also introduces the central notion of his own theological treatment of sex: 'spiritual bisexuality' (*dukhovnaya dvupolost'*) as a fundamental anthropological feature (Bulgakov 1917: 292–305). The Russian theologian adopts the notion of universal bisexuality in a very specific sense, admitting that the feminine and masculine coexist in creation at the level of every individual's spiritual constitution. Affirming the existence of a universal 'spiritual bisexuality', Bulgakov insists that one should not equate this phenomenon with androgyny or link it to sexual desire (as did his predecessors): biological sex as well as physical sexuality are occasioned only by creation's fallen state. Bulgakov defines the essence of the masculine and feminine in a Weiningerian key: the masculine element is 'solar, that of genius, logical' while the feminine is productive, it is the 'soil of the soul' (*zemlya dushi*) (Bulgakov 1917: 303). In later works, Bulgakov – just like Weininger before him – would make a special effort to disassociate the feminine as an ideal archetype from actual human females and their psychological character: by femininity he only means 'a certain spiritual element' 'a state of response, passivity, passive love, entirely unrelated to [… actual] women' (Bulgakov 1999: 318).

Opponents have criticized Bulgakov's sophiological system for being 'anthropocentric' (Lossky 1936: 41). Indeed, it is the observation of human 'spiritual bisexuality' that raises for Bulgakov the issue of the bisexuality of God. In 'The Masculine and the Feminine in the Divinity' ('*Muzhskoye i Zhenskoye v Bozhestve*', 1921) and 'The Masculine and the Feminine' ('*Muzhskoye i Zhenskoye*', 1921), Bulgakov argues that, created in the image and likeness of God, bisexual human beings reflect the differentiation and coexistence of the masculine and feminine in Divinity (Bulgakov 2003a, 2003b). Moreover, Bulgakov considers the trinitary structure of God and concludes that 'the Masculine and the Feminine are distinguished in the Divinity as properties ... of the Second and Third Hypostases', that is, the Son and the Holy Spirit (Bulgakov 2003a: 359).[17] As for the categories of feminine and masculine, Bulgakov keeps insisting that these notions refer to the transcendental properties that are expressed in *pol* ('sex/sexuality') but not derived from it (Bulgakov 2003b: 369).[18]

The transcendental feminine takes centre stage in Bulgakov's system. He finds its expression in the person of the divine Sophia – the Wisdom of God – a crucial character in his dogmatic theology. Mentioned in the Old and New Testaments, the Wisdom of God had been traditionally understood in theology as an allegory. For Bulgakov, however, Sophia is a Divine Person who links God with His creation. In *Unfading Light* Bulgakov comes close to seeing Sophia as the Fourth Hypostasis equal to the Three Hypostases of the Holy Trinity.[19] However, in his later works he suggests for her a special status as the feminine passive essence of God (Bulgakov 1999: 318). As a matter of fact, it is her feminine passivity that Bulgakov cites as the explanation for her non-hypostatic status. Sophia lacks an active element, and therefore she is not on an equal footing with the Three Persons of the Holy Trinity. Despite his insistence that Sophia not be understood as a reflection of actual human womanhood, Bulgakov nevertheless uses a strikingly sexualized language to describe her essence: she 'gives herself to love' (*otdayetsya lyubvi*), she is a 'receptive and responsive, passive love' (*priyemlyushchaya i otvetstvuyushchaya, passivnaya lyubov'*), God 'possesses her' (*Bog yeye imeyet*), and the 'ability to be taken' (*obladayemost'*) is her fundamental feature (Bulgakov 1999: 318). The language he uses to describe Sophia's status in the Divinity is reminiscent of the one used to denote the 'feminine' role in sexual intercourse. Nonetheless, Bulgakov presents Sophia as 'the eternal feminine' that is paradoxically and emphatically unrelated to the physical women of this world.

Bulgakov was all too aware that in his system the divine Sophia could potentially be confused with an earthly, sexual femininity. The grave danger of such confusion was exemplified for him by the worship of the eternal feminine as had been practised by Vladimir Solov'yev and the Symbolist poet Aleksandr Blok. Both recognized Sophia in the image of earthly women. Though mystically motivated, Solov'yev and Blok sought out earthly love affairs with these women. Bulgakov sternly condemns what he calls the 'heresy and spiritual lechery' ('*yeres' i blud dukhovny*') of his ideological predecessors. In his diary, he takes credit for 'overcoming' sexuality in his sophiology and creating a truly ecclesiastic concept of Sophia (Bulgakov 1998: 195, 199).

Vladimir Solov'yev famously had 'three encounters' with the divine Sophia. These meetings were in addition to at least two more mundane affairs with earthly women of the same name. Bulgakov had two transformational mystical experiences of his own, which he described on several occasions. One of them took place in 1898 when Bulgakov – then a young Russian Social Democrat studying in Germany – saw Raphael's Sistine Madonna for the first time. He was then a Marxist, but the contemplation of Raphael's Madonna brought him into a state of religious ecstasy. Day after day he returned to the Zwinger Gallery where he looked at the painting, cried, and prayed. It was then, claims Bulgakov, that the seed of his future return to Orthodoxy was planted in his soul. He came back to Russia a changed man (Bulgakov 1917: 7–9). In 1924, Bulgakov, by then an exiled priest and theologian in Prague, revisited Dresden (Bulgakov 1996: 389–96).[20] He looked forward to a second encounter with the Sistine Madonna, and hoped to experience again the mystical revelation that had descended upon him twenty-five years before. But no such revelation came. Instead of the sophianic icon, he only saw the lovely, masterful representation of a beautiful woman. Unlike Russian icons of the Mother of God, Raphael's Madonna was a mere woman of the flesh. In the painting, the disappointed Bulgakov even detected the traces of the artist's prurient gaze: too much uncovered body, too sensual a turn of the neck. In a special essay with a Solov'yevian title '*Dve vstrechi*' ('Two Encounters', 1924), Bulgakov likened Rafael's Catholic attitude toward the Mother of God to the Russian mystics' eroticism; to him, their 'impure' sexual approach to the divinity represented 'artistic Arianism' – a heretical overestimation of the human element in the divine incarnation (Bulgakov 1996: 393, 395). He condemned as sinful the introduction of the carnal and material into the spiritual sphere. In his view, artistic Arianism reflected the *oplotyaneniye* ('turning into flesh') of humankind, which had caused the 'religious decline of the modern age' (Bulgakov 1996: 395).

Bulgakov wrote in his diary about the political dimension of this decline: 'the mysticism of the Beautiful Lady ... has led straight to Bolshevism' ('*mistika Prekrasnoy Damy, kotoraya privela pryamekhon'ko k bol'shevizmu*') (Bulgakov 1998: 122). This striking thought becomes clearer in the context of his revised appraisal of the Sistine Madonna. Bulgakov saw the sexual element in such disparate phenomena as Russian erotic mysticism, Western Christianity, and Rafael's art as reducing the divine to the earthly, and therefore as heretical. In this reduction, all these phenomena shared the fundamental sin of godless Bolshevism. One remembers that Vasily Rozanov, Bulgakov's teacher, friend, and opponent, came to a diametrically opposite conclusion in his *Apokalipsis nashego vremeni* ('Apocalypse of Our Time', 1917–18). In this work – his last – Rozanov put the blame for Bolshevism and the collapse of the Russian state on Christianity. He believed that Christianity had failed to manage properly the affairs of *this* world, of life in the flesh (Rozanov 2000c: 12–13).

Bulgakov interpreted his path to sophianic theology as an obliteration of all traces of sexuality from his vision of Sophia.[21] He was convinced that he succeeded completely in banning sex from sophiology. The Church disagreed. In his 1935 decree condemning Bulgakov's theology on behalf of the Moscow Patriarchy, the Moscow Metropolitan Sergius Stragorodsky specifically denounced Bulgakov for bringing sexual differentiation into 'the simple Divine Being' (*prostoye sushchestvo Bozh'ye*) (as reprinted in Yeneyeva 2001: 116). Through the Moscow Metropolitan, the official Russian Church found a grave and dangerous temptation in Bulgakov's 'divinization of sexual life, as had been done ... by some of our secular writers, such as V.V. Rozanov' (Yeneyeva 2001: 116). The edict proclaimed that

'Bulgakov's teaching has nothing to do with the ecclesiastical tradition and does not belong to the Orthodox Christian Church' (Yeneyeva 2001: 116).

Conclusions

In this chapter, I have tried to show how some of the most influential twentieth-century Russian religious thinkers were 'infected' with modern European ideas of sexuality, and specifically with the notion of bisexuality. This concept had its origins in medical discourses, but it proved to be exceptionally productive in Russian religious philosophy. It made its way into Berdyayev's contemplation of the Russian national psyche, Florensky's model of the ideal Christian life, and Bulgakov's theology of Sophia. While Weininger and Rozanov were the first to give the notion of bisexuality its metaphysical interpretation, their Russian successors completed the job of ontologizing and transcendentalizing this notion. In a way, the biography of this idea repeats the trajectories of our philosophers' intellectual development: from their early materialist and scientific worldview to extreme idealism. Yet even in its most far-reaching mystical interpretations, the notion of universal bisexuality retained some of its original epistemological flavour as both modern and scientific. This peculiar modernism in the works of Russian religious philosophy accounts, I would argue, for its continuing impact as well as for its sceptical and often hostile reception by the official Orthodox Church.

In the context of today's discussions of (homo)sexuality, the Silver Age philosophers are commonly referenced as a Russian national philosophical authority and their views are cited as being dramatically different from the commonplaces of Western liberalism. Yet a deeper look into the genealogy and structure of those views reveals a substratum that is positivist and Western European in its origin. Striking and idiosyncratic as these philosophical positions appear to today's Russian reader, they are closely linked to the European tradition of thinking about sexuality. As I have tried to demonstrate in this chapter, the leading Russian thinkers of the Silver Age both actively partook of this tradition and energetically tried to distinguish themselves from it. Rediscovering the Russian erotic philosophers today, after the censorship of the communist era, we need to carefully consider the question of where their scientific anachronism ends and their original philosophical contribution begins.

Notes

1 See the examination of the Russian debates on sexuality in the early twentieth century in Laura Engelstein's groundbreaking study (Engelstein 1992); Dan Healey has recently investigated the scientific and legal treatments of homosexuality in modernizing Russia (Healey 2001, esp. 21–125). See also my analysis of the literary reflections of the sexual question in the Silver Age (Bershtein 1999).

2 On the discourses of the emerging sexual science in the Symbolist culture, see Matich (2005) and Bershtein (1999).

3 For the editions of Weininger's main work, see Weininger (1903), Veyninger (1908). On the history and significance of the 1908 translation, put out by the publisher Posev, and for the analysis of the Weininger cult in Russia, see Bershtein (2004).

4 For instance, the notion of bisexuality, crucial for Weininger, figured in contemporary medical and sexological literature and was popularized by Richard von Krafft-Ebing, Weininger's professor at Vienna University. In his book, Weininger referred to Magnus Hirschfeld's *Jahrbuch für sexuelle Zwischenstufen* as the authoritative source on the topic. The concept of bisexuality, while mentioned already in Krafft-Ebing's *Psychopathia Sexualis*, was hotly debated in the circle of young psychologists in Vienna in the first years of the century. This circle included Sigmund Freud and his co-author Wilhelm Fliess. Weininger's closest friend Hermann Swoboda underwent therapy with Freud and discussed the latter's ongoing research with him. After Weininger's suicide and the book's subsequent popularity, the question of the authorship of the notion of bisexuality led to painful tensions in Freud's circle. The most comprehensive analysis of Weininger's book and its sources can be found in Sengoopta (2000). See also Abrahamsen (1946), Le Rider (1982), Harrowitz and Hyams (1995).

5 See Olga Matich's examinations of androgyny in sexual ideologies of the Silver Age (Matich 1979a, 1979b, 1994).

6 Florensky (1990a: 715); other page references to this edition of Florensky's *Stolp* appear in the main text. Florensky's young friend, Vasily Giatsintov (see more about his role in Florensky's life later in the chapter) studied Weininger under Florensky's guidance; Giatsintov examines Weininger in his student composition 'Transcendental and Empirical Subject' written at the Moscow Spiritual Academy where Florensky taught (see Florensky's review of Giatsintov's work (Florensky 1911: 198)).

7 The voluminous correspondence between Florensky and Rozanov was published after I completed this chapter (see Rozanov 2010: 9–412). It contains a wealth of information indispensable for a deeper understanding Florensky's emotional life. I believe that Florensky's 'confessional' letters to Rozanov lend additional support to my reading of his personality. Another recent publication that adds to our knowledge of Florensky is Avril Pyman's biography of this Russian thinker. Informative and well-written, it does not address Florensky's sexual theories and his eros in much detail (Pyman 2010: esp. 41–84).

8 Further page references to this work are in the main text. On Raffalovich's scientific works, see Rosario (1997a, 1997b).

9 On problematic relationships between respectability and 'abnormal sexuality' in modern European culture, see Mosse (1985).

10 On the life of Raffalovich and his friendship with John Gray, see Sewell (1963) and Hanson (1997).

11 Also see Ellmann (1987) for a detailed history of the animosity between Raffalovich and Wilde.

12 Even the official Orthodox press found great religious meaning in Wilde's sufferings: the theologian Vasiliy Uspensky wrote in *Khristianskoye chteniye*, the official organ of the St Petersburg Spiritual Academy: 'Wilde suffered a lot and he suffered deeply … His blood joined the currents of blood, through which humanity was acquiring deep religious thought' (Uspensky 1906: 225).

13 Immediately after the London court sentenced Wilde to hard labour, Raffalovich published a pamphlet highly critical of Wilde and his sexual proclivities. He saw Wilde's activities as typical of effeminate inverts. He reprinted this text in *Uranisme et unisexualité*. In 1908, the translation of this essay was included in the first Russian scientific and popular anthology devoted to homosexuality (Ushakovsky (Psevdonim): 1908).

14 See Eric Naiman's analysis of the Weiningerian stratum in Berdyayev (Naiman 1997: 39–45).

15 In his *Diary*, Kuzmin relates an episode in which *banshchiki* show knowledge of his literary depiction of their trade in *Wings*: they have read about the novel in *Novoye vremya* (Kuzmin 2000: 343). I am grateful to N.A. Bogomolov for helping me locate this passage.

16 See a survey of Bulgakov's theological ideas and his bibliography in Kazaryan (2003: 340–57).
17 See also A.P. Kozyrev's thoughtful essay on the evolution of Bulgakov's thinking on bisexuality (Kozyrev 2003: 333–43).
18 Bulgakov's use of the polysemous Russian word *pol*, which can mean biological sex, sexuality, and gender, complicates his definitions. I believe that his *muzhskoye* and *zhenskoye* are the categories of gender which he understands not as socially constructed but as ontological and transcendental.
19 Bulgakov has been much criticized for this suggestion, which he himself characterized as heretical in his later works; see Yeneyeva (2001: 29–33).
20 See also S.S. Averintsev's study of this essay (Averintsev 2003: 251–65).
21 In her study of Bulgakov's early theological writings, Bernice Glatzer Rosenthal correctly notes the great role played in it by his 'metaphysics of masculinity and femininity'. However, I see a certain exaggeration in Rosenthal's claim that 'his positive view of sex distinguishes Bulgakov from Fedorov and Berdyayev' (Rosenthal 1996: 169). I believe that even in his early works, Bulgakov understood the feminine and the masculine as abstract principles, and nowhere did he approve of 'sex' in the English meaning of the word. In his works from the 1920s, Bulgakov's tendency to anathematize even the slightest trace of sensuality in the spiritual sphere became quite extreme.

Bibliography

Abrahamsen, D. (1946) *The Mind and Death of a Genius*, New York: Columbia University Press.
Averintsev, S.S. (2003) '"Dve vstrechi" o. Sergiya Bulgakova v istoriko-kul'turnom kontekste', in A.P. Kozyrev (ed.) *S.N. Bulgakov: Religiozno-filosofsky put'*, 251–56, Moscow: Russky put'.
Baer, B.J. (2009) *Other Russias: Homosexuality and the Crisis of Post-Soviet Identity*, New York: Palgrave Macmillan.
Berdyayev, N.A. (1909) 'Po povodu odnoy zamechatel'noy knigi', *Voprosy filosofii i psikhologii*, 3/98: 494–500.
——(1949) *Samopoznaniye (Opyt filosofskoy avtobiografii)*, Paris: YMCA Press.
——(1995) 'O "vechno bab'yem" v russkoy dushe', in A.A. Fateyev (ed.) *V.V. Rozanov: pro et contra. Lichnost' i tvorchestvo Vasiliya Vasil'yevicha Rozanova v otsenke russkikh mysliteley i issledovateley: antologiya*, vol. 2, 41–51, Sankt-Peterburg: Izdatel'stvo Russkogo Khristianskogo gumanitarnogo instituta.
——(1996) 'Stilizovannoye pravoslaviye (Otets Pavel Florensky)', in K.G. Isupov (ed.) *P.A. Florensky: pro et contra. Lichnost' i tvorchestvo Pavla Florenskogo v otsenke russkikh mysliteley i issledovateley: antologiya*, 264–82, Sankt-Peterburg: Izdatel'stvo Russkogo Khristianskogo gumanitarnogo instituta.
Bershtein, E. (1999) '*Psychopathia sexualis* v Rossii nachala veka: politika i zhanr', in M. Levitt and A. Toporkov (eds) *Eros and Pornography in Russian Culture*, 414–41, Moskva: Ladomir.
——(2004) 'Tragediya pola: dve zametki o russkom veyningerianstve', *Novoye literaturnoye obozreniye*, 65: 208–28.
——(2010) '"Next to Christ": Oscar Wilde in Russian modernism', in S. Evangelista (ed.) *The Reception of Oscar Wilde in Europe*, 285–300, London/New York: Continuum.
Bulgakov, S.N. (1912) 'Chelovekobog i chelovekozver'. (Po povodu posmertnykh proizvedeniy L.N. Tolstogo "D'yavol" i "O. Sergiy")', *Voprosy filosofii i psikhologii*, 2/112: 55–105.

——(1917) *Svet nevecherny: sozertsaniya i umozreniya*, Moskva: Put'.

——(1996) 'Dve vstrechi (1898–1924). (Iz zapisnoy knizhki)', in S.N. Bulgakov *Tikhiye dumy*, 389–96, Moskva: Respublika.

——(1997) 'Yaltinsky dnevnik', in V.I Keydan (ed.) *Vzyskuyushchiye grada: khronika chastnoy zhizni russkikh religioznykh filosofov v pis'makh i dnevnikakh*, 692–93, Moskva: Yazyki russkoy kul'tury.

——(1998) 'Iz pamyati serdtsa. Praga (1923–24)', in A. Kozyrev, N. Golubkova, and M.A. Kolerov (eds) *Issledovaniya po istorii russkoy mysli. Yezhegodnik za 1998 god*, 112–257, Moskva: OGI.

——(1999) 'Ipostas' i ipostasnost' (Scholia k "Svetu nevechernemu")', in S.N. Bulgakov, *Pervoobraz i obraz: sochineniya v dvukh tomakh, Tom 2. Filosofiya imeni. Ikona i ikonopochitaniye*, 313–22, Moskva: Iskusstvo.

——(2003a) 'Muzhskoye i Zhenskoye v Bozhestve', in A.P. Kozyrev (ed.) *S.N. Bulgakov: Religiozno-filosofskiy put'*, 343–65, Moskva: Russky put'.

——(2003b) 'Muzhskoye i Zhenskoye', in A.P. Kozyrev (ed.) *S.N. Bulgakov: Religiozno-filosofskiy put'*, 365–88, Moskva: Russkiy put'.

Chukovsky, K. (1909) 'Russkaya literatura', *Rech'*, 1 January (14): 7–8.

Ellmann, R. (1987) *Oscar Wilde*, New York: Vintage.

Engelstein, L. (1992) *The Keys to Happiness: Sex and the Search for Modernity in Fin-de-Siècle Russia*, Ithaca/London: Cornell University Press.

Florensky, P.A. (1911) 'O sochinenii studenta Giatsintova Vasiliya na temu "Sub"yekt transtsendental'ny i sub"ekt empirichesky"', *Bogoslovsky vestnik*, December: 193–202.

——(1990a) *Stolp i utverezhdeniye Istiny*, vols 1–2. Moskva: Pravda.

——(1990b) 'Popravki i dopolneniya Anonima', in V.V. Rozanov, *Lyudi lunnogo sveta*, 280–97, Moskva: Druzhba narodov.

——(1997) *The Pillar and Ground of the Truth: An Essay in Orthodox Theodicy in Twelve Letters*, trans. by B. Jakim, introduction by R. Gustafson, Princeton, NJ: Princeton University Press.

Florovsky, G. (1983) *Puti russkogo bogosloviya*, 3rd edn, Paris: YMCA Press.

Hanson, E. (1997) *Decadence and Catholicism*, Cambridge, MA: Harvard University Press.

Harrowitz, N. and Hyams, B. (eds) (1995) *Jews and Gender: Responses to Otto Weininger*, Philadelphia, PA: Temple University Press.

Healey, D. (2001) *Homosexual Desire in Revolutionary Russia: The Regulation of Sexual and Gender Dissent*, Chicago: University of Chicago Press.

I.I.V. (1908) 'Minskoye radeniye', *Novoye vremya*, 11533 (22 April).

Ivanov, V. (1994) 'Dve stikhii v sovremennom simvolizme', in V. Ivanov, *Rodnoye i vselenskoye*, 143–69, Moskva: Respublika.

Kazaryan, A.T. (2003) 'Bulgakov, Sergey Nikolayevich', *Pravoslavnaya entsikolpediya*, vol. 6, 340–57, Moskva: Pravoslavnaya entsikolopediya.

Keydan, V.I. (ed.) (1997) *Vzyskuyushchiye grada: khronika chastnoy zhizni russkikh religioznykh filosofov v pis'makh i dnevnikakh*, Moskva: Yazyki russkoy kul'tury.

Kolerov, M.A. (ed.) (1992) 'Neopublikovannyye pis'ma S.N. Bulgakova k V.V. Rozanovu', *Voprosy filosofii*, 10: 147–57.

Kozyrev, A.P. (2003) 'Androgin na "piru bogov"', in A.P. Kozyrev (ed.) *S.N. Bulgakov: Religiozno-filosofsky put'*, 333–42, Moskva: Russky put'.

Kuzmin, M. (2000) *Dnevnik 1905–1907*, N.A. Bogomolov and S.V. Shumikhin (eds), Sankt-Peterburg: Izdatel'stvo Ivana Limbakha.

Le Rider, J. (1982) *Le cas Otto Weininger: Racines de l'antiféminisme et de l'antisémitisme*, Paris: PUF.

Lossky, V. (1936) *Spor o Sofii: 'Dokladnaya Zapiska' prot. S. Bulgakova i smysl Ukaza Moskovskoy patriarkhii*, Paris: [s.n.].

Maestro [V.V. Rozanov] (1907) 'To zhe, no drugimi slovami', *Zolotoye runo*, 1: 56–60.

Matich, O. (1979a), 'Androgyny and Russian Silver Age', *Pacific Coast Philology*, 14: 42–50.

——(1979b) 'Androgyny and the Russian Religious Renaissance', in A. Mlikotin (ed.) *Western Philosophical Systems in Russian Literature: A Collection of Critical Studies*, 165–75, Los Angeles: University of Southern California Press.

——(1994) 'The symbolist meaning of love', in I. Paperno and J. D. Grossman (eds) *Creating Life: The Aesthetic Utopia of Russian Modernism*, 52–72, Stanford, CT: Stanford University Press.

——(2005) *Erotic Utopia: The Decadent Imagination in Russia's Fin de Siècle*, Madison, WI: The University of Wisconsin Press.

Merzheyevsky, V. (1878) *Sudebnaya ginekolgiya: Rukovodstvo dlya vrachey i yuristov*, Sankt-Peterburg: B.G. Yanpol'sky.

Mosse, G. (1985) *Nationalism and Sexuality: Respectability and Abnormal Sexuality in Modern Europe*, New York: Howard Fertig.

Naiman, E. (1997) *Sex in Public: the Incarnation of Early Soviet Ideology*, Princeton, NJ: Princeton University Press.

Pyman, A. (2010) *Pavel Florensky: A Quiet Genius. The Tragic and Extraordinary Life of Russia's Unknown Da Vinci*, London: Continuum.

Raffalovich, M.-A. (1896) *Uranisme et unisexualité: étude sur différentes manifestations de l'inctinct sexuel*, Bibliothèque de criminologie, 15, Lyon: A. Storck/Paris: Masson.

Rosario, V.A. (1997a) 'Inversions' histories. History's inversions: novelizing fin-de-siècle homosexuality', in V. Rosario (ed.) *Science and Homosexualities*, 89–107, New York: Routledge.

——(1997b) *The Erotic Imagination: French Histories of Perversity*, New York: Oxford University Press.

Rosenthal, B.G. (1996) 'The nature and function of Sophia in Sergei Bulgakov's prerevolutionary thought', in J.D. Kornblatt and R. Gustafson (eds) *Russian Religious Thought*, 154–75, Madison, WI: University of Wisconsin Press.

Rozanov, V.V. (1990a; reprint of the 2nd edn [1913]) *Lyudi lunnogo sveta: metafizika khristianstva*, Moskva: Druzhba narodov.

——(1990b) 'Opavshiye list'ya. Korob pervy' in his *Uyedinennoye*, 87–202, Moskva: Izdatel'stvo politicheskoy literatury.

——(2000a) 'Voyna 1914 goda i russkoye vozrozhdeniye', in his *Posledniye list'ya*, A.N. Nikolyukin (ed.) 253–343, Moskva: Respublika.

——(2000b) 'Posledniye list'ya. 1916 god', in his *Posledniye list'ya*, A.N. Nikolyukin (ed.), 5–236, Moskva: Respublika.

——(2000c) *Apokalipsis nashego vremeni*, A.N. Nikolyukin (ed.), Moskva: Respublika.

——(2010) *Literaturnyye izgnanniki. Kniga vtoraya. P.A. Florensky, S.A. Rachinsky, Yu.N. Govorukha–Otrok, V.A. Mordvinova*, A.N. Nikolyukin (ed.), Moskva: Respublika, Sankt-Peterburg: Rostok.

Sengoopta, Ch. (2000) *Otto Weininger: Sex, Science and Self in Imperial Vienna*, Chicago: University of Chicago Press.

Sewell, F.B. (ed.) (1963) *Two Friends: John Gray and André Raffalovich: Essays Biographical and Critical with Three Letters from André Raffalovich to J.K. Huysmans*, London: Saint Albert's Press.

Tarnovsky, V.M. (1885) *Izvrashcheniye polovogo chuvstva: sudebno-psikhiatrichesky ocherk*, Sankt-Peterburg: Tipografiya Stasyulevicha.

Trubachev, Igumen Andronik (1990) 'Iz istorii knigi "Stolp i utverzhdeniye Istiny"', in P.A. Florensky, *Stolp i utverzhdeniye Istiny*, Moskva: Pravda.

Ushakovsky (Psevdonim), P.V. (1908) *Lyudi srednego pola*, Sankt-Peterburg: [s.n.]

Uspensky, V. (1906) 'Religiya Oskara Uayl'da i sovremenny asketizm', *Khristianskoye chteniye*, February: 204–25.

Veyninger, O. (1908) *Pol i kharakter. Teoreticheskoye issledovaniye*, trans. by V. Likhtenshtadt, ed. and intr. by A.L. Volynsky, Sankt-Peterburg: Posev.

Weininger, O. (1903) *Geschlecht und Charakter: Eine Prinzipielle Untersuchung*, Wien/Leipzig: Wilhelm Braumüller.

Yeneyeva, N.T. (2001) *Spor o sofiologii v russkom zarubezh'ye 1920–1930* godov, Moskva: Institut vseobshchey istorii RAN.

14 Religious nationalism in contemporary Russia: the case of the Ossetian ethnic religious project

Sergey Shtyrkov

> Our people preserve an ancient and probably in former times world-wide religious teaching disseminated by ancient Indo-Europeans.
>
> (Makeyev 2007: 49)

During the last two decades the phenomenon of 'religious nationalism' has become a subject of academic debate. In many respects this has been caused by the outstanding role that religion and religious institutions have played in the dramatic political processes, which have occurred in the former Yugoslavia and the Soviet Union, as well as in the Islamic and/or postcolonial world. Understanding nationalism as a phenomenon, secular in principle and, therefore, competing with religion and even destroying it, came into conflict with observable social reality. So, standard theories of forming nationalist movements and national states have demanded correction. On the other hand, the supposed close connection between the processes of modernization and secularization was revised. A number of scholars have paid attention to the fact that such a correlation actually applies only to some European cases (Stark 1985). Such criticism caused the revision of widespread Eurocentric theories and the search for more flexible explanatory models to consider the specific character of local social contexts, starting with the peculiarities of understanding the social nature of religion in various societies and during different historical periods and finishing with the unpredictable and unexpected consequences of actions by supporters of secularization, which often stimulate the revival of religious life.

In modern social studies the analysis of religious nationalism is developing in several directions. A significant number of works is dedicated to relations and conflicts between a secular state and religious nationalism (Juergensmeyer 1993; van der Veer 1994; Asad 1999). In addition, connections between national identity and confessional affiliation are being studied in some research concerned with modern European contexts, where the adherence of practically faithless people to national churches ('belonging without believing') is marked (Botvar 1996; Davie 2000). As a special research direction one can consider work on nationalism (racism) in some neo-paganism movements (Shnirel'man 2004: part 3; Moroz 2005). There are some attempts to create a general conception of analysing the interaction of such concepts as ethnicity, nationalism, and religion (Baumann 1999).

Generally speaking, the prospects of creating a unified model of interaction between religion and nationalism look improbable at the moment – groups that have developed or are developing as nations have passed along such different historical paths, and the imagined social reality where the members of the various groups live is rather specific in almost each case. It largely concerns the question of forming relations between religion and nationalism or, to put it more precisely, the consequences brought about by the nation construction project for the religious life of various nations and ethnic groups; the attitude of religious institutions (existing or being created) to such projects; and the segments of social reality that define the trajectory of interaction between religion and nationalism (a religious institution and a national state).

Indeed, in most cases we may say that during the modern epoch nationalism, acting as a secular ideology and pretending to be a quasi-religion, has forced religion out of such important segments of social life as economy and politics. Religion finds itself in a kind of ghetto where it is expected to function as a keeper of tradition and spirituality, separated from economy and politics. But, as is well known, national projects during their realization essentially change public opinion and the image of social reality. So-called *cultural nationalism*[1] makes active efforts to change tradition (national culture), along with language (Shtyrkov 2011), into an absolute good in public opinion. When tradition starts to be taken as the main condition of preserving ethnic (national) specificity, the situation changes – a keeper of tradition becomes a socially significant figure. In this way nationalism creates preconditions for increasing the social importance of religion, which becomes one of the main symbols of an ethnic group (nation). In such circumstances, a world religion is often nationalized. For example, the image of Orthodoxy as the quintessence of Russian culture was formed in this way; consequently, it is now taken as the traditional religion of the Russian people. However in a number of contexts 'ethnic tradition' or, rather, its image in public opinion, is supervised not only by religious, but also secular institutions – first of all, by nationally orientated academic disciplines (ethnology, folklore studies). In that case, religious institutions try 'to assimilate' the knowledge of the 'spiritual culture of a people (nation)', which may well be secular in origin, resting upon its authority as the keeper of spirituality. The close connection between spirituality and religion that exists in the perception of people may allow a church institution to privatize a wide area of national spiritual culture. But sometimes nationalists, while not trusting religious institutions for various reasons but at the same time being sure of the religious nature of all spiritual phenomena, can undertake their own attempts to recreate a folk (ethnic, national) religion on the basis of folkloristic, historical, and ethnographic data.

Thus, religion and nationalism have a rather intricate relationship. Nationalism, to accomplish its tasks, may adopt some concepts from religion, which are useful by virtue of their high emotional loading – 'Chosen people', 'redemption and (national) resurrection', images of martyrs and prophets, to mention a few (Hutchison and Lehmann 1994). But religious activists, in turn, actively use nationalism's conceptual arsenal. They start using some images, which were religious in origin and than received certain new connotation in the nationalistic discourse (the idea of national Messianism). But many such images and rhetoric devices actively used by existing (or embryonic) 'nationally focused' religious institutions are invented by nationalist ideology itself – such discursive strategies include portraying the common people as the collective keeper of the higher wisdom, the nation as the only absolute value, and the ethnic tradition as the most important information base whose use can guarantee survival to an ethnic group (nation). In the social landscape created by cultural nationalism where the concepts of tradition, people, spirituality, and religion are closely connected, the activist supporters of a national (ethnic) religion can expect serious political dividends. For example, they can expand their religious group's borders to include the whole nation. The people who they present as their supporters do not always have any connection to the activity of a religious institution disposed to speak in their name. So, according to sociological research in Russia, 75 per cent of those questioned called themselves Orthodox, but only 40 per cent called themselves believers (Kääriäinen and Furman 2000). Thus, a sizeable number of non-believers defined themselves as Orthodox, using religion as an ethnic marker (Agadjanian 2001: 481).

Whether a national-religious project will be started and how effective it will be, depends on many factors concerning the spectrum of ideas about social reality. I will identify some of them:

1. The status of traditional national culture as national property. Here a lot depends on the activity of the scholars who create the image of tradition by collecting and publicly presenting data on national popular culture. In addition, a significant influence upon increasing the status of a national culture is exerted by public campaigns intended to popularize certain practices (customs, folklore genres, etc.).
2. The status of religion (religious institutions) as a source and controller of spirituality and public morals. In some social contexts these functions are perceived as the natural sphere of religious activity.
3. The degree of correlation of a certain religion and an ethnic group. If in some society the degree is high, we could say that religious nationalism is a special way of thinking about the social landscape, where an individual 'receives' a certain confessional affiliation together with his/her ethnicity. In these circumstances, the religious identity becomes 'natural' and practically obligatory, and an individual has either to let it be known demonstratively that he or she is not 'like everyone else', or to accept the identity 'by default'. In some cases the mono-religiosity of an ethnic group is considered to be the natural state of affairs; in the case of poly-religiosity, the confessional diversity is presented as an unnatural phenomenon, which should be eliminated. In such circumstance religious minorities are often regarded as potentially or actually dangerous marginal groups, and converts to another ethnic group's faith are regarded as traitors to their own nation.
4. The degree of development of national eschatology, that is, of ideas that the nation (ethnic group) is under the threat of disappearance and/or enslavement. It should be mentioned that I am not inclined to distinguish between

imaginary and real threats. All of them influence a situation irrespective of so-called expert opinion. A sense of national humiliation, an expectation of the loss of one's ethnic language (language shift), an obvious or latent ethnic conflict with unclear result, and various other factors in the image of social reality may all stimulate the creation of national-religious projects.

Let us take a look at the current situation in Russia from this general perspective. In the social consciousness of contemporary Russian society there is a very close relationship between the concept of religion and the concept of nation (or ethnic group). A nationalistic style of thinking about religious issues determines the logics of behaviour and discourse not only for the so-called radical Orthodox nationalists but also various new pagans,[2] who are trying to revitalize an allegedly ancient, even primordial, ethnic faith. One can come across such statements in very different, sometimes unexpected contexts. For example, the leaders of the main religious communities in Russia usually define the number of their followers just by the so-called ethnic principle, whereby Orthodoxy is presented as the religion of the Russians, Ukrainians, Belarusians, Chuvashes, Mordvins, Karelians, Komi, Ossetians, and so on; Catholicism as the religion of the Poles and Lithuanians; Lutheranism as the religion of Germans, Finns, and Estonians; and so on. Estimating the number of believers in this way involves nothing more than taking the data on ethnic identity from the latest population census and equating ethnic groups with religious communities (Filatov and Lunkin 2005: 35–37; Verkhovsky 2003: 120).

The easily recognizable rhetoric of nationalism is a 'natural' part of the discursive habits of many religious authorities. When one listened, for instance, to the late Patriarch Aleksiy II, the head of Russian Orthodox Church, who was persistently stigmatized by the so-called *revniteli Pravoslaviya* ('adherents of the Orthodoxy') as a traitor to the Russian people and faith, you could easily hear references about the 'unity of the Russian nation', the 'national originality of Russian Orthodoxy' and even about 'the extinction of the Russian people'. Some of his statements were not far from the idea of 'an international conspiracy against Russia': 'We must win in the war levied against Orthodox Russia; we must bring up a new generation of Orthodox Russians, who love Russia', and so on.[3]

Similar affirmations can be heard from ordinary, non-radical Orthodox people. And it is quite usual for these themes (a conspiracy against Russia, a secret war against Russia, a special predestination of Russian people, and so on) to appear in a conversation with an 'ordinary orthodox person', even when talking about such non-political things as children, food, or the weather.

Russian Orthodox believers are not the only social (or religious) group who represent religious questions in terms of ethnicity and nationalism. Evangelical missionaries, working among indigenous peoples of the Russian north, like to stress that their mission is not only the Christianization of these indigenous people but also the preservation of their ethnic culture. Many Muslim leaders eagerly talk about traditional ethnic Islam and even ethnic Muslims. So in contemporary Russia it is quite common to find that religion and ethnicity are represented through each other, when it comes to thinking about social groups and their corresponding social identities.

Under these circumstances, for some ethnic nationalists universalistic Christianity (and in some contexts Islam) is the main threat to national and ethnic cultures, to the very existence of ethnic variety. Some activists try to ethnicize the local variant of a world religion as far as possible; some create new ethnic religions (or, according to many of them, recreate old ones). The latter movement considers Christianity almost an absolute evil.

Here is an opinion of an Udmurt pagan priest from the Middle Ural region:

> The aggressive world religions led mankind into a deadlock. Russians and other peoples rejected their own gods and adopted Christianity. That is why there is no future for them. Their spiritual betrayal and the long domination of Christianity resulted in a deep corruption of the people's soul. The progress of mankind will make some peoples reject Christianity and will lead them to Paganism. If they still have the strength of mind to do it, they will be able to survive.
>
> (Filatov 2002: 147–48)

Supporters of ethnic religions proceed from the idea that every ethnic group has (or had or must have) its own particular religion, just as it has its own language and culture (Shnirel'man 2005: 8). For many ethnic activists it is very important to represent ethnic traditional beliefs, rituals, and practices as a particular religion or even religious system, because 'Only those people who created their own religious system are considered as a rule civilized. That system is testimony of an ethnic organism's maturity; it is evidence of ethnic integration's wholeness' (Salmin 2007: 5).[4] From this point of view, Christianity is dangerous and harmful for ethnic groups because it is an international and even cosmopolitan religion by nature. Sometimes it is considered as a forerunner and symbol of today's globalization (ethno-nationalists' worst nightmare).

Christianity is brought by aliens and their voluntary or deceived allies. Russian, Ukrainian, and Belarusian nationalistic new pagans are inclined to accuse the Jews and construct an image of an ill-intentioned invention of Christianity and a secret spiritual invasion. Non-Russian activists of ethnic religions prefer talking about an undisguised Russian cultural imperialism with Orthodox Christianity as one of its main tools.

One can continue listing particular accusations against Christianity (it suppresses human initiative by preaching humility; it humbles human beings through its concept of the original sin and Christian priests are, of course, greedy, etc). Essentially, none of these accusations are new: they can be found in the works of Nietzsche and Feuerbach or, for example, Soviet atheist ideologists. More interestingly, in some sense, such accusations seem to be superfluous. All of them lead to one simple conclusion: we do not need any alien values, beliefs, practices, and institutions, because we have our own. And they are better because they are ours.

My point is not to indicate the vicious circular nature or unoriginality of religious ethno-nationalists' arguments. I argue that activists of ethnic religious projects have a more complicated relationship with Christianity than a simple outright denial. First, they take their very concept of a proper religion from the religious traditions they would like to reject, and use it in their own creative way. Second, by constructing a new religion, they deny not Christianity but rather a modern Western category of religion. Thus the creation of new ethnic religions appears as a complicated and dialectical process. In support of my argument, I will now turn to two classical anthropological works.

The first work is Clifford Geertz's article '"Internal conversion" in contemporary Bali' (1973). Here he describes and analyses social transitions relating to changes in attitudes of different social groups of Indonesian Balinese society towards a local Hinduism. Those changes took place in the 1950s and early 1960s. Geertz talks about three main aspects of that process – 'the intensified religious questioning, the spread of religious literacy, and the attempt to reorganize religious institutions' (Geertz 1973: 189). I think it is worth adding some specific traits of this process – attempts 'to segregate religion from social life in general' (ibid.: 184), the systematization and interpretation of sacred texts (i.e. the creation of dogma and creed), the unification of ritual activity, and the organization of institutional control over local religious life (the local 'Ministry of Religion', qualifying examinations for priests, and a religious school). To include those processes into a more general conceptual scheme, Geertz uses Max Weber's dichotomy of 'traditional religion vs. rational religion' and names the transformation he writes about 'the rationalization of Balinese religion' (ibid.: 181).

Why did the rationalizers of Balinese religion choose those particular ways for their activity? Geertz did not give us a clear answer to this question. He seems to think about this issue in terms of general laws of religious rationalization, as when he writes about some 'social and intellectual processes which gave rise to the fundamental religious transformations of world history' (ibid.: 189) and compares indirectly the case of Bali with ancient China and Greece. However, I think that we have no need to look for some general laws and remote parallels for understanding modern and post-modern religious transformations. Probably, the Balinese know what they have to do to reform their religion because they have a bright and obliging model of a 'proper religion' not so far from them. I mean Islam.

Geertz notes that the Balinese are 'a people, intensely conscious and painfully proud of being a Hindu island in a Muslim sea, and their attitude toward Islam is that of the duchess to the bug' (ibid.: 181). But Muslims are a powerful majority in Indonesia, and they control all state institutions including the state Ministry of religion. The Balinese do not want to convert to Islam and they do not want their religion to be considered by the majority as a local and 'wild' one. They try to make their religion respectable in the eyes of their neighbours (and in their own eyes). In this context the outer model determines their activity and the Balinese have to accept the majority's rules of the game and communicate with that majority to achieve their aims. Geertz provides an example of such communication:

The Muslims say, you have no book, how can you be a world religion? The Balinese reply, we have manuscripts and inscriptions dating before Mohammed. The Muslims say, you believe in many gods and worship stones; The Balinese say, god is One but has many names and the 'stone' is the vehicle of God, not God himself.

(Geertz 1973: 188)

I would like to note that in these circumstances the Balinese have no opportunity to reply: 'So what? There are many religions without any holy scripture and there are many polytheistic religions.' It would break the rules of the dialogue and destroy it. But the dialogue is very significant for them. Through it arise Balinese Holy Writ, dogmatics, theology, unified rituals, and religious institutions. Such conversation does not necessarily take place in the form of direct contacts: religious reformers can imagine this discussion, but they have to imagine it quite correctly.

It is important to note that here I mean not just relations of direct obtrusion and, correspondingly, forced adaptation of a certain religious model. For the successful reformation of some religion that model has to be interiorized by reformation activists.

In the Bali case we are faced with a situation where a certain system of religious practices undergoes a substantial reorganization (or rationalization in Geertz's terms) on the external pattern. And we can say for sure that some form of Balinese religion existed before the reforms because the Balinese, not just Geertz, proceeded from the belief that some of their practices and ideas were religious. But sometimes we can see that an interaction takes place between a big religion and a society where almost nobody could say that their certain practices are religious. Nevertheless that interplay results in the creation of similar perception.

Here I turn to my Northern Ossetian subject. The official name of this Northern Caucasian national republic is Northern Ossetia – Alania. The last part of the name indicates the relation between contemporary Ossetians and their glorious militant ancestors the Alans. The population of the republic is about seven hundred thousand. Four hundred and fifty thousand of them are Ossetians. The Ossetian language is a Northern Iranian one and has no linguistic relatives in the region. In addition, Northern Ossetia is special because it is the only national republic of the region that does not have a Muslim majority. Sometimes, to outsiders, Ossetians appear to be the only Orthodox native people of the Northern Caucuses, but the situation is not so simple. There are many religions, traditions, and movements in the republic, including Ossetian religious traditionalists. To begin with I will try to describe briefly the context of public debate about Ossetian ethnic religion. Usually in this connection one speaks about creating a neo-pagan religion, similar to the one that may be observed, for example, in some republics of the Volga region (Shnirel'man 1998, 2002; cf. Filatov and Shchipkov 1996).

However, the situation only appears to be this clear in the absence of knowledge of the local religious and political context. The fact of the matter is that in

Northern Ossetia there is no distinctness about what is the Ossetian national (or ethnic) religion or what it should be.[5] Nor is there any public consensus on the existence of a specific Ossetian religion. The nature of phenomena ascribed to the area of Ossetian spiritual culture is a point at issue over which there are clashing interpretations. The complexity of the situation and the tension of the discussions in many respects are determined by the distinctive religious history of the Ossetians. The acceptance of Christianity from the Greeks by the ancestors of today's Ossetians in not later than the tenth century, and then the 'retreat' of church structures from Ossetia several centuries later (this event is often dated to the fifteenth century) defined the landscape of the religious life of the people during the following centuries. Without pastors, the congregation was left on its own. The expansion of Islam among a part of the Ossetians added some extra shades to the situation. Even the active propagation of Christianity by the Orthodox church, which 'returned' as a state religion in the nineteenth century together with the Russian Empire, has not changed the general picture: in Ossetian religious life it is easy enough to find elements corresponding with East-Christian (less often Islamic) culture and, most likely, going back to it and, on the other hand, practices and beliefs that can hardly be traced back to Christianity or Islam. Given this situation, the most widely used term to define the nature of the religious situation in Ossetian society was (and still is) 'mixture' – of Christianity, Islam, and paganism, or Christianity (religion) and superstitions. However, not everyone in Ossetia wanted to determine the nature of the phenomena, discussed by scholars and national leaders, in terms of religion. For the majority, practices that a researcher may recognize as indicative of the presence of a religious cult (for example, the practice of making a pilgrimage to local sacred places) are not essentially religious phenomena, but just old good ethnic (or local) traditions.

At the end of the last century such uncertainty has ceased to be convenient for a section of the Ossetian elite, and attempts were made to apply religious terms to traditional practices. Then one began to speak first about Ossetian paganism, and then about pre-Christian (ancient Aryan) monotheism. For many national activists that conception of an ethnic religion correlates directly with the conception of a particular spiritual path of the Ossetian people. Orthodox activists also joined the discussion and tried to represent Ossetian culture as Orthodox per se. Eventually, a significant section of the republic's establishment and the ordinary population consistently began to avoid applying religious terminology to the phenomena which some people take as demonstrations of religiousness, preferring to speak about ethnic traditions, customs, and so on.

So in the society under consideration, there are different interpretations of the republic's ethnic cultural heritage and different perspectives regarding its use for some national interests. Each of them formulates strategies for the perception and representation of the ethnic spiritual tradition. It often causes open public debates.

In any event, leaders and supporters of the Ossetian ethnic religious project occupy a visible place in the social landscape of the republic. Some words should be said about three particular features of their mission.

1. Their activity did not start in a vacuum but in a specific historical context. The concept of an Ossetian ethnic religion was created by academicians a century ago and was popularized since the 1950s by Soviet atheists who furiously fought against Ossetian paganism. It was Soviet anti-religious activists who drove certain local practices (pilgrimages to local sacred places, ritual feasts, etc.) from the field of ethnic tradition into the religious sphere in people's minds (Shtyrkov 2009, 2010). This now gives religious nationalists the right to talk about the persecution of their faith.

2. The leaders of the movement cannot just renounce Christianity as a religion of aliens, namely, Russians and Georgians because many Ossetians consider Orthodox Christianity as the faith of their glorious ancestors – the Alans. Hence, religious nationalists have to spend much time on explaining their anti-Christian position. Daurbek Makeyev, perhaps the brightest representative or even head of the movement, in attempting to be more persuasive uses, among other things, anti-Semitic stereotypes to connect Judaism with Christianity:

> There are no words about Honesty in the Jewish religion, but there is a description of how to achieve one's own self-interested goals. It is necessary to say that the conception of making profits through the corruption of other nations and their moral depravation is crucial for Judaism. It is the basic religion for Christians and Muslims.
>
> (Makeyev 2007: 19)

The other recognizable ideological image is related to the concept of the Jewish conspiracy: 'The degradation of the Ossetian nation is not a consequence of progress and technological revolution. It is a result of the successful work of Moses' followers and their gone astray assistants [Christians]' (Makeyev 2002: 56). It should be added that for Makeyev and his associates Judaism is the main enemy and a certain ideal at the same time:

> Moses understood perfectly that to betray some people's God means to break off their roots, to bring about universal debauchery, to loosen traditional values and thereby weaken their ethnic identity and make that people perish. He considered a betrayal of somebody's God as the ultimate crime – as a crime against the Nation.
>
> (Makeyev 2007: 25)

3. In their polemics with Christianity they stress the supposed vicious nature of the Church as a powerful institution. This argument makes their teaching attractive to some people, but at the same time does not permit them to speak openly about the establishment of a new priesthood.

It is no surprise that despite rejecting a world religion, Ossetian religious nationalists have to copy its main traits. They consider *Nart* folklore epic songs as Ossetian Holy Writ (Makeyev 2007; Chochiev 2009).[6] Through a very complicated exegesis of those texts they create their own dogma and theological system. The main methods of that exegesis are audacious etymological construction and drawing parallels between Ossetian linguistic, folklore, and rituals and those of Indo-Iranian (Aryan) ancient cultures. Activists of the religion, which is new and ancient at the same time, try to create a unified ritual system, every tiny element of which has a theological motivation.

It is not worth reducing this project to a simple blind imitation of 'big' religious traditions. There are some traits of this movement that make it, in my opinion, a bright and original phenomenon. Ossetian religious nationalists are not simply trying to create one more religion. They are trying to construct a system of faith that could go beyond the restrictions of modern Western conceptions of religion. And here is my second theoretical foundation – Talal Asad's discussion of the specificity of the Western modern conception of religion as an academic and, I would like to add, cultural category in his 'Construction of religion as an anthropological category' (1993). Here I mean that the scantiness of the modern Western idea of the nature of religion is conceived not only by the new generation of anthropologists but also by some leaders of new religious movements.

The Ossetian religious nationalists disapprove of a concept of religion as something that saves human souls and takes persons to Heaven, that is, as a teaching that places ultimate human values into another world. The religion of Ossetian traditionalists deals with this world, and its main function is to protect the ethnic culture and save the nation from assimilation and disappearance. The misdeeds of Christians and Muslims are sins against God; in the Ossetian ethnic religion they are sins against the nation because they result in, for example, the demographic crisis and extinction of the nation. And the main sin would be the abandonment of their forefathers' faith. 'A person who abandoned his people's God and adopted the alien faith (ideology) from Moses' followers brings damnation not only upon himself and his descendants but upon his whole people and all their lands and possessions' (Makeyev 2002: 57). As one can see, Ossetian religious nationalists deny that religion is a question of individual choice. The Ossetians' ancient religion is or must become a matter for the whole nation. 'If the people forget their [religious] tradition, it will lose its significance to God and be doomed to extinction' (Makeyev 2002: 47). The greatest sin is an apostasy from the national religion. Makeyev likes to cite historical examples where Ossetians' ancestors – the Scythians and Alans – killed apostates and believes that those acts were reasonable and legal (Makeyev 2002: 56, 2007: 25–26; see also Gazdanova 2007: 115–17).

The last, but not least, of the anti-modernist traits of this nationalist project I would like to mention is the refusal to accept a restricted function for religion in modern society, that is, to accept a situation where modern religious systems are forced to stay out of politics and where they have no actual working cosmology – they lose the battle against the Western modern natural sciences and political thinking. Ossetian religious activists need a total religion, a religion that is not just a part of social life or culture, but the whole life of the nation. The whole of Ossetian culture is religious by nature. Their religion is politics and they contend that they are able to create a system of faith where ethics, sociology, and cosmology are interrelated. 'We are talking about a three-level structure of the universe which is a psycho-emotional structure of the human being at the same time' (Makeyev 2002: 2).

The ideology of Ossetian religious nationalism is not new. Its slogan 'The nation is our religion' is well known. It is becoming more and more popular in contemporary Northern Ossetia. As one comment on an article by an Ossetian religious nationalist noted (the title is very characteristic – 'Truthful words against Christians' (Morgoyev 2006)): 'Today a supporter of the disappearing Ossetian culture can be forgiven for anything'.

In June 2009 the first community of the traditional Ossetian religion was officially registered in the Ossetian town of Mozdok. Daurbek Makeyev is its head.

Notes

1 This ideology proceeds from an understanding of nations as entities based on a mono-ethnic group with a common language, past (first of all, origin), and so on.
2 As shown in my discussion below, today some of them refuse to present their religious projects in terms of old or new paganism more and more often.
3 *Obrashcheniye Svyateyshego Patriarkha Moskovskogo i vseya Rusi Aleksiya k kliru, prikhodskim sovetam khramov Moskvy, namestnikam i nastoyatel'nitsam stavropigial'nykh monastyrey na Yeparkhial'nom sobranii 2007 goda.* Online. Available: www.patriarchia.ru/db/text/356093.html (accessed 29 March 2011). The following citation was taken from a normal (non-radical) diocesan newspaper:

> The West hates Russia unreservedly because the Russian land was and is the stronghold of the Orthodox Faith ... Now it is important [for the West] to annihilate the Russian man, who keeps the Orthodox world-view, Orthodox culture and Orthodox faith, and who will never permit the West to become the absolute ruler of the World
>
> (Opletnin 2009).

4 The metaphors of 'ethnic organism' and 'integrity (wholeness)' are very important and characteristic in this context. The former permits one to talk about some 'total amount of ethnic religious experience' and the latter, about perspectives of destruction of the ethnic culture because of the loss of a single element in the religious system (Salmin 2007: 610–11).
5 On some aspects of this discussion and on ritual and tradition in ethnic nationalism in Northern Ossetia, see Shnirel'man (2006: 182–85).
6 *Nart* epics are considered by most Ossetians as their main cultural heritage and one can find implicit and explicit references to these songs everywhere. For example, it is customary to name children after the well-known characters of the songs.

Bibliography

Agadjanian, A. (2001) 'Revising Pandora's gifts: religious and national identity in the post-Soviet societal fabric', *Europe-Asia Studies*, 53: 473–88.

Asad, T. (1993) 'The construction of religion as an anthropological category', in T. Asad *Genealogies of Religion: Discipline and Reasons of Power in Christianity and Islam*, 27–54, Baltimore, MD: Johns Hopkins University Press.

——(1999) 'Religion, nation-state, secularism', in P. van der Veer and H. Lehmann (eds) *Nation and Religion*, 178–96, Princeton, NJ: Princeton University Press.

Baumann, G. (1999) *The Multicultural Riddle: Rethinking National, Ethnic and Religious Identites*, New York: Routledge.

Botvar, P.K. (1996) *Belonging without Believing? The Norwegian Religious Profile Compared with the British one*, Oslo: Scandinavian University Press.

Chochiev, A. (2009) *Ir-As-/Alan/-skoye edinobozhiye: teologiya; teosofiya*, Tskhinval: n.p.

Davie, G. (2000) *Religion in Modern Europe: A Memory Mutates*, Oxford: Oxford University Press.

Filatov, S. (2002) 'Yazycheskoye vozrozhdeniye – povolzhskaya religioznaya al'ternativa', in S.B. Filatov (ed.) *Religiya i obshchestvo: Ocherki religioznoy zhizni sovremennoy Rossii*, 135–57, Moskva/Sankt-Peterburg: Letniy sad.

Filatov, S. and Lunkin, R. (2005) 'Statistika rossiyskoy religioznosti: magiya tsifr i neodnoznachnaya real'nost'', *Sotsiologicheskiye issledovaniya*, 6: 35–45.

Filatov, S. and Shchipkov, A. (1996) 'Povolzhskiye narody v poiskah national'noy very', in *Religiya i prava cheloveka. Na puti k svobode sovesti*, vol. 3, 252–56, Moskva: Nauka.

Gazdanova, V.S. (2007) 'Etnicheskiy mif osetin', in V.S. Gazdanova *Zolotoy dozhd'. Issledovaniya po traditsionnoy kul'ture osetin*, 110–20, Vladikavkaz: RIO SOIGSI.

Geertz, C. (1973) '"Internal conversion" in contemporary Bali', in C. Geertz, *The Interpretation of Cultures: Selected Essays*, 170–89, New York: Basic Books.

Hutchison, W.R. and Lehmann, H. (eds) (1994) *Many are Chosen: Divine Election and Western Nationalism*, Minneapolis: Fortress Press.

Juergensmeyer, M. (1993) *The New Cold War? Religious Nationalism Confronts the Secular State*. Berkeley: University of California Press.

Kääriäinen, K. and Furman, D. (2000) 'Religiosity in Russia in the 1990s', in M. Kotiranta (ed.) *Religious Transition in Russia*, 28–76, Helsinki: Kikimora Publications.

Makeyev, D. (2002) *Osnovy veroispovedaniya osetin. Tayny drevnikh Asov*, Vladikavkaz: RIA ANKO.

——(2007) *Religioznoye mirovozzreniye v Nartskom epose*. Vladikavkaz: IPK SOIGSI.

Morgoyev, Kh. (2006) 'Pravdivoye slovo protiv khristian', in *Iriston.com – istoriya i kul'tura Osetii*. Online. Available: www.iriston.com/nogbon/news.php?newsid=44 (accessed 29 March 2011).

Moroz, E. (2005) *Istoriya 'Mertvoy vody' – ot strashnoy skazki k bol'shoy politike: politicheskoye neoyazychestvo v postsovetskoy Rossii*, Stuttgart: ibidem-Verlag.

Opletnin, N. (2009) 'Neob"yavlennaya voyna', *Pravoslavnaya gazeta (Ofitsial'noye izdaniye Yekaterinburgskoy yeparkhii Russkoy Pravoslavnoy Tserkvi)*, 30.

Salmin, A.K. (2007) *Sistema religii chuvashey*, Sankt-Peterburg: Nauka.

Shnirel'man, V.A. (1998) *Neoyazychestvo i natsionalizm: vostochnoyevropeysky areal*, Moskva: Institut etnologii i antropologii RAN.

——(2002) '"Christians! Go Home!": a revival of neo-paganism between the Baltic Sea and Transcaucasia (an overview)', *Journal of Contemporary Religion*, 17: 197–211.

——(2004) *Intellektual'nyye labirinty: ocherki ideologii v sovremennoy Rossii*, Moskva: Academia.

——(2005) 'Ot "sovetskogo naroda" k "organicheskoy obshchnosti": obraz mira u russkikh i ukrainskikh neoyazychnikov', *Slavyanovedeniye*, 6: 3–26.

——(2006) *Byt' alanami: intellektualy i politika na Severnom Kavkaze v XX veke*, Moskva: Novoye literaturnoye obozreniye.

Stark, R. (1985) 'From church-sect to religious economies', in P.H. Hammond (ed.) *The Sacred in a Post-Secular Age*, 139–49, Berkeley: University of California Press.

Shtyrkov, S.A. (2009) 'Oblichitel'naya etnografiya epokhi Khrushcheva: bol'shaya ideologiya i narodny obychay (na primere Severo-Osetinskoy ASSR)', *Neprikosnovenny zapas*, 1/63: 147–61.

——(2010) 'Prakticheskoye religiovedeniye vremen Nikity Khrushcheva: respublikanskaya gazeta v bor'be s religioznymi perezhitkami (na primere Severo-Osetinskoy ASSR)', in

Yu. Karpov (ed.) *Traditsii narodov Kavkaza v menyayushchemsya mire: preyemstvennost' i razryvy v sotsio-kul'turnykh praktikakh*, 306–43, Sankt-Peterburg: Peterburgskoye vostokovedeniye.

———(2011) 'Lingvisticheskiy natsionalizm i akademicheskaya traditisiya', in *Radlovskiy Sbornik. Nauchnyye issledovaniya i muzeynyye proekty MAE RAN v 2010 g.*, 327–33, Sanet – Peterburg: MAE RAN.

Van der Veer, P. (1994) *Religious Nationalism: Hindus and Muslims in India*, Berkeley: University of California Press.

Verkhovsky, A.M. (2003) *Politicheskoye pravoslaviye: Russkiye pravoslavnyye natsionalisty i fundamentalisty, 1995–2001 gg.*, Moskva: Tsentr 'SOVA'.

15 Social networking on the internet: is the Russian way special?

Ilya Utekhin

In July 2009, *ComScore*, one of the leaders of digital world measuring, claimed that 'the Russian social networking audience had the highest engagement among the forty individual countries reported by *ComScore*, with an average of 6.6 hours and 1,307 pages consumed per visitor [per month]' (*ComScore* 2009). These figures are twice as much as the average for the forty countries studied. Some years earlier, before the epidemic arrival of social networking websites, blogging was among the pronounced trends in users' internet activities; in *Livejournal.com*, one of the largest platforms for blogging, Russian bloggers were the most active. Do data like those just mentioned mean that there is something special about the Russian way of social networking on the internet?

Russia, of course, is not an exception in terms of the general ways in which social and cultural factors influence the adoption of new technologies. That is why, along with a variety of economic, demographic, and cultural geographic factors, it would probably be useful to look for cultural features that might contribute to shaping the uses of information technology in this country. That is not to say that the internet or smart phones can be or actually are used in Russia in ways that sharply differ from what we find in other countries. However, although technologies are more or less the same in the global world, the pace of technology adoption and some ways of using technology in different societies might turn out to be different. Correspondingly, we can speak about culturally specific features of the use of technology. The social impact of technology might also vary cross-culturally, as might the social contexts in which technology is embedded.

As elsewhere in the world, technology is reshaping the practices of everyday life in contemporary Russia. The penetration of information technology into people's lives in post-industrial societies leads to important changes in their life worlds. These days, a significant part of the urban population of Russia inhabits an environment that is abundant in smart artefacts to interact with. To cope with all the challenges of this life world, one has no alternative but to actively use communication technology and a variety of virtual interfaces. Moscow and St Petersburg, on the one hand, and the *provintsiya* ('the provinces') and rural areas, on the other, differ much in this respect, but, in any event, mobile phones, personal computers, both at home and at work, ATMs, payment terminals, and so on, are now becoming ubiquitous.[1] People are also getting accustomed to using the internet, even though the speed of internet connection in Russia is considerably slower than has become normal in European countries. Generally, the amount of time that citizens of Russia dedicate to interaction with smart machines and to computer-mediated communication is growing fast, though it has not yet attained the average European level.

Younger generations of urban Russians are often acquainted with information technology from their childhood. For them, the use of the internet and many of its applications are mundane routines, almost to the point that the use of internet services does not require any conscious effort from the users, like the use of refrigerators and TVs. Broadband internet connection is taken for granted by many urban Russians these days, despite the modest speed of the connection. It should be noted that this leads to a new way in which the internet is used, compared to dial-up connection, potentially 'dissolving the structure of everyday life, mixing usually separate zones of study, work and recreation' (Petersen 2007: 85), and creating a habit of browsing the same sites, reading email, and logging on to social networking sites and messenger sites regularly, often several times a day.

Despite all the differences across social strata, ethnic and age groups, new phenomena related to information technology embrace the population of Russia as a whole. Let us take multitasking as an example. 'Multitasking is the simultaneous conduct of two or more activities, during a given time period', as formulated by Susan Kenyon, who studied the influence of internet use on scheduling daily activities and on perceptions of time (Kenyon 2008: 286). Parallel activities are often met in everyday life outside information technology, but Kenyon claims that the internet works as a 'time enhancer', providing opportunities for virtual mobility and thus losing 'the traditionally close links between activity, space and time' (ibid.: 290), so that many activities can be conducted anywhere, at any time. This opens radically new opportunities for multitasking and dividing one's attention between several activities.

For instance, multitasking is what a person is involved in when she or he is using a web-messenger while working on the computer while talking to a colleague. Moreover, constant scanning for activities and people brings about what is currently referred to as 'continuous partial attention': an overload of information of various kinds arriving simultaneously through different channels and thus making it impossible to be immersed in a single project. Like anywhere in the world where information technology is inseparable from people's daily lives, many contemporary Russians feel themselves to be constantly online, not only because their mobiles are always open for calls and text messages, but also because they feel obliged to check their email and social network websites several times a day.

Is this 'broadening of time' becoming common practice for a significant portion of the population in Russia? How does this relate to the usual chronemic patterns of Russian culture?

American anthropologist Edward Hall, who pioneered the cross-cultural study of time use, distinguished between monochronic and polychronic cultural orientations that roughly correlate to the amount and scale of multitasking, particularly in social communication (Hall 1977: 17–24). Russian culture and, particularly, Russian bureaucracy is not homogenous in this respect, as it combines spheres and contexts that display opposite chronemic orientations. In Russian everyday culture we meet both monochronic and polychronic approaches. Take queuing, for instance. The influence of Northern-European practices of queuing led to the appearance of a queuing system based on free numbered tickets in some banks and railway booking offices in Russia. In theory, this system is a guarantee that customers are served one at a time, in a strict sequence, according to the numbers on the tickets. However, as frequent visitors to Russia will have discovered, even if ticket-dispensing machines that epitomise monochronic scheduling are installed, they do not always work or, if the queue in the booking office is long enough, you will probably be approached by someone who will offer to sell you a ticket with a number that will allow you to be serviced much sooner than your own queuing ticket would. Polychronic communication by salespersons, that is, the situation when the salesperson takes part in a multi-party conversation with more than one customer at once and with fellow salespersons, is still a regular practice in markets, but is gradually disappearing from shops in Russia. In this cultural context, internet-related multitasking is readily accepted within essentially polychronic cultural ways at home and at work, but it may bring about conflicts given the monochronic orientation of labour organization in the work place.[2]

It is characteristic that the amount of time spent by office workers on social networking sites (SNSs) during the working day is not easy to evaluate by means of questionnaires and interviews, because people tend to report low figures for themselves while claiming much longer times for their colleagues' non-work related use of SNSs during the working day.

Since in big cities most offices are connected to the internet, employers began to feel that this practice was a problem. Generally, however, the penetration of the internet in Russia, according to data available in October 2008, is not very high (69 per cent of the adult population do not use the internet at all, compared to the US where 70 per cent of households have broadband internet connection).[3] In St Petersburg and Moscow, penetration is much higher and increasing fast: up to 750,000 households in St Petersburg had broadband internet connection in 2008 (cf. only 70,000 in 2005), and unlimited internet access is becoming as common a feature of everyday life as the telephone line. The bigger the city, the larger the proportion of internet users: 41 per cent (population older than 15 years) for Moscow and St Petersburg (and even higher according to other sources, e.g., Tagiyev 2008), compared to 12 per cent for rural areas. Mobile internet use (mostly WAP/GPRS) grew by 82 per cent in 2008 and the number of users has reached 32.5 million (data from J'son & Partners, quoted in Fadeyeva (2009)). Young people with a high level of education are more likely to be internet users than other social groups. The latest data available show that the daily internet audience in the summer of 2009 amounted to 22 per cent of the urban population older than 18 (*FOM* 2009).

According to what people say to sociologists, most often the internet is used by the Russians for work and study, for email and for reading the news; the number of those who get access to multimedia materials and communicate online is growing. Curiously, the survey by VTsIOM does not mention e-commerce and e-banking at all. Which is not to say that e-commerce does not exist in Russia: in 2007, the turnover of e-commerce in Russia was USD 3.2 billion (30 per cent up compared to 2006), and 85 per cent of active internet users said they shopped online. However, only 16 per cent of users shopped online at least once a month, and most of the shoppers (70 per cent) paid for online goods in cash upon delivery while only 12 per cent of responders used their bank cards online. The most popular shopping items include books (51 per cent of responders) and computers (43 per cent) (*Lenta.ru* 2008). According to a recent report by the *FOM* (Public Opinion Foundation) on internet trade and payments in Russia (Lebedev 2009), 87 per cent of the internet audience older than 18 said that they knew about paid services, but only 26 per cent actually used them, which means that 74 per cent of the internet audience had never paid through the internet. Among paid services, by far the most popular is the downloading of music and video, followed by buying software. Predictably, audiences that engage in internet activities such as content creation and socializing are more active in buying goods and services. It is interesting that one of the main reasons that people mentioned to explain why they didn't use paid services was that the same things could be found elsewhere on the internet for free. That is partly true, the more so as some SNSs, in a legally ambiguous stance, let their subscribers access for free multimedia content which, it is claimed, belongs to users' private collections.

Data quoted above are taken from representative polls. Sociologists know, however, that what people say about what they do differs from what they actually do, and people are sometimes not conscious about the real motives behind their behaviour, or are just unwilling to express their real motives in interviews and polls. In reality, Russians not only work and study, email and read news on the internet, they also, for the most part, socialize, play online games, and access multimedia and adult content. The most eloquent, though indirect, indicator of users' real interests is to be found amid the statistics of search queries submitted to web search engines.[4] The evolution of the top ten queries on the Russian internet from 2001 to 2008 is very impressive. In 2001–2, the most popular searches were for *порно* ('porno'), *секс* ('sex'), sex, mp3, and porno, followed by *эротика* ('erotic'), *знакомства* ('introduction'), *реферат* ('essay'), and *гороскоп* ('horoscope'). In 2006, the top five queries included *сонник* ('book of dream interpretations') *гороскоп*, *работа* ('jobs'), *знакомства*, and *порно*. Although in 2008 sex and dating retained their high position among the interests of Russian internet users, the first most frequent five queries were as follows: *одноклассники* ('classmates') (1.9% of all queries submitted), *odnoklassniki.ru* (domain name for classmates' social network site) (0.3%), *однокласники* (spelt mistakenly) (0.2%), *odnoklassniki* (0.2%), *работа* (0.2%). That is to say, in 2008, the top four queries had to do with *odnoklassniki*, or *www.odnoklassniki.ru*, which is an analogue of *Classmates* social networking service, one of the two most prominent Russian social network websites. Similarly, in 2008 and early 2009, another leading social network, *vKontakte*, was also among the most popular sites. From these data we can see that between 2006 and 2008 something important happened that reflected a significant change in the patterns of behaviour of Russian internet users.

Data on the monthly reach of the most popular services complement this picture. By the beginning of 2008 monthly reach figures were as follows: *Yandex* (search engine) 13.55 million,[5] *Mail.ru* 13.50 million, *Rambler* (search engine) 8.73 million, *Odnoklassniki.ru* (social network site) 9.52 million, and *LiveJournal* (blogging service) 5.02 million. At least once a month, social network sites or blogs were visited by 92.1 per cent of Russian internet users in 2008 (Tagiyev 2008). Social networking is gaining a more and more significant share of internet traffic in Russia, thus following the global trend. In Russia, by the autumn of 2007, 62 per cent of internet users said they used at least one social network site, and a third of responders said they used more than one (Vyrin 2008).

Generally, social network sites on the internet have a number of features that allow these services to be categorized as a separate phenomenon. However varied thematically and functionally the services are, their users have to build up a virtual self as a public or semi-public profile within a system. As part of this profile, a list of connections with other users ('contacts') is made available, so that contacts can be viewed within a user's network of contacts. The nature of the connections varies depending on the type of site. Identity-driven categories can underlie site design, which is particularly pronounced when a service's target audience strategy is aimed at the creation of a niche-community.

Users of social network sites are given opportunities to put (a part of) their offline extended social networks online, or to create new connections with various purposes ranging from establishing and developing professional contacts (e.g., in *LinkedIn*) to dating. Networking might involve the exchange of multimedia content (e.g., *YouTube*) and/or collaborative filtration as part of recommendation services that provide information and ratings based on audience's evaluations of products and services (e.g., *Imhonet*, the most prominent recommendation service on the Russian internet). Social networking usually supposes some kind of self-presentation and self-expression, especially in services based on user generated content. Socialization and communication is another dimension of users' activity on social network sites.

Interestingly, long before the internet, in the subculture of Russian schoolchildren, there was an instrument for playful networking that can distantly remind us of today's social networking on the web. This was the legacy of the old album tradition, mainly among girls. They used to have a copybook where they could copy their favourite lyrics and quotations, and a questionnaire that included questions about personal attitudes and tastes. This questionnaire was first filled in by the album's owner, and then offered to other people, often as a way to become more closely acquainted with the album owner's circle of friends. This, albeit in a rudimentary way, combined two crucial functions of SNSs self-presentation and communication. Although blogging on the *LiveJournal* platform was not a Russian invention, the Russian language is its second most popular after English: 29 per cent of all the posts are in Russian, compared to 66 per cent in English.[6]

The recent social networking boom on the internet started in Russia later than in the West, and its first manifestation was active blogging. The personal web publishing service *LiveJournal* emerged in 2001 and for several years was an important site for Russians active on the web. As Eugene Gorny writes in his study:

> The dialectic of private and public speech is a conspicuous feature of blogs. Since 2001, the blogging service *Livejournal.com* (or, as the Russians call it, *Zhivoy Zurnal* or simply *ZhZh*) has become the largest discussion centre of the Russian Internet. ... A host of Internet celebrities and intellectual and cultural figures also contributed to its popularity with the masses.
>
> (Gorny 2007)

It is characteristic that the audience of *ZhZh*, as can be seen from the rating of its interests and its social characteristics, is more 'literate' than that of other blogging services that appeared later. For Russian culture, its orientation towards the written language and texts is so important that blogging logically became an affordable way of virtual self-expression and socializing.

In 2007, the number of Russian-language users of *LiveJournal* was around eight hundred thousand, most of them residing in Moscow and in St Petersburg, and a few other blogging services were available on Russian internet.[7] *ZhZh* was and, to some extent, still is something different from a personal web-publishing service. For Russian users, it has become a means of socializing and communication, with posting comments, communities, friends, updates of friends' entries, and some other opportunities that were later realized and gained much success in micro-blogging and social network services like *Twitter*.

These days, although blogging in Russia remains an important platform for social activism, it is overshadowed by social networking by means of services analogous to *Facebook* and *Classmates*. Since 2007, the share of active blogs, that is, those that are updated at least once in three months, is decreasing, as well as the absolute number of active blogs.[8]

Blogging cannot be as attractive to the broad mass of users as *Facebook*-type sites are, mainly because writing and maintaining a blog presumes self-expression and requires a certain effort of creativity on the part of the blog owner, even though the content is not original but borrowed from elsewhere and linked. A potentially semi-anonymous milieu requires the active construction of a public face. *Odnoklassniki* and similar social networking services do not require this kind of effort, and hence their appeal: self-presentation, networking, and communication are made simple. Unlike blogs, the popularity of social networking sites in Russia involved such wide strata of the population that during 2008, in more than half of Russian offices, network administrators used to block access to social network services: similarly, earlier they used to block access to erotic content to prevent wasting work time and internet traffic. Instant messaging is also sometimes blocked in many cases to avoid the loss of working time, even if it actually could have increased the efficiency of interaction between office workers. It is worth mentioning that in Russian secondary schools SNSs are also blocked, by order of the Ministry of Education.

Launched in March 2006, Odnoklassniki.ru collected 3 million subscribers by the summer of 2007, and in October 2007 occupied the top position in terms of search queries in the Russian internet. It has held first position since then with up to 2.0 per cent of all web queries. It is worth noting that the users who submit this query to a search engine do not usually wish to find information about this service, but rather aim at navigating to the *Odnoklassniki* website. The fact that they do not use the URL field of their browser is indicative of their lack of knowledge of advanced web surfing routines: it is very likely that they do not clearly distinguish browser from search engine website interface. The level of computer and internet literacy of a large part of the subscribers of *Odnoklassniki* is probably lower than that of the users of *vKontakte*, and hence *vKontakte*, although also being a popular search query, does not attain the top position. This is understandable, if we take into account the difference between the audiences of both services. They are comparable in number. In August 2008, *Odnoklassniki* celebrated 20 million accounts registered, and in early 2009, the number of accounts went above 30 million.[9]

Another big social networking service, *vKontakte*, also registered 30 million accounts on 18 March 2009, and is still growing impressively, being far from saturation point.[10] *vKontakte* differs from *Odnoklassniki* in the structure of its audience: the proportion of students and younger age groups is significantly higher in *vKontakte*. It should be noted that the functionality of the service is much wider, especially when it comes to the storage and sharing of multimedia content. Compared to *Odnoklassniki*, the interface of *vKontakte* is more web 2.0 like, *Facebook*-style, but somewhat easier and more intuitive than *Facebook*.

Interestingly, the TNS Gallup 2008 study quoted above shows that the female share of the audience of *Odnoklassniki* is higher than that of the overall Russian internet audience, especially in the 25–34-year-old age group, and higher than that of male subscribers to this service. Compared to *Odnoklassniki*, the audience of *vKontakte* is not only younger, but the number of male subscribers is higher in various under 35-year-old age groups; in older age groups, females significantly outnumber male subscribers, both in *vKontakte* and in *Odnoklassniki*.

Despite its positioning as a site for socializing, the functionality of *vKontakte* allows the uploading of multimedia content and the accessing of content uploaded by other subscribers, hence a part of the SNSs' attraction. As in *MySpace*, a user's profile is eventually complemented with the multimedia content available from the user's page. As in *Facebook*, a growing variety of applications are offered to users.

The high popularity of SNSs can partly be explained by the fact that the average Russian internet is not fast enough for downloading quality online multimedia content, and thus cannot be compared in this respect to Western countries where internet users have a broader range of efficient services. At the same time, pay services on the internet are less widespread in Russia than in Europe, and Russians were not accustomed to paying virtually when SNS began to flourish. It should also be kept in mind that the number of active users of SNS is significantly lower than the number of subscribers. Interestingly, researchers who studied the spread of internet use in China have come to the conclusion that internet adoption and internet use are two different phenomena dependent on different variables. They consider that 'perceived social norms or perceived benefits may provide sufficient incentives for an audience to make the one-time investment, but may not be enough for the audience to sustain constant usage unless there is a felt need' (Zhu and He 2002: 489). The one-time investment, in this case, was the purchase of equipment enabling internet connection. This logic might also be true for the Russian situation when there is widespread adoption of internet technology. By the same token, a large number of subscribers register with a SNS at some point, but this is not to say that all of these people (and in some cases they can be counted in millions) really use the service: to create an account and to be an active user is not the same. A significant part of *Odnoklassniki*'s subscribers use the SNS irregularly – or don't use their accounts at all.

Some facts suggest that social networking in general, but particularly the use of *Odnoklassniki*, might be one of the first activities on the internet which beginner users of the web experience.[11] By the time public enthusiasm about *MySpace*, blogging, and *Facebook* started in the US, the penetration of the internet in the US was higher than in Russia, even when compared to St Petersburg and Moscow. Hence, what is special about the Russian case is the fact that the social networking boom coincided with the fast spread of broadband connection in big cities. Thus, for new strata of the population regular use of the internet started with social networking. Before that, the use of the internet positively correlated with high level of education and young age; with the boom of social networks, this correlation becomes much less pronounced.

Although putting existing social networks online and enhancing communication within them has been the declared aim of *Odnoklassniki* and *vKontakte*, this is obviously only one of the ways in which these services are actually employed by internet users. The services' functionality that allows the creation of interest based communities, as well as various means of introducing oneself to strangers, meet a high demand from the part of the users, so much so that users find their own ways of employing the services available.

Generally, advances of technology offer opportunities that users adopt, reject, or transform according to their demands. In this respect, it is highly informative to study the ways in which this technology is actually used, which may be very different from those envisaged or planned by designers. Such uses reveal the needs and expectations of users that had not yet been met by existing technology. For example, one of the networking activities available on *vKontakte* is to tag photographs and videos uploaded to the site with names of persons present on the photos and videos. When such tags are left as annotations of multimedia content, friends whose names appear among newly set tags get a message from the system offering to confirm the fact that they are present on that image. Since some images are not actually photographs of people – there are all kinds of images – system messages are used simply to attract the attention of one's friends to a recently posted picture or video. Another example is the way in which people embellish their accounts by displaying high profile friends and celebrities in their friend list; celebrities' pages of this kind are, of course, fake.

The two largest SNSs of the Russian internet put an emphasis on opportunities to link former classmates and colleagues, whereas interests and hobbies belong to secondary features; searching for them is available on *vKontakte* but not on *Odnoklassniki*. People's social networks that are being put online by means of SNSs involve people who belong to the Russian-speaking community living outside Russia, mostly in the US, Germany, Israel, Canada, and the countries of the former Soviet Union. An important share of *Odnoklassniki*'s subscribers live abroad and use the site to communicate with their friends and relatives, thus enhancing the idea of an international Russianness that is not linked to a particular residential location. Along with this global trend, there is another one, just the opposite: the use of the internet is becoming more local. People not only communicate over great distances because the internet allows them to do so, easily, but also (or instead) get to know their local community in a new way, by bringing their local networks online thereby adding a new dimension to their sociality. This is worthy of a separate study, as it involves more subtle forms of sociality than those which are covered by the terms 'community' and 'networking'.[12]

During the SNS boom in Russia, the owners of the social services made attempts to generate substantial cash flow for advertising and various kinds of service. Now subscribers are being asked to pay for advanced privacy settings (*Odnoklassniki*), for additional search opportunities, for additional features of applications, and for games (in *vKontakte*). Encouraged by the success of the two leading SNSs, several SNS projects were launched in an attempt to elicit those drives and needs that had not been exploited as part of virtualized sociability. Some services offered to Russian internet users are geographically linked to the users' locality, for example, with emphasis on becoming acquainted with one's neighbours whose locations are indicated on a map (*Mir tesen* 'it's a small world', *Vashi sosedi* 'your neighbours', *Sosedi online* 'neighbours online', *Pervaya Piterskaya* 'first St Petersburg's [network]'). None of them has obtained a level of popularity even remotely comparable to that of *Odnoklassniki*, but it is characteristic that the projects' authors are exploiting sociability linked with local identity and, apparently, eventual geo-targeting of advertising.

Privacy concerns related to users' personal information on SNSs have been discussed in the Russian media. Apart from hackers, who use SNSs to fish for personal information and for spamming, *vKontakte* and *Odnoklassniki* is an environment that contains valuable data for anyone seeking to pry into or control one's affairs, from the police and banks to one's parents, partner, and ex-partners. The privacy settings of *vKontakte* allow users to shut their list of friends not only from strangers, but also from their friends. New media thus allow essentially new forms of monitoring of one's behaviour, but their success would be unthinkable without some means of guaranteeing a certain level of privacy against unwanted intrusions. Monitoring and intrusions into privacy in SNS is a new kind of concern for many SNS subscribers. Thus, in 2009, monitoring services such as accessing information about a cell phone subscriber's location even if he or she had chosen not to disclose it, or even reading other people's text messages, became one of the topics that was actively advertised in spam and fraudulent ads displayed on SNSs and some other media. Services of this kind are not actually supplied by mobile providers, because they are against the law, but everyone knows that it is often possible to get round such laws in Russia. That is why people are inclined to believe that it is a real service that is advertised and follow links and instructions that deceive users who wish to intrude in their partner's privacy. At some point, users are asked to send certain sums of money in order to get access to the results. No results are sent to the fooled users, but demand is high enough to enable those behind the ads to earn millions.

This is an example of a new form of fraud that is nothing new in itself, like many other phenomena that are enhanced and given new shape and intensity on SNSs but do not represent a radically new form of social life. What is actually new is the role that virtual networking can play in everyday life, when it is coupled to and exchanged with multimedia content, entertainment, and self-expression. Russian culture has readily accepted this virtual dimension of human life. However, there is no single explanation for the fact that Russians are the most active users in the world when it comes to internet-based social networking.

To conclude, I would like to sum up some of my observations and draw some conclusions about the Russian way of internet-based social networking. First, fast growing SNSs extend the sociability of many Russians to the internet. For them, checking email and other activities on the internet are routines performed on a daily basis, but web-based sociability often becomes the most important motivation for their use of the internet.

Second, for a significant group of users belonging to older age cohorts SNSs have become the starting point of their acquaintance with the internet. This is linked with the fact that the social networking boom coincided with the widespread arrival of broadband connection in big cities, especially in Moscow and St Petersburg.

Third, SNSs are transforming the cultural norms as well as the stereotypes of private and public human relationships that now comprise communication and even friendship with people met on the internet.

Fourth, blogging and SNS interest groups are becoming an alternative platform for expressing opinions and for social activism in a country where the traditional media are under control of the state. They are an important resource for the development of civil society in Russia.

Notes

1 See some interesting observations on the use of mobile phones in Russia in Lonkila and Gladarev (2008).
2 It is not by chance that second place in *ComScore* list of internet audiences' SNSs activity is occupied by mainly polychronic Brazil.

3 The data on the structure of the internet audience in Russia from 2008 are available on the *FOM* social research service website (*FOM* 2008). According to this publication, only 29 per cent of the Russian population are internet users.

4 The data quoted here are taken from various sources. These are, first, official press releases by the largest Russian search engine *Yandex*, and, second, statistical data from the *Liveinternet.ru* service that tracks the number of transitions from search engine result pages for a definite query to web pages.

5 Compared to the total population of Russia of 142 million.

6 Data on the audience of Russian segment of *LiveJournal* are available from the corporate blog of the research department of SUP, the owner company of *LiveJournal* (http://livestat.livejournal.com).

7 The most popular competitor to *LiveJournal* is the *Mail.ru* blogging service that opened in 2005 and by April 2007 had 1.1 million subscribers (Bursak 2007).

8 Data on Russian blogging are from a report on the Blogosphere issued by *Yandex* search engine (*Yandex* 2008). Interestingly, according to that report, female blogs outnumbered blogs written by male users. For a comprehensive review of Russian blogging, see (Alexanyan 2009); see also (Etling et al. 2010).

9 The data on the structure of the audience of *Odnoklassniki* that I quote here are taken from the Gallup TNS study conducted in 2008. Slide show of the presentation was available for download from a page aimed at potential advertisers, but it is no longer available. More recent data from TNS are available from http://odnoklassniki.ru/dk?st.cmd=helpAdvertise&tkn=20.

10 By early November 2009, *vKontakte* claimed to have more than 48 million subscribers, against 40 million in *Odnoklassniki*. By October 2010, *vKontakte* had more than 94 million users, having left behind *Odnoklassniki* with its approximate 45 million.

11 One of the strategic initiatives of the Russian government related to the building of an 'information society' in Russia involves the organization of access points to the internet in all the country's post offices. In December 2008, in one post office in Irkutsk, I saw an announcement placed near the computer that was supposed to be used for connecting to the internet. It listed the web addresses of selected services in the following way: for search on the internet – < www.yandex.ru >, < www.rambler.ru >; for socializing (Rus. *dlya obshcheniya*) – < www.odnoklassniki.ru >, < www.vkontakte.ru >.

12 Using different material, this idea was proposed by John Postrill in his case study of a suburb in Kuala Lumpur, Malaysia (Postrill 2008).

Bibliography

Alexanyan, K. (2009) 'Social networking on Runet: the view from a moving train', *Digital Icons: Studies in Russian, Eurasian and Central European New Media*, 1/2: 1–12. Online. Available: www.digitalicons.org/Issue02/Karina-Alexanyan (accessed 30 March 2011).

Bursak, A. (2007) 'SUP poschitala auditoriyu *Zhivogo Zhurnala*'. Online. Available: www.adme.ru/blogi/2007/04/10/16777 (accessed 30 March 2011).

Classmates.com (n.d.) Online. Available: www.classmates.com (accessed 30 March 2011).

ComScore (2009) 'Russia has world's most engaged social networking audience'. Online. Available: www.comscore.com/Press_Events/Press_Releases/2009/7/Russia_has_World_s_Most_Engaged_Social_Networking_Audience (accessed 30 March 2011).

Etling, B., Alexanyan, K., Kelly, J., Faris, R., Palfkey, J.G., and Gasser, U., (2010) 'Public discourse in the Russian blogosphere: mapping RuNet politics and mobilization' (29 October 2010). Berkman Center Research Publication No. 2010–1 1. Social Science Research Network. Online. Available: http://ssrn.com/abstract=1698344 (accessed 27 May 2011).

Facebook (n.d.) Online. Available: www.facebook.com (accessed 30 March 2011).

Fadeyeva, A. (2009) 'V set' cherez trubku'. Online. Available: www.rbcdaily.ru/2009/03/17/media/406295 (accessed 30 March 2011).

FOM (2008) 'Internet v Rossii/Rossia v internete'. Online. Available: http://bd.fom.ru/report/map/bntergum07/internet/internet0802/int0802 (accessed 30 March 2011).

FOM (2009) 'Internet v Rossii'. Online. Available: http://bd.fom.ru/report/map/bntergum07/internet/_internet0926/leto2009 (accessed 30 March 2011).

Gorny, E. (2007) 'The Russian internet: between kitchen-table talks and the public sphere', *Art Margins: Contemporary Central & East European Visual Culture*. Online. Available: www.artmargins.com/index.php?option=com_content&view=article&id=145%3Athe-russian-internet-between-kitchen-table-talks-and-the-public-sphere&Itemid=133 (accessed 30 March 2011).

Hall, E.T. *(1977) Beyond Culture*, New York: Anchor Books.

Imhonet.ru (n.d.) Online. Available: http://imhonet.ru (accessed 30 March 2011).

Kenyon, S. (2008) 'Internet use and time use: the importance of multitasking', *Time & Society*, 17/2–3: 283–318.

Lebedev, P. (2009) 'Elektronnyye den'gi i platnyye uslugi v internete', Paper at *E-trade 2009* conference, 7 October, FOM. Online. Available: http://bd.fom.ru/report/map/bntergum07/intergum0703/eldengy09 (accessed 30 March 2011).

Lenta.ru (2008) 'Oborot elektronnoy torgovli v Rossii za god vyros na 30 protsentov'. Online. Available: www.lenta.ru/news/2008/07/02/etrade (accessed 30 March 2011).

Linkedin.com (n.d.) Online. Available: www.linkedin.com (accessed 30 March 2011).

Liveinternet.ru (n.d.) Online. Available: www.liveinternet.ru/stat/ru/queries.html?period=month (accessed 30 March 2011).

Livejournal.com (n.d.) Online. Available: www.livejournal.com (accessed 30 March 2011).

Livestat.livejournal.com (n.d.) Online. Available: http://livestat.livejournal.com (accessed 30 March 2011).

Lonkila, M. and Gladarev, B. (2008) 'Social networks and cell-phone use in Russia: local consequences of global communication technology', *New Media & Society*, 10/2: 273–93.

Mail.ru (n.d.) Online. Available: www.mail.ru (accessed 30 March 2011).

Myspace.com (n.d.) Online. Available: www.myspace.com (accessed 30 March 2011).

Odnoklassniki.ru (n.d.) Online. Available: www.odnoklassniki.ru (accessed 30 March 2011).

Petersen, S.M. (2007) 'Cyborg practice: material aspects of broadband internet use', *Convergence: The International Journal of Research into New Media Technologies*, 13/1: 79–91.

Postrill, J. (2008) 'Localizing the internet beyond communities and networks', *New Media & Society*, 10: 413–31.

Rambler.ru (n.d.) Online. Available: www.rambler.ru (accessed 30 March 2011).

Tagiyev, R. (2008) 'Auditoriya interneta v Rossii: yeshche odin god'. Online. Available: www.slideshare.net/segal/ss-398595 (accessed 30 March 2011).

Twitter.com (n.d.) Online. Available: http://twitter.com (accessed 30 March 2011).

vKontakte.ru (n.d.) Online. Available: http://vkontakte.ru (accessed 30 March 2011).

Vyrin, F. (2008) 'Pol'zovateli sotsial'noy seti – kto oni?' Online. Available: www.slideshare.net/segal/ss-398672 (accessed 30 March 2011).

Yandex (2008) 'Blogosfera rossiyskogo interneta. Vesna 2008'. Online. Available: www.slideshare.net/segal/yandex-on-blogosphere-spring-2008 (accessed 30 March 2011).

Yandex.ru (n.d.) Online. Available: www.yandex.ru (accessed 30 March 2011).

Youtube.com (n.d.) Online. Available: www.youtube.com (accessed 30 March 2011).

Zhu, J.J.H. and He, Zh. (2002) 'Perceived characteristics, perceived needs, and perceived popularity: adoption and use of the internet in China', *Communication Research*, 29/4: 466–95.

Index